# Anyone Can Sell:

## Creating Revenue Through Sales in the Fitness Business

**Thomas Plummer**

ISBN: 978-1-58518-049-3
Library of Congress Control Number: 2007925523
Cover design: Bean Creek Studio
Book layout: Bean Creek Studio

Healthy Learning
P.O. Box 1828
Monterey, CA 93942
www.healthylearning.com

*Life followed love and then happiness was set free*

*But it was the faith of a good woman that allowed me to finally see*

*All things are possible in the journey of life*

*But the adventure has new meaning with the love of my wife*


Thank you, Susan, for your love and support and the thought of forever.

**Dedication**

# Acknowledgments

My life has definitely been blessed. I live by my terms, run the path I choose, make my own mistakes, and enjoy a quiet success surrounded by a handful of people that really matter.

If there was only one lesson I could share with a seeker of knowledge and life, however, it would be that no matter how far you've come you and how much success you've had, you have had help and you are obligated to acknowledge those who've helped you along the way.

Perhaps the unwritten sin in business is that we forget where we came from and who has helped us along the way. If you are successful, you have had help. That first loan, the kind words of support from a friend, that caring person who answers your phone call in the middle of the night when you're afraid you can't go on, or maybe your first customer, all made a difference in who you are and where you are in life. And most people can't even begin to calculate the help from parents and how valuable that is over the span of your life.

You can, however, ruin your life on your own. Bad life choices are usually made when you go it alone and lose faith in yourself and those around you. We celebrate success together, but we often choose defeat alone.

I have tried to acknowledge most everyone who has helped me over the years in previous books, but the list just continues to grow and another book is just another opportunity to say thank you to those who have been part of the adventure.

If there is a negative to moving a lot and the fast pace of having a certain degree of success in business it is that important people in your life tend to get lost. I've had a great number of friends that are important to me, and who helped me more than they realize, but who are not currently part of my life.

We will meet again, but for now I do want to take this opportunity to say thank you, and I miss you all in my life, to Robin Dyche, Smed and Jamie Blair, Don Coleman, Matt Fox, Jerry Mastrangelo, Shawn Smith, Bill Clark, and Chuck Hawkins. You probably will never see these words, but somewhere in the future I will find you all again.

Contents

# Introduction

It's been about 30 years since I first started in the fitness business as a sales guy. During that time, I have gathered a few bits of information from all perspectives in the business, including as an owner, lecturer, consultant, and student of small business, as well as from time spent in the financial end of the business. I have also, by loose calculations, had more than 50,000 students go through the seminars that I have been teaching since 1980, and their questions and needs have guided much of my study and learning in the business.

The gathering of this information has led to this book on sales and selling in the fitness business, the third club business book I've written for Healthy Learning. Many people who get into the fitness business believe that many different paths will get you to the top of the mountain of financial success, but after all these years I think the roads to the top are few and are all based upon learning the principles of good business before you attempt to once again reinvent the fitness industry.

I was once asked why our company doesn't do case studies and publish them. My answer was "where?" The lack of any type of vehicle to gather data and study this industry has led us over the years to gather our own information and do our own analysis based upon those results. The International Health, Racquet and Sportsclub Association (IHRSA) is expanding into more research and you can look forward to great information coming out of that organization during the next few years, but for now most of what happens in an independent club is our domain, and we probably know more about these clubs than anyone else just because we started there and that is all we do as a company.

Because the research presented is the work of my company, the numbers and formulas used in this book are mine and are based upon my thoughts and the many years of experience I have had dealing with thousands of different owners and their business plans. If it works and can be explained through numbers, then I use it. If something works once but can't be duplicated in other clubs, then it isn't used because it's a fluke—and chasing flukes isn't a great business plan.

One of the debates over the years is that the information in my books won't work in the chain clubs and that these clubs have developed their own sophisticated operating systems. If you look back into the recent history of our industry, you will find that a number of big chains have failed, and a few are now in dire straits, and many of the mistakes they make are the result of simply ignoring the numbers and the business rules we all must follow.

The people who believe that many of the principles discussed in my books don't apply to them are simply wrong. There is nothing in any of my books that probably wouldn't benefit almost any type of small business as well as the chains. The touted business plan of the month by that next new and exciting group often fails while good owners who practice good business just seem to keep going.

This information also applies to nonprofits. In the age of accountability, nonprofit players, such as Ys and hospital-based fitness businesses, are now feeling the pain of having to generate revenue on their own without the eternal assistance from the community or profitable hospital. If you generate income and become profitable, you will be able to reach a bigger segment of the community rather than burn up your gifts covering operating losses because your management team refuses to operate like a real business.

Nonprofits, especially those who subsist by the goodness of those in their communities, have a moral and ethical obligation to learn how to make money, so money given in good faith is not wasted by inept management and the arrogance that leads to thinking that you are too good to practice the rules of business. If you deal with the public, then you need to learn how money works in the fitness business and you especially need to learn how to present your business in the best possible light and enroll the largest number of new members possible. Remember, you can't change lives if you can't even make the person a member.

The fitness business is actually very simple. Attract new potential members is decent numbers, learn to close approximately 55 percent of those guests with some type of ethical membership, collect the most money from the most members, and build a staff that works. All of these things are obviously based on creating a system that allows you to get the highest return per member that you can. It's a simple business, but so damn hard at the same time.

This book is written in the same format as the first two, meaning that it has separate chapters meant to be read in any order, each of which is filled with a lot of random ideas and hints sprinkled throughout the text. Pick up the book and start reading any chapter, but look for the new ideas buried everywhere.

If you are operating a fitness business of any type at this point in time, then you are part of the transitional generation of owners and operators. This status means that during your shift you will see the end of most of the old habits from our early history in this industry, such as pressure sales, sexist advertising, long-term contracts, and other practices from the 1950s and 60s, and the advent of a new generation of owners who are better prepared to do business than ever before.

Markets are maturing and most owners have more competition now than they ever dreamed of when they set out to write that first business plan. This competition has started the single most important change ever in our industry. This change is the validation process of the simple business plan. It doesn't sound exciting, but it is indeed an earth-moving shift in our entrenched way of doing business.

For years, most owners who didn't have a lot of competition were able to get by with a lot of business practices that were quite questionable. Many of these owners became industry names and spent a lot of time teaching new generations their secrets. Their only real secret, however, was to open in a town with no other fitness businesses where just about anything you do works.

In the age of competition, many of these owners will and should fail. Competition validates your business plan and many of the clubs that are failing now deserve to fail because most of them really never learned the basics of being in business.

In this business, you don't fail because a competitor got you; you fail because you never learned the business in the first place and what it takes to be successful over time. When your business plan meets the market, only the strongest and most prepared will survive.

The most fundamental skill in our business, and in the rest of the business world as well, is the ability to present yourself and your product. In the fitness business, selling is nothing more than learning how to talk to someone and help that person make a decision.

But you also sell in the rest of your life as well. Make a presentation to your boss and you are selling. Ask for a date and you are presenting yourself to another. Raise money at church and you are making a presentation and are selling. We all sell and it is a part of everyone's life.

If you are going to be successful in the fitness business, you need to learn to generate memberships. You also need to learn to sell the people already in your system (the members) additional products and services that will help them and also help your business. Anyone can learn to sell and this book is your first step in mastering this most basic of skills.

# NOTE TO THE READER

Use this material at your own risk. Much of what is written in this book is based upon my own opinions and my own experience in the business, and all of the information is offered as a simple resource to give you some new ideas about how to sell and how to run your business more successfully.

In all cases, and especially in legal issues concerning your business such as staffing, you are advised to seek the advice of qualified business professionals that support your business locally, such as accountants, attorneys, and other business professionals that may know your business and your situation on a more intimate level.

Neither the author nor publisher nor any party related to the information and development of this book assumes any responsibility or liability for the consequences, whether good or bad, of your application of this material.

# WHAT YOU SHOULD KNOW BEFORE YOU BECOME A SALESPERSON

Section One

# 1

# A New Definition of Sales

"Sales" is the one word that absolutely sends fear into the hearts of an employee in any small business, which is defined as any single business with fewer than 100 employees and revenues of less than $3 million annually. In such a business, everyone is somehow going to be involved in the sales process. The person who is answering the phone may be standing two or three feet away from the person who actually owns the place, and in a fitness business, the person taking the call might be the owner, janitor, head salesperson, or trainer.

When that phone rings, how it is answered directly affects the outcome of a later sale. A warm, enthusiastic greeting and a courteous offer to help will make the salesperson's job much easier, just as an impersonal and rushed answer might end up doing more damage than the best salesperson on your team can overcome.

In sales, everything counts and everyone who works in your company is part of the sales process. The delivery guy with a bad attitude negatively affects future sales. An employee who poorly packs a box for shipment, resulting in a broken order, just cost the company future orders, because the customer won't buy from that business again.

In the fitness business, every single person in the club is involved in driving revenue through sales. A trainer who is 15 minutes late and was assigned to handle a trial member's workout just cost the club a membership. The childcare worker who didn't show up, the group exercise person who wasn't prepared, and the janitor that did a lousy job of cleaning the locker rooms all cost that club money now and in the future.

Most of your employees will fight sales because they truly don't understand the word. When you say "sales," they hear "pressure," meaning that they must do anything possible, whether it is ethical or not, to get that sale now while the person is in the gym, including drop close them, pressure them, double-team them, and follow them home to get the check. If it gets the sale, then do it and we'll worry about ethics later. As the old sales dogs used to say, "No one leaves unless they're crying."

This industry has done a lot to earn the high-pressure, sales-at-any-cost image that it suffers from with the consumer. In this industry, owners and salespeople are often viewed as sales guys who couldn't make the cut at a car lot. People in the fitness industry have long used enormously negative sales tactics, especially the chain clubs that put their managers under the relentless pressure of having to do massive sales numbers each month to keep their jobs.

**In the fitness business, every single person in the club is involved in driving revenue through sales.**

Because these clubs have such poor business systems, such as memberships that can't be collected and few, if any, profit centers, the pressure to perform is pushed downward to the club managers. This pressure to achieve unrealistic numbers results in tactics ranging from writing memberships from any random name in the phone book to faking signatures on contracts from a guest who made the simple mistake of just stopping by to visit the club. If this industry is going to survive in future years, owners need to change their definition of what "sales" means to them and to their young staff members who refuse to have anything to do with such an old-style, unethical approach to serving the member.

How should the word "sales" be defined? Before you start the process of putting meaning to this word, you need to go back to why most people get into this business in the first place.

Most of the folks who get into the fitness business actually do so to make some type of change. This change may start as something as simple as working on their own bodies or working through personal fitness issues, which can range from being overweight to the extremes where bodybuilders live and where "fitness" takes on a whole new definition.

Once many of these folks get into changing their own bodies, they inevitably become that gym resource that begins to answer questions for other people. You may start with the single step of coaching your training partner or spouse, but eventually you are helping other people in the gym. This type of coaching, especially when your friends and clients get results and come back to you thrilled, may be one of the most addicting drugs in the universe. Nothing is more satisfying than watching someone change their appearance, their attitude, and even their life because of your help and guidance in the gym.

It's not hard to go from this point to somehow getting into the fitness business for a living. If you have the resources or connections, it may be as a gym owner. If not, your first step might be as a trainer or group exercise instructor, or even a salesperson. As long as you're helping someone, why not do it for a living and make some money doing something you love?

When you redefine sales, you need to get back to this caring attitude that got most people into the fitness business in the first place. Even those old jaded owners with multiple units and who are far removed from the workout floor need to reach back and explore those old feelings of why they're doing this job for a living and why they got into this business in the first place.

These experienced owners still can't get away from the need to coach and change people at some level. You may not be working people out daily anymore, but you are probably coaching some young employee in the business or giving a seminar somewhere on what you're learned from your business ventures. Once you are a teacher, you will always be a teacher in some form or another.

The core elements of coaching, caring, and helping are what sales are really all about in this business, and they are the key words that employees will grasp a hold of. The young people who come to work in the fitness industry instinctively want to help people, so you must avoid saying the word "sales" without defining it as something they can relate to in their work.

If you are going to expand your business and change the public perception of what you do for your life's work, you need to define sales as follows:

*Sales in the fitness business is the simple act of helping people get what they want from you. You help those people by always being ethical and professional. Every person who leaves your business should feel good about what he chose to buy from you.*

Owners still have to sell in this business and a cost is associated with this help. Just because you change the definition doesn't mean you stop selling memberships. It's how these memberships are sold that will determine if this industry survives over time or not.

If a member wants to lose weight, you can help, but a fee must be charged for that service. You should certainly offer coffee and healthy snacks, and while you may offer the best products you can find and afford, they must be offered to the member for a fee. In this new definition of sales, customer service is not free. Instead, customer service is about having quality choices available in your businesses.

If you think of sales as the act of helping people get what they want, most owners will have to change a lot of how they run their businesses, especially how they train their staffs. Every employee, not just the salespeople, will need sales training, because everyone is part of the helping process. Everything has to change, from the old limited-membership options to the guest's first experience with a trainer or group instructor.

Give the business a cold look and you will see an entire industry armed to sell memberships, but totally unprepared to actually help a person who comes

**If you think of sales as the act of helping people get what they want, most owners will have to change a lot of how they run their businesses, especially how they train their staffs.**

in for help in their quest to get what he wants. Just look at the things owners sometimes do to these people. They force someone to commit to a membership during the first visit and while under pressure, even though that same salesperson would likely take two days to shop for something that costs the same as a club membership. They only offer one avenue into the club: Buy a membership or hit the door. They even tell people that after two workouts they have to fly solo, even though the average deconditioned female needs seven or more workouts before she can work out on her own and feel comfortable.

Fitness businesses are not geared for member fulfillment, but instead are built as membership mills. "Turn and burn the numbers, and members be damned after they buy" has been the motto in the fitness industry for more than 50 years. Fortunately, fitness-business owners can change how they think and still make the same, if not more, money than they do with these antiquated business practices.

The process is actually simple. If you help the customer get what he wants, he will buy more from you and stay longer and pay longer. It's not an issue of money; it's an issue of building a system based upon helping an individual who is willing to trust you with his body, even when the person has a somewhat dubious view of what the fitness business is really all about.

> **If you change the definition of sales, you will attract and keep better staff members.**

Most importantly, if you change the definition of sales, you will attract and keep better staff members. Your young staff comes to the fitness business often looking for a chance to help people, and you get much better buy-in from these people if the first thing they learn is that the entire business is dedicated to helping the people who come to you get what they want.

Everything goes full circle and what is new was once old. That saying holds true in sales. Most people get into this business to help someone, but you may have lost your way somewhere over the years. Going back to the simple premise of helping people to be successful and meet their goals takes you back full circle to that higher standard that the industry was founded upon so many years ago.

## Key Points From This Chapter

- The word "sales" has a very negative connotation to many staff members.
- Most of the industry's current business practices are based upon closing memberships and not upon providing the help and guidance a potential member is looking for when he comes to the club for help.
- Go back to the reason why you got into the fitness business in the first place: to help people change their bodies, and even their lives, through fitness.

- If you change the definition of sales, you will also have to change many of the ways you train your staff and do business.

- By changing the definition of sales, you will make more money from more people over time while also changing the way the fitness industry is viewed by the consumer.

## You're the expert, so ask for the sale.

Potential members come to you asking for help and guidance. Give it to them.

Fitness is very confusing, even to fitness professionals. How many diets are out there and how many ways to work out are shown on television alone? Where do you start amongst the gibberish and sales pitches when you want to lose some weight?

Many people go to their local fitness center and ask for help, and it is surprising how few salespeople and trainers will actually tell people what they need to do to be successful. Do not confuse selling with leadership. Salespeople have no trouble pounding out some training sessions, but training is not always the solution the person needs to get started.

Fitness professionals are in leadership roles and are positioned as the experts who have the answers to what it takes to be successful in fitness. When a potential member asks, "How do I lose 10 pounds?" you should tell him exactly what he needs to do based upon what is available in your system.

And don't forget the learning styles. Many of your guests would greatly benefit if you wrote out a step-by-step process that covers the next 90 days of their efforts to reach their goals.

People will buy leadership, but only if it is shown. If someone asks for your opinion, then give him the best-case scenario based upon how you and your facility can really help him reach his stated goal.

# **2**

# **95% of What You Do Is Sell Somebody Something Every Day**

You sell. It's what you do every day. Selling has been an inherent part of the fitness business since it began and it will always be a vital part of what you do for a living.

In fact, 95 percent of what you do in this business, and virtually any other small business, is sell somebody something every day. Sales are how you make money and how you maintain cash flow, the lifeblood of a small business, flowing through your ever-needy business each day, each week, and each month you are operating.

Once you make this money from sales, you can then spend the other 5 percent of your time sitting up in your bed at 3 o'clock in the morning counting your money and trying to figure out just what happened in your business that day. You will usually make most of your money in the fitness business on the floor or behind that front counter, helping people get what they want and solving the problems they bring as part of their expectations of membership.

Most new owners drift away from this core philosophy at some point early in their careers. They start on the floor, but it's just a matter of time before they move to the office. They sit and look at statements, make deposits, return phone calls, solve member-service issues, make up their own ads, call their significant other, sneak a lunch, fix a toilet, and run a few errands. At the end of the day, they're sitting on the couch feeling really tired from putting in a full day at the gym.

The problem is that they forgot to make any money that day because they were too busy being busy. They started as production-based people, but they eventually became managers, and managers seldom make the money. Of course, you do not have to continue selling memberships in your own business forever, but you should be aware of the fact that you often lose this production mentality by moving off the floor and into the office setting.

Any time you find a business that isn't performing, one of the first questions that has to be asked of the owner is, "How many memberships did you sell in your own business last month?" If the business is flat, the answer is usually zero. This owner, who probably started as a driven salesperson putting memberships down every night and growing the receivable base and cash flow, now comes in at 10 o'clock in the morning, takes care of paperwork, checks the deposits, and is gone by 6 o'clock at the latest.

When times get tough, most owners just get more entrenched in their offices. "If I just sit here long enough and refigure these numbers, sooner or later they'll get better." Instead, get off your butt and go back to work, because one of the fundamental principles in this business is that no one ever made any money in the fitness business sitting at a computer in an office.

Even owners who are running successful businesses and are far removed from sales still need to sell a few memberships each month just to keep the feel. You can ask your staff a lot of questions about what's going on with the potential members, but when you do a sale yourself you get instant feedback from the person's words and expressions. This experience gives you the powerful information that you need to keep your business successful.

**In the fitness business, you make your money on the floor one membership at a time.**

In the fitness business, you make your money on the floor one membership at a time. You also make it by selling training sessions, soft drinks, supplements, tanning, and any other profit centers your club offers. The old staff-training line, "Can I get you a drink for the ride home?" is often more powerful than a whole lot of hours spent sitting at that desk wondering how much money the club will save by switching from three-ply toilet paper to the cheap stuff.

---

You can never save yourself into profitability.

---

Most fitness businesses can cut back, and waste exists in every small business. In fact, it is hard to find any fitness business that cannot trim 10 percent or so from its base operating cost.

The secret to running a successful fitness business, however, is not saving pennies. It's making dollars. You are in a production-based business, which means that every day the club is open someone has to sell someone else something. Again, 95 percent of what you do in the fitness business is produce. It takes work to maintain this mentality in most small businesses, especially if you get into multiple units or get big enough that you actually do work as a manager in your own business.

One of the main obstacles to keeping this production-based environment happening is that managers and owners take on too many responsibilities that get in the way of making money. The basic rule of thumb is that if it gets in the way of production, you should farm it out. Think of keeping your business a lean, mean selling machine. If something gets in the way of that mentality, then you probably shouldn't be doing it.

For example, many young owners, and even a few old dogs, insist on collecting their own memberships. Why would you not farm this task out to a specialist and then manage the results instead of doing the work yourself? In many cases, owners simply can't help doing this job themselves, since this industry attracts so many control freaks whose idea of running a business is, "Get the hell out of my way and I'll do it myself." The sad thing is that when an owner says, "I'll do it myself," it means doing everything in the business except the important things, such as selling memberships, training, and performing other high-dollar jobs that would give the club a cash-flow boost that day.

The goal is to keep the business simple. Farm out everything that gets in the way of production and keep the business totally focused on putting numbers up on the board every day. In the fitness industry, clubs make their money one day at a time and the focus should be on keeping the business on a set production track each day.

Another mistake owners and managers make in their quest to build a superior production-based business is that they forget *when* they make the money. Most clubs have a prime time, and it is usually not between noon and 5 o'clock in the afternoon. In other words, most owners go home just when business is starting to get good.

You will make approximately 70 percent of your money in a coed club between roughly 4 and 9 o'clock in the evening Monday through Thursday and between 8 and 10 o'clock on Saturday morning. If you have a women-only club, you usually have a second prime time from approximately 8 to 11 o'clock each weekday morning. If you are going to score each day, then you have to have your best players, without exception, in the club during these prime hours, which means that if you leave at 5 o'clock and let your otherwise unhirable brother-in-law run your business for the rest of the evening, you will eventually fail simply because no strong players are present to drive the business.

It is hard to make money if you're not in the business during the best production hours. Even if your business has matured, you still need to have a powerful driver in the business during these times. If you are an owner with a single club, then it is absolutely mandatory that you are in your business during the key hours when you make money.

When you explore ways to improve your business, always return to the key question: Am I doing everything possible to create a business that is totally production-based? Another way to look at this question is ask yourself: Is what

**In the fitness industry, clubs make their money one day at a time and the focus should be on keeping the business on a set production track each day.**

I am doing, or going to do, the best use of my time and my manager's time at this minute? If what you're doing is not driving production and sales, then you should be doing something else.

As you increase your knowledge about sales, always return to the most basic but powerful premise in the fitness business: 95 percent of what you do in this business is sell somebody something every day. Have this statement made into a huge sign that hangs over your desk. Also, make it one of the first things that all new employees learn, along with your new definition of sales, on their first day on the job.

**As you increase your knowledge about sales, always return to the most basic but powerful premise in the fitness business: 95 percent of what you do in this business is sell somebody something every day.**

# Key Points From This Chapter

- You are in a production-based business.
- Selling every day is what you do, and it is what you will always do in some form or another.
- Get rid of the things that prevent your business from being production-based.
- Have your key production people in the gym during prime production hours.
- No one ever made any money in the fitness business sitting behind a computer.

# Being on time means being 15 minutes early.

If you are one of those people who are always late and come running into a meeting or appointment scrambling with bags and a cup of coffee, you need to learn one important lesson: Grow up. When you are late, you've insulted everyone who is waiting for you. By walking in even five minutes after an appointment, you're stating that your time is far more valuable then theirs and that you are far more important than anything else that is going on at the time.

Treat your fellow staff, and especially your club appointments, with respect. Respect, when it comes to time, means being 15 minutes early for any appointment you might have scheduled.

For example, if you have a training appointment, arrive 15 minutes early, get your paperwork ready, brush your teeth, comb your hair, and show your client the respect he deserves for supporting you with his money. When the client walks in, you're ready to go and ready to demonstrate your professionalism by being totally prepared for the appointment.

# 3

# What Makes A Good Employee?

Because every employee in your business is a vital part of the sales process, you can't discuss sales without first having a discussion about what it takes to be a good employee. One salesperson doesn't make a sales team. Remember, that front counter person who was warm and friendly with her greeting often affects new membership sales just as much as the salesperson's words.

First, what does "good" mean? When most people hear the word "good," they think of warm and fuzzy people who help little old ladies across streets, suck up to their parents, and were often the most hated kids in their high schools because all the regular kids couldn't stand that one good kid who was every teacher's favorite.

In the real business world, good means effective. Can this person produce? Can this person be nice, provide customer service, and still get the job of making money done each day?

One of the biggest lies owners are told by their staff members is: "I'm good with the members. Everyone loves me, but I just don't think I should sell." These employees say this as if selling is just another form of spreading a hideous disease and that if they sell they are in some way hurting the members.

Most trainers are especially fierce in protecting this anti-sales philosophy. "I provide great workouts and have five certifications, but I believe that asking for money is wrong and not professional." Of course, they are overlooking the fact that someone had to sell to that person who is getting the great workout each day. As much as you may like to see it happen, very few members walk into the gym naked with a wad of cash in their teeth begging for training sessions. The reality is that at some point somebody sold someone something or no training sessions would be taking place.

In this case, being a good employee does not mean being an effective employee. You might be really good at making members happy at the front desk, but you still have to promote what the club has to sell. Trainers especially have to learn to produce and be able to generate revenue in their departments by learning to resell their clients and attract member referrals from their supposedly satisfied customers.

The difference between a good employee and an effective one is often determined by whether they truly understand that new definition of sales. Selling in the fitness business is nothing more than helping people get what they want without being afraid of asking for money to provide that solution. You want to help people, but some type of fee must be charged for that help.

One common denominator exists within every effective employee: no fear of trying. If you're willing to try, you can learn to be effective and graciously ask for money for the service, help, and solutions you are providing. The key element is whether or not you have fear.

A lot of ways are available to find out before you hire someone if a person has this fear of trying. What kind of jobs this person has had is your first clue. Back-office jobs, computer jobs, and other types of work where the person is not interacting with others provide a strong hint that this person isn't going to be that front counter dynamo you were looking for when you hired him.

Paperboys, customer service people, bartenders, fugitives from the Gap®, and other folks who are forced to interact with large numbers of people will do well in the fitness business. If you've worked with a lot of people in your face for long enough, you probably won't have any trouble asking someone if he wants a bottle of water for the ride home.

Another way to eliminate the fearful souls who think that a fitness job is just a matter of working out all day is to put the interviewee into a sales situation during the interview process. For example, an old interview game that can be used once you get an initial idea that the person can communicate is to pull the surprise sales skit. Right in the middle of the interview, and without warning, pull an employee in from the club and have the candidate sell her something without a chance to think about it. A favorite is to give the potential hire the worst parking place in the club and have him try to sell it to another employee.

You're not looking for a professional sales pitch at this point. You are, however, looking for people who give it a hell of a try without hesitation. If a person can fake it in this situation, he will probably do quite well if he has any level of training. If he refuses to play because he is too embarrassed, then he failed the test and doesn't make the cut. If a person can't do it in the office for fun, he certainly can't do it on the floor for real when it counts.

> Selling in the fitness business is nothing more than helping people get what they want without being afraid of asking for money to provide that solution.

Once you get past determining the potential employee's fear of sales, you then move on with your search for the single biggest trait a person must have to be an effective employee. Keep in mind that a trait is something the person brings to the job and is usually not something you teach, such as answering the phone, which is a skill. In other words, traits are who you are and skills are what you learn.

The single biggest trait needed to be an effective employee is strong communication skills. Can the person speak clearly, professionally, and with a wide range of people? If the communication skills are strong—a combination of a trait and a skill—then the person will probably be able to relate to a wide segment of the variety of people who come through your doors. This ability to relate translates into being better able to understand the person and help him get what he wants from you as a customer.

**The single biggest trait needed to be an effective employee is strong communication skills.**

How do you determine if a person has strong communication skills? This task is harder than it sounds, especially if you're a younger owner and don't yet have great communication skills yourself.

Again, the type of work a person has done in the past is a strong indicator of what type of communicator the person might be. Anyone who has survived in the retail or restaurant business for any length of time probably has mastered at least the basic skills it takes to communicate in a business setting. Bank tellers and other customer-intense jobs also produce the type of people you are looking for in this business.

Communication skills are also evident during the interview process if you know what you are looking for in a person. A common mistake is that most young owners don't interview properly. They simply ramble on about the job, their business, and the members, and spend the interview time talking instead of asking probing questions that get the candidate to talk and open up a little.

If you want the best results, use the same four or five questions for each person you interview and let the person answer. Then ask a few probing questions that keep the conversation rolling. For example, a strong question for an interview is, "What was the worst part about the worst job you ever had?"

Follow the initial answer with a probe or two. "That job sounds tough. How did you end up doing that?" or "Well, I'm glad that's your worst job. Now tell me about the best job you ever had." Probes keep the person talking while you gently guide the conversation.

What you're hoping to discover is the person's ability to talk. Is he clear? Does he sound like an adult or a kid? Would you want this person selling memberships or greeting people at the front desk? It usually only takes a few minutes of someone babbling away to get a real sense of the depth of his communication skills.

A strong case is made in a variety of literature that women are much better communicators than men, and that they are more competent at a younger age. Of course, if you've ever had kids or managed employees for any length of time, you know this fact without looking at some scientific report.

Consider a young male and female, both age nine, coming home from school. "How was school?" the mother asks. The young male grunts "Fine," reaches for the fridge door, and is done with the conversation. The young female, however, will tell her mother in great detail everything about the day, including who sat where, what color dress the teacher had, who was bad on the bus, and every morsel of what she had for lunch. Even at an early age, men mumble and women begin a lifelong communication process.

The question is: Who can relate to the largest number of members, and potential members, who come through the door? Many of the young males in gyms can only relate to other young males. Their dress, vocabulary, diction, and life experiences often limit them to relating to someone just like them. In sales, the ability to relate is everything. Even great training will leave such a person less than effective.

In many cases, women seem much better able to communicate and relate to more people at a younger age. This ability to talk to someone older, someone younger, and to folks of the opposite sex gives this person an edge in the sales game and is especially important to your front-desk workers.

Of course, you should not hire only young women in your gym. But you should hire the strongest communicators out of your candidates, male or female, because this ability will determine their success and your future sales.

A secondary, but still vital, trait that you are looking for in a potential hire is enthusiasm. Most owners and managers laugh at this word because it is so esoteric, but if you think about it, you do recognize someone who is genuinely enthusiastic and passionate when you meet them.

**In this business, someone who is enthusiastic but has moderate sales skills will often outperform an overtrained but bland salesperson who doesn't relate well to the consumer.**

Why is enthusiasm a must-have trait? In this business, someone who is enthusiastic but has moderate sales skills will often outperform an overtrained but bland salesperson who doesn't relate well to the consumer. People are drawn to enthusiastic individuals who have passion for what they are doing, and this enthusiasm will overcome a lot of deficiencies in someone's technical ability.

Enthusiasm is easy to recognize. In an interview, for example, the person is either leaning forward, talking with his hands, acting animated and in your face, or he is leaning back in the chair and just going through the motions.

While flaunting the eternally bored, low-energy look is everything in the baggy-pants set, this almost nonexistent energy level is the kiss of death in a mainstream fitness business. Can you imagine a low-energy person behind your front desk or trying to sell memberships? If a person is leaning back in his chair with his legs stretched out in the interview, he will very likely demonstrate even less energy when he's propped up on a stool behind your front counter.

The combination of strong communication skills and an enthusiastic, in-your-face attitude makes for a solid foundation for anyone who works in a production-based business. In other words, if someone can speak well, is excited about the job, and loves working with people, he will probably be more effective over time than someone who has more limited skills.

## Building a Culture of Sales

Successful sales in a fitness facility revolve around a common belief system that states that sales are important to the business and that selling memberships is part of everyone's job, not just the sales team. Consider the following cautionary tale: A club was advertising an interesting membership special, featuring bicycles as incentives to get new members and to drive buddy sales. The club was in a biking town and the incentive of getting a new mountain bike was almost too good to be true.

**Successful sales in a fitness facility revolve around a common belief system that states that sales are important to the business and that selling memberships is part of everyone's job, not just the sales team.**

The gym entrance was nicely decorated with posters of bikers and a piece of art displayed on an easel let the members know how each one of them could have a chance to get a bike of their own. The front counter was also part of the display and a mountain bike was hanging in the air about 10 feet above the desk. Behind the desk was a young counterperson glued to the computer. The following exchange took place when a group of customers walked in:

*"Hello, we'd like to get some more information about that ad in the paper and the bikes please." Three customers were standing in front of the young staffer at the counter.*

*"Those salespeople always have something going, but they never bother to tell us. What did you say the special was about? I'll see if I can get you a handout or something." Again, posters were hung in the entrance, an easel with information stood in front of the desk, and a bike was hanging over her head.*

*The customers pointed at the bike up over her head. She looked up, turned her back to the customers, and said, "I just got in. They must have put that up last night, but I don't know anything about it yet. Let me see if the manager is in."*

This story was not, as it first appears, about an exceptionally dumb staff person, although she probably should have questioned why a bike was hanging over her head. What is actually happening is that sales operates as a separate force in this business and doesn't bother to keep the rest of the team involved in the selling process. The feeling that salespeople are special or different and not part of the team is common in many clubs, especially in those with old sales systems that maintain the illusion that a salesperson is the most important person in the club.

This club will also have trouble selling memberships, because the counterperson probably feels somewhat embarrassed because she had to deal with questions that she was not prepared for. This embarrassment, and the associated feeling of being left out of the loop, builds an adversarial relationship between the salespeople and the rest of the team.

A simpler way to explain this relationship between the sales team and the rest of the staff is that anyone not part of the sales team will now do everything they can to make sure those jerks in sales fail. "Make me look bad and I will get even" is not just a random thought in her head, but becomes part of her job because she will share those feelings with every other person on her level in the club.

**Building a culture means that everyone in the club, no matter the level or job, at some point has the same belief system at the same time.**

Building a culture means that everyone in the club, no matter the level or job, at some point has the same belief system at the same time. In other words, you all work together doing those things, such as sales and service, that will make this business a financial success over time. This system only works, however, when you all share a common set of basic beliefs regarding how the business must be run each day.

Culture also has a broader meaning in the fitness business. How does the owner feel about training? How do the owner and management team feel about group exercise or weight management? How do you treat people in your business and how do you treat each other during the normal course of a business day? All of these beliefs, properly conveyed to your staff, lead to a culture in the club that is shared by all of the employees as well as the members who participate in the business.

Memberships are, and will continue to be, the basic financial driver of what you do. Sales are also where you start developing your basic thoughts regarding the role of an employee or team member in your business. Your culture in the club may grow to include other thoughts on these ideas, but the four items to follow are concepts that your staff members should learn on the very first day on the job.

Your role as a team member in this business can be described as follows:

- You sell memberships or support the people who do.
- You sell somebody something every day.
- You provide legendary customer service to every member and to every other team member.

- You treat every single member in the same way every single day: with respect, with a thank you, and with legendary customer service.

## You sell memberships or support the people who do.

Every employee is part of the sales process. When a guest decides to become a member, he is not just buying a membership but instead buying into the entire team. People buy memberships for different reasons and many of those reasons have little to do with the amount of equipment you might have or the number of classes you offer. Often a guest will buy because the staff was nicer and more attentive than the staff at the other club he visited, or perhaps the salesperson took more time to answer questions than the person who showed him the last place.

During an exit survey, which is a short questionnaire used to find out why a person decided to buy at a club, a 40-something female was asked about the reasons she picked a particular gym to join. Her answer was something most owners neglect because it falls outside normal sales training or is perhaps too touchy-feely for most male owners. "I visited several other clubs," she said, "and while this one was more expensive, the person at the front counter was so helpful and kind that I already felt like a member before I even met the salesperson. He also surprised me because he actually asked me questions about myself and what I wanted from a membership, which was different from the others I visited."

Who really got the sale, the salesperson who did her job or the front-counter person who paved the way? In sales, every employee is part of the process and everyone has to participate. In this case, the sale was probably made because the front-counter person did such a fine job of making the guest feel like part of the cub before she even really saw it for the first time.

The question is: How do you really teach this attitude to your staff? Hiring slightly older people with service experience helps because the communication skills are already developed. Creating an environment with an area for the guest to wait under the watchful eye of the counter staff also helps. The most important thing, though, is also the most simple: Slow the process down and make sure the guest is the most important thing in the club at that moment.

Many of the chain clubs, for example, pride themselves on being able to do a lot of volume, but many of the people caught up in that net don't stay long or pay long. One of the reasons might be that after a while the guest is no longer an individual, but merely becomes the next one up in the sales process. Run the person in the front, grind him up in the middle, spit him out the back with a membership, and then move on to the next guest. This process worked 20 years ago, but doesn't any longer because of the more sophisticated member and increased competition. The potential member wants a different experience and he wants to spend his money with someone who cares.

> People buy memberships for different reasons and many of those reasons have little to do with the amount of equipment you might have or the number of classes you offer.

In relationship sales, everything counts, because the person makes a decision to buy based upon a combination of factors, rather than just what a salesperson does or says. Owners and managers never really know what single factor made the sale. Therefore, you have to fix as many things as possible to be successful.

It is essential that you teach every team member that they are part of the sales process and that the job of a staff person is to make sure each guest has the best experience possible in the gym that day. For example, did you greet him quickly and with personality? Did you shake hands and make him feel comfortable in the club before the tour? Did you slow down the sales pitch and actually ask a few questions about the person and what he wants from the club? Were your staff dressed well and looking professional in their uniforms? Everything counts and every staff person is part of the process.

### You sell somebody something every day.

You are in production-based business, which means that you have to produce revenue each and every day to stay in business. Part of the job of any team member is to make sure that every member who visits the facility that day has an opportunity to get a snack, enjoy a service, or be informed about something new that the club is offering that might be of interest to that member.

You are not, however, forcing anyone to buy something that he doesn't want or need. Many young owners and managers, and most staff people, feel that asking someone to buy is putting pressure on that person to spend money. If you train your staff to ask the person about signing up for a specialty class, for example, a young staff person often says that she doesn't feel comfortable, because she feels she is bothering the person and pressuring him to buy.

The rule to remember is that good service is not free.

The rule to remember is that good service is not free. It means offering options to customers to save them time and money. If a person can buy supplements from the club, then he can make one less stop in an already busy day. If the person is a golfer and is informed about a specialty conditioning class you offer in the winter just for golfers, then you have offered an option and a service, even if the person declines.

The job of a staff person is to make sure that the member has options and is presented choices each time she visits the club. "Would you like a drink for the ride home?" is not pressure, but simply offering the member a service that makes her life easier and more convenient. What people forget is that she will probably stop anyway at a convenience store on the way home to get a bottle of water if you don't sell her one, so the option truly provides a service rather than a pressure.

You also have to remember that you need to make money in this business. New programming, more treadmills, and bigger pay come from a member buying something. You still, as a business, need to produce revenue each day to pay for all of these things. Learning to ask politely and with confidence for all types of sales not only provides a service to the member, but also helps generate cash flow.

## You provide legendary customer service to every member and to every other team member.

A difference exists between good customer service and legendary customer service in a club. The following examples should help you see where good service ends and legendary service begins.

> *Good service*
>
> Following a tour, on the way to the front of the club, the salesperson stops and introduces the new member to the head trainer, a training client who has been with the club for years, and the counterperson. The salesperson then walks the new member to the door, shakes her hand, and thanks her one more time for becoming a new member.
>
> *Legendary service*
>
> The counterperson notices that the new member is just standing at the door looking out and doesn't leave. He walks up to her and notices that it has started to rain outside. He gets an old umbrella out of lost and found and asks if he can walk her to her car. He walks her outside, opens her door for her, and runs back to the desk.

Most owners would roll over and die if they could just train their staff to deliver the service in the first example, and that type of service really is just common sense and training. If you want that type of service, then you have to train for it by asking, "How should we treat our new members?"

The second example, which is a true story, is what happens when the staff is taught to go beyond good service and be legendary. The issue is not how you can be of service to this woman, but rather how you can truly make her day. In the legendary example, the club staffer not only delivered legendary service, but actually helped the sales effort as well, because without a doubt that new member will tell a story about that service to someone the next day at work.

Owners and staff trainers often make customer service vague and hard to provide because they can't really define it to the staff. Many young staff members, for example, don't have a real concept of what you mean when you talk about delivering customer service. "Hey, I smiled and I was nice," is their universal answer and most really believe that they are providing decent service.

A difference exists between good customer service and legendary customer service in a club.

If you want to get the most from your staff, define the expected outcome by answering this question: What would good service look like if you saw it? When you define what you want in definite terms, it is easier to teach it and get results.

For example, how should you greet a person at the front counter? This simple act, as well as most other service acts in the club, can be broken down into three simple phrases:

- *Use a strong welcoming statement every time someone comes through the door or approaches the club.* For example: "Hello, we're having a great day at the Orion Y."

- *Use the person's name each and every time.* For example: "Hi Sarah, I hope you have a great workout today." Most check-in systems usually pop the person's name and picture up when the member scan her card, giving you the advantage of having the name prominently displayed on the screen.

- *Thank every member every single time.* For example: "Thank you for visiting the facility today, John, and thank you for buying that T-shirt. We do appreciate your business."

All basic customer service can be broken down into those three easy-to-remember phrases if you start with the concept of what good service would look like if you saw it being delivered. You also have to learn to deliver good service to other team members. Being nice to the members is one thing, but you also have to provide legendary service to each other.

In the club business, you never know when you're going to be really busy. One minute you might get overwhelmed with sales tours and an hour later the salespeople are bored and the counter team is getting slammed. Service to each other means that you understand what your teammates are going through and you work to help them when they are in trouble. Doing so also adds overall customer service to the club experience for the members, because they usually directly benefit from this team effort.

> Service to each other means that you understand what your teammates are going through and you work to help them when they are in trouble.

Consider a typical Monday night. Monday's the day most clubs do the largest percentage of their workouts for the week, and usually the most sales as well. It is later in the evening and sales are slowing down, but workouts are still jamming through the door. Your salesperson walks out of the back of the club and notices that the counter is three deep with people needing service.

This person has two choices: "It's not my job and I'll wander the floor pretending I am busy," or "My friends need some help and I am going to jump in and lend a hand."

Most staff members will automatically pick the first option, but with training and guidance anyone can learn that he should always provide service, not only to the members but to his teammates as well.

If this salesperson jumps behind the counter and takes care of some members, he is presenting the image that service is the ultimate goal in this club. Just as importantly, the team now knows that they can count on him if it gets rough and they will most likely be more interested in helping him with his sales clients in the future.

**You treat every single member the same way every single day: with respect, with a thank you, and with legendary customer service.**

Every member has to be valued to build a solid referral base as well as increase your member retention over time. Perhaps the strongest member-service phrase you can learn is: We treat every single member the same way every single day.

This phrase also solves many of your service issues on a day-to-day basis. Questions from members, such as: "Will you give me a deal?" "Can I get my friend a break?" and "Can't you do this for me just one time?" all go away when you simply state, "Sorry, we treat every single member the same way every single day, and giving you what you want wouldn't be fair to the other members."

> Perhaps the strongest member-service phrase you can learn is: We treat every single member the same way every single day.

# The Rule of Perpetual Motion

In the fitness business, the rule of perpetual motion is that no energy force shall ever come to rest while on the job. Assuming that your staff represents the energy forces, then this rule also means that everyone has something to do all day long. If this law of nature is true, then why do so many staff people stand in packs behind the front counter just waiting for something to do? Part of the culture in a successful club is that you are all in constant motion, which leads to improved service and improved sales.

In the old days of the fitness business, owners used to build bigger counter areas because a lot of the work of the club was done there. They also found, to their detriment, that the entire staff would hang out behind the counter, which scares new member to death when they walk in the club for the first time and see eight people standing behind a desk arguing about who is up next.

Thinking they were smarter, they started building smaller counters. All that change really did was force the staff to stand closer together so that they would all still fit. Eventually, they found that it wasn't the counters that were the problem, but the leadership the owners themselves were providing.

Look at the following list, which is not in any particular order, and rank each item in importance from 1 to 5, with 1 being the most important thing to do at any given moment:

* *Servicing members*
* *Cleaning* and maintaining the club as a service aspect
* *Selling* a membership
* *Following up* through email lists, sales follow-up, phone work, or other mailings
* *Preparing* for business, such as getting the club ready for business, getting each staff member ready for their next appointment, or preparing a room for a class

The law of perpetual motion means that everyone on the staff is doing one of these things at all times, unless the owner or manager puts him on another task. In other words, if the owner is not around, everyone must go do one of these things according to order of importance.

The list, which can be used as a checklist, should be ranked in the following order. If you think the order should be different, be sure to use the same sequence every time during your training sessions:

* Selling
* Servicing
* Following up
* Preparing
* Cleaning

If any employee is standing around with nothing to do, he should work through the list in the order he was trained in. For example:

* Is a guest in the house who needs to be sold a membership? If not, move on to number 2.

* Does anyone need immediate servicing? Is anyone waiting at the counter? Is anyone running late on the team and leaving a member stranded? If not, move on to number 3.

* Is any follow up needed in your department or can you help with someone else's stuff? Are the handwritten invitations done? Are the emails for the party out? Have you followed up with all of your sales leads for the day? If all of these things are done, then move on to number 4.

* Are you prepared for business today? Has anyone walked through the locker rooms during the past 30 minutes and closed the locker doors, checked the toilet paper, wiped off the sinks, and picked up the floor? Has anyone picked up the magazines in the cardio area? Has anyone picked up the clutter in the cycle room? If all of these things are done, move on to number 5.

> In the fitness business, the rule of perpetual motion is that no energy force shall ever come to rest while on the job.

- If all else fails, you should go clean something. Wipe down the equipment, wipe the fountain, pick something up, check the weights, or do something to improve the business.

If someone comes in and needs a membership, sell the membership and then work your way down the list again. If nothing else is left to do, then clean, which the members see and equate with good service anyway.

These things are easy to teach in a one-hour staff meeting. The list can be posted on the door in the break room or somewhere else out of the member's site. Teach your employees: If you don't have something to do, read the wall and get moving.

## Building a Culture of Success

Most staff members want to do a decent job, but they aren't really given a chance because the expected outcome is never defined. When clubs maximize their sales efforts, they do so because everyone on the team is involved in the sales effort and everyone understands that their job is to either sell or support.

This support can come from understanding the basics of the job, such as providing service, or from simple acts such as moving through the club and picking up a few old magazines. All these things combine to give the guest a perception of service that is beyond the level of your competitors and ultimately will sell you more memberships over time.

Remember, you are in an industry that is based on making money every day to stay in business. Your job as an employee is to help make this money by either selling memberships or by working the club's profit centers. If you're not doing either of those things at the moment, then make sure you are the best part of every member's day.

Most importantly, while you are doing these things, keep in mind that you are the real product in this business. You are what the club ultimately sells, since if a member, or potential member, gives up his money, it's because he liked the person he was talking to and trusted his help.

As the club's real product, employees have certain personal responsibilities they assume when they go to work for a fitness business, or for any other type of business for that matter. When you work for someone, you assume a responsibility toward that job and that employer. Whether the employee has taken this responsibility as something personal is always proven by the answer to a single question: "Is what you did today the best work you are capable of in this job?"

Any time anyone goes to work for someone else, an underlying agreement always exists between the two that this question is going to be answered "yes"

> **When clubs maximize their sales efforts, they do so because everyone on the team is involved in the sales effort and everyone understands that their job is to either sell or support.**

every day. What separates a good employee from a great employee is whether the person accepts this fact as part of the job. Teach this lesson on the first day of any new hire's training, because answering "yes" is also how the culture in your business should be defined from the first day forward.

Other personal responsibilities help define a good employee. These things can be taught and should be part of the club's culture, and therefore shared by all who work there:

- *A sense of timeliness.* Timeliness is defined as delivering the best customer service you are capable of when the member needs it and wants it, not when it is convenient for you. The team should always strive to make each member's visit to the club the best part of his day.

- *Being on time.* Being on time for any employee, and owners and managers too, means being 15 minutes early. One of the biggest insults you can give anyone is to disrespect their time. If you have a 2 o'clock sales appointment, then you should arrive 1:45. When the guest comes in, you should be prepared and ready to work. Coming in at 2 o'clock for a 2 o'clock appointment and then spending a few minutes cleaning up your desk is not professional and is an insult to the guest. This rule applies to salespeople, trainers, janitors, and every single employee in the business.

- *Everyone does everything.* To sell the Ferrari, you must drive the Ferrari. This statement translates in the fitness business to every employee being involved in everything the club has to offer. It doesn't matter if you do a cycle class every day, but it does matter that you hit a group class at least several times a month so that you, as a salesperson, are fresh and up-to-date about what the club is offering. If you have weights, then each employee should be working out with strength equipment. If you offer group sessions, then you must have at least a limited presence and experience with group training. If you offer tanning, then you'd better be bronzed. If you offer childcare, then you will be pregnant by the first of the year. A few limits apply to this theory, of course, but the point is that you have to be involved in what you sell to be effective in sales.

**You have to be involved in what you sell to be effective in sales.**

- *You must be a work in progress.* You don't have to be in the world's greatest shape, but you do have to be a work in progress. If you've lost 25 pounds but still have 25 to go, then welcome to the club. As long as you are working on yourself, you are credible and believable—two necessary traits for any salesperson or employee.

- *It's all your job.* In the fitness business, you are a team. Each employee watches the back of every other employee. If you're leaving at 7 o'clock, but the front counter is getting slammed, you jump in to help even though that is not your official job. In the fitness business, it's all your job and you do whatever it takes to keep production going for that day.

The question is, "What makes a good employee?" A club needs people who accept personal responsibility for their own work, can communicate well, are fired up about working with people, and who practice the fitness lifestyle in some form. If you have these basic traits and are willing to be coached, then you will be that salesperson that makes all the difference in your club, and reap the benefits that come with that success.

**A club needs people who accept personal responsibility for their own work, can communicate well, are fired up about working with people, and who practice the fitness lifestyle in some form.**

## Key Points From This Chapter

- Every employee is part of the sales process.

- A difference exists between being a good employee and being an effective employee.

- You help people as part of the sales process. If you have no fear of trying, then you can probably make it as a salesperson in a fitness business.

- The single biggest trait you need to make it in the club business is the ability to be a good communicator.

- The second biggest trait is enthusiasm.

- You are in a production-based business. A good employee can take a role in driving the production of the business.

- Every employee, in any business, who will excel accepts a personal code of responsibility for his work and for who he is.

- Selling memberships is part of everyone's job.

- Your role as a team member can be defined in three simple phrases: You sell or support, you help with cash flow, or you provide legendary service.

- A staff in motion adds to the culture of sales. In other words, if you're not selling, then you are helping create an environment for sales.

- The law of perpetual motion means that you are constantly doing something to either handle sales, service members, or get the club ready for the next guest.

**Tip of the Day**

# Don't forget what it's like to be a beginner.

You're at a family reunion and a seriously overweight relative asks you the following question about working out: "So, I'd like to get started walking, but I don't know where to begin." You stare at your relative, fighting the urge to tell him to just get his butt out the door and have at it. Come on, it's just walking and everyone knows how to walk right?

Wrong, and you just broke another important rule. The longer you're in the fitness world, the harder it is to recapture that beginner's mentality. Your relative asked a serious question, based up upon her perspective, but as you rolled your eyes and gave her that "you are so dumb" look, you lost the vantage point that would make you very successful in sales.

People in the fitness industry forget what it's like to be a beginner, which inadvertently colors their speech and mannerisms when they talk to potential members who are seeking their help. Rather than asking yourself how the person possibly can't know the answer, you would be better off telling yourself that the question is just right for their experience and abilities and answering the question at the level from which it was asked.

Another problem is that people like to show how smart they are. The worst perpetrator of this mistake might be a trainer who recently returned from a three-day seminar. Every sentence out of the person's mouth is filled with buzzwords and training jargon meant to prove his expertise and superiority in the fitness world.

Don't talk down to people, but learn to answer questions at the appropriate level and with language that the person might understand. It is scary approaching fitness for the first time and few people enjoy looking stupid or being embarrassed. Remembering that fear and stepping back to the beginner level will make you a better salesperson.

You would also benefit from putting yourself in the beginner's role once a year. For example, if you have never snowboarded, treat yourself to a lesson or two. That sport is guaranteed to make you feel like a beginner again and humble you in a short period of time. Remember those feelings and use them when working with your next deconditioned guest.

# 4

# Important Terms to Know Before You Get Started

Almost anything is easier if you have a basic idea about the important points that make up the system you are going to learn. The selling system presented in this book is based upon years of experience trying to ethically sell memberships in all types of fitness facilities.

Any system, however, is improved once you return to the core concepts that form its foundation. The terms that follow are ideas you will need to understand to get the most out of this system in the shortest period of time. If you study these terms and become familiar with them, mastering sales in a fitness facility will become much easier.

Most of these terms are used throughout this book and the other books I've written for Healthy Learning. Many of the words or phrases have a chapter dedicated to expanding upon the idea. Brief definitions are listed in the front of this section, as many of the terms are used in other chapters.

## Definition of Sales

In this book, sales is defined simply as helping people. Prospective members come to you for help and it is your job and duty to see that you find a way to give them the help they desire. Since you are working in a business, a charge is associated with this help, but the thing to remember is that you are in the business of changing lives and you can't help the person unless he first becomes a member. The old definition of sales is not used in this book. Sales is not slick and high-pressure techniques applied to a person to get him to buy something he doesn't really want or need. Help someone find a solution to his problem and he will be more than willing to spend money with you and financially support your facility.

# Production-based Business

You have to make money every single day in the fitness business. The term "production-based" means that you are in the business of generating revenue each day from a variety of sources. Remember, 95 percent of what you do in the fitness business is selling somebody something every day. The other 5 percent is the management of this money and the application of systems to make money. Part of your job in a fitness facility is to help generate this income. Actions such as getting someone a drink as he leaves the gym, being courteous to a guest as she waits for a salesperson, or patiently answering questions about fitness that you have heard a thousand times before, all lead to more revenue in the club. Production simply means that you have to produce revenue each and every time you work in the club as part of your job.

# Validate the Buying Decision

People want to feel good about what they buy, but most fitness facilities don't support that notion. When someone works hard for their money, and then decides to spend some of that cash in your business, you need to find a way to make him feel good about the buying experience. Most club owners sign someone up as a new member and then send him home with nothing more than a copy of a contract (pink), a copy of a copy of a copy of an aerobic schedule, and a business card in case he wants to call with a referral. Your goal is to validate the buying decision so that the person feels good about the purchase, and therefore feels good about buying again in the future and referring his friends to you without you having to pound him for names and numbers. The best way to validate any purchase is to reward that behavior in a positive manner.

# Discounting

Discounting, or
dropping a price to
pressure a person to
buy "now," is a
negative action that
does not make the
person feel good
about what he
bought.

Discounting, or dropping a price to pressure a person to buy "now," is a negative action that does not make the person feel good about what he bought. "If only I would have held out a little longer, then I might have gotten an even better deal," is the thought flashing through his mind on the drive home. This thought does nothing to drive referrals or win a long-term customer. Positively rewarding the person with gifts, such as gym bags and personal-training packages, while still sticking to the price and not making deals, lets the person know that you do appreciate his business and that he did make a good decision about spending his money with you.

# Support Materials

Support materials constitute a sales-prohibiting weakness in most clubs. These clubs rely on verbal assaults to get the sale, and fail to back up their salespeople with any type of supportive materials. For example, typical chain clubs spend hours teaching their staff members verbal ways to overcome objections, trial close, or probe for personal information up front, and then let the salesperson write the prices out for the prospective client on a yellow pad. Another example is a club owner who cites service as his biggest differentiator and then sends the guest home with a cheap, three-fold brochure and another copy of a copy of a copy of an old aerobics schedule.

Strong support materials, such as Welcome Guides, preprinted closing sheets, and well-done buddy-referral tools, all add significant points to a club's overall closing rate. Welcome Guides, which are discussed in Chapter 16, are approximately 70 pages of information contained in a smartly done three-ring binder. The information ranges from interesting articles that get people motivated to join a gym to a list of the club's complete service offerings and the associated costs. Most clubs also include testimonials, pictures from the club's last social event, and anything else of interest that makes your club stand out over the competition.

## Sales Presentations

Sales presentations were once based primarily on learning set pitches, ways to overcome objections, and tricks to lead the prospective member down the path toward an easy sale. Over time, the guest became more jaded and sophisticated, but most of these techniques were never updated. The modern sales presentation can be thought of in more complete terms and includes the verbal presentation aspects; how you physically meet and greet the guest; touring using a set, repeatable format; and other important details, such as developing strong support materials that make the sale easier for any salesperson.

Another way to think of a complete sales presentation is to remember that it's not just the words that you say that will get the sale finalized; it's how you say them, what you are wearing, how you present the club compared to your competitors, and the quality of your tools, including what you send the person home with after the sale or even what they have in their hand when they leave if they didn't sign up that day. When you think of an effective sales presentation, think of mastering all the details and remember that everything counts when it comes to improving your closing rate.

## Trial Memberships

You can use two methods to attract potential members to your club: price and exposure. Price ads are really just types of sales in which you hope that people who are interested in fitness in your market respond to your discounting. Several issues make price specials fail over time. For example, price ads are

**When you think of an effective sales presentation, think of mastering all the details and remember that everything counts when it comes to improving your closing rate.**

based upon the idea that you have a set price for a membership, but today you are going to discount that price to drive memberships. For example, a club might offer a "two-for-one summer membership fee" or a "buy one year and get a second year free" deal.

> **Once you come off your price and run a series of discount ads, it becomes hard to ever really charge full price again.**

Once you come off your price and run a series of discount ads, it becomes hard to ever really charge full price again. Most price-special owners have heard, "Hi, can you tell me what price special you are running this week?" You become known as the discount club, which makes it hard to ever run anything but specials. After a while, those specials have to get more extreme to work.

The second issue is that price ads assume prior knowledge. When a club first runs price specials, the ads actually do work for a while. After a few months, though, the return per ad drops because everyone in the market who has prior fitness experience and is looking to jump to another club has already done so. Each time the ad is run, the response becomes smaller. Price ads ultimately fail because they do nothing to attract new members who don't have any real fitness experience. If an overweight housewife has no fitness experience, what's price got to do with her joining a gym? She has no idea if the price is good or bad and she still has to pay before she even gets a chance to try out the club.

Exposure ads are based upon the concept of "try before you buy." You essentially say to the consumer, "Here is my service. Come try it. If you like it, then we will talk about buying a membership." Exposure marketing is similar to an attorney who might give a potential client some free time to see if he can handle the case before he takes the retainer.

The philosophy behind a trial is simple. You say to the potential customer: "We feel very strongly that we have the best gym in town, but talk is cheap. Would you like to come try our facility for a full 14 days with no risk, no obligation, and no money up front? We would like you to come meet our staff and meet the other members, and if at the end of 14 days we haven't earned your business, then we don't deserve to have you as a member."

Trial memberships, which are discussed further in Chapter 8, come in various forms, but the most common ones are as follows:

- *The seven-day trial* is for people who haven't used the trial before or for new clubs.

- *The 14-day trial* is the standard for most clubs.

- *The 21-day trial* can be used in conjunction with a club offering the 14-day trial. The 21-day trial could be used with business-to-business offerings or for situations where you want to add more value beyond the 14 days that you might be using in your regular marketing.

- *The 30-day trial* is the ultimate tool for the club owner who has solid systems in place and who has strong competition in the market.

# Risk

Risk is the biggest barrier to inquiry. You can define risk as how much money you will lose if you try something and don't like it or use it. Risk is an unusual factor in that it is hard to determine just what a person's individual risk tolerance is. Some people don't care and will throw a lot of money at something and then walk away quickly, while others won't risk anything until someone proves to them that they are going to love it.

When it comes to fitness centers, the perception of risk is extremely high for many guests, especially those with little or no real fitness-facility experience. These people always carry the fear that they will be pressured into something (a valid fear in most markets) and then get stuck paying for something that they aren't using for the rest of their lives.

Your leads will increase if you lower the perception of risk in your marketing. For example, trial memberships completely eliminate risk because the person can try the club with no risk, no obligation, and no money up front. This type of marketing attracts people who don't respond to traditional price-driven marketing.

Price marketing, for example, works off the assumption that someone already has decided that he wants a fitness membership and now he is shopping price. Price marketing does work for a little while in some markets because it sucks all the experienced gym people out of the market or out of other clubs. Price marketing eventually fails, however, because you eventually run out these people. These same price ads won't attract anyone who hasn't been in a gym, though, because price is not a motivator, or even relevant, to someone who doesn't have any experience and doesn't understand what it means to belong to a fitness facility.

Money-back guarantees sound very enticing. Theoretically speaking, this tool should work in your ads, but it doesn't. Why? Because money still has to change hands up front and the problem of perceived risk still exists. How does the consumer really know that he will get his money back if he quits? Money-back guarantees are also overexposed and every mail-order gizmo on television has a guarantee attached. This association with low-end products makes guarantees a harder concept to implement in a membership situation and means that they are not nearly as effective at attracting prospective members as a "try before you buy" offer.

**When it comes to fitness centers, the perception of risk is extremely high for many guests, especially those with little or no real fitness-facility experience.**

# Learning Styles

Learning styles are discussed in greater detail in Chapter 5 but the point to remember is that learning styles also impact how people make buying decisions. These styles—auditory, visual, or "doer"—and how people process information can dictate the decision-making experience. In the sales environment, an auditory person likes to hear the story, a visual person likes to take a lot of material to read or watch someone do it first, and the doer responds best to simply trying the place out for a few days. If you want to get the most out of your sales, you have to build a system that covers all three styles every time, as opposed to using older systems where you just try to talk (auditory) someone into submission, which is the style used by most clubs. The Plummer sales system is based upon all three learning styles and includes a well-practiced method of talking and getting to know the guest, strong support materials, and trial memberships.

# Sales Obstacles

**Anything that gets in the way of completing a sale is an obstacle.**

Anything that gets in the way of completing a sale is an obstacle. For example, out-of-order signs, dirty locker rooms, poorly dressed staff, bad music, poorly lit group exercise rooms, lack of support materials, inexperienced front-counter people, and a list of other things common to most clubs are all barriers that make it harder to get the sale. The important point to remember is that all of these things can be controlled to some extent by the club and, therefore, can be neutralized. The sad thing is that guests seldom ever mention these things during the tour. They just quietly disappear using one of the more common objections. These little things can kill your sales program and every effort has to be taken every month to identify and eliminate as many of the sales obstacles as possible.

# Cash Flow

Cash flow is something that happens even when sales don't. Most clubs only have cash in the register if the sales team scores that day. If the team doesn't score and no new sales money comes in, the club has no cash. This situation makes the club completely dependent on new sales, and if sales slow down for even a few days the club can run out of operating cash.

Balanced clubs have cash from three prime areas: new sales, dependable monthly money from the club's receivable base, and daily cash flow from profit centers. Profit-center cash is often neglected and yet can provide the biggest return to a club over time. Club owners who understand cash flow might not do any sales on Monday, but they always have people working out. These people are hungry, thirsty, and need other services, making each one of them a candidate to spend money (cash flow) in the club during each visit. The club might not have any new sales, but the same owner had 500 workouts and put $2000 in the register from members who visited that day and bought something. Successful clubs develop cash flow every day and lower their dependency on new sales as their primary source of income.

# Expected Outcome

If you don't know where you are going, how will you know when you get there? It is common for many owners and managers to start an event or task without any idea of what a successful conclusion might look like when they reach it. For example, owners and managers often give their young staff tasks to do in the club, but they seldom give them an idea of what that task will look like when they have completed it. A directive as simple as, "Clean the storage closet" becomes easier when it is coupled with, "and when you're done we should have the drinks lined up on this side by brand, the supplements over here, cleaning supplies in the cabinets, and anything that is old or broken in the dumpster. You should be able to finish this job by 4 o'clock this afternoon."

Do you really have to paint a picture for your staff? Yes and no. Visual people work better when they have an idea, or picture, in their heads of what something looks like when it is completed. Such a person will simply be more successful and effective if he has a mental image of what a successful conclusion looks like when he hits it.

Bigger tasks are also easier to accomplish if a person has an idea of what he is trying to do. For example, the owner tells the manager that the club needs to increase sales over the next few months and then sets an arbitrary goal for the sales team. The team is not likely to hit this goal because it has no ties to current numbers or the situation in the club.

The owner and staff might be more successful if the owner first ties the goal to the reality in the club at the moment. For example, if the club averaged 75 new sales per month during the same time period last year, the team might be able to increase that number by 10 percent. In this case, the owner needs to state: "We averaged 75 new sales per month last year during the fall. This year I am increasing my marketing by about 20 percent, we have added one new salesperson, and we have had a lot of extra sales training. Based upon those things, I feel that we can increase our monthly average by 10 percent. In other words, we need to make between 82 and 85 new sales per month average for the fall selling period to be successful."

This simple example illustrates nothing more than, "Here is where we are, here is why we can do better, and here is the exact number we need to hit" (expected outcome). If the team hits this number, it has accomplished the mission. If the team doesn't hit this number, then it has failed. The expected outcome is a clearly stated range, 82 to 85 new sales, which must be hit for the team to achieve success.

The expected outcome is also like a goal in the sense that the term can be applied to many other aspects in the club. For example, consider an owner trying to get a staff person to address envelopes by hand. "Hey Janie, will you address these envelopes today while you're here and put them in my office

> **If you don't know where you are going, how will you know when you get there?**

when you're done?" This owner is most likely going to be frustrated with the result of this instruction, because he isn't clearly stating to his staff person what he wants done, when it should be done, and what it might look like if it was done correctly. It might be better to say, "Janie, please block out two hours and sit in my office and hand address these envelopes for our special promotion. Here is a sample one to model from. You should be able to have these finished by 3 o'clock. I will check on you in an hour. If you have any problems, please find me. Seventy-five envelopes are in the box. When you're done, they should be in the box and in the order they are on the list. Thank you."

# Delivery System

Old-style aerobics programs are perfect examples of a good idea delivered in a horrible manner.

Old-style aerobics programs are perfect examples of a good idea delivered in a horrible manner. When aerobics first became a hot idea in the club world in the 1980s, the concept was so new and strong that it carried itself without a lot of packaging. Get a talented instructor and some decent music and you were good to go. In those days, the owner could get by with a room with white walls, eight-foot rectangular mirrors turned sideways, and even carpet on the floor. Aerobics was the next big thing and the environment in which the classes were delivered was far less important than the fact that you had classes and some of the new music from the West Coast.

Flash-forward to today and you'll see the rules have changed. Aerobics is dead and has been replaced by the magic of group exercise, and the delivery system is now much more important. If you try to offer classes in an old white room with standard mirrors, little baskets of sweaty bands on one wall, piles of worn dumbbells in the corners, and bikes and stability balls in the back, you will find that you're getting your old-style aerobic butt kicked in the marketplace.

You might as well dress your instructors in leg warmers and play old Sylvester music, for all the financial good you'll gain from this worn-out business plan. Yes, you may still have 12 old aerobics queens out there jumping up and down and wearing the same clothes they had on in 1986, but you can't build a successful group program on the past.

The business has matured and the consumer has gotten more sophisticated, not only in her expectation about group exercise, but also in what she expects from any experience she pays for. Consider children's birthday parties, for example. In the 1980s, a birthday party for your child might be a simple affair with a few kids, a cake Mom made, and a few small presents. The kids played games for entertainment and went home full of cake and ice cream. Today, a birthday party thrown for a one-year-old might have giant rented castles, entertainers, a full-blown party for the adults, and way too many gifts.

The same changes have taken place in the restaurant industry as well. When you read a review about a new restaurant, you have to read through a half-page about the ambience, the décor, the experience gained from the lighting behind the bar, and the uniforms before the writer even mentions the food.

These days, it's not just about the food. It's about the experience that surrounds the food. The same is true in your gym. It is not only about fitness, but also how fitness is delivered to the consumer. If you want to be successful in the fitness business in the coming years, you have to understand that offering equipment, classes, and a friendly staff is not enough to buy and maintain market share. The future will belong to anyone who understands that the consumer wants her fitness to be an experience that delights her, entertains her, and leaves her feeling that she has gotten her money's worth.

Apply this understanding to the old-style aerobics example. Owners and managers once were able to get by with a 1980s-style aerobics room, but not anymore. Group participants want décor, an amazing music system, and athletic classes developed by teams of experts, such as those offered by Body Training Systems®, that tantalize the soul during each visit. Classes are not enough. You must focus on how the classes are delivered and the environment that supports the classes. It is no longer just the instructor that matters, but what the instructor is wearing, how she interacts with the class, and the training she has had.

More sophisticated members want a more sophisticated experience, and this experience is offered through a delivery system that matches your consumers and their desires. Mastering the art of building a unique delivery system also gives you an advantage in a crowded marketplace, where even the average group class is made better by its better delivery.

## Trigger Factor

Fitness doesn't sell. Fitness has never sold and will not sell in the future. Owners who attempt to sell fitness for a living probably will not make it. Owners who do make it, and make it big, understand that selling the *results* of physical fitness (selling the benefit) is how to make money, because this philosophy actually gives the consumers what they want.

No one—aside from an occasional older adult—joins a gym to live longer, because most people looking for a membership are trying to solve other problems that are more urgent in nature and more personal in need. These issues are also usually more emotion-based.

A potential member walks into a fitness facility because of one simple reason: Something snapped in his life and triggered an emotional reaction that

**Mastering the art of building a unique delivery system also gives you an advantage in a crowded marketplace, where even the average group class is made better by its better delivery.**

led him to say, "Today's the day I'm joining." This emotional driver is called a trigger factor, because even after years of neglect, something happened in the person's life that led him to seek out a fitness source.

A trigger factor usually isn't far off in the future, but rather something that is immediate in the person's life. For example, a woman in her 30s who is going to be in a summer wedding in just six weeks may worry about her bare arms being visible to all 200 guests during the wedding and for hours afterwards at the reception. The trigger is the wedding and the insecurity about being out of shape, and the reaction is a distraught woman standing at the front counter looking for a fitness membership.

Of course, many other trigger factors exist, such as divorce, vacations, birthdays that end in zero, and even the simple pain of having to suck in your gut to button your pants on the morning after a long weekend of too much food and fun. All of these events trigger emotional responses that can lead to action.

**Understanding trigger effects is important in the sales process.**

Understanding trigger effects is important in the sales process. Not being aware of them leads to missed opportunity and disappointed guests who leave without a solution to their problems.

A major disconnect occurs when a guest comes in looking for a solution to a specific problem and you end up trying to sell her fitness delivered over a long period of time. "You just don't understand," she quietly thinks during the sales tour, as the club's employee talks about equipment, long-term memberships, and the need to start thinking about whether her husband wants to join too.

"I have to be in a wedding in just six weeks, which means that I only have six weeks to get into the best shape of my life. Why can't you, young salesperson who has never been out of shape, hear my pain?" She doesn't actually voice this plea, however, and instead just mumbles that she needs to think about it and disappears. Her next solution is magic weight-loss pills, starving herself, or some other stupid human fitness trick that might lead to short-term success but long-term failure.

The very nature of the fitness business prevents you from helping this woman be successful, not because you are unwilling to do something harmful, such as offer her a questionable solution like diet pills, but because you have been taught, as a member of the fitness industry, that you fail in your job unless you get her tied to a long-term membership. Most clubs simply don't have any way to help this woman, because her problem falls outside the typical membership structure.

First of all, you need a short-term solution in your price structure that handles the pressures of the trigger effect. This woman, from a technical viewpoint, can't achieve very much in just six weeks. The other side of that issue, however, is that with your guidance, she can get further than she could if she attempted it on her own. Most owners are just too pure for their own good and can't stand the fact that she is not willing to commit to fitness for the rest of her life.

In other words, the club that failed her sells fitness and the club that helped her sells hope, which will win out over fitness every single time. "Janie, I don't know how far we can get you in six weeks, but I do guarantee this; if you get started moving today with a little cardio, get a little help on your nutrition for the next six weeks, and are willing to try, I know you will feel better about your shape than you have in a long time by that wedding."

Long-term fitness may be the right thing for her over time, but the step is just too big. Many people that don't have a lot of fitness experience need a shorter, baby step into the fitness world. She might soon be able to see that the next, longer step is not so intimidating. And if you really believe in your product and your facility, why aren't you willing to risk it by giving her a chance to start with a smaller step rather than forcing a long-term commitment?

The solution could take the form of a three-month Total Support membership. This membership could be the step before your regular annual membership. The Total Support membership would include a trainer every week, perhaps in a semiprivate situation but not necessarily one-on-one, nutritional guidance, and some free gizmos such as a T-shirt and water bottle. Think of this membership as a way for someone without a lot of fitness experience to explore the club, get started with full support, address the trigger event, and then have a chance to roll over into a regular membership at the end. Don't overprice this type of membership. For example, if your monthly membership is $49 per month, this option could be priced at $329 as an introduction-to-fitness program that is only available once to an individual.

> Closing rates are defined as how many people out of every 100 you talk to buy annual memberships within 30 days of the first visit to the club.

It is important to note that, in most situations, the person never tells anyone about the emotional driver that brought her through the front door that day. She may mention the wedding, but not say that she is afraid of short-sleeve dresses. Another customer may mention in passing that he is divorced, but never tell you that he is horribly embarrassed about how he looks without a shirt. Understand that the triggers exist, but also understand that you might not hear the words you are looking for that would make your life easier as a salesperson.

# Closing Rates

How good do you have to be to be considered an effective salesperson? The answer lies in the closing rates. Closing rates are defined as how many people out of every 100 you talk to buy annual memberships within 30 days of the first visit to the club.

For example, if a sales team encounters 100 guests during a month and ends up with 38 annual memberships, then the team's closing rate is 38 percent, which is the national average for most clubs. This number is based upon clubs using trial memberships, which are the most effective way to attract the widest number of potential members over time.

When you are using trials, you should calculate your closing percentage using a gross average, because some guests start at the end of the month but don't become members until the following month. Using a gross average means that you simply count the enrollment during the actual month the person signed up in rather than trying to backtrack and count the membership during the month the person first visited the club, since the numbers will all average out over time anyway.

This method of calculating the closing rate also assumes that you are focused on annual memberships. Only count annual memberships, since, while the short-term memberships do help cash flow, they don't help the club grow over time because they don't impact the receivable base. The exception might be a club using the Total Support three-month membership described in the Trigger Factor section. This tool is often financed by the club and helps build the receivable base.

**Your goal should be that 55 percent of all qualified members buy annual memberships within 30 days of their first visit.**

Your goal should be that 55 percent of all qualified members buy annual memberships within 30 days of their first visit. Out of this number, 30 percent, which is the minimum acceptable standard for judging your sales team's efficiency, should buy their memberships on the first visit.

These numbers are tracked daily for each member of the team and for the team as a whole, and then totaled for the month. Use this number as your training indicator and as the standard you seek to achieve in your business.

## Drop Close

The drop close is an old tool from the early days of sales. Drop closing is a form of pressure applied during the sale to get the prospective member to buy "today." For example, a salesperson might say, "Normally our membership fee is $150, but if you are willing to get started today it is only going to be $50. I am only going to offer this deal today because I know you are serious and ready to make up your mind."

A number of problems existed with this system, but the most important was that the consumer became more sophisticated and the scheme just stopped working. Who really believes that if they come back tomorrow they won't get some type of deal? Does anyone still believe that any type of percentage discount is real? Furniture listed at 50 percent off was marked up before being marked down. Clothing at a severe discount is nothing but leftovers the store couldn't sell during its first three sales. Major chunks of money or percentages off aren't perceived as real, and the average consumer doesn't trust or respond to these gimmicks.

Secondly, drop closing doesn't work with two of the three learning styles. Visual people need time to look at and study materials and doers need to get a few workouts and experience the club. If a drop close works at all, it only does for the auditory folks who interact well with salespeople. Drop closing also fails to work with people who have money. Knocking off $50 is just plain insulting to these people, and anyone with any money is not going to go crazy and sign a membership under pressure based upon saving a few fictitious dollars.

## Features and Benefits

These two terms fall into the "lost art" category. Much has been written over the years about features and benefits in a variety of sales and marketing books, but they are still probably the most abused and confused words an inexperienced salesperson encounters.

Features are the components that make up a product or service. Benefits are what the product or service does for you. Benefits sell stuff. Features don't sell anybody anything.

> Features are the components that make up a product or service. Benefits are what the product or service does for you. Benefits sell stuff. Features don't sell anybody anything.

In a fitness business, features include all of the programs and products you have in the business. Owners usually list these things using bullet points in their ads. For example, some typical copy for a newspaper ad might look as follows:

- More than 100 classes per week
- Personal training
- 50,000 pounds of free weights
- Wood lockers
- Tanning
- Childcare
- Nutrition bars and supplements

These points are the features of this particular fitness business. This ad is also an example of bad marketing. Can you imagine a hotel running an ad that states: "We have beds and toilets"? This example may sound silly, but is it any worse than stating: "Come to our gym, we have fitness stuff"?

Listing features assumes that the person reading the ad is a complete gym dog who is looking for 50,000 pounds of weights and had trouble with his last locker. Feature ads do nothing to drive new business to a club because this type of ad doesn't build interest for the inexperienced user.

Benefits, on the other hand, provide the answer to the most basic question: What's in it for me as the consumer? Features don't answer this question, because stating a component of your business, such as classes or training, doesn't directly relate to a potential customer's problems or needs.

The way automobiles are sold is a great example of features and benefits at work. Expensive sports cars might list their suspension, engine output, or 0-to-60 speed, but they are advertised toward their target market with an indirect approach. The announcer, for example, might be talking about speed and quality, but the ad shows a guy ripping through curves with a beautiful woman sitting in the seat next to him. The implied message is: Buy this car and you too, you middle-aged, second-childhood accountant, can get the adrenalin rush from this car's sheer speed and smooth cornering, and that young babe will be yours too for only $65,000.

Most tours in the fitness business are nothing more than extended features lists. "Here are our 80 treadmills, here is our group room where we hold 100 classes, and here is our locker room with real wood lockers." All of these features are supposed to dazzle the potential buyer.

As a side note, why do most club owners insist on touring their locker rooms with the guests? Think of your current members for just a second and you'll see that touring the locker rooms is not such a great idea. Imagine being a member standing with one foot up on a bench drying off after your shower when a salesperson comes through with a tour. "Hey, here is Joe, one of our great members. Joe, this is Melvin, a guest today." Joe is naked, part of the tour, and now feels obligated to shake hands with Melvin. Keep in mind that naked people in your locker rooms shouldn't be part of any sales tour. Let the guest walk through your locker room on his own, exploring quietly without disrupting your members. Female guests especially like to wander and see how clean the place is, and may actually want to use the facilities without you continuing your rap outside the stall door.

Everything on the tour, and everything in your marketing, should become benefit driven. The ultimate benefit involves trying before you buy. "How would you like to try the club with no obligation or any money up front?" This type of ad powerfully answers the question: What's in it for me as the consumer?

## Selling Stations

**Selling stations are tools that can be used to increase sales effectiveness, train new sales people more quickly, and ensure that every guest in the gym sees everything during each tour.**

Selling stations are tools that can be used to increase sales effectiveness, train new sales people more quickly, and ensure that every guest in the gym sees everything during each tour. Selling stations are pieces of artwork, usually about 2 x 3 feet in size, that list the benefits of each area of the club. During the tour, the salesperson stops at each one and relates that information in benefit form to the guest. For example, the salesperson might stop at the station outside of the childcare area, where the following benefits are listed:

- Our childcare area is open during the following hours for your convenience:
  - √ Monday–Thursday: 8:00–11:00 am and 4:00–7:00 pm
  - √ Friday and Saturday: 8:00 am to 12 noon
- We have planned activities four nights a week for your child.
- We guarantee one childcare provider for every eight children during our peak hours.
- We have three video monitors displayed throughout the club that provide constant monitoring of our childcare area.

If the guest is a mother, the salesperson might spend several minutes at this station highlighting the service and how it can benefit her. If the guest doesn't have children, the salesperson still must stop at the station and at least say, "Bill, I know you are a serious fitness guy and don't have kids, but we just want you know that we have this service available in case you ever have a guest that might need it." Chapter 18 further explains selling stations and includes sample copy for all of the key club areas.

## Behavior-Modification Tools

What do you send home with a guest who doesn't become a member that day? The standard issue for most clubs' sales teams is an aerobic schedule, a price sheet, and a business card. Even club owners who think they masters of the membership don't send the person home with much more than a three-fold brochure or even a stack folder of some type. All of these items are cheap and can't convey the message that you want the person to receive. Are these items really what you want in front of the person when he sits down at home to make a buying decision?

**Behavior-modification tools change how the guest perceives the club and how he reacts to traditional club materials.**

If your price is $39 or higher per month, 70 percent of your guests will need two or more visits to the club before buying. In other words, once your memberships get up to $500 or more per year, the large majority of your guests need to think about it for a day or two before they will commit that much money. The learning-style theory also kicks in at this point. Your visual types want to go home and review your materials, while the doers will have a very hard time making any type of decision based upon what has been given to them so far.

Behavior-modification tools give the person something more to think about after visiting the gym. Perhaps he has visited a couple of gyms and is sitting at home with his wife talking about which gym they want to try first. Again, it is in this setting that the person makes the decision and the club with the best support materials will likely earn his membership.

The recommended tool is the Welcome Guide. Remember, Welcome Guides are information books that are handed out to each guest before he takes the tour. These tools are called behavior-modification tools because they change how the guest perceives the club and how he reacts to traditional club materials.

Welcome Guides contain approximately 70 pages of information, including basic club information, pictures from the club's last party, testimonials, a list of club services, motivational articles about getting started in fitness, information about why the club offers a trial and how to take advantage of it, and, yes, a list of prices. The average person is way too busy for you to leave the prices out the kit that he takes home after the tour, but you should also show value in the form of the trial membership offer. All of this information should be packaged in a high-quality three-ring binder with color. It's recommended that you use a three-ring binder system so that you can change the piece often rather getting it bound but never changing it or updating the information. Keep in mind that you might be spending $5000 per month on marketing. Shouldn't you spend another $2.50 to increase your chances of closing the sale?

Imagine the same customer going home and talking to his significant other. "Hey, I got that club information today. Look, the first club gave me a yellow piece of paper with the prices written on it, the second club gave me a cheap-looking three-fold brochure, and the new club gave me a 70-page information book in a classy three-ring binder with color pictures. And look, he put in a full 14-day trial for you, too. I don't know, honey, which club do you want to try?" The choice is obvious and easy because the best club had the best information in front of the potential customers when they made their decision.

**Welcome Guides provide another way of extending your brand outside your walls.**

Welcome Guides provide another way of extending your brand outside your walls. If done correctly, these tools can travel from friend to friend or from relative to relative because they have interesting information, and they are high-quality, so someone is more likely to pass it on rather than throw it away.

## Immediate-Response Tool

In the future, one of the sales keys will be who can get relevant information to the customer the fastest. People are busier now than they were in the past, and people shop less now than they did just a few years ago, especially if it involves physically going to look at something. Computers can be used to get this information to someone quickly and, if used correctly, can help prevent the person from even shopping your competitors. Consider the following exchange:

*Bill:* I would like to get some information about your club.

*Sales:* Of course, I would be happy to help you with that information. By the way, have you ever been in our club before?

*Bill:* No, I haven't. I just received your flyer in my newspaper and thought it was worth the call.

*Sales:* Yes, that flyer just went out and we have been receiving calls all day. Hey, I'm sorry, I haven't introduced myself. My name is Kelly. Any you are? (Bill responds) I'm sorry Bill, we are busy today and I just picked up the phone and started talking. So, you received the ad. Was it the trial offer that made you call?

*Bill:* Yes. How does that work?

*Sales/Kelly:* Well, we feel strongly that we have the best club in the area, but everyone is going to say that. We are the only club, however, that will let you try the club absolutely free with no money up front, no obligation, and no risk on your part. We would like you to come meet our staff, meet the other members, and at the end of 14 days, if we haven't earned your business, then we don't deserve to have you as a member. How does that sound, Bill?

*Bill:* I like it. I just moved here and I would like to get started so I don't miss my workouts.

**In the future, one of the sales keys will be who can get relevant information to the customer the fastest.**

*Sales/Kelly:* We can get you started today Bill, if you like. By the way, are you near a computer? If so, I can email over a Word document that really details everything we do here.

*Bill:* Yeah, that sounds good. I am at Bill@aol.com.

Kelly sends the material over and, within seconds, has five pages of quality material in front of a prospect, including information about getting started with the trial. She has tied him to the club and reduced his incentive to keep shopping, because he already has a 14-day membership that he can enjoy first. Kelly also has information that she can review on the phone with him that allows her to build value with Bill that will make it more likely that he will show up for his workout. Remember, you aren't trying to sell him a membership at this point, but merely to increase your chances of getting him in front of a salesperson.

# Summary

The terms discussed in this chapter are the key words and phrases used throughout this section and the rest of the book. Most of the important points are detailed in their own chapters so you will be able to study and immediately apply them to your business.

# Take responsibility and develop yourself.

At some point, you move beyond your teachers, your parents, and others that drive you to learn and grow. The responsibility to continue to grow as a person then shifts to you.

Don't wait for your boss to tell you to learn something new. You should force yourself to grow as a person each day by learning a new skill that will help you somewhere in your life. Work on how you dress. Work on how you talk. Work on a business skill you need. Learn to sell and present yourself, which is a fundamental skill for almost anything you want to do in your life.

Many young staff people get out of school thinking that they know everything, but the harsh reality is that once you leave school your real education begins. If you want to be successful as a person as well financially, it's what you learn after you get out of school that counts, and you must take personal responsibility to learn those lessons.

# WHO ARE YOU DEALING WITH AND WHAT DO THEY WANT?

Section Two

# 5

# How and Why Do People Buy?

When someone first learns sales, he will spend hours learning how to handle objections, take a phone call, correctly fill out all the necessary paperwork, and even upsell services and products. Very few new salespeople, however, will actually spend very much time trying to understand how and why people make that final decision to buy something.

Old pressure-sales guys believe that if you just pound on someone hard enough they will eventually buy. Locking them in an office, double-teaming them, in-your-face handling of objections, and phone harassment at home are all fair-game tactics for these low-ethic sales dinosaurs.

Yes, these guys can put some memberships on the board each day, but the truth is that a significantly large number of memberships sold under extreme pressure go bad, giving the owner a false impression of what is really happening in the business. The members that fold under the pressure don't sign because they want the membership; they sign because it seemed like the only way they could actually get out of the office alive. The club owner is excited because he thinks he got a new member for the club that day, but the buyer, because of the pressure sales tactics, defaults and the contract goes bad.

Mastering sales, especially in a competitive marketplace, requires that the owner and sales team take a much more sophisticated approach to learning and mastering the sales process. These old sales tactics, especially the need for pressure, don't hold up with a more sophisticated buyer in most clubs.

A sophisticated buyer can be defined as someone from the top 60 percent of the demographics in the market, as determined by household income. This person also has buying experience in real-world products such as insurance and possibly a house, and in typical consumer purchases, such as an automobile. This buyer has been sold to before and understands the selling game.

The exception to the rule of needing to learn more sophisticated selling techniques exists for the club owner whose business is focused on the lower end of the market. This owner offers low-end memberships costing $19 a month or less. Most of the customers for this type of fitness product aren't necessarily sophisticated buyers and will respond to many of the older types of sales tactics that give the industry such a bad name but that still work on a younger and less world-experienced buyer.

**Most buyers of a fitness membership, however, are people who have buying experience and who have outgrown the antiquated selling systems many owners just refuse to let go of in their businesses.**

Most buyers of a fitness membership, however, are people who have buying experience and who have outgrown the antiquated selling systems many owners just refuse to let go of in their businesses. This statement is validated by a lot of the research provided by the International Health, Racquet and Sportsclub Association (IHRSA) and others who all agree that the higher the household income, the more likely an individual is to join a fitness center. The more money a person makes, the more sophisticated he is as a buyer. It is also true that the more money a person makes, the more likely he is to value fitness and join a fitness center. The combination of a more sophisticated and affluent buyer is why you need to have a more advanced understanding of this new consumer and how you have to change your strategy of selling to him.

# How People Make Buying Decisions

The information in this section doesn't tell you "why" people buy the things they do. Instead, this information explains the processes of "how" people make the decision to buy something, learn something new, or even why they might be attracted to someone.

When trying to learn something new or buy something, each person has his own unique learning style. This style is defined by how an individual takes information in and processes it before taking the leap to buy or fully grasping new material. Each person does it a little bit differently, but most people fall into three broad categories: the auditory person, the visual person, and the "doer" person.

### The auditory person

The auditory person is someone who learns through listening. This type of person learns best, or makes a buying decision, based upon having someone explain things to him. In other words, you talk and this person listens and bases his decision to act on what he hears.

This person is often hated in high school or college. He sits with his feet straight out in front of the chair and his head laid back and appears half asleep in every class, but miraculously gets great grades. No miracle is taking place—just a true auditory learner at work.

## The visual person

A visual person learns through seeing. This type of person wants to read or study new information himself instead of having a teacher, or salesperson, explain what's going on.

This type of person is all about books, consumer reports, and Internet searches, and wants to gather all the material possible before buying. Visual people are great note takers in school and want to do all the research possible before buying that new television.

## The "doer" person

A doer—more technically called a tactile, kinesthetic person—learns through touch or movement. Tactile/kinesthetic means that this type of person learns either through reacting to the environment around him or by having the environment react to him.

While the auditory learner was faking a nap in class and the visual learner was filling her notebook, the doer was in the lab blowing stuff up. This person usually learns "the hard way."

For example, a mother yells to her three kids, "Don't touch the iron, it's hot and you'll get burned." The auditory child will listen to that warning and walk away in fear. The visual child can see that the iron is hot by the steam coming off the clothes when the iron touches them. The doer, however, just *has* to touch the iron. It is the only way he will learn and as soon as Mom is looking somewhere else, his little hand is reaching toward the iron. He will get burned, but only once. The problem is that this person usually learns all of life's lessons one beating at a time.

Every individual fits predominantly into one of these categories and has a blend of the other two. Look at another example and see where you fit.

Three people in a ski class are standing in front of the instructor on the slope, waiting to get the lesson underway. The auditory person listens to the instructor's words and tries what he has heard. The visual learner listens, but then says, "Can I just ski behind you down the slope and follow in your tracks?" which is just another way of visually grasping the new material. The doer, on the other hand, is just standing there looking anxious and digging his poles into the snow. He just wants to go and try it and see if he can figure it out on his own. He heads down the hill, blows up halfway down (the person reacting to his environment, perhaps the first bump in the snow), and then gets up and wants to do it again. The instructor gives him a few words of instruction and off the student goes again. This time, he hits a tree (the environment reacting to the person), gets up, and mumbles, "That hurts. I don't want to do that too often," and then off he goes again.

> When trying to learn something new or buy something, each person has his own unique learning style.

When these people buy, they all do so while applying their personal learning style. The auditory person wants to interact with a salesperson, the visual person wants to get a lot of cool information and do her own research, and the doer just wants to try it a little before he buys it.

> The biggest negative of salespeople in the fitness business is that they often only cover one style of learning, usually the auditory style.

The biggest negative of salespeople in the fitness business is that they often only cover one style of learning, usually the auditory style. Most owners won't let a person try the club more than once (not enough for most doers) and most offer a mediocre brochure or handout for the prospective member to take home. "Why should I put a lot into handouts when the salesperson told the person everything anyway?" he asks. The result is that the visual person, when she is sitting on the couch reviewing the material and trying to make a decision, really has nothing to go on except some cheap, low-rent brochure that cost the club about six cents for a three-fold say-nothing piece.

The auditory person, however, is really happy because he got to spend an hour chatting with some overcaffeinated salesperson who was also an auditory person. In this scenario, you limit your potential memberships to one-third of the guests you actually get through the door, because you don't understand how a person gathers information to make a favorable buying decision that benefits the business.

# Cover All Three Learning Styles Every Single Time

If you want the best chance to close as many sales as possible, you must learn to cover all three styles in your sales presentation. Don't bother trying to guess which person is which type of learner. Instead, just cover all three every time.

### The auditory customer

This person needs to talk to a prepared salesperson before he will buy, but the rules have changed. Instead of relying on old sales techniques that do nothing but upset the buyer during the sales process, a good salesperson will have a mastery of the material and be able to individualize the gym to match the consumer's needs and wants. The prime question to ask a prospective member, which is discussed throughout this book, is "What is the single most important thing you want from a membership at that this gym?"

### The visual customer

You have to send this person home with something more powerful than a copy of a copy of a copy of an aerobics schedule and a handwritten price sheet. The question to ask yourself here is, "What do you want to place in front of the person when she is sitting at home making the buying decision?"

She needs detailed information about the history of the club, a list of services, testimonials from other real members, schedules, club rules, staff pictures, a floor plan, and just about anything else you can think of to give her. Keep in mind that more is better and remember to put the prices in the handouts. You old sales dinosaurs who continue not to give the prices over the phone and who won't send a price sheet home with a guest need to get out of the gym business and apply as the gatekeeper of the Jurassic Park Fitness Center. Of course you should give the prices over the phone and you must always give every potential customer a classy price sheet to take home.

The tool of choice is a Welcome Guide, which is a three-ring binder full of current and fun information, including random fitness articles that inspire the person to workout. This book is given at the beginning of the tour as a gift from the club and as a way to change the person's expectations about your gym. In other words, before you even walk the person through the gym, you give him a cool gift from the club that he can take home. This gift has everything a customer needs to know about the club in case he misses something on the tour or wants to refer to something special later on.

These books should always be three-ring binders. Binding them does save a few pennies, but they look cheaper and won't be current a week after you get them done. Three-ring binders can be changed monthly to highlight club activities, specials, and other items that you might want or need to change.

Most of these binders can be made for two or three dollars, depending on how classy you want them to be, but keep in mind that you are probably spending thousands of dollars in advertising to get people in the door. Wouldn't you spend a few dollars more to increase your sales closing rate? You can increase your closing rate by as much as 15 percent by using classy support materials.

**If you want the best chance to close as many sales as possible, you must learn to cover all three styles in your sales presentation.**

## The doer

A doer is simple. He won't buy until it feels right, and all the talking in the world doesn't help him make the move to buy unless he can drive that little baby first. Doers simply have to try before they buy, and they don't buy until they can get first-hand experience with the product.

The key question is, "How much experience do they need with a product or service before they will buy?" For some buyers, it could be as simple as a little test drive around the block. Others just may have to keep that demo car overnight.

In the fitness business, start with the premise that one workout is just not going to be enough to get the feel of the club, especially when the price is $39 a month or higher. It takes two or more visits to a club before most people will make a buying decision if the price is $39 per month or higher. Salespeople should keep in mind that it's not the $39 they're selling or that the person is buying. For the more sophisticated buyer, the purchase equates to agreeing to the concept of fitness and the commitment it takes, in time, energy, and money, which is what makes the decision so difficult.

It is interesting to note is that none of these people will respond to price-driven ads without some type of prior experience with a fitness center. Price ads assume prior knowledge of fitness. In other words, if a consumer responds to a price ad, it's because he already has fitness experience and is shopping for the right facility at the right price. Keep in mind that only 16 percent of the population in this country, as of 2005, belongs to a health club, which means that 84 percent *don't* have fitness club experience. Price is not an effective tool to bring these people into the club.

Doers need trial memberships of some type. The recommended trials are seven days, 14 days, and 30 days if the market is right and the club is ready. The gist behind trials, which are covered in detail in Chapter 8, is that the customer can try a club before being forced to make a buying decision. The doer may respond after one workout, but it also might take two, three, or even more. This person makes the buying decision only when the product or service feels right to him.

## Why a Person Buys

This interesting question never seems to be asked: Why does a person visit several clubs and pick one over another? What was that deciding factor in the person's mind that swayed him to choose one over the other? If you can get some grasp of what is in the consumer's head when he is making that buying decision, then you can become much better at training your sales team and at designing sales systems that will hold up over time.

**One of the common misconceptions is that price is always the deciding factor for the consumer.**

One of the common misconceptions is that price is always the deciding factor for the consumer. This false assumption states that every single consumer is looking for price first and that all other factors slide down the priority list.

The influx of low-price/value competitors in the marketplace that are applying the theory of commodities to the fitness business will change how many consumers look at the fitness product, especially when it comes to price. When you commoditize something, you strip all the differentiation points away and just compete on price. In the case of the low price/value competitors, they offer a basic club with no frills that is clean and has decent locker rooms, but they sell fitness as a generic product that can't be differentiated from anyone else's fitness product. According to their theory, walking on a treadmill is just walking on a treadmill, no matter where you do it. This attempt to commoditize the fitness industry, or bring the product down to its lowest common denominator, will force many owners to reevaluate what they offer and what they charge for that offering.

Four classes of clubs, categorized by price, currently exist in the industry:

- The low-priced providers with prices under $19 per month offer big box facilities but no programming or support. These facilities are usually big box clubs with endless equipment and cardio, but not much else.

- The mid-priced clubs in the $29 to $39 range   provide a box-type facility with limited programming and amenities. This type of club might have some group classes, childcare, and other limited programming, but is often just another big box full of equipment.

- The full-service facilities in the $49 and higher range provide extensive programming and full amenities. This type of club offers full group exercise schedules and perhaps other facilities such as a pool or basketball court.

- The landmark clubs that are in the $89 and higher range offer just about anything you could want, including full racquet and pool facilities. These clubs are often measured in acreage rather than square footage and might have everything from restaurants to day spas as part of their offerings.

Specialty clubs, such as personal training studios, are often price immune because they appeal to a limited market in the upper-level demographics of the area. The clients who use these clubs don't mind paying extra for personal service and the expertise of the trainers.

What does all of this information mean to the potential customer? Price should not be the deciding factor for consumers, as long as they are in the right club for their needs. Where this theory breaks down is in the conflict between the first two categories: the low-priced and mid-priced clubs. In many cases, clubs in these two categories are exactly alike. Both are big box clubs full of equipment and both offer limited, if any, support or programming.

**Price should not be the deciding factor for consumers, as long as they are in the right club for their needs.**

Price wins out and becomes a factor for the consumer when two such clubs go head-to-head in the market. If the physical plants are similar and the offerings are limited, the cheaper price will win because, in essence, the low-priced provider is offering exactly the same service with exactly the same equipment for less money.

In the coming years, these two categories will blend into one: the big box that really offers nothing but a rent-a-treadmill for about 10 bucks per month. If the owners who are already charging in the $39 range want to survive, then they will have to figure out ways to strongly differentiate themselves from the no-service, no-programming, big box, equipment-rental gyms

This differentiation will have to be much more distinct and much stronger than it is currently in the industry. One bland room with stark white walls, eight-foot mirrors turned sideways, and little baskets of nasty bands and rusty weights, lorded over by instructors who haven't changed music or outfits for the last 20 years, is not group exercise and will not justify someone paying an additional $20 or more per month for a membership.

The thing to keep in mind is that you can't win the equipment war, because someone else can simply out-buy you somewhere down the line. You can out-service, out-program, and out-train a box competitor, but you have to rise to a higher standard than most gyms practice in that $39-per-month category.

In most markets, this category of clubs is the mediocre class that might have a little of everything, but nothing that is done very well. They have group exercise, but it is weak. They have training, but only make a few thousand dollars a month. They offer tanning, but it is in two old beds at the end of the hall in a shabby room with no music and poor ventilation. The reality is that you can have everything in your club and still do nothing well enough to justify your price. Given a choice between a clean big box with a $19 price and a mediocre club with the same equipment and weak support services, the consumer will choose the low price every time.

Some people do want a low price. They are either looking for value for their money, can't afford a higher price, or this type of low-priced gym is all that is offered near their home.

When these people are given a quality/value difference, however, things will change. The people in the upper ranges of the demographics, when given a choice, will often support the club with the higher price if it is indeed different and offers a wider range of programming and services. These folks join a club because it has what they want beyond just equipment and more people like themselves work out there (likes attract likes). The higher price also has the connotation of increased value.

The negative side of this equation is that this club truly has to be different. If group exercise is one of the club's points of separation, then the club has to master group exercise by offering multiple rooms, advanced training from companies such as Body Training Systems®, and systems that will dominate the market. The same rules apply to personal training and other club offerings that are never found in the low-priced providers. You either master that segment of the business or you get your business dragged down to a lower level of play.

**Price is only important if a customer has limited money or if the other providers in the market are offering the same product for a higher price.**

Again, price is only important if a customer has limited money or if the other providers in the market are offering the same product for a higher price. When given a quality option that happens to be higher priced, enough folks in the upper 60 percent of the population by household income will support that business.

## If It Isn't Price, Then What Is It?

People who are considering joining a gym and are in the process of visiting clubs usually bring their own hidden agendas with them. These people have an idea of what they want, what they want to get done, and, although they may be armed with bad information gleaned from some magazine article, they often think that they know exactly what they are talking about despite having little, if any, actual gym experience.

The following sections represent a short list of the hidden agenda questions that people often want addressed before they buy a fitness membership. While you will face countless such questions, these sections cover some of the more common ones a salesperson in a fitness business will encounter in the actual process of selling a membership.

## Is it convenient to my home?

The first thing most people think about when they seek a fitness center is convenience. Is it close to my house? Is it easy to park? Can I get in and out quickly and easily? Owners don't really think about the convenience aspect of fitness. You're here to work out anyway and that little extra walk from the far end of the parking lot shouldn't be a factor. The member, however, has a completely different thought process. He wants to park next to the door and if he has to walk, then he is upset from the moment he walks into the club. It doesn't make sense, but it is the reality of the member mindset.

**The first thing most people think about when they seek a fitness center is convenience.**

The biggest issue is convenience to the customer's home and this factor is the first thing a potential member looks for when visiting a gym. According to IHRSA, 85 to 90 percent of a club's members live within a 12-minute drive of the club during primetime. In other words, between 6:30 and 7 o'clock in the morning and around the hour of 5 o'clock in the evening, the customer needs to be able to get to the club in less than 12 minutes.

As a salesperson, you have to demonstrate often during a tour that you are indeed convenient. If you have parking problems, you need to have a site map for the potential member to look at during the tour that highlights the best parking spots.

If you have unusually heavy primetime traffic, you need to gently suggest that if the new member can time his workout differently, he might do better coming just a little before or after the heavy-traffic hours. By painting the picture of convenience to your potential members, you address one of those hidden agenda items that the person may be wondering about but not asking. This item could be the one that prevents the final sale, but you might never know it as a salesperson.

## What's the risk?

Risk is the single greatest entry barrier to a potential member. Some clubs try to eliminate risk by offering a low rate, such as the $19 clubs. If the customer is an experienced gym member, this price range may work. Even if a customer is totally clueless and has no idea what fitness really is or how it works, he might join a gym that costs $19 or less per month because he really doesn't have a lot to lose by trying.

The low-risk/low-price group is small, however. Remember that only 16 percent of the population of this country belonged to a health club as of 2005. Price might be an entry barrier for a certain percentage of that population, but it's doubtful that it is the prime deciding factor for the other 84 percent of people who aren't in clubs.

No one wants to spend money that might be completely wasted. The question the potential member asks is, "What if I join this thing and don't like it?" The cost of joining a club may not be a lot of money to some folks, but it is considered substantial by others. Either way, spending money and not getting anything for it is still a waste and salespeople seldom know what a person's tolerance for risk really is.

**Risk is not only an entry barrier once a person is in the club, but more importantly it can also be a barrier to inquiry.**

Risk is not only an entry barrier once a person is in the club, but more importantly it can also be a barrier to inquiry. In other words, the perceived risk outweighs the benefits of inquiring about a fitness business. These people don't even check out their local fitness center because they have no working concept of what belonging to a club is really about, so they simply avoid the subject altogether.

Risk can't be solved by lowering the price, because you simply can't go low enough with your pricing to please everyone. If any money changes hands, then risk is still involved. The issue is that for more than 50 years the fitness industry used price as the bait to attract new prospective members to its businesses. When that tactic is taken away, many owners don't have any backup plan. The contradiction is that price-driven ads, including price specials such as two-for-one deals and discounted membership fees, do work when a club first opens, because a new club drains all the folks from the market who have some type of club experience.

These folks are gym savvy and will jump from their present club for a price deal if they are simply looking for a place to work out with fresh equipment, new people, and decent locker rooms. Toward the end of the first year, however, the owner starts to run out of potential members in the market who will respond to price ads.

In other words, everyone who will respond to price-driven ads already has, and each time you run a price ad it becomes less effective. This situation demonstrates the Law of Diminishing Returns, which states that after repeating the same action over time, the results of that action begin to decline. You've burned the market and each new price ad attracts slightly fewer prospects.

If you want to attract new members in sufficient numbers, you have to find a way to eliminate risk but still make the club and its offerings attractive enough for someone to want to get involved. You can accomplish your goals in a number of ways. The following sections present techniques to eliminate or lower the perceived risk factor and that open the door to potential members that the club wouldn't normally attract through a traditional price-driven marketing plan. Potential members who are touring the club are always considering the risk factor, and by keeping the risk as low as possible, you increase your chances of selling more memberships.

## Trial memberships

Trial memberships are discussed in depth in Chapter 8, but warrant attention in this context as well. A trial membership is an offering to potential members to try the club absolutely free, with no risk or obligation, for a set period of time. The most effective time is 14 days (do not say "two weeks," as 14 just sounds more substantial than two). During this period, the club attempts to close the prospective member after that person has had a chance to try the gym, meet the staff, and interact with other members. Trials are especially important to those people who are from the doer category of learning styles, because they need to experience something before they will buy it. Trials eliminate all risk, since no money changes hands.

## Paid trials

A paid trial can be used to create a course format for the client, which is similar to someone signing up for a six-week computer course, for example. The club charges a fixed fee for a specific period of time, which lowers the risk for the customer because he is only committing a small amount of money and has no obligation beyond the trial period. An example might be "6 weeks for $69" for a group exercise-only membership or "8 weeks for $249" for a golf-conditioning program that runs during the winter and includes group lessons with a local teaching pro.

## Solution programming

Solution-based programming can be used to attract a person to the gym to solve one specific problem. For example, a club might offer weight management in a separate mailing, distinct from a normal club membership. Another example might be a club owner who offers a fall ski-conditioning class for eight weeks just prior to ski season. Again, little risk to the client is involved because the person came to the gym for a narrowly focused program that has a definite end and no further obligation is required beyond that timeframe.

**Solution-based programming can be used to attract a person to the gym to solve one specific problem.**

## Guest incentive programs

If you like your members, you will probably like their friends too. Most guest incentive programs simply don't go far enough to be effective. No one, for example, is going to drag a friend to the gym just to get a free month added to their membership if that friend decides to join.

Guest incentive programs need to be aggressive and should offer incentive packages that match or exceed your normal cost per sale to attract a new member. For example, if a club spends $5000 per month on marketing and attracts 150 prospects, its cost per lead is $33 ($5000/150). Add commissions (using $25 per sale, for example) and $5 for support materials (Welcome Guides), and the combined cost per sale is $63 ($33 + $25 + $5 = $63). In this example, the club is spending $63 to buy a sale in the open market. Why wouldn't the club spend at least that amount, or slightly more, to buy a buddy referral sale? For example, you could buy a very high-quality backpack and offer a T-shirt, the pack, a water bottle, a towel, and three free training sessions as an incentive to bring in guests. This package can be purchased by the club for less than $50 but have a retail value of $150 or more.

### Newsletter marketing

Newsletter marketing is a unique concept pioneered by the Susan K. Bailey marketing company from Canada. This company developed a newsletter-format marketing piece that a club can stuff in local newspapers as an insert. The format is a four-page mini-newspaper that the club can use to create interest, not only in the club, but also in fitness in general. A basic rule of business is that before you can attract someone to your business, you first have to create interest. The newsletter format does both at the same time.

### Are other members like me?

Likes attract likes. It's an elementary concept that is often overlooked in the club market.

If I am 30-something guy with a decent job who is married to a 30-something girl who is working on her career as well, we probably don't hang out with 20-somethings without jobs or the CEOs of the companies we work for each day. Most likely, we hang out with people just like us—other 30-somethings that have the same interests and make about the same salary that we do.

When someone tours the club as a potential member, one of the things they are looking for is other people like themselves. No one wants to be embarrassed, and working out with a group where you don't fit in is a sure way to make yourself feel uncomfortable.

You can do several things to help potential members feel more comfortable and more at ease in the club. The first step is to neutralize your staff, which means that your staff should match the target demographics of your club. Neutralization means that your staff becomes a positive part of the sales effort rather than a negative force working against it.

**Likes attract likes. It's an elementary concept that is often overlooked in the club market.**

For example, if your target market is 30 to 50 years old and your counter staff is all around 20 years old, this mismatch will work against you during your tours. In other words, your staff is not enhancing the sale, but instead working against the process because they are different in age, affluence, work experience, and other key factors as compared to your club's target demographic, which usually makes up approximately 80 percent of your club's members and is defined by age. For example, you might target the 24 to 40 market, the 25 to 45 market, or the 30 to 50 market. If your market is the 24- to 40-year-old age group, then your club will eventually have approximately 80 percent of its members fall within this range and this group will also become the club's primary marketing focus.

Most people have a higher expectation from their club than just a place to work out. A good club provides socialization, relaxation, and an escape from the normal routine of someone's day. If the club is doing its job, then it should be living up to the simple mission statement: "We promise to always be the best part of your day."

> **Most people have a higher expectation from their club than just a place to work out.**

If this statement is to come true for the members, then they will expect most of the other members, and most of the staff, to be somewhat close to them in age and other demographic factors. Likes attract likes, and while someone may not openly inquire about the other members during their tour of the club, you can be sure that each person is checking out the other people in the gym to make sure folks like themselves are already members.

## Will the staff understand me or be like me?

This question is similar to the previous one, but a few subtle differences warrant discussion when it comes to staff and the sales process. Two of the hidden aspects of the sales process rarely discussed in typical sales books are empathy and product experience. Both factors are important, but they are often overlooked by most sales trainers and owners.

Empathy can be defined as a sensitive understanding of what the other person is going through, or has gone through, in his life. Empathy is the ability to say, "Yeah, I know what you're going through because I understand (or have been there myself) and I can feel your pain."

For example, if a deconditioned 35-year-old mother of two comes into the gym—usually the hardest sales situation, largely because no one on the staff has the life experience or patience to sit and get to know her—and is toured by a 21-year-old female who has never been out of shape and doesn't have kids, then the empathy level will be very low. The younger woman has never been out of shape, never had kids, and doesn't know how hard it is for a mom to find that 45 minutes a day to get to the gym.

The sales process breaks down in this example when the mom describes how hard it is for her to lose that last 15 pounds from the latest baby and the young staff person starts selling the club's weight-management program without really listening. Since the staff person hasn't shared that experience, she cannot identify with the mom, and no relationship-building and no real communication occurs between the two beyond a problem delivered and an unemotional solution provided.

Of course, you can't have someone on your staff who exactly matches every possible sales situation the club might encounter. It does mean, though, that your staff should match the target demographics of the club and have people closer to the prospects' age group who are more likely to be able to identify with the people you are tying to sell to.

The second question is one of product experience. Sales trainers often refer to this aspect as "living the lifestyle," but sometimes that definition causes trouble, as it conjures images of fanatical fitness people trying to convert the heathen fat people.

It is surprising how many people who work in fitness facilities don't really take part in what the club offers or don't really practice fitness in their own lives. And if you work in a club and don't take part in what the club offers, how can you really sell it to someone else?

Group exercise is one of the best examples. Many clubs, for whatever goofy reason, end up with a whole herd of young, overdone male salespeople. Maybe it's because clubs are a great place to meet women or maybe clubs hire exclusively from this population because these guys are perceived as being more aggressive, and therefore better, salespeople. How persuasive can these guys be on a tour, however, when they are trying to explain a group program that none of them have even tried during the past year? You simply can't sell the Ferrari if you have never driven the Ferrari, and you can't sell fitness if you don't somehow participate in the lifestyle.

On the other hand, you don't want your salespeople to be born-again fitness fanatics either. Some of the worst salespeople, in fact, are often people who have radically changed their lives and are now going to tell everyone how they did it.

The example you see in almost every Gold's Gym® or World Gym® is the 40-something female who lost 30 pounds and entered her first bodybuilding contest. She inevitably has the pictures of her posing in a small bikini on her desk and, instead of listening and communicating with the potential member, she spends all the time telling about her personal journey and what fitness means to her. She doesn't inspire, and in many ways turns off the prospective member to fitness because it seems that a person can't be successful unless she is fanatical.

Simply remember that you don't have to be super-fit to work in a gym. If you've lost 30 pounds but still have 20 to go, welcome to the team—you're a work in progress. But if you're not part of the fitness world, you won't be

> Your staff should match the target demographics of the club and have people closer to the prospects' age group who are more likely to be able to identify with the people you are tying to sell to.

successful in the fitness business no matter how well you can talk.

If your staff is close in age to your club's target membership and your team members, including the front-counter people, are lifestyle people who believe in the merits of fitness and who take part in the club's offerings on a regular basis, then your sales efforts will be more productive, and you will acquire more members over time. The potential member wants to know that he will fit in to your business and that a place exists for him. One of the strongest cues comes from who greets him at the front counter and who tours him in the club.

## Are a variety of activities available to keep me from getting bored?

Over the years, a constant effort has been made to reduce fitness down to its most simplistic form. The Curves® chain has tried to get women to go around and around in the circle to complete their workouts in 30 minutes or less. The Curves imitators, which followed in droves following the success of the first wave of Curves gyms, went for the 27-minute circuit; another offered a the 22-minute circuit; and one men-only imitator claimed that you could do their circuit in 19 minutes. Fitness is truly easy when it gets to the point that it's over before you get there.

The low-price gyms, meaning those in the $19 per-member per-month range, try to reduce fitness to a room full of fixed workout equipment and cardio machines, eliminating group fitness, weight management, and childcare. These clubs rent space to trainers, but virtually anyone who claims to be a trainer is allowed to rent space, and how good can a trainer be if he is trying to troll the $19 membership group for business?

Except for runners, and even the running magazines pound the benefits of cross-training to prevent injuries and keep people excited, people in mainstream fitness look for multiple tools to get the fitness job done. Literally hundreds of articles have touted variety as the way to stay consistent with a fitness program and to get the best results for the time you spend.

This tenet is becoming even more important as functional training makes its way back into the mainstream. Functional training, or lifestyle-enhancement training, means that whatever you do in your life, the folks at your friendly neighborhood fitness center can make it better. If you want to be a better golfer or tennis player, the club can help. And if you simply want to be a better parent and keep up with your four-year-old son, the club can help you solve that problem as well.

The boring box-style gyms that offer limited options, especially those low-price clubs with only cardio equipment and dated, fixed, single-joint equipment, suffer the most over time because nothing can be done after a certain point to keep a member entertained. You can only get on that seated

**If your staff is close in age to your club's target membership and your team members, including the front-counter people, are lifestyle people who believe in the merits of fitness and who take part in the club's offerings on a regular basis, then your sales efforts will be more productive, and you will acquire more members over time.**

chest press and treadmill so many times before you're bored, and bored members, no matter what the price, don't keep paying.

It's even worse when the entire gym is only 1500 square feet and you simply go around and around through the same circle of circuit equipment. At some point, the member just has had enough and quits because the club can't offer anything new to change up the routine. The circle is the circle, and nothing will change it no matter how long the person keeps coming.

When a potential member shops, he is often looking for a variety of programming choices, although members always start with just one or two and build from that point as they get experience or as boredom sets in with their routine. The new member might be excited about the lines of cardio, the functional-training areas, the resistance-training areas, and the weight-management center, but he might want to get started with group exercise and then add things as he gets comfortable in the club.

**Variety lays the groundwork, but highlighting the member's favorite activity closes the deal.**

To add to the illusion of variety and multiple offerings in the gym, show the club and tour the facility using the mall concept. The mall concept means that you always show the separate businesses within the business, just like when you visit the mall and then wander from business to business within that mall.

You probably already have a number of businesses within your gym but don't use them as sales tools. For example, you have your lifestyle-enhancement center (personal training), your weight-management center, your tanning center, your juice bar, and your childcare center. All of these areas should have separate signage that brands them as distinct businesses within the gym, with their own logos and hours posted.

When you tour the club, you tour from business to business. "We have a variety of things in the club to help you get the most out of your fitness membership. Here we have our Apex Weight Management Center and here we have our Endless Summer Tanning Center."

If this technique is done properly, the guest leaves with a feeling that this club really has a lot to offer compared to other clubs she visited that did the old "walk to the back, walk to the front, point at the cardio, and then hit the office" tour. In the first case, you are selling a complete support system that can help the person get the most out of her fitness program, while the second scenario has nothing to sell but the workout. Guests instinctively know that they may need some help, and knowing that the club has all of these separate components under one roof gives them a sense of security when they tour.

## Does the club offer "my" activity?

Variety lays the groundwork, but highlighting the member's favorite activity closes the deal. It's actually amazing how few club salespeople take the time to find out why the person is in the club and what he actually wants to do once he becomes a member. Granted, some guests may not know and may be looking for guidance from a trainer or other staff person, but most do have an idea of what they want to do and what they think is fun.

Chapter 18 covers the procedures for profiling a prospective member. It is essential that you realize that everyone coming through that door has done something somewhere in the fitness world that they think is fun. For example, a deconditioned woman may say that she has never really been involved in fitness and that the closest thing she does to any type of consistent activity is walking the family dog with her husband in the evening, which is something she really enjoys.

Why would a club take this woman and automatically put her on some type of antiquated weight-training program? She obviously enjoys movement and walking, so why not get her grounded in some type of program that supports her lifestyle activity instead of going purist and giving her some type of activity that has no relationship to her experience or enjoyment?

The club could get her a pedometer, talk to her about how much walking is enough to make a difference, and perhaps steer her toward group classes such as cycle, yoga, or even a more challenging functional class that combines on-your-feet movement with some gentle core training. These activities enhance her movement rather than distracting her from pursuing her favorite type of activity, which currently is walking. Later, once she is grounded in the club and has obtained a modest level of success, a trainer can introduce strength training and other options that might make more sense to her at that point of her fitness journey.

Many clubs make a major mistake by being too pure, and too out-of-date, with their approach to fitness. Traditional strength training, which entails having a trainer fill out an old workout card with a certain number of exercises and reps, is not what the majority of people who come to a gym actually want. If it was, the industry would be way past the 16 percent membership level after more than 50 years of existence, since strength training and rooms full of equipment have been the primary offering since the 1970s.

> **Many clubs make a major mistake by being too pure, and too out-of-date, with their approach to fitness.**

Muscle for the sake of muscle, and the isolation training that builds this type of showy muscle, is not for everyone and doesn't sell well over time in a fitness environment, except to a small segment of the population that makes lifting weights their primary hobby. People who want showy muscle become bodybuilders, which usually make up a very small percentage of the membership of any gym. The fitness world is open to the clubs that go beyond this type of training and help people develop fitness programs that truly enhance their lifestyles and that match what they like to do in the real world. For example, if a person is a cyclist and that's his hobby, then your job is to help him become better at his sport.

Remember that the average person coming to a gym only has so many hours available to commit to fitness, especially if he is someone in the higher-affluence demographic. If he's in this group, then he is probably working longer hours than people with similar jobs did in the past. A 1997 survey by the Families and Work Institute showed that a typical father was working approximately 51 hours per week and the typical mother was working about 41.4 hours per week.

People who are working long hours only have so many hours left that they will give up to nonessential activities during their week. If a person plays golf, for example, and he only has four or five hours per week that are his own, then he will most likely spend this time playing golf rather than going to the gym, even though he knows that working out would be better for him in the long run.

> What people in the fitness business don't understand, and the reason why clubs don't attract golfers, bikers, runners, and dancers, is that clubs are asking those people to do something that competes against their hobbies, instead of something that enhances those lifestyle choices.

What people in the fitness business don't understand, and the reason why clubs don't attract golfers, bikers, runners, and dancers, is that clubs are asking those people to do something that competes against their hobbies, instead of something that enhances those lifestyle choices. The only way clubs will ever attract those people is by offering things that will make them better at what they do, rather than trying to get them to sacrifice their valuable and limited time doing something as boring as fitness training.

Embracing functional training and understanding how to build saleable programs that attract the people who want more from their training are big steps for many club owners. For example, winter bike-conditioning classes, late-winter golf conditioning programs, walking clubs housed at the gym, alliances with ski and tennis clubs, and other sport-specific training will attract these people and ultimately sell them memberships once they are in the gyms and have experienced how much you can help them beyond the simple fitness experience.

Almost everyone has had some type of favorable fitness experience at some point in his life. What you have to understand is that this experience might not have been something you consider part of the mainstream fitness world or part of the gym business, but it is something that people who seek you out enjoy and will embrace in your business if given the chance.

## What about the little extras?

Oh, how those small things make life so much better. Think of that oversized coffee cup at your favorite shop, that extra pillow on the bed in the hotel, or the seat by a window with a great view in a new restaurant. All of these little extras add value to your purchase and to the experience itself.

Most fitness facilities don't do well in this area, and in fact most owners don't feel that these extras are worth the effort or cost. These operators often feel that rows of equipment, classes, and basic services should be enough for most members and that it is a waste of time and money to go beyond these things.

The problem arises when a prospective member tours several clubs and they all start to feel the same. Everyone has rows of equipment and most group rooms have that sterile, white wall, out-of-date feel that screams, "This club is still locked into the old aerobics world and nothing is going to force us into modern group exercise." When a person tours several clubs, all the base components start to look alike and the person therefore loses the ability to differentiate each club from any other. For example, if you see three clubs, you have probably pretty much seen every piece of equipment you want to see. If you're a novice exerciser, this equipment not only starts to look alike, but it also may become overwhelming because so much of it is crammed into each club. Throw in three or four group class schedules, a few generic locker rooms, a whole bunch of black rubber flooring, and you have blended everything the person has seen into one confusing image.

The little extras are those things that go beyond the basic fitness offerings, and, most importantly, are the things that the customer might actually remember. They will separate your club from anything else he has seen. Think of these things as a club's signature items that the owner uses to gain a distinction over other competitors in the market.

One offering a club can use to gain that distinctive edge is childcare. Childcare is something almost every club in the country loses money on, but it is also something that most owners simply can't live without in their businesses.

Childcare rooms in fitness facilities across the nation look like the product of the same inexperienced designer. These unworkable rooms consist of lousy murals, piles of mismatched toys, worn-out videos, stacks of who-knows-what on shelves, and bathrooms that would make even the most heartless parent cringe.

Childcare in a fitness facility has the potential to be a true signature item for the club and something that will stand out for the prospective member over other clubs he has visited. Since most clubs offer childcare, why not make it a standout item on the tour or that little extra the person didn't expect that adds value to a potential membership?

Most childcare rooms are too small for a parent's taste. The minimum size should be approximately 600 square feet. Feature unusual flooring (no carpets), a bank of computer games, oversized bathrooms with kid fixtures, and bright, bold colors that are easy to maintain, rather than a chipped-up mural that no one wants to deal with after a few months of wear. Add security cameras and monitors throughout the club, a secure infant area, and scheduled activities, and you might end up with a true signature that sets you apart from your competitors.

**The little extras are those things that go beyond the basic fitness offerings, and, most importantly, are the things that the customer might actually remember.**

Another example of where you might be able to add something extra is in the group-exercise areas. Despite what many owners seem to think, no law states that a group room has to be white, have eight-foot mirrors turned sideways, and have little plastic milk crates around the walls full of sticky, sweat-stained bands and little dumbbells. Line up the bikes against a wall and add an old dusty stereo in the corner, complete with broken tape boxes and confusing wiring, and you have an all-too-typical group-exercise room.

What most owners don't understand, since most are men who never do group exercise, is that if you are a group fitness person, that is all you do. Machine people are machine people and group people are group people, and that is it. The thing to remember is that when group people tour a club, they are looking for things that will enhance their group experience—those little extras that separate your program from everyone else's.

Group rooms are energy rooms and should be treated accordingly. Colors should be bold and dynamic and mirrors only have to be on one wall. If possible, keep all the tools stored outside the room so the students can pick them up on the way in and return them on the way out. At the very least, build storage into the walls so the room is always clean and energized rather than cluttered with that dirty feel that comes from having too much stuff lying around.

When it comes to sales, never tour a quiet room. Every group room should have music going in the background whenever someone tours and the lights should be on to give the room a used feel.

It doesn't take much time or money to turn a flat group presentation into something bold and energized as a signature feature for the club. Group people get it when they see it, and the look and feel of the room is that little extra the might sway their choice away from another club on their shopping list.

> **Every club, no matter the size or price level, can develop a few signature items that provide the illusion of added value for a prospective member.**

Every club, no matter the size or price level, can develop a few signature items that provide the illusion of added value for a prospective member. Larger, higher-priced clubs can get into oversized towels, locker room amenities, and even valet parking during the prime traffic months (i.e., January through April, when clubs are the busiest). Lower-priced facilities can concentrate on their group or childcare presentation and even the low-price/value clubs can add items such as an extensive entertainment system to their cardio areas. Every club can and needs to find those little extras that separate it from its competitors.

## Does the club offer weight-loss programs?

Weight loss is commonly acknowledged as the number one reason people seek out a fitness facility. The problem for salespeople, however, is determining why a person seeks weight management. Is it for cosmetic reasons or in response to health issues? Could it be as simple as the customer wanting his pants to button without having to suck in his gut? All of these issues are valid reasons to become interested in a gym, but each requires a somewhat different sales approach.

Salespeople make the mistake of assuming that weight loss is weight loss, and that one size fits all. If you truly want to help the person in front of you, and sell a membership to the club, you have to go beyond the initial statement of, "I just need to lose a few pounds," and ask, "Why?"

Most people in the fitness business realize that getting in shape is 15 percent working out and 85 percent getting a better nutrition plan. The issue is that the consumer doesn't know it. Customers think that they have a weight issue of some kind and that all they have to do to change their shape is join a gym and start working out a few times a week.

This misconception not only leads to a number of lost sales, but also eventually costs the club a significant amount of member retention because members never achieved success at the gym. A person joins to get in shape and, after several months of running on a treadmill or lifting a few weights, nothing really noticeable happens to his body, so he quits coming and eventually quits paying.

As noted by John McCarthy of IHRSA in his *Guide to Member Retention*, relatively few clubs have an integrated exercise and weight-management program. Most clubs only sell one side of the formula, the exercise portion, which yields the smallest net gain for the consumer. In other words, gyms are great for maintaining weight loss, but they aren't very good at helping someone lose the weight in the first place.

When you are selling a membership, you must explore the weight-management issue by first asking, "What is the most important thing you want from a membership at this gym?" and then asking, "Why?" For example, a middle-aged man who is 20 pounds overweight visits the gym. Before the tour, the salesperson asks the first question and gets the standard answer, as the man pats his stomach: "I just need to lose a few pounds of this."

If the salesperson stops here, he will assume that weight loss is the answer and that the solution is to get the guy a membership and get him moving on that treadmill. Unfortunately, most clubs *have* to stop at this point, because they don't have a weight-management program in place (keeping in mind that writing diets on the back of a clipboard is not the same as providing a valid nutrition/weight-management program).

If he asks why, however, the salesperson will have a better chance of getting him into the club and really helping him. For example, the salesperson notes the pat on the stomach and follows up with, "Why is weight loss important to you?" The answer might be "I want to run my first road race,"

**Most people in the fitness business realize that getting in shape is 15 percent working out and 85 percent getting a better nutrition plan.**

which might mean that he is in the club because of health reasons and his doctor or wife made him come). On the other hand, he might reply by saying, "I just got divorced and need to drop some weight now," which means that his primary goal might simply be looking good.

How this person would be sold, how he would be trained, and the options he has in the gym should be very different depending on which answer he gives. In the first case, you might have a trainer that specializes in runners and have a running group he can join. In the second example, the guy might immediately be turned over to your club's Apex Nutrition Professional or some other weight-management expert on staff.

Weight management sells, and almost everyone touring a club is looking for some type of guidance in this area. Part of a successful sales approach is to first determine the interest the person has in losing weight, followed by what he hopes to accomplish through that weight loss. If the salesperson knows this information, he can then individualize the sales process to increase his chances of getting the sale. He can also actually help the person get the results he is looking for, even if he doesn't seem to understand the relationship between exercise and a solid nutrition program.

### Did the person connect with the salesperson or someone else in the club?

In many cases, salespeople tend to complicate the sales process. Thousands of books cite every sales technique in existence, describing complicated closes, weird body language, and in-depth follow-up. According to these books, sales are nothing more than putting the right combination of magic words in the right order to make people do almost anything you like or buy anything you are selling.

What can be learned from some low-tech research (i.e., asking someone why they bought a membership) is that successful selling in a fitness business is often based upon a few simple premises. Did you greet the person politely as he came in the door? Was your salesperson properly dressed and did she actually listen and respond to the customer's questions? Did you clearly explain what you offer and did you have high-quality support materials for the person to take home and look at before committing to a membership?

One of the most important things to understand is that the number one reason a person actually buys a membership from a business is that he likes the people he talks to in the club. It isn't price, and it isn't the club's offerings. Simply stated, "The people were nice and they spent a lot of time with me." This statement assumes that the clubs in the area have somewhat comparable services and offerings, although lesser facilities will still sell memberships if they have better people.

> One of the most important things to understand is that the number one reason a person actually buys a membership from a business is that he likes the people he talks to in the club.

This type of finding throws a wrench into the training plans of those owners who like complicated sales theories and who spend hours teaching their salespeople to write upside down so they can present prices across a desk. Mediocre salespeople who are nice have a better chance of succeeding than good salespeople who aren't patient and caring.

More importantly, everyone on the team has to be involved in the sales process. If you remember, customers buy because they like all of the people they talk to in the gym, not just the salesperson. In other words, everyone from the manager to the janitor is involved in the sales process and affects the outcome of each and every membership tour.

Of course, you can't just have nice people and expect great sales numbers. But someone with a caring attitude coupled with good sales training will get more sales than an old-style sales dog who is more concerned with pounding out memberships than taking care of the customer.

Someone visiting a club is usually a little nervous anyway, because he is in a place he hasn't been before or because he doesn't really know anything about fitness or what people do in a club. This type of person is very susceptible to salespeople who slow the process down a little and demonstrate a caring attitude.

For example, your front-counter person is your first line of offense. If this person doesn't do his job, then the salesperson's job is that much harder because he has to overcome the negative impression the customer has from the encounter with your desk people.

Prospective members look for someone like them at the counter. If your target market is 24 to 40 years old (target market is defined as 80 percent of your membership coming from one defined demographic), then all of your staff should be in that group as well. The mistake owners make is hiring people who are too young and inexperienced. They hire the cheapest employees they can find for the desk and then undertrain them for the job. Why train them if they are just desk people? They come and go so often anyway.

The reason you should hire an older, more business-mature person for the desk, even if it does cost a few more dollars per hour, is that this person makes or breaks the sales process. If the prospective member is an adult and sees someone who is also an adult at the counter, he starts his tour of the club with the impression that this club caters to people like himself. Add some training and the desk person will give a cordial greeting, seat him at the counter, chat with him for a few minutes before a salesperson appears, and even buy him a bottle of water if he has to wait a few minutes, and you have just greatly increased your chances of selling more memberships.

**All management people, including the owner, should be introduced to every prospective member who tours if they are available.**

Everyone else on the team is also involved in the sales process. All management people, including the owner, should be introduced to every prospective member who tours if they are available. For example, if your lead fitness professional is on the floor working with a member and sees a tour going by, he should take this opportunity to add to the experience by saying, "Hello, my name is David and I am the lead fitness professional at the club. If you have any questions about your programs or how to get the most out of your membership, please come and find me."

David steps in, introduces himself, gets the guest's name, says his piece, and steps back to his client. That process takes less than a minute, yet the guest has met another friendly face on the tour, which is something he probably didn't see at your competitor's club.

People like to buy, but they don't like to be sold. Most folks would rather give their money to a group of people who seem nice and who demonstrate a caring attitude, as opposed to just a hard-line salesperson who obviously only cares about writing a membership.

People who buy memberships do so for all sorts of reasons, but the most important common thread is that they buy more often from people they like and who were nice to them when they inquired. Slow the process down, train all the staff to be involved in the sales, and be especially mindful of having people work in your club that can demonstrate an attitude of caring about the client.

## How and Why Do People Buy?

**Successful sales in the fitness industry are based upon your ability to individualize the sales process.**

Everything presented in this chapter adds up to the fact that successful sales in the fitness industry are based upon your ability to individualize the sales process. In the past, owners and managers have taken the approach that no matter who the customer is or what he wants, only one solution exists in the gym: buy a membership.

Hopefully, this industry will reach a point where it finally starts to attract those new people who have never before been in a fitness center. If you want these people as members, then you will have to master the art of taking something most fitness people take for granted as simple—fitness and exercise—and effectively translating it to potential customers who have no idea what you're talking about or how it works. All they know is that they need fitness, you sell it, and they're here to buy it if it makes sense.

As these first-time people enter the market, owners and managers will have to fill their staffs with caring and patient people who will take the time to meet the different wants and demands from this new membership population. Understanding how and why they buy is the first step toward being financially successful while working with this new breed of potential member.

## Key Points From This Chapter

- The potential buyer is changing in the fitness business. He is more sophisticated about sales, but less knowledgeable about fitness.

- People make buying decisions based upon their individual learning style.

- You can increase your chances of selling more memberships by covering all three learning styles during every tour of the club.

- Every potential member brings his own agenda to the gym with him. Each one has certain things he is looking for or expects to see, and a good salesperson is aware of these things and covers each one during the tour.

- You will be more successful in sales if you learn to individualize the sales process.

# Consider making fitness your life's work.

People change lives every single day in the fitness business. At some point, you will probably want to decide on a career. Before you leave this industry for something else, consider making the fitness business your life's work.

Fitness is booming and opportunities will continue to come in the next few years all around the world. This industry provides you with an opportunity to spend the rest of your life helping other people improve theirs.

If you want to make fitness your career, start by working to master the components of what people in the fitness industry actually do for a living. Understand these things and you become more valuable as an employee and will be more successful as an owner:

- How to sell memberships
- How money works and arrives in the fitness business
- How important weight management will be in the coming years
- How to train people as individuals and in group settings

These components—management and sales, weight management and training—are the base-level skills that will make you a well-rounded employee and open the door to becoming a manager or owner in the future. You may never completely master these skills, but you could spend the rest of your life working on each one and, along the road, change a few lives as well.

# 6

# Either They Get It or They Don't

Some people understand the concept of health and fitness and do something about it. Most people don't. Approximately 16 percent of the population has taken the first step and actually joined a fitness center. The other 84 percent of the people in this country have never belonged to a fitness facility.

Examining the difference between someone who "gets" fitness and someone who doesn't provides a very simplified way to look at the fitness business. After approximately 55 years of existence, the fitness business has hardly penetrated the total population and most fitness centers are in reality nothing more than a place where fit people go to stay fit and the deconditioned people of the world fear to tread.

If you think about it, just how brave are those heavy, sweat-suit-wearing, out-of-shape people who do find the courage to join a mainstream fitness center? How much does someone want change in her life if she is willing to face the fact that she is out of shape and then join a fitness center, where she just knows that everyone in the place is going to be in better shape than she is?

Think of 500 naked, in-shape fitness women on the beach and one, lone 5′4″, 230-pound female streaking through the middle shrieking, "Look at me, I don't belong here and never will." When you're out of shape, you often think that everyone else in the world is in shape but you, yet this person somehow finds the strength and courage to walk through the door and buy a membership. Even if she is thinking about joining a softer facility with an older clientele, the fear still remains that she will be the only one who is out of shape. Exceptions exist, of course, and every mainstream fitness center has that group of deconditioned people that you can point to and use for your newspaper testimonials or news stories about how you are changing the world by attracting those uninformed folks who aren't your typical fitness people.

Some of the newer pocket clubs, which are small 1500-square-foot facilities such as Curves, are doing a fair job of attracting the first-time people to their clubs, but they suffer from the same retention issues as the rest of the industry. But overall, the fitness business still only attracts and focuses on people who already understand and appreciate physical exercise and a healthier lifestyle.

But what about the other 84 percent of the people in this country? These people don't belong to a club, sometimes practice fitness by following whatever is hot in the tabloid magazines, and wouldn't even consider joining a fitness center until they get in shape. They think that everyone at the club will be in shape except them and that people don't join a fitness center until they get into decent shape first. These people aren't in the 16 percent who get it and the industry doesn't really do anything to help them figure it out.

Do you think your club is different and your membership is a little softer? The wellness and recreation folks always believe that they do a better job with this population than the mainstream fitness facilities, but both groups need to spend Saturday morning at a big box retail store to get the ultimate reality check.

What you'll see on a typical Saturday morning are a lot of big folks with carts, who represent the people you never see in the clubs. These folks don't respond to typical fitness ads and aren't represented in large numbers in any type of facility. In other words, these people are not in the 14 percent who "get it," and the fitness industry doesn't really do anything to help them begin to understand what fitness can do for them in their lives. The industry has failed these people, yet in many ways they represent the future of the entire industry.

## Who Are the "Get It" People?

Who are the "get it" people, why are they in your club, and how did they find you? The answers to these questions are not yet understood in great enough depth to help the industry very much. Enough is known, however, about the people in fitness facilities to make some bigger leaps that can help you with the sales process.

**Household income is a big predictor of whether someone will join a club.**

First, household income is a big predictor of whether someone will join a club. IHRSA has done some pioneering work in this area and found that the higher the household income, the more likely a person is to join a fitness facility. In fact, if household income is over $60,000, then approximately 23 percent of people join clubs. The lower the household income, the less likely the person is to join.

Other assumptions can be made about who is more likely to join a gym. More money might give a person more time to work out, especially if he has enough money to declare a portion of it discretionary, which simply means that all bills are paid and he has a little cash left over that he might use to join a gym, go the movies, or go out to dinner.

Higher household income might also connote a higher perceived status in the community, and looking good is part of maintaining that status. People with more affluence in their lives might also have the type of jobs that put them in front of other more affluent and successful people more often, creating the need to maintain a better image at work and in their circle of friends.

Education is also an important issue. The higher his education level, the more likely a person is to be involved in fitness. Similarly, the higher a person's education level, the less likely he is to smoke. A pattern quickly emerges. If a person has some money and a good education, he at some point becomes more interested in taking care of himself than someone with less income, who might be struggling to simply get by on a day-to-day basis. This less affluent person might be much more concerned with paying his bills than with joining a fitness facility.

These assumptions quickly break down, however, when they hit the real world. Many people who make a lot less than $60,000 in their households join gyms. At some point, awareness and desire overcome income, which is what makes selling memberships in a club so difficult. One tour may be given to a middle-aged woman who drives a nice car but gripes about the cost of a membership and leaves. The next tour is given to a nice working kid who doesn't look like he could ever come up with the membership fee, but who joins during the first visit because having a place to work out is important not only to help him look good, but also because the gym is his country club and social center all rolled into one.

The 16 percent of the people who do belong to health clubs understand the process. Even your newer members, who may have little gym experience, have read an article, perhaps have started walking, or were involved in some type of fitness program in the past. These folks may have never been in a gym before, but they at least understand what a gym is supposed to do for them and what kind of help they can anticipate from a full-service facility. They may not have the answers, but they most likely know some of the key questions.

## Where the fitness industry goes wrong

Where people in the fitness industry go wrong is that they can't believe that someone out there just doesn't "get" fitness. With everything society knows about the evils of smoking, who can believe that people out there still light up? With more than 60 percent of the population overweight, how can anyone who is even vaguely cognizant not be aware of fitness and its benefits in a person's life?

**Where people in the fitness industry go wrong is that they can't believe that someone out there just doesn't "get" fitness.**

Who in the fitness business has not berated a relative about their weight or bad personal habits, screaming in disbelief that the person you are talking to just doesn't understand how bad it is to be overweight? If you get it, then everyone must get it, and no room exists for those who don't.

The reality is that you may have forgotten what it is not to know. In other words, you have forgotten what its like to be a beginner. The purist in you emerges during these conversations. Your life is fitness and everyone should come on the path with you.

The industry ignores the people who don't get what it does and instead concentrates all of its efforts on those who do. In fact, almost every decision made in the fitness business is designed for the target population that already understands what clubs are designed to accomplish.

Consider this issue again from a different angle: Everything you do as an owner or manager is directed toward the 16 percent of the population that already understands fitness in some form or another. Nothing that you do, including you owners who think that you speak "beginner" in your facility, is truly targeted toward those people who don't get it. For example, consider these common missteps:

- You give a new member two workouts and then he has to go solo or buy training.

- Your ads include a few bullet points listing your stuff, a picture of a fitness model of some type, and a price offer. Doesn't offering price assume that the person has already made a decision to join a gym and is just shopping for the best deal? Doesn't price in an ad assume that the reader already "gets it"?

- You scare new people who come into the gym by having equipment too close to the counter or door, so that they walk in and are just a few feet from someone on a back machine. Too much, too soon scares a lot of people.

- You sell memberships using a feature tour, which is nothing more than showing everyone your stuff and brand names. This technique also assumes that the person has fitness experience and is expected to know and care about the choices you have made in your gym.

- More than 60 percent of the population cites weight loss as their major motivator to go to a gym, but very few clubs have a true weight-management system in place. In fact, less than 10 percent of the clubs in this country have any type of true weight-management system in place.

- You hire a staff that is too young and inexperienced, dress them badly, and undertrain them to deliver service, a vital component for someone who is new and needs a lot of help to get grounded during the first 30 days.

**Almost every decision made in the fitness business is designed for the target population that already understands what clubs are designed to accomplish.**

- You run Yellow Page ads with bullet points and more feature lists.

- You don't provide orientations to your club. Even the smallest club needs to spend 30 minutes with someone before he works out to get him grounded and to simply tell him, "Here is what is going to happen to you. This is what we will do during your first workout. Here is what we think you should wear. Yes, you may bring a friend. This is where you send your monthly payment. This is who to call if things aren't going your way. These are the club hours."

This list of instructions that you provide to a new member could go on and on, but the point is that most of your new members will start their memberships with just enough information to hate you in about 30 days. An important point in this book is that these questions need to be answered before the person becomes a member so that you lower that barrier of fear that keeps many people from trying anything new. Many clubs provide a Welcome Guide, which is a 70- to 80-page support book that answers these questions and more, as a gift for the prospective member during the tour. This type of support tool breaks down a lot of barriers and gives the person a higher perception of the service in your business.

If you step back and review your operating plan, you'll find that most of what happens in a typical fitness business is geared toward the people who already understand the concept of fitness. If you want to be more successful in sales over time, you need to eliminate as many barriers as you can and start all of your club's decision-making with this question: Would this make sense to someone who has never worked out before?

## Who Are the "Don't Get It" People and What Do They Want From You?

Start with the premise that approximately 300 million people live in the United States. Out of this number, roughly 45 million belong to fitness facilities of some type. Research conducted by IHRSA has shown that another 30 million people may have belonged to a fitness center at some point in their lives, but currently do not.

Using these numbers, approximately 225 million people are out there who are not currently members of a fitness facility. If the industry only converted 5 percent of these people, or 11.25 million, it would change the very nature of what you do for a living. Divide those 11.25 million people among the 29,000 mainstream fitness centers that exist as of 2006, and every gym currently in business would get 387 new members, which is a significant number for most clubs.

Where the industry goes wrong is in trying to change the world by going too big too soon. Not everyone is a fitness candidate and not everyone will join

> If you want to be more successful in sales over time, you need to eliminate as many barriers as you can and start all of your club's decision-making with this question: Would this make sense to someone who has never worked out before?

a gym. You need to think about the fitness business as more of a continuum, with those who will never, ever join fitness centers on the extreme left and the hard-core workout fanatics on the extreme right. You live and work on the right side and your potential markets exist closest to that side (Figure 6-1).

Figure 6-1. The fitness business continuum

According to IHRSA, the number of people joining gyms has been slowly rising at a rate at approximately 5 percent per year. The industry's growth, and its future, rests with those folks closest on the continuum to the 16 percent number discussed earlier. These folks fit the rest of the demographics and partially understand what the industry does, but fitness hasn't become important in their lives yet.

For example, consider a former housewife who has raised her kids, returned to the workforce at age 40, and wants to spend some time working on herself. She might have never belonged to a gym, but she is a strong candidate because she has everything you need: awareness, income, education, and opportunity.

IHRSA published another report, called *Why People Quit*, that is important to your sales efforts. This report discusses the reasons people quit a gym after spending the time, money, and energy to get started. The reasons people quit are important to the sales effort, because if you are proactive in your efforts to address these issues, it would be easier to generate new sales, and those people who did become members would stay longer and pay longer.

These issues are also extremely important to the "don't get it" people. Such a person asks a simple question in English and you answer in Japanese, which is how a trainer sounds who just got back from a three-day seminar on advanced training techniques. Because of your experience, you operate at a higher level than your potential members, which helps keep them away from your club. The brave souls who join gyms despite not being hardcore fitness people quit at alarming rates. You can learn from their reasons and change how you talk to people, how you market, and how you design your gyms and sales tours.

# Some People Quit for the Same Reasons That Others Never Join

The reason that one member quits a club after a few months is often the same reason why another member never joined in the first place. Some reasons are personal, but many are merely entry barriers set up by the club that can easily

> The reason that one member quits a club after a few months is often the same reason why another member never joined in the first place.

be fixed with a little thought. All of these issues need to be addressed during the tour, or in your support materials, as they represent real entry and retention issues for your clients.

## It's too hard.

*Newsweek* published an article in January of 2006 about how simple fitness really can be. Clubs make it harder than it has to be for most people to get results. A deconditioned woman may be thinking about dropping a few pounds for a wedding, but your trainers are talking to her about her first amateur bodybuilding contest in six months. Many club employees err toward the hardcore side of the fitness world, which isn't where most of your clients want to reside. You should talk often during the tour, in your ads, and in your support materials about how simple fitness is when a person first gets started. Make the following points as often as you can:

- We want you to move a little each day. Walking, group exercise, some light workouts using a stability ball, and a variety of other activities all count toward your daily movement goal.

- We want you to think about eating a little healthier. You don't have to give up all of your favorite things to change your shape, you don't have to starve, and you don't have to go on any extreme diets. A number of easy little tricks will make a difference and you can choose what you want to apply depending on how much weight you want to lose—and how quickly. All of our memberships begin with a session with a personal coach and a nutritional professional.

- Getting moving and eating a little healthier is a lot easier when you have a professional guide to help you, which is what we do here at the gym. We're the key for many people who look for guidance and support to get started on a healthier, and thinner, lifestyle

Fitness should be this simple, and you should explain it to the consumer as simply as possible. Most club owners and managers make mistakes, however, by trying too much too soon and thereby killing the feeling that the person can do what it takes to be successful.

> **Most club owners and managers make mistakes, however, by trying too much too soon and thereby killing the feeling that the person can do what it takes to be successful.**

Consider these two versions of the same story:

- "Well Kristen, you want to lose 15 pounds, so let's get you started on a three-day-a-week program. It takes about 45 minutes and you should plan on working out Monday, Wednesday, and Friday." Kristen does fine on Monday, makes it on Wednesday, and then has a soccer carpool on Friday and doesn't show. Because her trainer said she had to work out three times a week, she is now a failure. She couldn't make it on Friday, so what's the sense of even going back? She already knows that Fridays are always going to be tough.

- "Well Kristen, we hope that you start moving a little each day, and that includes doing some light medicine ball work at the gym twice a week. We realize, however, that you're a mom and getting here on a set schedule will be tough, so I'm going to give you two plans, one for here and one that includes things you can do at home. For example, you mentioned that you have to drive your kids to soccer practice after school a few times a week. When you're at the soccer field, try to walk around the field for about 30 minutes. That walk will count for your workout for the day and make it easier for you stay on schedule. If your trips here are going to be limited, then let's try to do just some light strength training here at the gym…"

In the first example, you gave Kristen enough help to fail. In the second, you built in success, because no matter what Kristen does, she is doing the right thing: she is moving.

## I don't have time.

This reason comes up often, and not just among working people. Students, mothers, and almost everyone else has a hard time finding the time to go to a gym. This play on time is one of the primary reasons the "30 minutes or less" clubs have found a niche.

The response to this common complaint goes hand-in-hand with the response to "It's too hard." Many people associate going to the gym with spending hours instead of minutes. This myth comes from many sources, but even some long-term members help perpetuate it. These members might spend several hours a night at the gym, but they do so because the gym is their social outlet. When they talk with their friends about working out, they talk about spending hours in the club, when their actual workout takes only 37 minutes to complete, including the shower.

**All of your salespeople should be able to explain the fitness experience as a quick "in the gym and out again" sequence.**

Again, fitness can be made simple. All of your salespeople should be able to explain the fitness experience as a quick "in the gym and out again" sequence. It is also important to get the concept across in all of your support material that fitness can take hours for a specialty athlete who is training for a triathlon or minutes for a deconditioned accountant during tax season who is just trying to be a bit healthier.

If all a person has to do to get on the path to fitness is move a little each day, then more people will realize that they have the time. The accountant may not have an hour for cardio, but he does have time to walk for three 10-minutes sessions each day, which is better than he has been doing for the past year. It is success, even if not in the heart of a purist trainer.

## The gym has broken and out-of-date equipment.

While this critique may be fair, many club owners will respond by asking themselves, "What does this person, who doesn't 'get it,' know about out-of-date equipment? Actually, he may know much more than you think about what he is looking for and what he wants to do when he comes to a fitness facility.

In the fall of 2005, a popular morning show ran a three-minute feature on training. One of the women on the show came out in a workout suit and told her co-hosts that she had just had the workout of her life at a local gym and she was going to show them the hottest thing in training.

After the inevitable commercial break, the woman then preceded to do walking lunges with a medicine ball twist, followed by more walking lunges with some small dumbbells and curls. She sweated, groaned, and talked about how these core exercises build the strength that women need to live better lives and that functional training was the next big thing. The show has three women co-hosts and obviously targets the morning female crowd.

If you own a fitness center, how much more help do you need? Several million women who previously didn't "get it" now have a clue and a target: They want to do that cool stuff they saw on television.

You can only guess at how many women who were watching that show decided to reach out to a fitness club for the first time. Now think about how many women were bitterly disappointed by their experience during their gym visits.

These women walked into clubs across America looking for functional training, racks of medicine balls, and other cool functional stuff they had seen on this show. Instead, they were baffled when they discovered that most gyms have lines and lines of fixed equipment and one little rack of duct-taped medicine balls in the corner.

They were further discouraged when many trainers laughed at their questions and told them that they didn't need this functional stuff, and that they would be better off with traditional weight training. And many were further let down when they noticed members doing walking lunges in the walkways in the club. Because most fitness facilities don't have any designated space for these exercises, such as a short two-lane track near the workout floor, members have to do them wherever they can find the room.

The "don't get it" crowd may not understand advanced training techniques, but they do know instinctively when your club is dated and your training concepts are out of date. The disconnect exists because the potential member was driven to go to a gym by something she thought was new and exciting, only to find that the club is five years or more out of date because the owner refuses to keep up with current trends and training information. The club lost

> The "don't get it" crowd may not understand advanced training techniques, but they do know instinctively when your club is dated and your training concepts are out of date.

a sale, not because the woman wasn't really interested, as the sales report will read later that day, but because she was actually smarter and more current than the owner.

People quit because they get tired of out-of-order signs, broken TVs, duct tape on the seats, and other signs that the club isn't keeping up. They leave you for fresh competitors with fresh equipment that works and for other clubs that have sufficient enough resources to service their membership.

## The facility is not clean.

Your club is never as clean as you think it is, and it has to be cleaner than you think it does. Lack of cleanliness is the first reason that many members quit, especially women, and is perhaps the biggest barrier to joining, because you can't hide or overcome a dirty club with words.

It is important to note that many of your potential members will first check out the club with a drive-by. Remember that the tour starts before the guest gets inside, and if the barriers are strong enough beforehand, the person never will never even get there.

You can control the outside impression more than you think, or have previously been willing to do. Clutter and garbage around your door is a sign to many people of the experience they will get inside. Dirty mats, greasy door handles, and cluttered counters seen through the windows on a Sunday afternoon when you are closed, but still getting shopped, lead to fewer in-person inquiries.

One small suburban club in Chicago ran a picture of an elderly lady with glasses in the corner of every advertising piece, with a little bubble overhead with the words: "This club certified clean by my own mother." If it's clean enough for your mother, then it must be truly clean. This owner obviously had encountered issues with cleanliness somewhere in the past and wasn't going to tolerate it anymore. No data are available proving this tactic worked, but it definitely gets the point across that this club does understand the importance of being clean for its members and guests.

## I don't like dishonest or harsh business practices.

Your world is always smaller than you think. Most clubs attract approximately 85 to 90 percent of their members from within a 12-minute drive time of the club. These people live close to each other, work in the same neighborhoods, and have kids in the same sports leagues. If something isn't right in your club, or the perception exists that something may be slightly shady, then word will spread into your market faster and more deeply than you think.

The simplest rule is to put everything in writing. Print out your prices, have a clear, legal contract approved by your state, list all services and member rules in your Welcome Guide and post them in the club, and if you promise something to your members, write it so that both sides understand the deal. Members leave because they had an expectation and you either changed the rules or the communication was poor. Don't take the chance. Be clear about what you're offering and what the person will get for the money.

Because the pressure sales guys who have been so instrumental in destroying the image of the club industry for so many years have laid such a rough foundation for the rest of the owners, the perception of many of the "don't get it" people is that when you go to a gym to inquire about prices you should take a bat, because you will have to beat your way out of the sales office.

The only way to overcome this legacy in the industry is to offer a trial membership. "Try this club absolutely for free for 14 days with no money up front, no obligation, and no risk. We are proud of our club and would like you to come meet our members, meet the staff, and give us a chance to earn your business. If we haven't earned your business at the end of 14 days, then we don't deserve to have you as a member."

If you offer trial memberships, your positive image will build over time in your market. Unfortunately, most people who don't have any working experience in a fitness facility associate the people in the fitness industry with used car salespeople, or worse. The perception of pressure is big and it has to be eliminated in your marketing and covered within the first three minutes of a guest's visit. "By the way Joe, have you heard about our trial membership? We are so proud of our club that we want you to try it free for 14 days with no risk…"

You still are going to write memberships that day and you are still going to sign people up, but by referencing the trial up front, you take the pressure off of the guest during the tour. He will spend more time listening to you, rather than worrying about being beaten senseless with a hard sell later in the office.

## I don't like the staff at the club.

Ask yourself this difficult question: "How many memberships do you think your worst staff person costs you each year?" Few owners ask this question because they are usually just happy because the person actually showed up for his shift. Beyond that issue, it is easier to just ignore the problem and keep moving.

The bubble effect costs you the most money in terms of your staff. The bubble effect means that a staff member comes to work each day, does her job with the least amount of pain, and then goes home. You might even consider this employee a good one, because she is on time, decently dressed, and reliable. The problem with this employee and others like her is that she fails to connect with any of the members. She operates in her own little world— her bubble—and only deals with people around her who need immediate

> Members leave because they had an expectation and you either changed the rules or the communication was poor.

attention. She is polite to the members, but she really just fills a position instead of delivering the service that would lead to increased member retention.

People are acknowledged, but this staff member never learns names. Members are serviced quickly at the counter, but never thanked for what they bought. The employee might even be so efficient that she can take care of the counter while carrying on a conversation with a fellow employee behind the desk, thereby failing to focus any attention on the member in front of her at the time.

Hundreds of similarly negative actions are masked each day by the illusion of being a good employee. Slowly, over time, she erodes the club's relationships with its members, and eventually some will leave because they don't feel that they have built any connections that warrant continuing to spend money there.

People look for and want these small, positive acknowledgments from the people around them, especially when they are spending money with that business. Members also want to earn the feeling of being a regular who is recognized in the business, as opposed to a new person who has not yet earned his stripes.

How powerful are these small things? In our seminars, we tell the story of a visit that a group of us made to a new deli near our offices. Being in the seminar business means that everyone represents a potential story that will be told somewhere, especially when it's a negative story that powerfully illustrates a point.

**Common courtesy is nearly dead in many small businesses, so it is interesting to extend some to the people who are doing the actual work in a business.**

Common courtesy is nearly dead in many small businesses, so it is interesting to extend some to the people who are doing the actual work in a business. Many of the working people who man counters, reception desks, and even the front counters in fitness businesses, are often neglected, or rudely treated, by stressed-out customers.

We stress the importance of extending extreme courtesy to everyone whenever anyone from our company is out, in hopes of possibly receiving it back in kind. Therefore, the counter person at the deli was greeted with a strong hello and "How is your day going?" No one else was in line, so being busy wasn't an excuse for totally ignoring us and looking back with a blank stare. The order was placed, again without acknowledgment, and the sandwich was slid across the counter. Our staff person said a positive "Thank you" and again the counter person simply stared. As we walked out of the deli, our staff member said, "Well, we can take that place off the list."

How much business does that one employee cost the business over time? She was quick and efficient, and the food was good, but who would ever want to go back to deal with someone so rude? The issue is that too many of these people are working the front desks of clubs all around the world because owners don't train them, or even hire them, properly. They associate being a good employee with the wrong things, such as efficiency, which is certainly good, but is only one of many skills the person needs. Instead, owners should focus on the employee's ability to positively impact every single person she comes in contact with each day.

Beyond costing the club existing members, the bubble employees cost clubs a lot of money in new sales. Your guests, especially those who don't yet "get" the fitness concept and who have no experience in fitness centers, are looking for those small, interpersonal connections that make them feel welcome and gain a sense of belonging over time.

All salespeople seem nice, especially those involved in the actual sale, and being nice on a tour should be a base expectation. And all owners and managers expect the front-counter person to be trained enough to greet each guest and be sociable, which is becoming more of a lost art. What the guest doesn't expect, however, is a trainer stepping away from a client to shake hands and welcome her to the club. She also doesn't expect the owner or manager to stop and introduce herself, and she would never expect the salesperson to take the time to introduce her to some of the regular members encountered on the tour.

If the salesperson is doing his job, he will send a handwritten note the day the guest visits thanking her for visiting and he should have already sent her a thank you email (with a different script) before she even left the parking lot. All of these things help build an emotional connection to the club and make the person feel that not only can she do it, but also that she will fit into the club as a person.

Again, the "don't get it" crowd needs this bridge. Without these connections, and with no other base to draw upon, the leap from never being a member to being a fully functional member of the club is just too big.

## Summary

The key concept to remember is that the things that drive members out of the club are often the same things that lower your chances for new sales. The issue of staff, for example, illustrates that if you aren't treating your members correctly, you are not very likely to treat your guests any better, even though you are on your best behavior when trying to get money out of their pockets.

The most important thought regarding this issue is that you probably focus almost all of your energy in your businesses on the people who are like you and who already understand what you do. After 50 years, the fitness industry has only managed to attract about 16 percent of the people in this country to its clubs. They bought memberships and they "get it," although owners and managers don't yet do a great job of keeping even these people.

> If you aren't treating your members correctly, you are not very likely to treat your guests any better, even though you are on your best behavior when trying to get money out of their pockets.

The future of this business, and where the bigger sales numbers are going to come from in the near future, is in diverting some of this focus to the 84 percent of Americans who don't yet get it. How you market, how you lay out your club, how you train your staff, and especially how you tour and sell new memberships has to change or you won't be able to take advantage of the individuals in this huge, untapped market, who will eventually find fitness.

## Key Points From This Chapter

- Clubs owners and managers focus most of their efforts on people like themselves who understand fitness and the fitness lifestyle. Currently, only 16 percent of the people in this country belong to fitness centers.

- Owners tend ignore the other 84 percent of the people who don't belong to fitness centers. They give lip service to this group, but their marketing, their clubs, and their staff are all designed to support people with prior fitness experience.

- The reasons why people quit clubs are often the same as the reasons and barriers that prevent others from ever joining in the first place. Addressing these issues as part of your marketing and sales tour will enhance your penetration into the "don't get it" group.

**Tip of the Day**

## Sales is part of everything in your life.

You want to go to the beach on vacation, but your significant other wants to go to the mountains. A sales pitch will determine your ultimate destination. Either you have the best pitch or your significant other does; whoever presents the best is going to go where he or she wants.

Ask for a raise and the outcome is based upon your sales presentation. Speak at your church to raise money and the outcome is determined by the strength of your sales presentation. Talk your kids into a trip for the day and it all comes down to how well you present yourself.

Almost everything you do in your life might be a little easier if you learn to present yourself more effectively than the other guy. Sales is nothing more than mastering presentation skills, and these skills will serve you well in both your professional and personal life.

# 7

# Will You Please Tell Me What's in It for Me?

Never give a feature without giving a benefit. You've probably heard this rule over the years from anyone who has more than a week's worth of sales training. But what does this overused statement really mean and why is it so important to how you sell in the fitness business?

Before learning about features and benefits, you first have to explore what you are really trying to sell in any type of fitness business. It's a basic rule of any sales encounter that you probably won't be any good at selling if you don't know what the product really is.

Many salespeople also make the mistake of starting out thinking that they always know just what the consumer wants from them. The reality is that the majority of consumers don't really know what fitness centers are all about and don't have any idea of what they need when they first come through the door. Most people have a vague idea of fitness, they know that they need to do something, and a health club seems to be the logical place to start.

If you want to be successful in sales of any type, including selling in the fitness business, you must first understand what you are selling and how it relates to what the consumer thinks he is buying. This dichotomy between what you think you sell and what the consumer thinks he is trying to buy is what make sales so much harder than it needs to be.

People in the fitness business are selling intangibles, which are things that you cannot grasp, hold, take home, or play with. Tangibles, on the other hand, are real things that the consumer can pick up, put in the shopping cart, and then throw it into the trunk for the ride home. No discussion of the differences between features and benefits can take place without first understanding the difference between a tangible and an intangible.

For example, a consultant who sells information or guidance deals in intangibles. No physical goods are involved in the transaction, even though money changes hands. The client pays the consultant for her time and information that might be shared over an hour, a day, or perhaps through a visit to the client's business.

A tangible, on the other hand, might be something like a set of tires. You bring your car to the shop, the guy in the back pops off your old tires, and an hour or so later you head home riding on your new set. In this exchange, you paid money and received something that had substance, as opposed to the previous example, in which the client paid money and received information that has no physical shape or form.

**The always-fatal mistake salespeople make in the fitness business is that they think that they are selling something tangible and the consumer believes he is buying something intangible.**

The always-fatal mistake salespeople make in the fitness business is that they think that they are selling something tangible and the consumer believes he is buying something intangible. Where owners and managers fail in the sales process is when they build a system based upon training their people to sell tangible items to prospective members who are intent on exploring the intangible quality of fitness and what it can do for them.

Compare opening a fitness business to having a child. Most first-time parents truly believe that their child is the most beautiful child in the world, and they even invite all their friends over, the same friends who the couple used to go to bars and great restaurants with in the BB days (before baby), to simply sit and watch the kid sit on the floor and burp and slobber. The process of having a child, through the long months of pregnancy and then birth, has consumed their lives and now everyone else must be sucked into their shrinking world, which now entirely revolves around their child.

Opening a fitness business for the first time is very similar. It consumes your life for years, as you raise money, write your business plan, hire your first staff, and then finally, after months of intense labor, you finally get your gym open.

When you tour this owner's new gym, it's never about the client. It's always going to be about the club. If you tour this club as a prospective member, you can be sure that you are going to hear about the quantity of equipment, including brand names, how new the locker rooms are, and how this club compares to any competitor in the area. It's all about the club, because it's really all about the owner and the years it took to get this dream up and running.

This rule does not, by the way, apply to only small independent owners. Big chains make this same mistake by assuming that all the millions they have spent on each unit are what finally sell the consumer a membership. The only really difference is the scale, because the mistake is the same: Both are selling from the tangible viewpoint that states that the consumer is buying the physical plant and the emotion it took to build each club.

You can see this rule in action by simply taking a tour in one of these clubs. The excited single club operator points out the 50 treadmills and their brand name, the size of the group rooms, the size of the workout floor, and the number of classes held each week. This type of tour is the basic, "buy my club/I built it/I am proud of it/I need the money to pay for it" tour. His tangible is the gym itself and he is selling equipment and the physical plant.

The chain guys give the same type of tour, but they go one step beyond selling equipment to selling memberships. It's very simple and very obvious that this physical plant exists for the sole purpose of turning and burning memberships all day long. Their tangible is selling a membership, something you can hold and take home in the form of that rip-off-the-back pink sheet of the membership agreement.

When a consumer enters a gym, he may not know exactly what he wants, but he does bring some base expectations to the situation. Fitness is a nebulous concept that often doesn't have any concrete substance for the consumer. Fitness is what someone else has, defined by someone on the beach looking better than he does, or it may be as simple as that fantasy the person has that last five minutes before he goes to sleep, in which he is someone famous that always is in shape and looking good.

Beyond appearance are health and wellness, which are even harder ideas to conceptualize. Most people only recognize wellness when it is gone and they don't feel so good. Being fit, healthy, and happy are very difficult concepts to verbalize for the consumer and most wouldn't want to share their most intimate thoughts about how they really view themselves and what they really want to look like at some distant point in the future when the club staff declares them "fit."

It's an odd concept, to grasp but what you are actually selling to most people is hope. Diets have failed them, working out has failed them in the past, and in many ways they have failed themselves because they haven't yet found the discipline, or the guidance and support, they need to succeed in fitness and weight management.

Walking into a fitness center for the first time, especially when you're not feeling good about your body and the way you look, is probably one of the most emotional events you can have in your life. Compound this experience by having a 20-something, rock hard, never-out-of-shape counter person, who turns the person over to another hard-body salesperson, who again turns the emotionally distraught prospective member over to a semi-naked trainer with a bare midriff, and you basically have everything that's wrong with the fitness business in one very horrible sequence of events.

If you get it right, you sell hope, which is translated as, "This time you won't fail because we are going on this journey with you. We'll hold your hand, we'll

**Walking into a fitness center for the first time, especially when you're not feeling good about your body and the way you look, is probably one of the most emotional events you can have in your life.**

guide you, we'll make the big decisions for you, and most importantly, when you stumble we will be there to pick you up and get you back on the right track." The hope states that things will be different this time and the person won't fail because you're there for them. Hope sells, and it sure beats the hell out of selling "fitness" or "memberships."

The intangible hope, if understood and sold properly, becomes your benefit. This benefit answers the single most important question a potential client might ask: "What's in it for me as the consumer?" This question is the foundation for selling an intangible and for mastering the benefit-based sales process.

When you sell tangibles, such as equipment brands and memberships, you almost always end up selling features. Instead, you should be focusing on the benefits that what these things can provide to a new member. Feature-driven sales focuses on what the product is or the means by which the consumer does something, such as the number of treadmills or the number of classes offered each week. Benefit sales, on the other hand, always clearly answer the question of what is in it for the consumer.

For example, a feature of most fitness centers is the equipment. When a salesperson talks about the 50 treadmills, the brand names of those treadmills, the amount of free weights, and the number of classes, what he is really doing is listing the components of the business (what the product is or parts of the product). This same salesperson might talk about having trainers available and the packages available for that department (the means or process by which you do something).

Almost all fitness tours, in almost all clubs anywhere in this country, are feature driven. This statement is broad, but after years of taking fake tours, the pattern becomes obvious. This default to feature tours doesn't occur because they are the most effective way to sell, but because this situation is where you end up as an inexperienced or uneducated owner. Feature tours are simply the path of least resistance. In other words, if you don't know what else to do, just show the customer all the cool stuff you have in the gym and brag about the brand names.

These feature-based tours all focus on the things that the owner wants the customer to see and everything is sold from the club's perspective. Building an effective sales system is based upon changing your perspective from what you want you to see as a gym owner or sales manager to what all of these things can do for the potential customer. Always be sure to answer the magical question, "What's in for me if I buy from you?"

Remember the first line of this chapter: Never give a feature without giving a benefit. If you don't eventually grasp this perspective shift, then you are doomed to weak sales and ineffective marketing.

> **Benefit sales, on the other hand, always clearly answer the question of what is in it for the consumer.**

Keep in mind that marketing is nothing more than a process to get someone through the door. Feature-based marketing, such as a typical club Yellow Pages ad with a picture of a fitness model and a string of bullet points, is not an effective way to bring new people to your business. Good, effective marketing is benefit-based and a benefit headline always answers the question, "What is in it for the consumer?"

For example, "Try our club absolutely free for 14 days with no risk and with no money up front," is an example of a benefit-based headline. The benefit in this case is that the person can try the club before buying, thereby eliminating risk, which is the biggest barrier to inquiry for most people. What's in it for the consumer? Try before you buy without risking a single dollar is the best possible answer.

The following story has floated through many business books and best describes the difference between a feature and a benefit:

*"Ever go fishing?" the marketing instructor asks his student.*

*"Yep."*

*"Use worms when you fish?"*

*"Yep."*

*"Why?"*

*The student thinks a moment and answers: "I guess because they attract the fish."*

*"Do you eat the worms?"*

*"No, I can't imagine ever eating a worm."*

*"Well," the instructor says, "All the fish care about is what they like and if you're fishing and hope to catch fish, then what they like is all that matters and what you like doesn't really count at all."*

In the fitness business, consumers can get the same features at almost any club. Any decent club is going to have a lot of equipment and services and be at least moderately clean. What sells memberships is that the consumer can only get the benefit question answered at your club. Remember that whoever best answers, "What's in it for me as the consumer?" will sell the most memberships.

**Whoever best answers, "What's in it for me as the consumer?" will sell the most memberships.**

# Marketing

When owners don't know what else to do, they often put together a list of everything they have in the gym. This list always comes out in the fabled bullet format: Draw a dot followed by some component in the club. For example:

**Jim's Gym**

- 50,000 pounds of free weights
- Hammer™ strength equipment
- Personal training
- Group classes
- Locker rooms

This ad is an example of feature marketing at its worst. List everything you have, add a semi-naked model, and you have the typical health club Yellow Pages ad.

Another term for features is base expectation. These products and services are an expected part of that type of business. For example, would a Ford® dealership have to advertise that it has cars for sale? Just imagine these ads: Come to Lighthouse Ford, we have cars for sale. Stay at the Sheraton®, we have beds and bathrooms. Eat at Anthony's Restaurant, where we serve food every day.

The epitome of this type of ad, of course, is come to our gym, where we have all types of fitness stuff you can use. Fitness businesses that list all of their fitness stuff with bullet points in their ads are no different from hotels that would advertise beds or restaurants that talk about items on their menu. These features are expected in that business, and are base expectations from the consumer's viewpoint. Features do not sell memberships, rooms, cars, or meals.

What does sell is what all this stuff can do for you, which is the benefit of dealing with that business. Restaurants that describe their atmosphere and service are far better at attracting new customers than those that merely list their menu items. Similarly, health clubs that talk about what the customer gets from the business are far more successful than those that simply list all of the stuff in the gym.

> Health clubs that talk about what the customer gets from the business are far more successful than those that simply list all of the stuff in the gym.

## What every marketing piece has to do to attract new customers

Good marketing of any type for almost any business should address the following four questions. (These questions are also important throughout the sales process, and each one should be addressed during the tour.)

- What's in it for me?
- What's the risk?
- Are any other people like me using this product?
- How do I get started here if I am interested?

These questions reflect the thought process of a potential client who is approaching your business for the first time. If I buy this membership, what do

I get out of it? I work hard for my money and don't want to waste it. Am I the only sucker who has ever bought this membership? Are other people like me using this service? Will I fit in? Hey, this sounds nice, but how do I get started?

Someone new to your business starts his analysis with something very similar to these four questions in mind. The person looks, thinks, questions, and either buys or doesn't buy based upon how well he can get those questions answered. The following sections take a closer look at each of these questions.

## What's in it for me?

Features are the tools in the business. The benefit is how the business uses those tools to help the customer get what he wants.

**Features are the tools in the business. The benefit is how the business uses those tools to help the customer get what he wants.**

The ultimate benefit, which is discussed in other books I've written for Healthy Learning, as well as in Chapter 8 of this book, is "try before you buy." A trial provides a chance for the customer to get involved before he goes far enough to be unhappy. The benefit is that he gets a chance to validate other claims before totally committing to the opportunity.

Building an emotional bridge between the business and the potential client is usually the goal of an experienced marketing person. For example, consider an ad that features an overweight person on a beach walking in a swimsuit with the headline: Your reason to get fit just might be right there behind you. This ad is edgy, but it also taps into the emotional aspects of weight management and why people seek fitness.

Most consumers aren't looking for a gym with 50,000 pounds of free weights; they are looking for a place that will help them ease their pain. If this edgy ad continues by offering a 14-day trial membership that includes a personal coach and a few nutritional lectures, you have not only tapped the emotional bank with the picture and headline, but you have also given the person a chance to validate your claim that you are the club that can help him compared to other fitness businesses in the area.

## What's the risk?

Risk is the greatest barrier to inquiry for most people who are considering fitness club memberships. "What if I sign up and don't like it? I will lose all of my money and be stuck." This fear is so strong, perhaps due to the image the industry has developed of being high-pressure salespeople, that many people simply don't even try.

Risk has to be eliminated to get people to try your club, and the illusion of risk also has to be eliminated during the sales process to get more people to become members. This statement will be especially true in future years, when the industry begins to attract more and more people with absolutely no fitness experience whatsoever.

You eliminate risk by offering the trial membership. "Try before you buy" is far more powerful than "try and we will give you a money-back guarantee." "Try before you give me money" eliminates risk. "Give me money and then hope that I will give it back if you don't like my service" doesn't lower the perceived risk at all, and might even accentuate it.

When you use trials in your marketing, you lower the perceived risk from the start. Look at this sample ad copy and think about the risk factor from the consumer's perspective.

**We are so proud of our facility that we will let you try it absolutely free with no risk, no obligation, and no money up front for a full 14 days. We would like you to come meet our other members and our staff and, if we haven't earned your business at the end of 14 days, then we don't deserve to have to as a member.**

This copy, coupled with a 14-day trial membership and some gentle pictures that indicate the type of target market you are chasing, should attract people who wouldn't normally respond to a price ad. In this case, the copy spells out the benefit very clearly for the consumer: Try us before you risk a single dollar and if you don't like us just walk away and you won't lose any money.

If you are still using price-drive ads, you should consider some type of money-back guarantee, even if it is only for seven days. Money-back guarantees are not as powerful as "try before you buy" presentations, but they are still much better than those clubs that aggressively try to bag the client during the first visit and then trap him in membership hell.

Much of this same verbiage could easily be adapted to your sales tour, no matter what type of marketing you are using. Are you willing to stand behind your memberships? Are you willing to let the customer have a reasonable chance to try this facility before making the total commitment? These questions are in the consumer's head and have to be addressed before he ever gets to your club and then several times more during the actual tour.

*Are any other people like me using this product?*

**People want to hang out and work out with their own social group.**

Likes attract likes. People want to hang out and work out with their own social group. According to IHRSA's *Why People Quit*, one of the main personal reasons that people quit a facility is that they don't get socially connected to the other members or the staff. They come for a while, do a few workouts, but never really form any types of friendships or recognition factor from others in the club.

This problem is easy to address through marketing. Keep in mind that if you address the problem in your marketing it is a lot easier to be successful in the sales process later. The fewer perceived barriers that the client brings to the gym, the easier it will be to individualize the sales process and build that emotional bridge necessary to get people to join and to stay longer and pay longer.

Be sure to use pictures that match your target market, which is that demographic population that you are targeting with your marketing. A club's target market is usually defined as 80 percent of its membership. For example, if your target market is the upscale adult, you might have 80 percent of your membership in the 30 to 50 age range. In comparison, many of the national chains specialize in the 18- to 34-year-old population and wellness centers and hospital-based facilities often have target markets in the 35 to 55 range.

Where the disconnect comes for the client is when your club talks about being an adult club, but you run pictures of models that are too young or too fit. Before the potential member even gets into your club, she is already afraid that she will be too old to be a member, or worse yet, the only one who is not in shape in the gym. The images you use in your ads should convey the types of people you are targeting and who are actually using the gym.

Another way of conveying your target population is by better utilizing your kick line, which appears under your club's name. Consider this example:

**Center City Fitness**
**Serious Fitness for <u>Every</u>body**

This secondary line, called a kick line, has been used, including the underline, a thousand times and is a complete waste. It says nothing to the consumer and wastes an opportunity to further identify the club's market.

You can get more out of your kick line by thinking of it as an identifier for your club's name. Catchy or cute phrases don't sell memberships and don't lower the potential member's perceived barriers of not fitting into the club. A better use of the identifier line might be as follows:

**The Woman's Workout Company**
**Upscale Fitness for the Women of Boston**

This name clearly states who should use the club (women) and how much they're going to pay when they get there (upscale). Give the consumers an actual hint and let them know what they're getting into before they visit.

The common objection from many owners, and even some marketing people, is that they purposely want the name and identifier to be generic in hopes of opening the market to everyone. The rule to remember is: If you try to be everything to everybody then you become nothing to nobody. The point

> **The rule to remember is: If you try to be everything to everybody then you become nothing to nobody.**

is clear: Use your name and kick line to let the customer know if they indeed fit into your business.

Consider this next example:

## World Gym North Beach
## The High-Energy Fitness Alternative

This one actually scores twice by adding a locator to the franchise name and by stating through the identifier that it is an alternative to the boring box facilities. Identifier lines can easily be used to position your club in a mature—that is, crowded—market and state your target market in relationship to other clubs in the area.

If a lot of women's clubs are in the area, then take the upscale position if you can. If a lot of big old-style box clubs are around, then become the alternative. No club can be everything to everyone because, again, likes attract likes and people want to hang out with other people like themselves.

During the actual sales process, you have to demonstrate that the prospective member will fit your gym's environment. Several strategies are effective, but always return to the basic thought that the person you are touring is glancing around the facility as you tour, looking for other people like himself. He simply wants the connection of being with people struggling on the same path as he is.

> One of the biggest mistakes salespeople make is forgetting that everything counts in the sales process, especially the power of first impressions.

One of the biggest mistakes salespeople make is forgetting that everything counts in the sales process, especially the power of first impressions. When the prospect enters the gym for the first time, whoever is at the front counter sets the stage for what happens next. If the front-counter person is too young, too inexperienced, and working for the cheapest pay you could get away with, then you are going to have that image as the first impression of every guest who walks through the door.

This type of counter person is fine if every prospect you have is young and in a lower economic class. But if you deal with other clientele, then you have a serious disconnect right away.

Consider the arrival of a female prospect in her 40s. The counter person is 19 and hasn't even had time to get out of shape yet. The guest's first impression of your gym is that you are staffed with people who really won't be able to identify with someone who is a little older, has kids and a career, and who is fighting that last 10 pounds that just won't go away after the birth of her last child.

No matter what the salesperson says during that tour, the guest is going to carry that first impression with her. This situation compounds itself if you have a young male provide the tour and a number of hard-body trainers on the floor.

Simply put, your staff should match your target membership. If your target market is 30 to 50 years old, then every employee should be as close as you can get to those numbers. It's hard to build a fitness business for a group of people in their 30s and beyond with a staff that is all under 30, because no connection exists between the people you are trying to acquire and the people you hired to sell and service them.

One other hint is to make sure your club's dress code matches your target group. If you are seeking an older clientele, meaning over 30, then you should have the appropriate dress code in place. You don't want to be touring a 35-year-old businessman through a room of people working out in cut-off jeans and work boots.

If the work-boot crowd is your market, then you don't have a problem, but if you are seeking another type of clientele you need to set restrictions on dress that will hurt your chance of giving a successful tour. Once again, don't forget that everything counts on a sales tour and your club is judged by the first impression of your staff, the look of the members, and even the age and shape of everyone the prospect meets on the cruise around the gym.

*How do I get started if I am interested?*

"What do I have to do to get started? I like what I see, but I am not clear on what to do next."

This question represents one of those obvious issues that are so neglected in the sales process. Properly responding does not mean closing and asking for the sale, which is discussed in Chapter 18. It also doesn't mean just becoming an expert at filling out a membership contract. What this question does mean to the consumer is, "Now you have my attention, what is the clear, logical way to move forward one step?"

Marketing exists to get the attention of a consumer. The biggest mistake owners make in marketing their fitness business it putting too much in the ads. The thought process must be that if I put enough crap onto this postcard the person reading it will simply surrender due to being overwhelmed, or maybe just beaten into submission.

**The biggest mistake owners make in marketing their fitness business it putting too much in the ads.**

This thought process was mentioned earlier in this chapter. Feature-based ads, which are nothing more than a list of everything you have in the walls of your gym, don't work because they are just so self-obvious. Nothing is powerful or attention-getting about a fitness business that has fitness stuff in it, which the customer now knows about because the owner has listed everything he owns on the postcard he sent, and nothing listed excites the customer enough to move to the next step. The consumer might go to the Sheraton this weekend because they are offering a getaway package that includes a great dinner and some champagne, but she is not likely to respond to an ad for that hotel simply because they have beds, toilets, and a phone in every room.

Marketing is similar to dating. If you're in a crowded room and catch the scent of a nice perfume (advertising), and find that the wearer of that perfume is dressed to kill (marketing), and you chat and find out she is single and likes to ski (benefit), then you become tempted to move to the next step, which is to call her (how do I get started if I am interested?). This process is clear and most people understand how to play the game.

Typical fitness business ads, however, make this process harder than it has to be. Club marketing rarely states a benefit, keeping in mind that price specials are not benefits of that business, and merely rely on the features. Price is only important once a person decides to join a gym and is an attraction only if he already has prior knowledge of how a gym membership works and is a very experienced gym person.

**Your ad should be designed to get the customer's attention, make him want to learn more, and encourage him to come in or pick up the phone to take that next step.**

Your ad should be designed to get the customer's attention, make him want to learn more, and encourage him to come in or pick up the phone to take that next step. Most fitness ads discourage the next step because no next step is really presented due to the nature of how the ads are designed: random pictures that don't match the members, a list of everything in the gym, a phone number, and a price special that is supposed to drive the customer wild.

In the dating example, you walk up to the woman and she hands you a list: single, 35, work at a bank, divorced with two kids, pick nose in public, and have a mother that will be a terror in your life. In this case, she may be a great person but you now know too much information too soon and make a decision that you are not interested from just the list. The problem might be that you misread the list, weren't really familiar with the terms, or just didn't see something you were looking for that is part of who she is but didn't make the list.

This same thing happens with the feature ads. The consumer may look at your list and not see something your club is good at, such as delivering that personal touch in service, and then not respond. Simply put, nothing was listed that made him want to find out more.

With fitness ads, just listing price and bullet-point features doesn't get a customer's attention. Even assuming that you do run a decent ad with a strong trial offer and artwork that matches your club's demographics, most owners still leave out a very important part of the ad: "What do I do next now that you have my attention? Okay, so you got me. You have my attention and this fitness stuff sounds interesting." If you want your marketing to be effective over time, you have to clearly state what to do next. For example:

**To get started with your trial membership, call 555-1234 today. We'll set a time for you to meet with your personal coach and get your individualized program going today. If you'd like to simply stop by. We are at 0000 Main, behind the Wal-Mart®, and we're open until 10:00.**

People like a sense of being in control, and knowing the next step gives the customer confidence that he can join the gym and not be embarrassed. The emphasis is on the word embarrassed. The fear of looking bad often freezes people into inaction. They feel that the risk is just too high to take the chance that they will embarrass themselves by trying something new.

Most people reading this book have made fitness a significant part of their lives. You may not be a fanatic, but you're at least comfortable with the process, understand how it works, and own the right clothes for the right workout. Who would want to show up for a long bike ride wearing running shorts? You'd get laughed off the course before you even got started.

The fear of looking bad in front of others already familiar with the activity or sport is bad enough that the average middle-aged person who is successful somewhere else in his life won't subjugate himself to looking out of place or wrongly dressed in front of younger, less successful people. The key is that if any doubt exists whatsoever, he won't risk it and, therefore, won't try it at all.

**If you want your marketing to be effective over time, you have to clearly state what to do next.**

Look at some of your mysterious first-visit no-shows and you'll see the pattern. "If I haven't been in a fitness center in years, or at all, where do I start? What do I wear? How long will that first workout be? Will I die or puke in front of my instructor, who I know will be younger, prettier, and more fit than I am?" If any chance exists that the consumer can't figure out the answers to these questions and feel good about them, she will not show up.

Give the person some help. It's the least you can do, and it will help your chances of closing more deals:

*Well Bob, we'll see you tonight at 7 o'clock for your first workout with the trial membership. If you would like to change here we have day lockers available at no charge. Once you're a member you'll need a lock, but tonight we'll give you a loaner.*

*Most of our members wear simple workout shorts and T-shirts with some type of running or cross-training shoe, but we don't see many sweat suits in here because you'd get too hot. Your first visit is usually light on the workout and focuses more on getting you orientated to the gym. You don't want to go too hard during your first visit. Many new people expect it to be harder than it really is.*

*We'll look for you a few minutes before 7 o'clock. Crystal is at the front desk tonight and will get you going in the right direction. Again, my name is Kirk and I'll be showing you around. Bob, you said you drove by us on the way home from work, so I'll assume you know where we are located. Are there any other questions you need to have answered before we see you tonight?*

This show of personal concern greatly enhances the prospect's anticipation, because he has a plan and knows that someone on the staff is already looking out for him. It makes the first workout, and the membership sale, much easier when the person understands the next step and knows how easy it will be.

### The ultimate benefit question

The future of sales in a fitness business relies on learning how to individualize the sales process.

The future of sales in a fitness business relies on learning how to individualize the sales process. Many owners currently offer a one-size-fits-all solution to fitness. You want to lose weight? Buy a membership. You want to run a marathon? Buy a membership. Your dog got run over by a car? Buy a membership. Memberships are the answer to questions that aren't even being asked yet. You can start to individualize the sales process and change your approach by asking two simple questions:

**What is the single most important thing you want from a membership at this gym?**

**Why is that issue important to you?**

These two questions help you uncover the hidden layer beneath the first layer. The first layer is the almost superficial level at which most sales people operate, which keeps them from building any type of emotional bond with the potential member.

People come to you for help and they are not buying a sofa for their house. They are concerned about looking good naked, being in weddings, and being on the beach in a bathing suit. What they are really talking about is emotion. Emotion is what brought them into the club and emotion is what will help sell them a membership and other services in the club.

Tapping into this emotion is not something that most young salespeople want to do. It's much easier to avoid it and talk about types of equipment, hours, and classes than it is to actually get into a conversation about why the person really came in that day and what he really wants from a membership.

You want to acknowledge that the person is an individual and that you do care about the reasons that drove him to seek out a fitness center. Owners and managers like to kid themselves and think that people are really in the club to embrace the fit lifestyle and to seek a higher level of being through fitness, but most are there for darker reasons that the owners and managers simply don't want to bring up.

For example, it is easier for a young salesperson giving a tour to talk about working out than it is to hear a story about a nasty divorce from a middle-aged housewife who gained 30 pounds from the stress. Instead of listening to her story, most salespeople find it easier to stick their fingers in their ears and go "na, na, na, na" and just point to the treadmills as they walk by.

A level of compromise can be reached, and the two simple questions introduced in this section will help you recognize the person as an individual without getting too deep into their issues. Most importantly, validating this emotion with the person also makes her feel that you care. Ultimately it comes down to who do consumers want to spend their money with, someone who cares and who can individualize the process or someone who just wants to sell a membership?

If you want to be really effective in the sales process, however, you have to get to the layer under the layer. This next step comes from asking the follow-up question: Why is that important to you? This question taps the person's emotional base and begins the process of individualizing the sales experience for the guest.

You should also remember that your best chance of getting a sale will come from answering these questions in the member's mind: What's in it for me as the consumer? What is the benefit of joining this gym? Every gym has equipment and classes, but the salesperson who can help the guest see what's in it for him will have the best chance of a successful sale.

Remember, the strongest benefit you can offer is that you really care that the person is here, and more importantly, you care why he is here. A caring attitude is perhaps the strongest benefit and one of the easiest things to demonstrate. Consider the following example:

*Salesperson*: So, Sarah, you've been working out for a number of years, but you've taken a year off because of your new baby. Now that you're back, let me ask you a question. What is the single most important thing you want from a membership at this gym?

*Sarah*: This was my second child and I just can't seem to lose that last 10 pounds this time. With the last kid I just went back to my old routine of jogging and exercise tapes at home and it worked. This time, those pounds just won't go away. So I guess if I have to give you the single most important reason it would be weight loss.

*Salesperson*: Okay, so your most important reason is weight loss. Why is that important to you (the layer under the layer)?

*Sarah (with tears forming)*: Well, my younger sister is getting married this summer at the beach, in fact in about eight weeks, and I am in the wedding. We're wearing sleeveless dresses and then the family is staying for a week on vacation and I just don't want to put on a swimsuit looking like this.

*Salesperson*: Sarah, I don't know if we can get a full 10 pounds off of you in eight weeks, but I bet we can get close. By just working with a personal coach (trainer), you will get much further with us than you would by trying to do the same old fitness tape over and over again. I would also like to set an appointment for you with our nutritional person. What you're eating may be a big part of that 10-pound block and we should take a look at what's going on there too, so you can get the most out of your workouts in the shortest period.

> Every gym has equipment and classes, but the salesperson who can help the guest see what's in it for him will have the best chance of a successful sale.

If you've never encountered this scene, then you have never sold a membership in a fitness center, because real life is played out this way every single working day at some club somewhere. If you sold this woman the old-fashioned way, with a features-driven tour and a lot of first-visit pressure, you most likely would never have a chance to make her part of your business.

Many of your customers will want to be heard before they part with their money. Spend a little time, listen for a few minutes, and show some sincere interest, and you might get them as members. Rush the tour, point out the equipment list during the walk-through, and finish with your polished sales pitch learned from a pressure-themed sales course, and you are guaranteed to lose this woman, and many others like her, because most customers don't respond to traditional fitness-center sales techniques.

## So what's in it for the potential member?

Features are the various components that make up a product or service. Features are the easiest concept to grasp and are what every new salesperson instinctively moves to when they first start to sell anything. "Did you know that this car has the new parktronic electro illumination brakes? Our company just developed those and my job is to tell everyone who comes in here about them because we spent $4,000,000 to invent them and we're going to tell somebody about it."

**Features don't sell anybody anything.**

Features don't sell anybody anything. Features don't get people excited. Features don't tap into the emotional experience. And features definitely don't differentiate you from your competitors, because you all have basically the same list of fitness stuff.

What does sell memberships is learning to define the benefits. What is in it for the consumer? How will he benefit from using your product compared to the guy down the street? And most importantly, how can you individualize this experience so that for just a few minutes he feels like you really care about him joining this club?

When you can answer these questions, you're on your way to a higher level of helping people get what they want. This effort translates to a higher level of sales productivity for your business.

## Key Points From This Chapter

- Never give a feature without giving the benefit.

- You sell intangibles, or things that will happen to the person in the future, versus tangibles, which are things they can hold in their hand and take home. Intangibles can't be sold using strategies designed for tangibles.

- Salespeople naturally gravitate toward feature-driven tours because of their pride in their facilities.

- Base expectations are things the consumer already associates with your business, so you really don't have to tell the person you have them. Owning a tire store and then listing in the Yellow Pages that you carry tires and do tire repair is not only bad marketing and a waste of money, but kind of silly too.

- The four major questions of marketing have to not only be answered in your ads each and every time, but should also be built into your sales presentation.

- Risk is the greatest barrier to inquiry. "What if I sign up and then don't like it? Will I lose my money?"

- Use an identifier as the kick line with your club's name instead of wasting it on something cute and mostly irrelevant.

- Potential customers are more likely to respond if they have an idea of what to do next without the possibility of embarrassing themselves.

- Individualize the sales process by asking the guest the following question early and often: What is the single most important thing you want from a membership at this gym?

- Get to the layer under the layer by asking the follow-up question: Why is that issue important to you?

# Tip of the Day

## Think about the learning styles.

As you progress through your sales training, always return to the learning styles. Remember that people learn new things and make buying decisions in three ways: an auditory person learns by listening, a visual person learns by reading or watching someone else do something, and a doer learns through experience with what is going on around him.

People are usually primarily of one type, with a blend of the other two mixed in. To be successful in sales, you have to cover all three styles every time, because you will not know which one of these categories your guest falls in. In the system presented in this book, a good presentation covers the auditory folks, the Welcome Guide is sent home to provide visuals, and the doers benefit from the trial memberships.

Most salespeople make the mistake of assuming that everyone is like them and they base their entire presentation upon that one style. Again, cover all three every time and, as you progress, always return to review the learning styles.

# 8

# Why Trial Memberships Increase Sales

In the ancient days of the fitness industry, meaning prior to 1990, marketing was somewhat simple. You ran an ad and people showed up. You used draw boxes (e.g., enter here to win 50 gallons of gas) and people not only picked up the phone, but also actually came in and joined. Even better were the referrals from members, who gladly gave out lists of their friends who needed to join the gym, and those friends really did respond.

All of these things worked then, and don't have a fat person's chance in a naked marathon now, because the market was different. This difference can be simply explained by this formula:

$$\frac{\text{High demand}}{\text{Limited choices}} = \text{Almost any marketing will work}$$

Simply put, this formula shows that if you own the only bar in a college town you'll make a ton of money. In other words, if you have high demand (thousands of thirsty college students) coupled with limited choices (you own the only bar), you will make a fortune no matter what specials or advertising you run, if indeed you have to run any at all.

In the early days of fitness, this formula held true for this industry as well. There were more people who wanted to join gyms than there were choices. Therefore, any fitness ad worked and no matter what ad you ran you looked like a genius.

The issue is that no one ever realized that it wasn't the ads, it was the market at the time that made clubs so successful. The sad thing is that many of the people who worked in the industry in those days are still around, or trained people who are now running businesses, and the industry as a whole still believes that those ads and that type of marketing should still work today. The harsh truth is that this lie might be the biggest ever told in the fitness industry.

Ads in those days were price-driven ads, which entail running some type of special that deviates from the normal pricing structure. For example, your club might have a regular membership fee of $69, but in your ad in the paper you feature a two-for-one summer special during which two people can join for just one membership fee split between them.

This ad might work for a month or two and then the club owner would switch to another special, such as "join now (during the summer) and get the fall free." The member would join in the summer and defer the first payment until after the first of the year. This situation would go on month after month, as the owner grinded out deal after deal after deal. "Hey, what special are you guys running this week?" was a common question in those days.

But everything you did in those days worked, so it had to be the marketing right? Wrong again. Price-driven marketing, as illustrated in the previous formula, will always work as long as the demand stays higher than the choices available. In other words, if you own something that is limited or rare you can charge a lot more for it than you could if it was more common. If you have a high demand for fitness, which was the case in the 1980s, and limited fitness choices compared to what the consumer has now, then almost any ad or special you ran would work.

Things changed in the 1990s and into the early 2000s. Demand stayed flat compared to the percentage of the total population, but the number of clubs began increasing. The market was still somewhat strong, but it was becoming harder to do the old-style marketing and still drive big numbers. Other factors, such as an increasingly sophisticated consumer, also started to change the way marketing worked. The new formula for those years looked as follows:

$$\frac{\text{Flat demand and growth}}{\text{Increasing consumer options}} = \frac{\text{Decline in the effectiveness of}}{\text{traditional marketing}}$$

**Pressure selling has always been a part of the industry, but it became worse when the marketing became less effective.**

Pressure selling has always been a part of the industry, but it became worse when the marketing became less effective. If you have fewer people responding to your ads, then the pressure had to shift to the salespeople. The chains in the late 1980s and 1990s were notorious for the pressure their salespeople had to apply at the point of sale, as well as the stress felt by those sales teams to make their 100 cold calls each day and keep their personal appointment sheets filled. When the marketing began to fail, the pressure was on for the salespeople to fill the shortages.

In today's market, another formula can be applied:

$$\frac{\text{Slightly increasing demand}}{\text{Virtually unlimited fitness choices}} = \frac{\text{Failure of traditional price ads}}{\text{to drive revenue}}$$

The market is at this point in 2007 and will be for a number of years to come. When you have an increasing demand for fitness by the consumer, yet one that is not keeping up with the increase in club openings, price-driven marketing works even less effectively than in the other models.

Price-driven ads are by design meant to generate volume. You can't sell your product at the regular price so you discount it and hope to sell more units to make up the difference. In other words, if your price is $40 for an item and it doesn't sell, can you discount it and hope to sell a higher number to make up for the lesser money earned through the lower price?

Two key elements are in play that lead to the failure of price-driven advertising in this model. A finite number of people are joining clubs at any given time. At this point, only about 16 percent of the population in this country belongs to a health club or fitness facility of any type. Even though this number is increasing, it is not rising as quickly as new clubs are opening.

As an owner, you are locked into competing for a finite number of members that might join, and if you are using price alone to attract new members, which again is a system designed to generate a high volume of new memberships, your business plan fails because of the lack of enough new people interested in joining a fitness facility. In other words, you are running ads to attract people who aren't there.

The second reason you would be on the track to failure is that price-driven ads work off a false assumption from the beginning. This assumption states that price ads are created to attract people who *already* have fitness experience, not to attract new people who have never been in a fitness facility before.

For example, a typical price ad might look roughly as follows:

### Join now and get the rest of the summer free!

- Large free-weight area
- 100 group classes a week
- Free childcare
- Certified personal trainers
- Weight loss available
- Tanning included with every membership

Couple this copy with a picture of a semi-naked woman and you have the typical fitness ad you would see in a shopper, newspaper, or Yellow Pages ad. Besides being somewhat illogical in the sense that a fitness center is advertising that it has fitness stuff in it, this ad is also ineffective because it targets the wrong market. Think of a hotel advertising that it has beds or a car dealership advertising that it has cars for sale. "Hey, come to our fitness center… we have fitness stuff."

**When you have an increasing demand for fitness by the consumer, yet one that is not keeping up with the increase in club openings, price-driven marketing works even less effectively than in the other models.**

Think about this sample ad carefully: All of these bulleted points are aimed at whom? Would a deconditioned female respond to this ad, or is the more likely respondent a person who already has fitness experience and is looking for these things in a gym.

Also think about the statistic that state that only approximately 16 percent of the population belongs to a fitness facility. If all clubs run this type of ad, which most do, then all fitness owners do is target the same small population of people who have fitness experience. This advertising is doing nothing to attract people who don't have any experience and who don't respond to these ads.

# Exposure Marketing

**If you don't advertise price, then all you have left is exposure marketing.**

If you don't advertise price, then all you have left is exposure marketing. Remember that only two ways exist to attract people to a fitness business: You either offer a price special of some kind or let you let the person come and try your club, see if he likes it, and then sign him up.

Non-ads are out there that run pretty pictures and let people know the business exists without offering any type of special. Think about Coke™ and its traditional bear ads during the holidays. These ads are cute, but they don't feature any special offer. You watch, smile, and maybe connect with the company somehow.

You aren't Coke and you don't have the money to run ads that merely look cute. In this business, you have to run ads that drive people to the door in big enough numbers to feed your business, so every ad has to have some device to elicit a response.

Exposure marketing means that you let someone come try your business for free and see if the person likes it enough to join. This type of marketing is called trial marketing, and it is a common form of advertising that you will see almost everywhere.

Full trial memberships, meaning those that last seven days or longer as opposed to just a single workout, have been used in the fitness business since about 1990 and are an effective way to attract people who normally wouldn't respond to any type of traditional fitness advertising. A sample trial ad might contain copy as follows:

**Never been in a fitness club before?**
**Afraid to take that first step?**

**Would you like to try the area's only upscale fitness center for 14 days with no risk and no obligation?**

We are so proud of our club that we would like you to come try us absolutely free for 14 days with no risk and no obligation. We're proud of our club and feel that it is the best in town, but talk is cheap. We would like you to come meet our staff, meet the other members, and try us with a full membership for a full 14 days. At the end of this trial, if we haven't earned your business then we don't deserve to have you as a member.

All memberships include a personal coach, a session with a nutritional professional, and a full membership to the club for 14 days.

This type of copy is aimed at the people in your market who aren't fitness people and who again don't respond to typical price-driven ads. The thing to remember is that people with fitness experience will find you anyway, since fitness is part of their lives and those folks are out there looking for a gym as soon as they move to a new area or get bored with their existing facility.

Exposure ads also eliminate risk, which has proven over the years to be the biggest barrier to inquiry for people who don't have any fitness experience. Risk pops up in the form of "What if I try this and don't like it? Will I still have to pay for it? Why can't I try it first and see if I like it?"

All of these legitimate concerns and questions don't get answered through traditional price-driven ads. Traditional ads, coupled with traditional sales techniques that slam hard on the first day a new person inquires about the club, set up an almost impenetrable wall for someone without fitness experience who might be nervous about inquiring at a fitness center for the first time.

> Exposure ads also eliminate risk, which has proven over the years to be the biggest barrier to inquiry for people who don't have any fitness experience.

## The Trial Philosophy

The trial philosophy is really nothing more than stating, "We have a good club and we'd like you to come try it because we know that once you try us you'll want to become a member." The trial philosophy can be explained simply, as it was in the ad in the previous section:

Would you like to try our club absolutely free with no risk, no obligation, and no money up front for a full 14 days? We'd like you to come try our club, meet our members, and meet our staff. At the end of 14 days, if we haven't earned your business then we don't deserve to have you as a member.

This type of marketing not only generates a larger number of leads, but it also makes the salesperson's job a lot easier. Trials are targeted at people who don't have a lot of fitness experience, which is a much larger number than those who do. Trials done correctly feed the club sufficient leads, which allows the salespeople to concentrate on closing the ones already in the system rather than wasting time trying to develop appointments that never show.

## Types of trials

A club owner can use two types of trials.

A club owner can use two types of trials. A regular trial simply lets anyone in the market who is qualified try the club for the set trial period. A paid trial let the consumer pay for a short segment of time, such as six weeks for $69, and try the club with more of an all-inclusive course format that might include a trainer and other help.

Qualification is usually determined by using these restrictions:

- Must be 18 or older, depending upon the club
- Must live in the club's market area and be able to prove it with a driver's license or equivalent identification
- Must show the ability to buy at some point by flashing a credit card
- May be used once a year

These points represent the fine print. You will still have a small percentage, usually approximately 3 or 4 percent of all the people who take the trial, who don't really have any intention of actually becoming a member. This situation is acceptable for two reasons.

First, these people might actually buy something while in the club, such as a bottle of water or personal training, so the risk is acceptable. The cost of actually servicing these members is low compared to the upside of what they might spend in the club during their trial visits. It is also important to remember that just because a person doesn't join during this trial period doesn't mean that he might not consider joining in the future based upon his current experience with your club.

Second, this very small percentage is nothing to worry about if indeed the volume does increase the number of potential members coming through the door. In other words, if the volume goes up for potential members, it doesn't really matter if a few of them are just passing through looking for a free workout or two. The key is to not lose focus on what you're trying to accomplish with a trial: The goal is to drive more guests, from a different group, than you would get with regular advertising.

## Lengths of trials

A number of variations can be used with trial memberships. The ones listed in this section are most commonly used in the market today.

❑ _The seven-day trial._ This length of trial would be used by clubs that just opened or for someone who has never used the trial before and is a little nervous. The guest has total use of the club for seven consecutive days.

❑ _The 14-day trial._ This trial is the standard for most clubs. It's long enough to attract more people than the seven-day trial, but also the right length for most clubs to service without losing control.

❏ *The 21-day trial.* This specialty trial could be used by a club owner in conjunction with the 14-day trial. The 21-day trial would be offered to small businesses or as a special pass and would have more value as a handout, as compared to the 14-day trial that anyone can get from a direct mailer or ad. For example, a sales manager might visit a small business and offer the owner and her eight employees a chance to come try the gym as a group. Rather than handing out almost worthless business card–sized passes, and to show more value than the 14-day offer available in the paper, the salesperson would hand the owner eight 4 x 5 cards hand-signed by an employee, each one of which is good for 21 full days of fitness.

❏ *The 30-day trial.* This trial is the ultimate tool for an experienced club owner who has great control systems in the club. In this case, you are boldly stating that you have the best club in town and that you are willing to prove it by letting anyone in the market try you absolutely free for a full 30 days. This tool is strong, especially in markets that have heavy competition, with multiple clubs running price-driven ads.

## Extreme trials

Experienced owners who have strong systems can also adapt the trial concept to certain market conditions. For example, an owner of a small chain of successful clubs had the chance to buy a smaller, 3500 square foot women-only facility in a market he wanted to expand into in the future. He took the club, which had a small membership, and offered a 90-day trial to every qualified buyer in the market. Out of a market of approximately 50,000 people, this owner saw more than 500 trials show up during the first three months he offered the deal. Out of this number, he was able to convert more than half into memberships and literally doubled the club's membership during his first 90 days. Word of mouth was also good, because he was willing to prove the club's worth from the outset.

## Paid trials

Paid trials are a form of target-specific marketing, which means that you are using a specially designed tool to go after very small segments of the market. In other words, imagine a single bullet rather than the shotgun approach. Traditional marketing done through newspaper ads, for example, works off the principle of sending a mass message to the entire market with hopes that someone out there reading the paper will see your message. Target-specific marketing, on the other hand, assumes that you can identify one specific person—or group of people—who is an ideal candidate for your club. You then

Target-specific marketing, on the other hand, assumes that you can identify one specific person—or group of people—who is an ideal candidate for your club.

deliver a specifically designed marketing piece targeting his needs and concerns.

Sample paid trials, such as six weeks for $69, also represent a finite course of action. One of the problems with traditional fitness membership offerings is that they often don't match what the consumer is actually looking for when she walks through the door. For example, a deconditioned female may have the specific concern of losing 10 pounds before being in her sister's wedding in a few months. She has a specific need, a specific goal, and a set timeline in her mind when she comes through the door.

The sale breaks down 30 minutes later when a salesperson hammers her on a long-term commitment, or even a simple month-to-month membership, both of which fail to meet the goal she had when she came through the door. She wants to buy a specific solution for a specific problem, and that solution is what you should be selling her. Solve her problem first and she is more likely to stay beyond the initial program. The trial membership, again a short-term course for a flat fee, gives her what she wants and also helps the club in that it exposes its services and programs to someone who might not sign up through standard fitness offerings.

Paid trials can be used throughout the year and work especially well in softer delivery systems that cater to women, such as Val-Paks® and other coupon- or value-driven tools. Sample paid-trial copy might look as follows:

**We know the first 10 pounds is always the hardest...and we also know that you may not know how to get started.**

**Our "6 weeks for $69" easy-start program includes everything you need to lose that first 10 pounds, including a personal coach who will guide you every step of the way.**

**Need to lose weight for that special event?**

**Interested in fitness but don't know where to start?**

**Overwhelmed by too much information about fitness?**

**Our six-week course is the perfect way to get started on the right path to fitness and weight management with no risk or any further obligation.**

# The Law of Diminishing Returns

Price-driven ads do work for a short period of time in most markets, but ultimately fail in almost every market. This failure happens because of the law of diminishing returns.

Price-driven ads do work for a short period of time in most markets, but ultimately fail in almost every market.

This theory, which is derived from an agriculture concept born in Europe, states that when you plant a crop in a new field, your harvest from that same crop in that same field will go down in each succeeding year. For example, you might plant corn and generate 20 bushels per acre the first year. If you plant corn again in the same field next year, your harvest will drop to maybe 18 bushels per acre and continue to drop each year after that until your harvest reaches a sustainable low point.

In other words, by repeating the same action over and over again, you get lower and lower responses. Over time, you will ultimately hit a low point where the action generates the lowest possible number for that field or market. In the corn example, you might get down to a few bushels per acre, at which point it bottoms out.

Price-driven ads emulate this same theory in the fitness business. Run the same type of ad over and over again and slowly the market is burned up and the ad fails. For example, when an owner first runs price-driven ads, he will get results. But if he continues to run price ads, over time, the market becomes burned, and the ad response continues to drop until it hits the lowest sustainable number.

For example, if an owner offers a one-year membership at $489 in the paper, he will initially be successful by attracting everyone in the market looking for a membership who is willing to pay $489. After the owner burns up that segment, however, then what are his options? If everyone in his market who wants to, or can, pay $489 has responded, then each time he runs that ad it will be less successful, as fewer people are left to respond.

This owner's next step would be to lower his price, perhaps to $449. He would thereby open up his market to a new segment that didn't respond to his previous ads at $489 per year and he might generate a little success with this ad for a short period of time.

But what happens when new sales falter again? When an owner is dependent on price-driven ads, he will ultimately burn up his market, which is nothing more than the law of diminishing returns kicking in. Eventually he will be forced to lower his price to the lowest common denominator, which might be $249 or even less in this example.

**When an owner is dependent on price-driven ads, he will ultimately burn up his market, which is nothing more than the law of diminishing returns kicking in.**

## Every market will have a limit, no matter what the price.

Can you use a low price based upon a monthly membership that resists the theory of diminishing returns? What happens, for example, if you run prices so low that everyone in the market who has ever thought about a fitness membership has no excuse left? The ads will still fail over time, but it will take longer for it to happen.

For example, an owner runs prices in the $9-per-month range. This price will obviously attract the widest number of potential members who are interested in price, and the theory is that this price is so low that he should be able to attract new members practically forever. This type of pricing is the purest form of a volume-driven business plan, because almost all of the revenue is coming from building up a large membership check based upon thousands of people paying $9 per month.

The reality is that every market still has a limit. If you use the low price of $9, then you might be targeting a huge number in your market. This number is called the penetration rate and is the total percentage of the population that you can attract to your business.

**Penetration rate has two limiters: drive time from your business and turnover in your market.**

Penetration rate has two limiters: drive time from your business and turnover in your market. Research shows that the average person will only drive about 12 minutes from his home to get to a fitness facility. Typical facilities, for example, usually have about 85 to 90 percent of their membership living within a 12-minute drive time from their club. Specialty clubs, such as women-only or lifestyle-enhancement centers (personal training) draw from a slightly larger area, with a drive time potential of up to 20 minutes.

In other words, every club has a geographical range that limits its drawing power to an equivalent of approximately three to five miles from the club. Potential members simply won't drive any further than that to go to a club for a workout.

The turnover in an area also is a factor. Some markets, such as parts of Orlando and Atlanta, have extremely high turnover in their younger segments. These areas have a larger than normal amount of apartments and other multifamily homes, which turn over often due to the large number of young workers coming into and out of the area. This number is usually constant, however, and once accounted for becomes a normal part of the business plan.

For example, the owner using the $9-per-month per member price is targeting 20 percent of his available market. If his five-mile market ring contains 60,000 people, then his business plan is based upon attracting approximately 12,000 members paying $9 per month. He would hit this number near the end of the second year if his business plan came together, meaning that his monthly check before collection expenses and losses would be about $108,000. It is possible for the owner to get to this point and several low-cost chains have clubs that do these numbers. The hardest part is sustaining these numbers over time.

Once this owner hits a certain penetration rate, he has gone far as he can with this type of business plan. Everyone who wants a membership at $9 has already joined and, over time, the owner will reap lower and lower responses from the same type of advertising.

Also remember that his market has geographical limits that prevent him from pulling more members from further away from the club. If his club has unusual turnover numbers, he might be able to sustain the higher volume over time, but eventually that number will also top out because of loss rate.

## Loss rates correct a faulty membership system.

Loss rates are discussed at length in the other books I've written for Healthy Learning, but they do need to be mentioned briefly in this context. Loss rate is a term that simply explains the difference between money you expected to collect and the money you actually did collect. Unfortunately, not all the members who join a facility actually pay as promised.

Each tool an owner might use, such as open-ended memberships, 12-month contracts, 24-month contracts, and low-price monthly memberships, has some type of loss associated with it. For example, open-ended memberships have losses that range from 4 to 5 percent per month, which doesn't sound bad until you realize that losses are calculated monthly but compounded annually. In other words, you may lose 4 percent a month, but compounded over 12 months you have 48 percent annual losses, or approximately half of the members you signed up in the first place.

Some pricing systems, such as the $9-per-month plan, seek to offset these losses by keeping the price so low that it becomes almost irrelevant to the member who supposedly will continue to pay even if he isn't using the club. Low-price memberships do delay the losses by a number of months, which means that people do delay in canceling their memberships if they aren't coming in, but eventually the losses do kick in and affect the overall membership collections.

In this scenario, the owner achieves a large membership receivable base, collecting more than $100,000 per month. This number will ultimately correct itself downward, because the losses and cancellations will still occur at some point, but just a little later than regular club pricing systems. In this case, the owner is still bound by numbers. His market has limits and loss rates happen to everyone and in every system.

Going into the third year, this owner will feel the losses hit and experience the limits of his market. If you are losing 4 percent of your membership per month, you have to at least replace this number to keep your income stable, and then you have to try and sell more memberships on top of that to stay profitable.

In this example, the owner might lose approximately 480 members a month during the third year due to losses associated with open-ended memberships. Remember that open-ended memberships mean that no contractual obligation exists and the member can quit at any time. If this owner

> Loss rate is a term that simply explains the difference between money you expected to collect and the money you actually did collect.

is losing 480 members per month, then he has to get at least that number of new members each month to cover the loss, which is referred to as replacement mode, since all he is doing is replacing the members he once had. But, can an owner sustain 500 new members a month forever to be successful?

The key in this scenario, as with price-driven advertising of any type, is that at some point you run out of potential members due to the limits of the marketplace, the law of diminishing returns, and the effect of loss rates. Any system based upon shear volume will ultimately fail because of these limiters.

## Don't forget how price ads work compared to trial memberships.

What everyone who uses price ads forgets is that price ads are designed to attract people who have previous experience with fitness and do nothing to develop new business. If a customer knows about fitness and is looking for a place to work out, then price ads will work. Price ads won't work, however, for people who don't have this experience and who aren't sure whether fitness is really for them or not. Again, price ads work for an owner over a short period of time and then slowly fail, because everyone who is looking for a place to work out based upon price has already responded, and each rerun of a price special will attract fewer potential members.

Trial ads are based upon an entirely different theory. Trial memberships, and the variety of ad copy that supports them, are designed to develop interest in people who have not yet taken the next step toward fitness. The most important thing to remember is that price ads fail over time and trial memberships don't.

In summary, trial memberships that are done correctly help drive new sales, because over time these ads will continue to increase the number of potential members who visit a gym. Trial ads also don't weaken over time, as repeated use doesn't burn the market as price-driven ads do.

The major weakness of price-driven ads is that eventually the responsibility to fill the club with potential members will fall upon the sales team, since the price ads will fail to bring in enough new bodies over time. Sales teams in clubs with trial memberships should concentrate on getting the potential members in the midst of trials into the club and then spend time servicing these people. Keep in mind that trials repeat and clubs using trials will always have a combination of new business and reoccurring leads in the club each night, which takes away the need to fill that appointment book each day with fresh leads that have to be closed during the first visit or be lost forever.

> Sales teams in clubs with trial memberships should concentrate on getting the potential members in the midst of trials into the club and then spend time servicing these people.

## Key Points From This Chapter

- In the early days of fitness, almost anything owners tried with marketing worked because of high demand and limited fitness choices for the consumer.

- Eventually, the demand flattened and the effectiveness of many of the old tools that owners used to attract new members began to decline.

- Owners are now faced with the fact that many of the old systems to attract new members simply fail in a modern marketplace.

- Price-driven ads are an example of old technology that fails in today's market.

- Price-driven ads are based upon the assumption of previous experience with fitness and fitness facilities.

- Price-driven marketing of any type has limiters that kill their effectiveness.

- Trial memberships are based upon the concept of developing new business—not previous experience—and do not fail over time.

- Trial memberships shift the emphasis away from salespeople having to fill the club with potential members and onto the marketing and advertising.

**Tip of the Day**

## Walk the person to the door.

Send each guest home with a positive image by walking him to the door and thanking him for coming in today, even if he did not buy a membership. This final touch sets you apart from the other clubs your guest visited, and on the way home he might have that one final feel-good thought about your kindness and courtesy. It's a small gesture, but it is powerful and will set you apart from the salespeople you compete against.

# 9

# What Is Expected of You as a Salesperson?

Your job is to be part of the team and help the club make money. It really is that simple, and that difficult.

In the past, many club salespeople gained superstar status in their clubs. In the early years of fitness, if you sold, and sold well, you made money that was way beyond all of the other employees in the club, including the club's manager. Good salespeople in the 1970s and 1980s, working in the golden years of selling memberships when the picking was easy, sometimes even made more as individuals than the rest of the club's employees combined.

Things have changed, however, for both the salesperson and the club owner. Sales is harder due to mature, crowded markets. The cost of operation is higher due to increased rents, much higher payrolls, and other rising costs, such as marketing expenses.

The cost of training and other profit centers has also increased, but head trainers that perform in their departments can now make good money in an area that was almost nonexistent in early club business models. In those days, clubs simply gave training away as part of the membership and very few people were charging enough to derive serious revenue from that neglected area in the club.

How people sell has also changed. Many clubs once used scripts and techniques gleaned from other industries, such as insurance and the old dance studios, and these techniques and scripts were designed to inflict the maximum pressure possible on the potential member in the shortest amount of time.

Fewer job choices existed in those days for people who liked to sell and who didn't mind a little pressure. The fitness industry often attracted people who would today be selling phones, copiers, real estate, and other large-ticket items where the rewards are higher and the number of needed sales was smaller than is seen in a typical modern-day fitness center.

These old sales dogs were ruthless, well-trained, driven, and could sell enough memberships to make real money in their lives. But the industry changed slowly over the years and it became harder to find sales dogs that could learn the old tricks. In addition, many of the old techniques stopped working because of the increasing sophistication of the consumer and the overall selling environment.

When you drop closed in the 1970s, the consumer really did believe that if he came back the next day he would have to pay more money. The club, and the club's salespeople, benefited from the fact that most of their clients in those days were somewhat naïve when it came to dealing with a polished and relentless salesperson.

Drop closing means that you state one high price, such as $150, as your joining fee, but tell the customer that if he is willing to make up his mind today, and today only, that cost will only be $50. "We are willing to drop that price because we know you're serious and want to join this gym, so we're going to give you the incentive you need to make that final decision. If you come back tomorrow, however, the price will be back to $150 and you, my new friend, will have lost out."

Try that technique with a 40-year-old, Beamer-driving, financial-service person as a potential member and you would not only get laughed at, but you also might end up buying $50,000 worth of stock from someone who really knows how to sell. Everyone, including most people over 18, knows that if they came back tomorrow the price could be almost anything, but it won't be $150. The consumer is just too sophisticated in sales and gets pitched too many times by too many people every day of his life.

**Selling is more difficult and salespeople in today's clubs function as part of a balanced team that combines with the other departments to drive the overall revenue of the club.**

Selling is more difficult and salespeople in today's clubs function as part of a balanced team that combines with the other departments to drive the overall revenue of the club. System selling, meaning that the club has a set method of presenting the club and its prices, has replaced the more freestyle approach designed to let the big dogs roam and do their own thing 30 years ago.

Most importantly, the sales dogs are gone and have been replaced by people who want to make their living in the fitness industry, but also want to be proud of their work and how they help people each day. Remember the new definition of sales used throughout this book: Your job is to help people get the help they need to achieve what they were looking for when they came to you. You should always do the right thing by helping people. Of course, you are in a business, meaning that a fee is charged for that help, either in the form of a membership or as a fee for your other services, such as weight management or training.

# What Is Expected of You as a Team Member?

Because being a salesperson in most facilities carries more responsibility than many of the entry-level jobs, more is expected of those staff members who pursue sales as a career choice—and with good reason, since sales drive revenues for the club. These expectations begin with simple concepts, such as who you are and how you dress, and end with higher levels of play concerning performance, leadership, and the ability to get the job done each and every day.

## You are the product.

Ultimately, when a person decides to buy, the decision is often based upon the answer to one simple question: Do I like and believe the person who just gave me all of this information? If you are believable, then the person might buy from you. If you are patient and caring, the potential member is more likely to want to buy from you, especially since most membership people are too focused on presenting the club and what's in it, as opposed to spending a few minutes to develop the rapport needed to get the sale done.

Rapport is defined as a relationship marked by harmony, but very few of the old hardcore salespeople understand this concept, since their goal is to sell at any cost. Nothing harmonious is developed in that old-school atmosphere due to the pressure applied. Over time, the club suffers as well, because someone who buys something under extreme conditions will ultimately punish the club by refusing to pay their membership fees or by refusing to spend any money in the club while they silently suffer until the end of the membership.

Your job is to build rapport, which is more easily stated as building a relationship in which both parties win and get what they want from this new alliance. In this case, you are the product you sell, since a potential buyer is much more likely to buy something from someone he trusts and likes and who has spent time to genuinely get to know him as a person.

## Don't overlook the power of sincere interest.

It can't be overemphasized—or laughed at too often, for that matter—how bad a typical fitness facility tour really is. On the low end, a presentation ranges from, "Go look around and I'll give you a price sheet when you get back" to high-pressure lockdowns in offices, which is still being done by some of the old chain clubs. Not many clubs have a set tour that is done professionally and with class.

One of the most common mistakes is that no one takes the time to get to know the person who is inquiring. Salespeople are so busy trying to sell that they don't listen, which would make the sale much easier. The skill that is

> Your job is to build rapport, which is more easily stated as building a relationship in which both parties win and get what they want from this new alliance.

needed is the ability to convey sincere interest, which is simply defined as the ability to take the time to get to know the person as an individual and apply the business to his individual needs.

Countless ways to demonstrate sincere interest are discussed in the endless sales books on the market. The common flaw is that most of these methods involve nothing more than learning more aggressive sales tricks that actually defeat the attempt to build rapport. In lieu of these relationship breakers, consider the following simple methods that anyone can use to build that essential relationship between the club representative and the guest.

## Slow down.

The faster you go, the less personal you will become. "Speed kills"—that old high school driving slogan—applies to sales in any type of fitness facility. The faster you go, the less effective you will be.

Speed increases for several reasons, and most of them are bad for sales over time. If you give too many tours without thinking or refreshing your approach, you will get faster and more impersonal. If you are so into the sales techniques you just learned from the latest and greatest sales guru, you will focus on those things instead of building a quick and efficient friendship with the person sitting in front of you.

Most importantly, you get fast when you forget the mission. You change lives for a living and the person in front of you is there because he is looking to you for help and guidance in changing something that isn't right in his life. When that person becomes a membership number rather than an opportunity to provide help and change, then the process becomes quick and impersonal and your sales efficiency drops over time.

> When that person becomes a membership number rather than an opportunity to provide help and change, then the process becomes quick and impersonal and your sales efficiency drops over time.

It is especially important to work on the first five minutes with your guest. Later chapters provide in-depth coverage of techniques for being effective during the first two to four minutes, which is called the pre-tour. At this point, simply think about relaxing yourself and your guest by talking about something besides the gym and membership options. For example, "Have you been in our facility before?" "What type of workout are you doing now?" "So, you haven't worked out in a few years. What is giving you the incentive to get started again now?"

## Individualize the process.

As discussed in Chapter 8, individualizing the process is the simplest and most powerful way to build rapport. The best question in this regard is, "What is the single most important thing you want from a membership at this club (facility)?" Follow this question with a second one designed to get to the layer below the superficial layer: "Why is that important to you?"

Individualizing the process—or taking time to care about the person you are talking to and who needs your help—seems obvious, but seldom occurs in any sales process. Salespeople become so focused on their procedures and ways of doing things that they seldom ask the person what he really wants. Tour a typical club and you will find out how many classes they offer, the number of cardio pieces, the amount of strength equipment, and the offer of the day, all wrapped around perhaps one question that actually is aimed at the prospective sale: "What are you looking for?"

Individualizing the process must not be confused with asking old-style sales questions. These questions, such as, "Is this for yourself or for you and your spouse?" aren't asked to get to know the person and make him feel comfortable with you and the club, but rather as part of the sales process. In the case of this question, what the salesperson is really doing is scouting to see if he can write a family deal rather than a single membership. Sales questions are designed to enhance the sales value to the club and increase the overall sales dollars. Individualizing the sales process uses questions designed to build a relationship that will lead to the sale anyway, but also start the club on the road to attracting a new member who will stay longer and pay longer over time because of that relationship.

## Kill the adversarial nature of the sale.

The most intrusive thing you can do to kill the mood and the budding relationship is to take someone you have gently guided around the club and chatted with and throw him into the office, where you sit across from each other on different sides of a desk. Nothing says that you are going to get your butt kicked more than when a sales guy pulls up his seat behind the desk and starts in on his pitch.

Sales offices in general, and especially when the two of you are sitting across the desk from each other, instantly set up barriers that are hard to overcome with even the best sales techniques. Bad news and bad sales techniques are almost always associated with someone pounding you from across the desk. For example, you never see a car salesman on television that isn't sitting across a desk and working his not-so-exaggerated sales nonsense.

People come to a fitness facility for socialization, for help with personal problems (weight and image), and to escape their daily routines for an hour or two each day. These people will respond better to someone they trust and respect and who can guide them on their path to fitness. In other words, people are looking for some leadership and they are hoping that you, the club representative, can provide it. How do I work out? How hard is fitness? Will I like the people in this gym? Do I really belong here and do you have other members like me? These very real questions are rattling around the prospective buyer's head, and by answering these questions you are providing the information, or leadership, they seek.

Sales offices in general, and especially when the two of you are sitting across the desk from each other, instantly set up barriers that are hard to overcome with even the best sales techniques.

Setting the tone for this leadership can be as easy as just dumping the traditional method of selling in an office while hiding behind your desk, which again is the ultimate barrier to getting the sale and making the person feel comfortable in the gym environment. The first step is to use a high café-style table near your juice bar or near the edge of the workout floor. All sales tours should start at this table. Use a high table, because people tend to lean forward and rest their arms on it, as opposed to a regular table, where everyone kicks back with their feet out in front of them. In a sales situation, you want the person to be leaning in toward you as you ask questions and guide him through the sales process. Leaning toward your guest is a simple way to show interest. "Hey, I like you, you're interesting, and I am going to lean in so I don't miss a word," is the message you are sending by using this type of setup.

All sales could be done at this table, but if you absolutely have to have an office then take out your desks and replace them with round tables where you can sit side-by-side, which is far less threatening to your guest. Women especially find sitting across from males, who still comprise the majority of all club salespeople, more threatening than being seated side-by-side, where the two of you are more of equals and where she feels that you are helping her rather than selling her. The obvious hint is that using nontraditional sales people, or anyone except mid-20s white males with gold shirts on, would give your club a different look and appeal to a wider variety of people over time.

Desks, offices, enclosed spaces, and guys who write upside down on yellow pads are all barriers. The more barriers you eliminate, the more comfortable the guest will be and the stronger the relationship will become.

## Build success and avoid failure.

**Many clubs inadvertently build failure into almost everything they do during the sales process by selling purism rather than hope.**

Many clubs inadvertently build failure into almost everything they do during the sales process by selling purism rather than hope. For example, a young salesperson, usually male and in pretty good shape, automatically thinks that his workout is the workout for everyone he talks to during his sales day. If he works out five days a week, doing strength for three days and cardio for two days, then he is going to share that fact during the tour. The problem is that doing so puts failure into the guest's head before she even gets started.

Consider the typical soccer mom and mother of two who is 10 to 15 pounds heavier than when she got married. She is in her 30s and that last 10 pounds she so easily lost after the first kid just won't leave this time no matter what she does. She comes to the gym, hears the story from the salesperson, and goes home to think about it and never comes back. Why?

What she heard was that she can't do it. In his purist quest to save everyone from eternal fatdom, the salesperson laid out what he thought she needs to do to be successful: "Well, you need strength training at least twice a week and you definitely want to do cardio the other three or four days." *"The other three or four days?"*

"Let's see," she thinks, "each of the kids has soccer three days a week, I have my job, I have to shop because my husband is worthless, I have to do laundry because my husband is worthless, and of course I have to clean the house because my husband is worthless. Work out four or five days a week? That kid must be snorting protein powder from behind the counter, because he sure doesn't live in my world."

The salesperson told her what she should really do in a perfect world, but what he didn't tell her was about fitness in *her* world. You should build hope, not failure, from the first contact. Keep in mind that simplifying everything about fitness and the fitness experience will help a novice feel better about something she has never done before in her life:

*"Fitness is actually very simple. Most people make it harder than it really has to be. Our view is to make it as easy as possible and still allow you to be successful. First of all, move a little every day. We hope it is with us, but we realize you can't make it to the gym some days, although you still might have a chance to get moving. For example, during your kids' soccer games, get a few of the other mothers and walk around the field while your kids are playing. If they are moving, you can be moving. We'd like to help you get started moving each and every day. To make it easier, here is a little gift from the club. This pedometer counts steps and is easy to use. I've enclosed an article about walking, which you will find simple but effective."*

*"Next, eat a little healthier. Many of our new members want to make better choices, but due to the overwhelming information out there they don't really know where to start. Part of every membership here is a free introduction to nutrition from our weight-management specialist and there is more information in your Welcome Guide, a gift to you from the club that has articles and information concerning everything we do here."*

*"Finally, to get the most out of working out, you need a guide. Fitness is a great adventure, but like anything new in your life it helps to have a guide for that journey. That's what we do here at the club. We will get you on the right path so you can get the most from the time you do have and make fitness something you look forward to rather than be afraid of or avoid until your kids get older."*

If the customer moves, you win. If she looks to you for leadership, you win. If she isn't pure in her approach to fitness but still does a few laps around the soccer field with the other moms while wearing your pedometer, you win. Fitness isn't being about being pure. It's about getting on the path and moving every day for the rest of your life. This definition is what you should be selling to the consumer who is already afraid that she won't be able to do it anyway.

**Fitness isn't being about being pure. It's about getting on the path and moving every day for the rest of your life.**

### Give the person a solution.

People want and
expect leadership
from the
professionals they
choose to work with
in their lives.

People want and expect leadership from the professionals they choose to work with in their lives. For example, you don't go to an attorney, pay $150 per hour, and walk out of the office without a specific answer to your legal issue. You picked a professional and you expect an answer for your time and money.

The same is true for the person who comes to the fitness center looking for help. The mistake owners make is that they often confuse the experienced 20 percent of their members who understand working out, or at least think they do no matter how horrible their form is, with the rest of the new members who might need some help.

Most new members fall into three different categories. First, you have the 20 percent discussed in the previous paragraph. You may think that these folks need help, but they don't want it and mostly want to be left alone. Unless they are actually endangering someone in the gym, including themselves, they should in fact be left alone unless they ask for help. You can always expose these members to new ideas by offering free clinics and workshops to all members, but most of the people in this group will do their own thing year after year and are happy doing it their way.

The second group comprises approximately 40 percent of your new members and could be classified as those who have had some exposure to fitness somewhere in their history. They may be rusty and out-of-date, but they have had at least a little experience, including prior club memberships, somewhere in the past. These people are open to help, but often waste a lot of time comparing what they did in the past with what you are talking about now.

An example of this second group is an old high school football player who is 10 years out of school and 20 pounds overweight. He only wants to work out exactly the way he did in high school and will remind your trainer (personal coach) of that fact the entire time he is getting help. Eventually, however, he will see the light and become a born-again fitness person who is addicted to the new ways and results—or he might not adjust and will find himself reclassified with the 20 percent in the first group.

These people will respond well to group orientations or a few sessions with a good personal coach who will spend time showing them a few new ways to get it done while not negating their previous experience. "You're right, 10 years ago that workout was right for a young high school football player, but now that you're a young business professional who plays golf more than he plays football, you might want to change some of your workouts to fit who you are and what you are doing now." These guys also love the boot camps and functional work in the club, such as rolling big tires and pulling sleds on your track. Just present this activity as manly men wanting to do manly men stuff and these guys will be first in line with their wallets open.

The third group is the 40 percent of people who may not have any experience at all or were frustrated with their last attempt at fitness and simply want to start all over again. Put your time and money into this group. The mistake made with this group is that club employees sometimes try to apply a general rule to every new member.

For example, the club might use the anti-customer-service rule of "two workouts and then you have to solo." You'll give the customer a little help, but not enough to really get going because of your effort to keep the costs down. Ways exist to give help and still keep the expenses under control.

The first group doesn't need or want help, so give them a simple orientation to the equipment and get out of the way. The second group might respond to a few sessions to dust off their technique and will do fine in semiprivate groups with two to 10 people. Group sessions keep the costs down, allow the club to group new members by experience, and give the new member a chance to meet some new friends.

The third group needs as much help as you can provide during the first 30 days of their membership. Remember, if you set them up correctly they will stay longer and pay longer. You can usually solve the cost issue by offering set times for group orientations. A dedicated orientation room stocked with a line of functional equipment, free weights, and a wide array of functional toys allows you to start new people in a safe and nonthreatening environment.

Set specific times during the evening and daytime when a personal coach will meet the group and teach them not just what to do but how to work out. You want to give them more general information, rather than just giving them one specific workout. You don't have to make them trainers, but most new people like to know *why* they are doing something instead of just *how* to do it. This room can also double as a room for the trainers when it is not scheduled for group orientations.

The key to working with all of these groups is that people are seeking leadership from you, their chosen fitness professionals. Your job is to provide an exact solution to the problem and then let the consumer decide whether he can afford it. The key phrase is to "tell, not sell." In other words, offer a set written solution to the problem rather than simply trying to upsell everything in the club.

For example, a woman who is 20 pounds overweight from her last child, and who is frustrated because what she did to lose the weight from the first

**Your job is to provide an exact solution to the problem and then let the consumer decide whether he can afford it.**

child just isn't working this time around, wants you to lay out a specific plan of attack to get it done now. You will fail this client if you try to sell her bits and pieces instead of designing a specific program just for her and her needs (individualizing the process). Consider the following example:

*Club person:* So Kristen, what is the single most important thing you want from a membership at this club?

*Kristen:* Well, I just had my second baby and I can't seem to lose the weight the way I did after my first baby.

*Club:* Why is this important to you?

**The key phrase is to "tell, not sell." In other words, offer a set written solution to the problem rather than simply trying to upsell everything in the club.**

*Kristen:* Last time I lost the weight easily by just doing a few of my old workout tapes at home and eating a little better. This time, it just isn't working and it's frustrating because summer is coming and I find it a little embarrassing that I can't get into my swimsuit this summer.

*Club:* How much weight loss would make you feel better about yourself?

*Kristen:* I need to drop 20 pounds to get back to my old weight from before the baby.

*Club:* Well, based upon what you've told me, let's lay out this solution. I recommend that you sign up for eight weeks with our Apex weight-management consultant. She is patient and has worked with a number of members who have gone through just what you are feeling at this time. I would like to couple that with a small training package that would take you through your first month with us. This personal coach will get you grounded and help you find ways to challenge your body that will work for you. If we get you set up properly, you'll get the quickest results in the shortest amount of time.

*Kristen:* I don't know if I can afford all of this.

*Club:* Your total cost would be an additional $850, but the club makes it very easy for you to fit it into your budget. Simply put one-quarter down and you can pay the rest in three payments over the next 90 days. Remember, based on what you've told me, this is the best solution we can offer you to get that 20 pounds off in the shortest amount of time.

She may not always buy, but you offered her the best solution for her problem in a straightforward non-sales way. She wants guidance and ideas from her fitness professional and then she will process this information and make a decision about whether to buy. Many sales rookies simply try to upsell on too many options or prejudge by assuming that the person won't be able to afford the solution. Give her the best solution that fits her problem in a professional manner and you will sell more memberships and services over time.

## Remember that it's not about you.

Absolutely nothing is worse than a born-again fitness enthusiast selling memberships in a health club. On such a woman's desk are four or five pictures of her when she was overweight and several others of her looking orange from her painted-on tan, half-starved, and posing at her first bodybuilding show. She is 44, lost 40 pounds, had a trainer who set the show as her personal goal, and now she proud as can be with these pictures all over her desk and her office.

Is she a personal success? Yes. Does the person sitting at the desk as a guest, with her own agenda and her own personal problems, really want to hear 30 minutes about the salesperson's personal journey from being fat to being a bodybuilder in a show? No.

This salesperson is not a role model. She is an entry barrier to this sale and almost all others, because it is not supposed to be about her. It should be all about the person sitting in front of her and what she wants and needs.

This form of egomania is not just restricted to this type of employee. For example, think of the diploma monster who decorates the wall with every certificate and every diploma from every school and course he has gone to since he left grade school. You also see the homesick person who has a dozen pictures of her family, her dogs, her last vacation, and other assorted shots with meaning only to her, strewn all over her office and desk. And the workout geek who insists that walking right off the floor and into the office, still sweaty with a towel over his shoulders, shows that the he embraces the lifestyle. And don't forget the nutrition idiot who eats every two hours and has the Tupperware® and oversized water bottle on his desk to prove it.

In other words, it is not about you, so get rid of all the personal stuff that gets in the way of the sale. Your selling space should be professional and dedicated to the sole purpose of making the guest feel at home and secure with you as her professional choice. If you are an oversized person, as in overbuilt, dress down a little with oversized shirts, perhaps even one with a collar. Your personal approach to fitness might be considered scary and too much for the smaller person just looking to change the way she feels about herself.

The old concept that extreme fitness is motivating to the rest of the population is a myth. Most or your guests would pick slim and vital over bodybuilder big and scary any time, and lifestyle fitness, meaning the ability to get more out of life, sells a lot more memberships than cosmetic muscles that serve no purpose except to fill up the sleeve of a golf shirt.

## Everyone is different.

One of the hardest things about being in sales in a fitness center is that after a few months you have heard almost every story in existence. Most of the

> Absolutely nothing is worse than a born-again fitness enthusiast selling memberships in a health club.

problems your guests bring to bear are somewhat similar in nature, so after a few hundred prospects all the versions begin to blend together. Once in a while you get surprised, such as the time the hooker in a club in California asked if the club would rent her the sauna for an hour for her and her client, but mostly it's overweight people or the vastly unfit who are just trying to make changes in their lives.

The problem is that you may tend to start taking shortcuts with your guests because you have heard the story so many times before. A guest begins to weave her tale of quiet frustration and before she gets out a dozen sentences you are cutting her off and telling her just what she needs.

In these situations, remember to take a breath, sit back and listen, and remember that you might have heard this story before, but you haven't heard it from her. Rushing and stepping on another person's conversations is a sure way to kill the individualization process, and it makes the person feel devalued. This conversation might be the first time she has ever really opened up about her weight and how she feels about herself, and she is hardly into the story before you are stomping on her with the right solution.

Listening validates the person, makes her feel special, and in a business sense sets you apart from any competition that just does the point-and-shoot feature tour of all the equipment. Remember, you may have heard the story many times before, but you do need to hear it again from this special individual in front of you.

## The Image You Need to Have as a Viable Employee

**The number one reason people buy from a specific fitness center is that they like and trust the person, or people, they talked to last.**

The number one reason people buy from a specific fitness center is that they like and trust the person, or people, they talked to last. Put another way, if they like you then they will buy from you more often.

You are also a team member in a community that sees you every day and knows who you are. Except for those salespeople who are somewhat invisible in big cities, it is hard to escape in a town where the club has 3000 members out of only 50,000 residents. It does seem, however, that for most club owners and their staffs, no matter where you go and what you do, a member is going to be in your face watching what you eat, how much your drink, and with whom.

One club owner and his wife from the south suffered a particularly horrible fate at the hands of a member. This couple owns several clubs, with a total of more than 12,000 members, and has been active in their community, the church, and other civic organizations and charities their entire lives. It is hard to walk with them anywhere in their rather large town of 250,000 people without a member, or former member, greeting them.

These owners like nothing more than to escape by themselves, and after all the years that they have been in the business, a week or two away from the clubs and members is nothing short of a miracle. During one trip to one of the small islands surrounding St. Thomas in the Caribbean, they were walking on a deserted beach near the villa they had rented for two weeks. It was early in the morning, the beach was deserted, and they dropped all their clothing and ran into the surf for a morning dip before breakfast.

As they walked hand-in-hand back to the villa, enjoying the beautiful sunrise, still naked with their clothing in their beach bag, they were startled by the sudden appearance of another couple from behind a bush near the path back to their place. "Hi y'all. What a surprise seeing you two here." Of course, they were members who were staying in a house a few miles down the beach, also naked, and also out walking on the supposedly deserted, but now quite crowded, beach.

The lesson is that if you work in a club, people take notice and the pressure is on to maintain the professional and lifestyle image that people expect from you as a fitness person. In other words, who you are outside of the club is often as important as who you are and how you act in the business.

Fitness is a lifestyle choice, and most employees embrace this lifestyle. How you choose to pursue fitness and what you do outside of the business does affect the overall success of that business, especially in smaller markets. Think about the following issues and how they affect your image in the fitness business:

*Dress for success inside the business, but don't forget that you are a professional outside as well.* Professionals usually put a little more thought into their personal presentation, and each generation has its own thoughts about what "dress for success" actually means. In the club, dress as if you are professional no matter what your job. People look to you for support, and how you dress in the club reflects on the business and your own ability to be successful. This rule is especially important if you are younger and working with an older clientele. They expect professionalism from someone they trust with their money and you are no exception as a salesperson, trainer, or even front-counter person who delivers member service.

*Live the lifestyle.* Personal vices, such as sneaking out to smoke behind the club dumpster, don't always send the right message to your guests and members. If you want to have a career in the fitness industry, you need to be aware of your personal image and how those in the community who look to you for leadership perceive that image. On the practical side, it is a lot harder for a salesperson who is severely hung over or who smells like his last cigarette to sit and rationally discuss the merits of fitness with someone who might already be somewhat doubtful.

> If you want to have a career in the fitness industry, you need to be aware of your personal image and how those in the community who look to you for leadership perceive that image.

*Have pride in everything you do.* Have you ever asked yourself why some employees really succeed and others work year after year and don't get much further any place they work? The answer to this question has been written about in many books, and hundreds of success seminars try to get people to solve this riddle of life, but if have ever owned a small business that employs a number of mostly young employees, then the answer is somewhat easy to decipher.

Those people who are successful bring everything they've got each and every day. The difference between being someone who is average and someone who makes more money, gets more opportunities, maybe starts your own business, and is progressing further in life is simply putting everything you have into the job each and every day.

Many employees resist this notion, using the reason: "Why work this hard for someone else? It's not my business and I'll just cruise as long as necessary to get by." The success factor requires you to bring it all, your best effort and best work every day, and if the owner doesn't respect that work, or pay for it, then take your effort somewhere else. Someone will understand and see the difference.

Bring it all every day and you will be more successful than those who don't. If for no other reason, give your job your best effort because to do otherwise is a waste of your talent and your life. At the end of every work day, if you honestly can't say, "That was my best work," then you have failed your business, and most importantly, you have failed yourself.

> The difference between being someone who is average and someone who makes more money, gets more opportunities, maybe starts your own business, and is progressing further in life is simply putting everything you have into the job each and every day.

## Your Personal Responsibilities in the Club

You also have a number of personal responsibilities as a salesperson in the club. You may be a salesperson at the moment, but if you want to be a manager, or even an owner, in the future, the cultivation of these responsibilities now will help you be more effective and more successful in the future.

These responsibilities are personal in nature because you have to bring these traits with you rather than have them managed by someone else. You have to figure these things out and only you can really have the personal initiative to live with these traits and responsibilities every day.

### Be on time.

The greatest insult you can give to most people is to abuse their time. If you have an appointment and are late, you've made a statement to that person that he isn't nearly as important as you are and that your time and personal agenda are much more critical than his. "On time" as a professional means 15 minutes early. If you have an appointment with someone at 2 o'clock for a sales or training appointment, for example, walking in at 2 o'clock is not on time, because it still takes you a few minutes to get organized and to get your act together.

You need to give yourself 15 minutes to get prepared, organized, and ready to take care of business. Being perpetually late cancels out a lot of other good work you might do and eventually most supervisors will have had enough and ultimately replace you with someone who can arrive on time and get the job done without insulting the clients and guests.

## Understand the club.

If the club offers something, you have to be involved in it or you can't sell it. For example, it is hard to express the power of a good group class if you have never set foot in a group-exercise room. It is also hard to talk about cardio equipment if you don't use it regularly.

**The greatest insult you can give to most people is to abuse their time.**

Sales are even more difficult when it comes to amenities if you aren't personally involved. Tanning, for example, is a tough sale if you've never used a bed or been sprayed. You don't have to be tan to sell tanning, or a bodybuilder to sell strength training, but you do have to have a working knowledge of the activity and how it feels.

As a side note, it is often the more functionally athletic people who turn out to be the best salespeople, because more regular people can relate to them. A good example is a 57-year-old trainer/salesperson/group fitness instructor from a club in Florida. He is a lean runner and biker who loves to work out with functional tools, teaches cycle classes, and fills in as a salesperson when the regular team is out of the club. He is successful because so many people can relate to him on so many levels.

He is also a retired businessperson who has strong communication skills and can patiently answer questions about fitness from many angles, because he is involved in so many fitness activities. Young, overly done bodybuilders, for example, are often less successful over time in sales because they can only discuss the club from one perspective, which limits their ability to build rapport.

An old saying states that you can't sell a Ferrari if you have never driven a Ferrari. Some things, such as the fitness experience and what it can do for you in your life, are easier to sell if you as a salesperson are actively involved in the lifestyle and are frequently taking part in everything the club has to offer.

## Remain a work in progress.

You don't have to be a perfect physical specimen to be a fitness-facility salesperson, but you do have to be a work in progress. Fitness is a constant journey and many people fight their weight and fitness level their entire lives.

If you are working in a fitness facility and gain a few pounds over the holidays, then welcome to the crowd. Like most people, you pick up your cardio after the first of the year and get on with your life.

If you don't work out and are losing the battle, or just don't work out at all but think being an employee in the fitness business sounds fun, you probably won't last long or be too successful. Remember, it doesn't really matter if you are in shape. What does matter is that you are constantly pursuing fitness on some level and that you remain a work in progress.

## Remember that it's all your job.

One of the airlines used an unusual trick to hire flight attendants. All the applicants were left in a waiting room that opened to a long hallway. As the group sat waiting for their turn to interview, a person with an armload of stuff would struggle past the office. The person doing the hiring was amazed at how few people who were trying to get into the "helping people" service business would actually get up and offer to help the person with the burden. Those who did immediately got the job, because in their business it is all about helping the customer, and most importantly, it is about being a good team member and helping those you work with as well.

Being a team member is not always about the big things. It is often the small details that make you stand out to the members and to those you work with every day. For example, a salesperson is leaving the club at the end of the day and walks past the juice bar. He notices that they are still busy and that the trash is running over because no one has had time to get it bagged and to the dumpster. He has two choices: Walk past the mess while saying to himself, "It isn't my job," or taking a few extra minutes to bag the trash and throw it in the dumpster on the way to his car. The first choice isn't wrong, but it doesn't help the team either. The second choice isn't the most convenient thing for the salesperson, who has worked his shift and just wants out at the end of his day, but it is the right thing to do as a team member.

Fitness facilities are unique places to work. One minute you're busy and the next you're bored. One day you're swamped with sales and the next day it is all about the juice bar or the trainers. The very nature of what you do and how you interact makes it a hard business in which to just do your job and leave. Instead, the business almost forces you and your coworkers to think and act more like a team that is all in it together.

> When it comes to sales, it is even more important to realize that you are part of a team, because every employee is involved in the process.

When it comes to sales, it is even more important to realize that you are part of a team, because every employee is involved in the process. If you walk through the locker room on the way to the bathroom and notice a mess, then clean it up, or get the right person to do it, because five minutes from now a sales tour will be in the gym and the club will lose a prospective member if she thinks that the locker room is dirty.

The same rule holds true with the garbage behind the juice bar. It isn't the salesperson's job to handle the juice bar's trash, but by not helping people who are very busy doing their jobs, he is setting up failure for the next sales tour that might stop for a minute at the bar if a guest notices the trash and decides not to buy because the place is filthy.

Remember, it is all your job. You most likely have a job description, but keep in mind that anything that gets in the way of providing good customer service or prevents a sale is a responsibility shared by the entire team.

In summary, as a salesperson you are a vital part of any fitness business. You will be more successful and more effective if you are aware of the role you play and the preparation needed to do your job. Ultimately, you are what you sell, because the guest is more likely to become a member if he likes you, believes you, and feels that you have taken the time to demonstrate a caring attitude.

> **Anything that gets in the way of providing good customer service or prevents a sale is a responsibility shared by the entire team.**

## Key Points From This Chapter

- The client is more sophisticated and you need more sophisticated techniques to sell in today's mature markets.

- Individual sales dogs have given way to better-trained salespeople who are able to help people get what they came into the club for.

- You sell (or support others who do), provide legendary service, and learn to professionally present all of the club's offerings.

- You are the product. People buy because they liked you better than the rude person at the other club.

- Showing sincere interest is nothing more than slowing down the process and getting to know the person in front of you.

- Understand that many guests view the sales process as adversarial.

- Clubs sometimes make fitness too hard for the typical person who has little or no experience.

- Individualizing the sales process is the first step to becoming a more effective salesperson.

- Your image, in and out of the club, affects the success of the business.

- Have pride in your job and "bring it all" every day you work for anybody anywhere in your life and you will be more successful.

- You must have certain traits and behaviors, such as being on time for appointments, for which you are responsible and which often can't be coached by an owner or manager.

> **Tip of the Day**

# It isn't about you.

A woman became a salesperson in a fitness facility after losing weight and entering her first natural bodybuilding show. She had the pictures to prove it on her wall and all over her desk. She finished third out of three in her class, but had accomplished her goal to compete and was very proud of her commitment to fitness and how much she had changed.

A few of the pictures showed her before she started training, but most were taken during the period when she was training for the show and on the actual night of the show. Quite a number of shots showed her in her red posing suit, all oiled up like the real bodybuilders. She had that particular orange color people get from applying too much self-tanning lotion.

Every tour she did ended with her at the desk showing her pictures, with tears in her eyes, telling the guest how fitness had changed her life. The bad news is that she was a lousy salesperson because she broke a very important rule:

### It is not about you. It's about them.

Take down your certificates and all of your personal pictures from your journey through fitness, because the guest doesn't want to talk about you. He wants you to talk about himself. Your pictures are not inspirational; they are egotistical and set a negative tone with the guest that states that everything in this club will always be about you, your fitness journey, your degrees, and how special you are.

If you want to inspire, show testimonial pictures from actual members who have been successful at your club. Leave out the extremes, however, because as exciting as it is to have someone lose 100 pounds, such an event is rare and is not as valuable as having 20 people who have lost 10 to 15 pounds and who are real, normal folks.

# 10

# Sales Is About Doing, not Thinking

Thinking is overrated in sales, especially when you're trying to train a young staff member without any prior sales experience. A "thinking" salesperson makes educated choices that match certain situations or comments from your guests.

For example, many sales trainers teach a variety of methods to go for the cash sale. These methods are based upon the salesperson taking a read of the prospective member and then applying a variety of phrases, or closes, that work to get cash from the person. The salesperson might have the latitude to go for a range of cash and can drop or add time depending on the guest's responses or resistance. Look at the following example:

*Salesperson:* Our memberships are based upon a $59 one-time membership fee and our monthly dues are just $49 a month, based on an annual membership ($59–$49 x 12 = $647). If you would like to pay in full for your membership today, you will pay only $549, a savings of almost a $100. Which one of those options is best for you?

*Guest:* I like the idea of paying for my membership up front, but that price still seems a little high. How about knocking off another $50?

*Salesperson:* I really can't reduce the price, but I can add some time. If you are really serious about paying for your membership in full today, I'll add three additional months, which gives you 15 months for the price of 12 and saves you another $147 ($49 x 3 = $147).

In this situation, the salesperson has the flexibility and training to work through the process, go for the cash, and make deals to get the most cash from the most people. You may not be going for the cash in your system, but you are probably giving your salespeople similar methods to make the deal, such as combining an enrollment fee for two friends who are trying to sign up at the same time.

The problem is that it takes a long time to train a salesperson to use these methods. Keep in mind that the salesperson is probably given the option to make decisions at a number of places in the sales pitch, all requiring extensive role play and practical experience. The nuances of this type of sales are difficult to teach and it is a difficult system to maintain over time.

The end result is the second issue that makes this type of training and system suspect. If you train a salesperson long and hard with this method, you end up with what is called an old sales dog. This person may actually be young in age, but is old in attitude. Over time he becomes the ultimate salesperson who can close deals under almost any conditions time after time.

The question is: Where do you find these guys and how do you find enough of them to keep your business going? In the early days of the fitness industry, these people were common. These days, a good salesperson with that type of personality and skill set has just too many other options where he can make more money. If someone is that good, he'll sell real estate or something with a big upside, which is why the majority of fitness salespeople are young males who are getting experience for their next job—after they leave you just when you get them trained.

The other side of this question is that if you do find this person you are almost always held hostage by his success. How do you replace a person who has taken you two years to develop and who does the bulk of your sales? As an owner, you are faced with the prospect of spending another two years developing the next guy or simply paying this person too much to keep him because you live in fear that he will leave you—a classic "can't live with them, can't live without them" scenario.

**If you want to be successful with sales in the future, then you have to change the rules.**

If you want to be successful with sales in the future, then you have to change the rules. In other words, you have to stop trying to apply the same old technology to what is happening in the business today.

First, you need a system that will let you develop effective, nontraditional salespeople. Housewives returning to the workforce, kids from the Gap® who like people but hate retail, and retirees who like helping people be successful with fitness but can't see themselves drop closing someone in an office, are all people you should be using in you club, but who don't usually fit the young male, aggressive sales mode.

Second, you need to develop a system that will let you develop people more quickly. You should, with the right system in place, be able to make that energetic housewife effective in a sales encounter in only a few months, rather than two years. Most importantly, you should be able to duplicate this training with anyone who has the basic sales traits, such as an outgoing personality and enthusiasm.

Lastly, you must create a system that is effective, yet makes the buyer and salesperson feel good about what just happened. Most sales systems used in fitness businesses don't have this outcome and, in fact, most make the customer feel horrible. He just spent an hour getting pounded in an office by a slick sales dog and now he's driving home mad with a pink copy of a membership form and an aerobic schedule lying on the seat beside him. "Damn, I should have asked for more months or free training or something."

It is pretty well documented that most people leave a car dealership feeling like they were just violated by a Mongolian horde. Many new fitness club members also feel that their first experience with a fitness center leaves them feeling damaged and bitter, and many punish the club by canceling their memberships or skipping payments. You will seldom get any referrals from someone who hates you because of the sales experience.

Many fitness facilities, especially the Ys and wellness centers, in reaction to this high-pressure stereotype, go too far the other way and just hand out price sheets and let the person take a self-tour. This method fails the client just as much as the other one, because someone came to the club for help and you end up hoping the facility can sell the membership for you rather than actually spending time helping the person get what he wants and needs.

## The Linear Training Method

The alternative to the hard-to-maintain sales system based upon teaching people to cover every contingency and to have to think their way through every situation is what is called a linear training method. This method is based upon teaching exact steps and progressions that anyone can easily master in a short time. Due to the nature of mastering set steps, a person can be more effective in this system in a much shorter period of time.

Linear means a straight line, so developing a linear training progression means you develop a step-by-step process with limited choices at each stop on the path. For example, many sales systems have an option where the salesperson can adjust the cash up front:

*Salesperson:* Well Joe, how much would you like to put down today toward your membership?

*Prospective member:* Let's see, I have $150 on me I can give you.

*Salesperson:* Okay, so let me readjust your monthly dues.

The salesperson is probably getting some type of commission based upon how much cash he can get up front. The more cash, the more commission he gets, so he is willing to ask for more from the member and will push for credit cards and checks if the guy actually doesn't have any real cash on him. The

**Many fitness facilities, especially the Ys and wellness centers, in reaction to this high-pressure stereotype, go too far the other way and just hand out price sheets and let the person take a self-tour.**

problem is that this system adds another layer of complication to the sale, making training this person harder and more extensive. Using a linear model makes the training simpler and the sale easier. For example:

*Salesperson:* Well Joe, our memberships have a $59 one-time membership fee and our monthly dues are just $49 a month EFT and are based upon an annual membership. If you would like to write a check each month, simply add $5 to your monthly dues. It costs a little more to process checks, but you can save the $5 with our automatic withdrawal memberships if that is more convenient for you. Which one of these options would be best for you?

In this example, the salesperson only has to master the price and the explanation, rather than how to fish for cash and then adjust the monthly dues. The second model has fewer steps for the salesperson and fewer decisions for the buyer.

## Train progressions for each and every step

**Developing a linear training progression means you develop a step-by-step process with limited choices at each stop on the path.**

Another example of the difference between the option model and the linear model is how you greet people when they first arrive at the club to inquire about memberships. In the option model, you tell your salesperson to greet strongly and take control at the door. You train for this scenario by teaching a variety of phrases and comebacks for all the standard questions you might hear. In this model, more time is spent on the sales words and a lot less time is spent on how to actually meet and greet the guest.

Thinking allows for freestyle, and freestyle is dangerous in the sales environment. For example, a young, classically trained salesperson meets someone at the door, another young male, and gives him the current version of a handshake and states, "What can I help you with?" Since almost all of his training is based upon sales talk, little time is spent on the actual procedures of meeting someone and making the guest feel comfortable in a new and stressful environment. This same salesperson also applies some version of this loose greeting to any potential client, no matter the age or sex, since again he has been trained extensively on the use of sales words and closes and very little on how to interact with someone.

The linear method would have a set greeting that a new salesperson uses over and over again and can therefore master. Since you train specific steps and actions with this method, you would also work on how to shake hands, approach people of different ages, sizes, and sexes, and properly use voice and dress. All of these factors add to the sale and are core basics that you would neglect with the other type of training and sales system.

The following is another way of looking at the differences for you sports-minded people. Assume you are training people to play baseball. In the old-style sales training, you spend a lot of time teaching people to prepare for any option that might come up. If the bases are loaded, do this strategy. If you have two outs, you might try this play. If a left-handed batter is up, you might want to bring in this pitcher. The options are endless and to properly prepare someone in this situation you have to train for each and every option. The sad thing is that you are not training for the most important elements of the game with this type of training.

Someone who understands linear training understands that the basics make you successful. When you are eight years old and playing on your first real team, if the coach is any good he spends time practicing the core elements of being successful in baseball: you hit the ball, you throw the ball, and you catch the ball. Do these things better when you are eight and you win more games than the kids that don't practice these basics as much.

When the kid makes the high school team, and the coach is wise and tried, the young athlete practices hitting the ball, throwing the ball, and catching the ball. If he does these things better than the other kids he might get to play ball in college.

In college, his coach makes him hit the ball, throw the ball, and catch the ball. If he excels at these skills in college he might make the pros. During his first week at the Boston Red Sox camp, after years of practice and years of coaching, his new coach puts him out on the field and they spend hours hitting the ball, throwing the ball, and catching the ball. If he does these skills better than the other players, he is more successful on the field—and better off financially off the field.

Selling in a fitness facility is nothing more than mastering the basics. You greet people, you show sincere interest, you tour based upon benefits using a set tour with specific steps, you explain the prices the same way every time, you don't make deals, and you ask for the sale using one set close that you practice over and over again. "Let's get you signed up today?" Each and every one of these things is done the same way each and every time in a normal progression. You follow the steps rather than learn to think about the game. Think about the greeting again and how it can be done with a linear style:

**Selling in a fitness facility is nothing more than mastering the basics.**

*Salesperson:* Hello, welcome to the club. My name is Eric. You are… (pause/wait for name).

*Prospective member:* My name is Bill.

*Salesperson:* Bill, it's nice to meet you. What brought you into the club today?

Couple this conversation with a handshake (that is taught), while standing a certain distance from the prospect (also taught). Remember that your voice is a tool that can work for you or against you.

If Eric the salesperson says anything else but this greeting, he is in trouble. Learn this one simple greeting, master it, and no matter how tired or burned out you get, your training will always save you.

It is thought that American troops are the best in the world, but when you read about them you realize that they are also the best trained in the world. When you are young, scared, and entering your first combat, your training takes over and you know what to do because you practiced the basics to the point where you can't stand them.

**In sales, you practice the basics, such as how to shake hands, until it seems silly.**

In sales, you practice the basics, such as how to shake hands, until it seems silly. But on a Monday in March, after several months of endless prospects, when you're just getting ready to go home for the night, in walks a guest. You are tired, cranky, and done for the day, but your training, due to repetition of the basics, takes over and you walk over and say: "Hello, welcome to the club. My name is…"

Your chances of getting the sale will be higher because less room exists for sloppiness and errors. Owners can train salespeople more quickly because they constantly work on the basics, such as answering the phone, rather than trying to master an endless array of sales options.

The following list provides samples of core basics, the fitness industry's version of hit the ball, throw the ball, and catch the ball. These basics should be practiced no matter what your experience level and no matter how long you have been in sales:

- Greeting at the door with a set welcoming statement
- Learning to shake hands properly
- Practicing the handoff between the front-counter person and the salesperson
- Letting the guest know about the trial membership before you tour the club
- Spending two to four minutes getting to know the guest before the tour by asking questions based upon simple rules. What kind of workout are you doing now? When was the last time you felt you were really in shape? Have you ever been in the club before? How did you hear about us? These questions are nothing more than simple who, what, where, when, and why questions that demonstrate sincere interest and that can be taught in a one-hour meeting and repeated as necessary.
- Touring following a set system of stops (selling stations that are discussed in Chapter 18) so that everyone sees everything every time and owners can get an idea of how long it takes each salesperson to present the gym. The idea time is 30 to 40 minutes for most gyms. The most common error is that most salespeople shorten the process and rush through in under 30 minutes.

- Using a classy, standardized closing sheet rather than writing the prices on a yellow pad or worse

- Memorizing a few paragraphs so the prices are presented the same way each time, building consistency and confidence in the words for the salesperson

- Asking for the sale using the same simple phrase each time

This list represents just a few examples of the basics of sales. Put together, you have the basis for a sales system that can be taught easily to any new salesperson. Remember that the heart of an effective sales system is developing a repeatable sales process that can be broken into simple steps.

Most of the newer owners who have entered the industry in the past few years, as well as those in the nonprofit sector, find that the old-style sales system is just not something they want to learn or do in their businesses. In fact, most of the newer owners from other industries find that high-pressure, slick sales is somewhat sleazy and is something they don't want to be associated with in their business.

In summary, keep it simple and break it down into steps. Teaching your people to follow simple steps is much easier, and much more effective, than trying to teach slick comebacks for everything a potential member might say or do. Most importantly, you can create a new breed of salesperson that is badly needed in the industry and that will respond to an ethical sales system based upon presenting the club in the best way possible and truly helping the person who has come to you for help.

> Teaching your people to follow simple steps is much easier, and much more effective, than trying to teach slick comebacks for everything a potential member might say or do.

## Key Points From This Chapter

- Thinking is harder to teach than simply getting someone to follow set steps.

- It takes too long to develop the model of an old sales dog.

- Nontraditional sales people will respond well to a system based upon following set steps and showing sincere interest in the guests.

- Linear training is nothing more than teaching the salesperson to follow fixed steps (a straight line) in the sales process.

- Limiting options makes it easier for the salesperson and the prospective client.

- New staff members feel more confident when they have mastered a step rather than trying to master endless verbiage designed to cover every sales situation they might face.

- Building a repeatable sales system should be the goal of every owner.

## Tip of the Day

# Couples are always equal.

Nothing will ruin a potential sale faster than a young male salesperson who spends all of his time on the tour talking to the male half of a couple and ignoring the woman. Couples of any mix are equals and you must talk to both of them at the same time and explain everything to both of them. Also ask questions to both equally and find out what each one wants from the club and from their membership.

Assuming that the man is in charge or that the woman won't "get it" is the fastest way to unemployment in today's market. Treat everyone in front of you as equals and with respect, and you will be much more likely to sell both people memberships.

# 11

# Never Separate Marketing and Sales in Your Business Plan

Marketing can be simply defined as getting qualified butts in seats in front of your salespeople. Look closely, however, and you will see that this simple statement actually takes two distinct parts of the business to complete.

First, you have to have a marketing plan in place that will attract new prospective members to the gym. Second, once the prospective member is in the facility, you have to have a trained salesperson in place to take advantage of the marketing dollars you spent to drive that person to the seat.

Marketing and sales are totally dependent on each other in your club's business plan. Unlike other areas of the club, such as personal training and group exercise, where you can excel in one and be terrible in the other and still run a successful business, you cannot be strong in marketing or sales and weak in the other and survive over time. You have to master both to be successful and these two areas, along with staffing, may be the most difficult areas of your business.

## What happens if the marketing is weak but sales are strong?

This type of club usually shows low volume, but a strong closing percentage. The sad thing is that this club's team is not made up of great salespeople. Instead, they are great order takers.

If you're not marketing, most new members find you through referrals, or a guy simply turns himself in because he just moved in around the corner. In other words, most new members are already somewhat pre-sold before they ever enter the place.

In this case, you falsely assume that a little more volume would fix the situation. "Hey, we can sell but we don't get enough leads," is the cry of the frustrated owner or manager. In reality, if this club obtained more leads the closing rate would be pathetic, because no one really ever learned to present the gym and sell memberships based upon any repeatable system. The staff in this club can fill out paperwork well and close a high number of the few leads they get, but if any number of prospects showed up at once the flaws in this system would be exposed quickly and with a negative result.

True sales expertise is based on experience with volume. If your team can convert 55 percent of all qualified leads to annual memberships over a 30-day period, then you really do have a system and really can sell. Most low-volume clubs can't maintain this number if the number of leads increases, because salesmanship was never really in place from the beginning.

The other interesting question is, why doesn't this owner simply increase the volume of marketing, leading to a greater number of potential members through the door? Most of these owners won't risk more marketing capital because of prior experience. "We tried more marketing last year and it didn't work for us. All we got through the door were a bunch of unqualified people who really weren't serious." What he is really saying is that the marketing did drive new leads to the facility but his staff wasn't trained well enough to get the job done. Therefore, he is correct in saying that the marketing didn't work for him, but not for the reason he believes.

### What happens if the marketing is strong but the sales are weak?

**You can never spend enough marketing dollars to overcome a weak sales system.**

You can never spend enough marketing dollars to overcome a weak sales system. For example, which one of the following examples has the competitive edge in this marketplace?

Club 1:

- Has 150 leads per month and closes 38 percent (the national average)
- This club writes 57 new memberships a month.

Club 2:

- Has 150 leads per month and closes 55 percent (average with sales training and systems)
- This club writes 82 new members a month from the same leads.

Marketing is expensive and Club 1 is wasting a large portion of its marketing money because it is getting leads but can't convert. Club 2 has a 25-members-per-month advantage over Club 1, or 300 new members a year, in the same market and from the same number of leads.

Where club owners go wrong, however, is when the person who owns the Club 1 simply keeps throwing more dollars into the marketing pool to get a higher sales number. But marketing is expensive and it gets to a point where you can't throw enough dollars over a long enough time to keep buying marketing share.

The owner of Club 2 has a huge advantage in a number of ways. First and foremost, at the end of the year she has 300 more members than her competitor. The secondary advantages are that she also has more new sales income per month, her receivable check will increase, her chances for a higher number of renewals each year is higher because more members are in the pile, and the money she saves because she doesn't have to buy more marketing could be used elsewhere in the club. All of these advantages exist simply because she did more sales training than her competitor, given that their marketing is somewhat the same.

## How many leads does a club have to generate to be successful?

Over the years, a number of different ways have been proposed to determine how many sales a club has to get each month to be successful. Most of these old formulas were based upon the number of salespeople the club hired.

For example, a good salesperson in the 1980s and 1990s might be able to generate 50 sales per month. This number was based upon how many lead boxes he put out (cardboard boxes put in businesses where the customer enters to win a prize), how many cold calls he could generate, how many appointments were set, the show rate of those appointments, and most importantly, how many buddy referrals he could get from the members in the gym.

An owner would figure out this formula and then just keep adding salespeople until she got enough sales. Theoretically, no limit existed to the number of sales an owner could get from her business, since all she had to do was keep adding salespeople and then make sure each one maintained his appointments for the day.

The problem is that the cold-call process is mind-numbing work with a high burnout rate. The pressure was also enormous for the salespeople. One of the national chains, for example, held weekly meetings for the sales staff and the low man that week was fired in front of the group. This technique was supposed to drive the survivors to do better the following week, but no matter how hard everyone worked, a low man always was fired each week.

**The problem is that the cold-call process is mind-numbing work with a high burnout rate.**

The entire burden for generating leads for the club was centered on the club's salespeople and not on the club's marketing, where it should have been focused. Over the years, this system has become progressively more difficult to work.

Not too many people with any type of brain power enter a draw box at Denny's® expecting to win the free trip to the Bahamas. This system has a corresponding formula generated by those people who still believe that boxes work. If you are good with a draw box, you call 100 leads from the box, make 10 appointments, and one shows up.

Calling 100 leads takes a lot of work, especially compared to the expected outcome of only one appointment. And remember the quality of this lead; this guy entered a draw box at a low-end restaurant, expecting to win the big prize and settled for two weeks at the local fitness center as the second prize. Just entering a draw box may make this guy one of the least qualified leads coming through the door, and don't forget about all the work you had to do to get him.

Other options for the salesperson, such as buddy referrals and cold calling someone's home, are also getting much more difficult. Not too many people are left who will give you a list of their friends' phone numbers, and the "do not call" lists and high-tech answering machines make it so much harder to actually get a hold of anyone by phone at home.

All the techniques developed in the 1960s and 1970s and then honed in the 1980s and 1990s fail in 2000 and beyond. The technology is old, insulting to the more sophisticated consumer, and worthless as a tool to the club owner. Most importantly, it is difficult to find and train enough salespeople willing to do these high-failure-rate activities.

> **In today's market, you as an owner or manager have to generate enough leads to keep your sales staff fed.**

In today's market, you as an owner or manager have to generate enough leads to keep your sales staff fed. Higher-return marketing, such as trial memberships, generates more traffic into the clubs, giving the salespeople more time to work your actual guests instead of putting in 100 calls to nonqualified buyers.

## The Single Most Important Rule in the Fitness Business

If you want to be financially successful over time, no matter if you are a nonprofit facility or a traditional for-profit operation, you have to understand and apply the following rule to your business.

---

### The 1 per $1000 Rule

You must write one new annual membership, with a price of $39 per month per member or higher, for every $1000 of expense per month.

---

For example, assume your club has a monthly operating expense of $73,000, which includes all debt service, payroll, rent, and any other expenses you incur each month to pay all your bills and keep your operation open. If you are the owner and are taking out more than you would pay a manager to do the same job, adjust your budget number using the manager's salary. For example, if you are an owner and take out $100,000 per year, but would pay a manager $40,000 to do the job, then use the $40,000 as your budgeting number.

This total number is called your base operating expense (BOE). Once your business is established, this number may fluctuate at different times of the year, but once you find this number it normally doesn't change all that month over time, unless you add new profit centers or somehow fundamentally change the structure of the business.

In this example, the club would have to write an average of 73 new annual memberships (one per $1000 of expense) each month over time to be successful. The owner may write 150 sales in March and only 50 in July, but the average has to stay at 73 or above throughout the year.

## Adjustments

In this example, 73 is the net number. If the club has certain losses each month, such as members who quit with a permanent medical excuse, then the owner needs to adjust his sales number. This adjustment number is referred to as a loss factor. Once you establish this number as an average you only need to refigure it once a year. The components of a loss factor are as follows:

- Cancellations on contracts within the first three days (a federal law gives the consumer a cooling-off period after signing a retail installment contract of any type) Permanent medical excuses

- Cancellations made because the member moved more than 25 miles from the club (the law in most states that you must cancel this person with proof of the move)

> Important note: The loss factor number does not include non-renewals. The 1 per $1000 rule is only used to determine new sales needed for a typical fitness business. Renewals are handled in member retention and are not included in the new sales process.

You must adjust the $73,000 per month BOE according to the loss factor:

- $73,000 BOE = 73 new annual sales per month net goal
- The club has a price of $39 per month per member.

**Once your business is established, your BOE may fluctuate at different times of the year, but once you find this number it normally doesn't change all that month over time, unless you add new profit centers or somehow fundamentally change the structure of the business.**

- The club has a loss factor average of 10.

73 new sales needed (1 per $1000)
+ 10 extra sales needed because of the loss factor
83 new adjusted number of annual sales the club must average

## Other deviations

> Clubs with higher member prices can still stick to this rule, because the formula would err toward the club simply setting a higher membership goal each month.

This example is based upon a club with a basic membership price for an individual of $39 per month per member. Clubs with higher member prices can still stick to this rule, because the formula would err toward the club simply setting a higher membership goal each month. If your monthly membership price is higher than $39 per month per member and you would like to fine-tune the formula, then use the following list for adjustments:

- $39 = 1/$1000
- $49 = 1/$1200
- $59 = 1/$1400
- $69 = 1/$1600
- $79 = 1/$1800
- $89 = 1/$2000

Using these numbers, a club with a BOE of $73,000 and a monthly membership price of $59 for an individual would need one new sale per every $1400 of operating expense.

### $73,000/$1400 = 52 new annual sales needed per month

Club owners with monthly prices lower than $39 can also adjust the formula using the following numbers:

- $39 = 1/$1000
- $29 = 1/$800
- $19 = 1/$600
- $9 = 1/$400

For example, if a club had a BOE of $73,000 and was using a monthly price of $19, the club owner would need to write and average of 121 sales per month to survive.

### $73,000/$600 = 121 new annual sales needed per month

This formula gives you the *minimum* number you need to survive in business. Once you determine this number for your club, you need to then create a sales process that will allow you to average that number over the prior three-month period. If this three-month average falls below that number, then it is time to troubleshoot, because if you consistently fall below the needed average your chance for failure becomes much higher.

## What Is a Qualified Buyer?

The old view is that if he has a pulse and a dollar then he is qualified to buy a membership in your gym, but you really only care about the dollar. Most owners are now a little more selective, because they have learned over time that if you start with a weak sale, the chances of the membership going bad early in the collection process is much higher. High-pressure tactics, for example, generate more sales, but these tactics also generate a much higher rate of first-payment default and total failure during the first six months of collections.

These failed memberships are an expensive waste to the club owner. She paid commission on the sale, adsorbed the cost of advertising, and then loses 20 percent or more of all new memberships because her sales team uses too much pressure during the first visit. These false numbers can erode your business plan over time because most owners simply try to compensate by turning up more pressure to write more sales to cover the losses, which results in even larger losses.

Qualified buyers, coupled with trial memberships, create a higher return per member over time. Trial memberships, or "try before you buy" offers, are covered more extensively in Chapter 8, but the key point to know about trials in this context is that you still have to generate memberships to survive in this business. The difference between the old-style traditional system and a system based upon using trials is the timing of when the membership is written. The old-style approach mandates that you write it "today" and do everything you can to force the person to sign while he is in the club during his first visit. The trial system still scores during the first visit, but it also increases the chance of getting another shot at the person tomorrow if he walks out today to think it over.

The secret in this business, if a secret really exists, is how can you write memberships during the first visit and still have a strong chance of getting those who don't join today to come back tomorrow? Old-style pressure sales that load up the first visit with an all-or-nothing approach, may generate sales, but those who don't join on that first day hardly ever come back. The pressure for most of these salespeople is leverage in the form of dropping the price today, and today only: "Normally our price is $150, but if you and your friend are ready to go today then I will let you both join for $50."

What happens if the person truly wants to think about it overnight? Research shows that when the price gets to be $39 per month or higher, 70 percent of potential guests need two or more visits before they will join. In

**The secret in this business, if a secret really exists, is how can you write memberships during the first visit and still have a strong chance of getting those who don't join today to come back tomorrow?**

other words, 30 percent of your guests might join during the first visit, but 70 percent would like to think about it and come back the next day.

What is the incentive to come back tomorrow when they were beaten so badly today? High-pressure guys who drop the price drastically during the first visit don't have a backup plan, because supposedly if you came back the next day you would have to pay the higher price. It is an all-today approach for the salesperson, because no one wants to come back and pay more tomorrow.

This scenario leads to the salesperson making pathetic calls for weeks after the person's visit, trying to offer more deals and incentives. "Hey, I kind of lied to you. We really will give you a deal if you come back again. I was just kidding around with you during your first visit." How good does the prospect feel about the salesperson, and the club, if the relationship begins so dishonestly and with so much unneeded pressure?

You can still generate a significant number of first-visit sales with enhancements rather than discounts. Enhancement selling is discussed in Chapter 15, but the theory is that you can get more sales by offering strong incentive packages versus insulting the person and making the sale harder over time by discounting on the first day.

> **Protecting price protects integrity, and people still feel good coming back the next day because they don't have to get into a used-car-guy negotiation with the club's salesperson.**

The key is to never come off the price, but instead change the incentives. The price today will be the same tomorrow, but the incentive package will be reduced. Protecting price protects integrity, and people still feel good coming back the next day because they don't have to get into a used-car-guy negotiation with the club's salesperson.

Qualified buyers are easy to determine, especially if you are using trial memberships:

- You must be 18/21/23 years old, depending on the type of club and the owner's desired target market.

- You must live in the club's market area and present an ID proving that you do.

- Anyone wanting to take advantage of the club's trial membership program must present a valid credit card.

- If you are qualified, you may use the trial once a year.

The age factors are used for certain clubs and in certain areas. For example, if you own an upscale adult club you might want to limit your trials to people 21 years or older, because you wouldn't want anyone younger than that using the facility. If you are in a college town, you might want to use 23 years or older to keep the local college kids from taking advantage. The ages depend on the target market and demographics. Remember, you can't build a club that makes everyone happy, so it is important to keep the mix in mind.

The driver's license limits those using a trial to only the people who actually live in the local market. In other words, if you are stopping through on vacation, you can't use the 14-day trial because you aren't a real qualified buyer.

Flashing a credit card is a way to limit the trial to only those who are qualified to buy later. Only those people who are sincerely interested in trying the club will offer to show you a valid credit card, while folks living in their cars looking for a place to shower probably won't show you their IDs.

# Closing Rates

Closing rates are simple. How many people do you sign up out of every 100 qualified prospects? The national average is 38 percent. Your goal is to make sure that 55 percent of all qualified people through the door end up with annual memberships.

Out of this 55 percent, at least 30 percent should close during the first visit. For example, if the club gets 100 qualified leads in a month, then the owner should end up with at least 55 annual members, of which 30 percent, or about 16 people, buy during their first visit.

You don't count other junk memberships because selling a short-term membership for a few hundred dollars may help cash flow today, but this type of membership doesn't have the power to help the business grow over time. Annual memberships drive growth, fuel the club's receivable base, and are what you should be focusing on as owners and managers.

## Once you know needed sales, and know your closing rates, you can project needed leads.

Once you calculate your needed sales using the 1 per $1000 rule, and you have tracked your closing rates, you can use this information to project the number of needed leads. Knowing your needed leads will give you better control over your marketing budget, because you would be able to adjust the amount you are spending in correlation to the leads you are buying.

Don't forget that the 1 per $1000 rule gives you the minimum sales needed to keep your business alive over time. If you have been in business for a while, you might be doing better than the minimums and these numbers should be used instead, but always remember that you have to average the minimum to stay in business. Chapter 14 explains how to project sales using existing sales numbers for those owners and managers who are achieving numbers above the minimum needed. The following formula can be used to project needed sales:

**Needed sales x 100/Closing rate = Needed leads**

> Once you calculate your needed sales using the 1 per $1000 rule, and you have tracked your closing rates, you can use this information to project the number of needed leads.

For example:

- The club has a BOE of $73,000.
- The club has a price of $39 per month per member.
- This club has a −10 loss factor based upon an average of:
    - √ The three-day right of cancellation
    - √ Permanent medical excuses
    - √ Cancellations based upon moves of more than 25 miles from the club
- The club's sales team closes 55 percent of its leads.
- This club needs to average 83 new sales a month:

> 73 new sales based upon 1/$1000
> +10 adjusting for additional sales needed due to loss factor
> 83 total sales the club needs as a minimum number

Based upon these numbers, you can project the club's needed leads:

$$83 \times 100/55 = 151 \text{ new leads}$$

This club needs at least 151 new leads per month to hit its target sales number. The owner or manager's focus should be on achieving this number of leads via the club's marketing. Not many things are more important in the daily life of a manager or owner than figuring out how to hit this number, because if the club gets this much traffic and the sales team stays at this closing rate, then almost everything else should come together.

Where many owners get off track is with the closing rate. What happens, for example, if the club has a less successful sales team?

$$83 \times 100/38 = 218 \text{ new leads}$$

In this example, the club's sales team only closes 38 percent. The difference is that 218 leads are needed versus only 151 in the previous example. If these numbers came from two different clubs, the first club could write the same number of annual contracts per month with 67 fewer leads. This difference is a huge advantage in a competitive marketplace where a number of clubs are fighting for market share.

The possible solutions are to either buy more leads or do more sales training. In today's marketplace, it is easier to learn to sell than to keep throwing additional marketing dollars at the problem.

*In today's marketplace, it is easier to learn to sell than to keep throwing additional marketing dollars at the problem.*

## Key Points From This Chapter

- Sales training and marketing can never be separated.

- Owners usually blame the marketing when they can't effectively sell memberships.

- Weak sales put a burden on marketing dollars that most clubs can't handle.

- The burden in the old systems has always been on the salesperson to generate enough leads for the club. Most of those old techniques, such as draw boxes, don't work anymore.

- The 1 per $1000 rule is the single most important rule in the fitness business. Break it and your chances of failure are much higher.

- One of the most important tools a club owner has is the ability to track qualified leads in the club each month.

- If you know your needed sales number, and your team's closing rates, you can project the needed leads for your club.

- Sales training, which raises your team's effectiveness and closing rate, lowers the cost of marketing and makes you more competitive over time.

## Build your own sales notebook.

**Tip of the Day**

Most salespeople rely strictly on their ability to talk their way out of anything and pride themselves on their ability to have an answer or explanation for almost any question that arises. If you sell for a year or two, you realize that not many unique questions will get thrown at you by the potential members. With a little experience, you can come up with an answer for just about anything that pops out of a person's mouth. But why do all of your answers have to be verbal?

The sales notebook is a tool that you can use to project some of your personality into the sales encounter, while also allowing you to answer many of a prospect's questions with a pertinent article, cartoon, or picture rather than relying on verbal responses alone. Develop your own notebook that you carry with you on every tour. As you get more experience, start to add interesting articles you find that answer a commonly asked question on the tour.

For example, a female might say, "I know I should lift weights but I don't want to get too big." Anyone can respond to this comment after a few months of experience, but a verbal response is not nearly as powerful as showing pictures of some actress who trains with weights along with an article that discusses the benefits of weight training for women.

Give your guest copies of anything relevant and then reload the notebook from your file before the next tour. Also keep a membership agreement, price sheet, and other closing materials in your notebook, because you don't always have to present the prices at the table. If someone is excited about your group room, then take her there and present the prices and try to close her in the area of the club that she most likes.

# 12

# The Fable of Ugly Jim

This fable is based upon a true story from early in my sales career. It's a story about how, despite the fact that I was young and foolish, the sales gods looked after me anyway and gave me a lesson that all new sales people can learn from in the future. Keep in mind as you read this fable that I was young and dumb and had the perspective of a guy in his 20s who knew nothing, but thought he had a definite superior advantage in the world. I am glad I am not this guy anymore.

One of my first jobs in the fitness industry was managing a small martial arts school with a fitness center in San Diego. The owner of the school, Chuck Hawkins, was a talented martial artist, a motivating person to work for, and was the type of leader that coached you when you needed it but also gave you room to experiment and grow. Looking back, he was a good man and someone a young guy wanted to work for because of his leadership abilities and his generous, caring attitude.

The school was located on El Cajon Boulevard, which is a main street, but our end of it wasn't full of class A businesses at the time. Most of our neighbors were car repair places, local bars, and small restaurants, with a smattering of second-class businesses, such as discount car insurance guys.

One of the great things about this job, besides being in my 20s and living in San Diego, was the endless stream of hookers who paraded past our front doors during the lazy southern California afternoons. Leaning against the front counter watching the girls go by was our team's favorite way to dog a few hours before evening classes began. My previous home was in Arkansas, so I, along with my coworkers, often stood big-eyed while commenting on the variety of options strutting past our two glass front doors.

Friday afternoons were particularly slow, and during the summer they became almost lethal when it came to finding the energy to do anything but lean and kill time until the Friday night all-school workout began. June is an especially beautiful time to be in San Diego and on one memorable Friday it was even more inspiring as the sun faded in the west, flooding our doors with the golden rays of a late afternoon.

Lined up at the counter at the usual perches were two sales guys, with me in the middle. The sun was dropping, the doors backlit with warm light, when an apparition appeared silhouetted in the glass as both doors slowly opened. The backlighting made it like an old western, when the good guy with the white hat slowly opens the swinging doors with his face hidden by the blast of light from behind him.

Our doors slowly opened and a small man, perhaps no more than 5'4", approached the counter with the shuffling walk of someone with a bad back or bad hips. His feet never really left the floor, but merely scooted along as they powered him toward the counter.

Once in the door, his features became clear. He was obviously a flashback to a distant time in earth's history, because moving toward me was a true Cro-Magnon man, complete with the low forehead and one eyebrow running across his face.

As he approached the counter, the salespeople disappeared in a flash of light, like the hookers who were there and then suddenly gone every time a police car cruised our street. I was alone and face-to-face with one of the homeliest human beings I had ever seen. He looked up at me and spoke in a sharp, nasally voice that could only come from the combination of a broken nose and a harelip. His unusual twang added extra letters in places where they shouldn't have been and made for bizarre words and sounds. "Heeellow, I'd likke to geet some in-for-ma-tion about your meembershiiips," he said. I just stared for minute, not sure what I just heard.

**Couldn't this guy see we were serious gym people here and that I was busy?**

I couldn't believe the voice. I couldn't believe the look. And I just couldn't believe that I had to waste my time with this obvious loser when I was busy watching hookers on a Friday afternoon. Couldn't this guy see we were serious gym people here and that I was busy?

He was persistent, so I gave him the famous "you're a loser" tour. Every young jackass who has done sales anywhere knows this tour. It's the, "You want a tour? Okay, you'll get a tour, buddy," attitude combined with a quick, 10-minute walk through the gym.

I walked quickly, throwing tidbits of information over my shoulder as he shuffled along behind me around the gym. Occasionally, he would ask a question in that comic voice, which the staff and any member within earshot found hilarious.

The tour was over in minutes and I gave him the prices. "It's $498 cash." He was a loser, so I saw no sense in giving him the monthly prices or taking the time to really explain the other options in our little gym. He was wasting my time and now it was time for him to go. "Ooookay, I'll beee back," he said as he shuffled off into the California sun from whence he came.

The rest of the afternoon was a combination of frustration and painful humor directed at my former tour, whose name, Jim, was only discovered after I looked at his guest slip after he left. Every time I would leave my office, two or three people would be lined up behind me, shuffling along. Members and staff would take turn sticking their heads in my door to ask questions while trying their best to mimic the voice. Even recently arriving members got into the act despite not being around for Jim's tour, having gotten the word from others who couldn't wait to share the story.

I opened by myself on Saturday mornings. We were usually slow except for classes and one guy could handle the entire gym until the first class and first instructor arrived. We opened at 8 o'clock, and just a few minutes after I opened the door for business Jim came sliding on in, wearing the same blue work shirt he had on the day before and shuffling with a purpose toward the front desk.

"Heellow, I'm backkk and I'd liiike to geet started," he said. He then proceeded to lay $498 in cash on the table. It was then that I began to notice that Jim wasn't nearly as homely and as much of a loser as he seemed to be the day before. "My girlfreeend is in the car. Can I bring her in and geeeet her and her kiiiids signed up for karate too?"

All I had left was a nod. He painfully slid toward the door and reappeared in minutes with a small, but extremely beautiful, Mexican-American woman and her two kids. She was short, gorgeous, and crazy about Jim, or maybe just crazy, but she hung on his arm and mentioned that they had been together for years and were getting married soon. Jim laid more cash on the desk. I had four memberships and hadn't been open for 30 minutes yet. Most importantly, I was really beginning to like good ol' Jim.

By the end of the month, I had signed up a total of 11 members, including Jim himself, and all of them had paid cash. It seems that Jim, or UJ, as the staff and members called him, was a crane driver at the piers where they unloaded fish. The cranes were small, high-speed vehicles that sped around the docks emptying fish boats as fast as they landed. The cranes were also cramped and horrible for your back, which came to explain Jim's shuffle. The voice, however, was never explained, and was simply a part of Jim that we chose to ignore.

You also had to be short to drive these little babies. Every one of Jim's friend who joined the gym was under 5'5" and on afternoons when they were all working out together before work, I would walk through the gym feeling like

> I had four memberships and hadn't been open for 30 minutes yet. Most importantly, I was really beginning to like good ol' Jim.

a god, towering over the mere mortals at my enormous 5'10". I'd look out my office window when all of them were together and it would seem like the filming of a Keebler® cookie commercial in which the elves have taken over the forest.

UJ stayed with the gym and was still there when I left a year later. He was still referring friends and brought the gym and karate school thousands of dollars worth of business during his time there. Being the thoughtless, insensitive kids we were, we never told UJ that those initials stood for Ugly Jim, but that didn't stop us from calling him that every time he stopped by to work out. He enjoyed the nickname and his friends picked it up as well, but I don't know if he ever knew what it meant.

# The Moral of the Story

The moral of the story is that by being young and stupid I could have cost my owner several thousand dollars in business by falling into one of the biggest traps in sales: prejudging. Prejudging means that you as a salesperson predetermine by looks or personal biases that a prospective member doesn't really qualify to be a part of your business. In Jim's case, I made up my mind when he walked in that he wasn't one of us and that he didn't belong in the business. In fact, I did everything I could to discourage him from joining the gym, including not even giving him all the price options.

This attitude is a part of every salesperson. Even those of you who think that you have grown beyond the baggage of discrimination still have those subtle, under-the-surface prejudices that cost your business money. If you're an owner, you have the right to make the final decision about who will ultimately be a member in your facility, but keep in mind that discrimination under any guise is still wrong and works against what the core belief in the fitness business really is: We help people who need help to make changes in their lives.

Prejudging is also just plain bad business. In the case of Jim, my young stupidity could have cost the business probably more money than we even knew about at the time. How many friends did Jim tell about the gym because he was happy? How many people did he tell about his success? And how many other parents did he tell about how well the kids were doing in the marital arts? Once Jim was in, we treated him well and he became family, like most members do in a small facility, but we made it hard for him to get his foot through the door. Only his persistence overcame the uncaring attitude of a young, thoughtless manager.

> The moral of the story is that by being young and stupid I could have cost my owner several thousand dollars in business by falling into one of the biggest traps in sales: prejudging.

## Your Job

Your job as a salesperson in a fitness facility is to treat everyone fairly and with a caring attitude. Your job is not to predetermine who fits your model. Prejudging costs money in the short run and over time can even take down a business that develops a bad reputation of being prejudiced against certain groups in the community.

**Your job as a salesperson in a fitness facility is to treat everyone fairly and with a caring attitude.**

The only exception to this rule is that you should never tour anyone through the club that has obviously been drinking or doing drugs. Otherwise, sign them all up and let the owner sort through them later. Your job is to do everything you can to get the sale in an ethical manner and to give the best tour you can to each and every guest.

## Key Points From This Chapter

- Prejudging means that your personal biases get in the way of making money in the facility.

- Your job is to give the best tour you can to everyone who comes through the door.

- Prejudging can cost the facility huge amounts of money, because you may refuse qualified people just because they do not look like you or sound like you.

- The only exception is that you do not tour people who have obviously been drinking or doing drugs.

**Tip of the Day**

## Don't chew gum.

Chewing gum is bad at work. It can make you look like a cow.

Smacking gum is worse and often irritates people.

Use mints, and stop with the gum.

Enough said.

# THE CORE ELEMENTS OF THE PLUMMER SALES SYSTEM

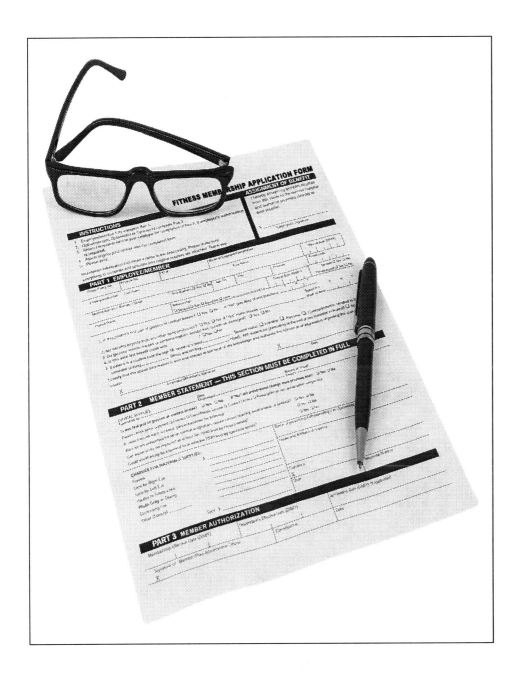

**Section Three**

# 13

# Superstars Usually Aren't Worth the Effort

The early days of fitness were based upon the star system. In those days, if you ran a successful club that could generate a lot of sales, it was usually because you had a team of ultra-hot salespeople who slammed customers at the point of sales, made a hundred calls a day, and still prowled the nightclubs spending their cash at legendary parties.

The glory days of the 1970s and 1980s produced some of the most successful salespeople in the history of this business. Sadly, most of those people went on to become owners, which led in many ways to much of the negative attitude that modern-day owners and operators encounter.

An old saying states that if all you own is a hammer, everything you see is a nail. This statement was especially true of the salespeople that came to maturity during these easy days in the business. In the 1980s, very limited competition existed, the running boom was on, and fitness was just emerging. If you couldn't sell memberships in the early 1980s, then you could never sell, because it truly was easier than it is in today's mature—meaning heavily competitive—markets.

Everything worked in those days. If you called out of a lead box, people actually took your call and came in to buy. When you ran price-special ads, the public believed them and responded in droves. If you drop closed people, they went home and got friends so you could do it to them. It was legal to use almost any contract length and some of the chains were selling lifetime memberships. Cash was plentiful, competition was scarce, and every high-pressure sales gimmick you could think of worked.

It was also easier to find great salespeople in those days because they really had nowhere else to go. Computer stores, copier companies, phone stores, excessive retail options, companies selling phone systems, and the many other choices that a salesperson has today didn't yet exist. If a salesperson wanted to make big money working for serious commissions, he worked in a gym or sold real estate. Sales jobs existed, but the choices were mostly for the serious, career-driven folks, while the mid-level sales choices that clubs compete against today for their staff members weren't around in great numbers.

Hard-working salespeople were gods among the rabble and made fortunes that were unheard of even in other businesses. Regional sales guys drove Mercedes® and their more peasant-like employees, the club sales guys, only drove Cadillacs®. If you could sell, you had status, power, a chance for promotion, and a lot of cash in your gym bag. If you couldn't adjust to the tactics and pressure necessary to put your numbers up every day, then you were gone and the survivors gained even more status over time.

Jump ahead a few years and these same superstar salespeople owned clubs in the late 1990s and early into 2000 and beyond, and were getting their collective butts whipped in most every market they were in. This list includes the now middle-management players in the chains, who were superstuds when they worked in the clubs, and who started the long decline of their new companies.

When all you own is a hammer, everything you see is a nail. When all you know how to do is pressure sell and call prospects out of drop boxes, then no matter how the market changes, you still wield your big sales hammer.

The sales techniques no longer match the new consumer, the ads fail to draw enough to feed the sales efforts, and only guys living in their trucks put their names in a lead box. The reign of the super sales dog is over, but the legend and legacy continues today.

The legacy of the sales dog is still alive in the industry, as illustrated by the dream of many owners to find that team of superstars that can light up the sales numbers at the end of every day. But these guys don't exist very often anymore, and if you can find one of these guys, he is a lot more trouble than he is worth to your business.

> To secure your future, you must understand how to hire and train nontraditional salespeople who can competently get the job done without the associated hassles that go with the diva mentality.

Sales dogs and sales divas are the highest maintenance employees you could ever hire, especially in exchange for what they actually produce. To secure your future, you must understand how to hire and train nontraditional salespeople who can competently get the job done without the associated hassles that go with the diva mentality. Consider the following problems associated with having a super sales dog on your staff:

- He needs constant attention, because he is always unhappy about some commission, time slot, or marketing problem that is your fault— and unless you fix it he will leave.

- He won't follow the club's sales system because he has been successful in the past with his—and that is the way he is going to do it or he will leave.

- No matter where you get your new ideas, what you read, or how much training you provide to grow your system, he once had a boss that was legendary. Your guy learned directly from him and any other training is worthless because his guy invented sales in the club business—and if you don't leave him alone he will leave

- He will poison the rest of your staff, because no matter what you teach the team, the superstar will bad-mouth it or do it his own way—and if you correct him he will leave.

- Sales dogs can sell and close higher percentages than the rest of the team, but these numbers are false due to the pressure he has to apply to get the sale. Sales dogs have higher loss rates in their file, more first-payment defaults (the person just signed anything to escape and then won't pay), and more complaints from the guests—but if you say anything or point out the losses and try to get him to back off, he gets mad and threatens to leave.

- If you promote him to sales manager, he can't really teach because the techniques he wants to use, such as high-pressure drop closes, don't work anymore. He gets by because he has years of experience beating people senseless, but what he does can't, and shouldn't, be taught to your team. The sales dog manager is a poor leader and ends up just going club to club in your organization, jumping in to sell himself to prove how good he is, but no one is ever really trained—but if you try and help him develop an easier system to implement, he gets mad and threatens to leave.

- Owners constantly live under the pressure that if this guy leaves, the club will fail, because even though he is a pain in the butt he puts up numbers. You are now held hostage in your own business—but can't say anything because he will threaten to leave.

**Sales dogs can sell and close higher percentages than the rest of the team, but these numbers are false due to the pressure he has to apply to get the sale.**

Put the book down right now and go fire this guy. It will be the best thing that ever happened to you and your business. And yes, you can build a business that is not dependent on sales dogs and old divas left over from the 1980s. The easiest way to think about this issue is that you need to replace your stars with rocks. Stars shine for a while and then burn out. Rocks are forever. Hire rocks and forget about the stars.

Rocks are those strong secondary players that show up every day, are loyal to your business, and are coachable to new ideas. Rocks are those B players that you take for granted but are the strength behind any successful small business.

One of the many issues with the old sales dogs, the supposedly A players, is that the only way they became effective was that they had to learn to think. These guys were taught a variety of closes, sales techniques, and ways to handle objections that became polished over time. The more experience they received alongside a master sales dog that had been in every sales situation conceivable and who trained them, the more effective they became over time. Put in a few years talking to a 100 or so guests per month, coupled with the need to sell or get fired, and if you survived you became effective. Review the following lists and you can see where the system fails today:

Sales dog with five years of experience:

- 60 months x 100 guests average = 6000 learning situations
- 60 months x 10 hours of training per month = 600 hours of training

New hire with three months of experience:

- Three months x 50 guests = 150 sales encounters
- Three months x 10 hours of training = 30 hours of training

What do you teach the new guy? Do you teach him the old techniques that don't work for young salespeople anymore, but that the sales dog still uses and can get away with because of his experience? And if you start him down the sales dog road by teaching him how to think and apply each sales technique to every different sales encounter, what happens when he leaves you in a few months for a better job with a greater benefit package selling high-ticket items for more money than you can pay?

The answer is that you can't spend the time or money trying to buy or develop sales dogs. Many owners waste a lot of their time trying to find these guys in the market and when they do they become immediately frustrated because the sales dog introduces countless problems.

## You don't have to look like a salesperson to be a salesperson.

**Don't teach people to think. Instead, teach them to follow the steps of a sales system.**

Don't teach people to think. Instead, teach them to follow the steps of a sales system. Use nontraditional salespeople and limit their options. Systems and steps, defined as using set patterns and responses rather than thinking, allow you to build a more effective salesperson in a shorter period of time.

For example, when it comes to presenting the prices, a thinking sales dog would profile the prospect and then present the prices as he sees fit to get the most money he can out of the guy today. The sales dog is getting paid on the amount of cash he generates each day, so he has to learn to read people and apply the pricing system to the guest at hand. Again, how long would it take to get a new salesperson to this level? And if you did, what would happen if you lost him after a year or two of that type of training?

An owner using a set system would use a different approach. For example, the new salesperson would be taught to present the prices in a set manner that is exactly the same each time. This salesperson would be able to learn and master this system much more quickly because he only learns one thing: Present the prices this way during each encounter. Because he only has to master one method, he can become more efficient, and more confident, in a much shorter period of time, which will lead to more sales success.

The club owner still benefits, because while he may get less cash, he will probably get more overall memberships from a wider range of employees, leading to a higher receivable base. He is also less vulnerable to staff changes because he is teaching a system that can be ramped up with new employees faster than the old way of developing sales dogs.

Another question is begging to be asked: Why are most salespeople in clubs all across the country young, white males in their late 20s? And why do most of these guys dress so badly?

The answer to this question is probably pretty straightforward. The sales dog system is a very aggressive system that needs someone not afraid of pressuring and pushing a little on a client, and who better to do that job than a young guy in his late 20s? Guys in this category account for most of the car wrecks, bar fights, ski crashes, and other activities that lead to testosterone-driven behavior, making them prime candidates to sell memberships in an office using an in-your-face attitude.

When it comes to hiring salespeople, break the traditional hiring rules. Your staff should match the target demographics of your club. If you focus on the 30- to 50-year-old target market, for example, then the bulk of your employees should also be in that age range.

Remember, target market is defined as the population you are seeking for your business and usually makes up approximately 80 percent of your club's membership. You may have members outside your target market, but the core of your membership will come from this narrowly defined group. For example, your target market might be 24 to 40, 25 to 45, or 30 to 50. If you specialize in upscale adult fitness, 80 percent of your members might be in the 35- to 55-year-old range. In comparison, chain clubs often seek the 18- to 34-year-old market.

The key point is that likes attract likes, and it is a total disconnect when your guest is 50 years old and your salesperson is 22. This disconnect prevents the building of rapport, which is perhaps the strongest element of a successful sale. These two people really have nothing to talk about except the club and the sale. Their ages are too far apart for there to be a connection in most cases.

Most young male club owners would also benefit from hiring more women for their sales positions due to their communication skills and ability to

**When it comes to hiring salespeople, break the traditional hiring rules. Your staff should match the target demographics of your club.**

multitask. Women are better communicators at an earlier age, which allows them to build rapport with a wider range of people during the sales encounters.

Think of having two children: a boy who is 10 and a girl who is nine. The boy comes home from school and sits at the table eating a cookie. "How was school?" you ask. "Fine," is his reply. "Do anything fun?" you try again. "No," he grunts and out he goes.

Your daughter then comes home and sits at the table eating her cookie. "How was school?" you venture. "Well," she replies, "I sat next to Nikki today and we drew houses. Then during recess we talked to Bobby, but he wasn't any fun. Our teacher wore a red rose today because it was her birthday but we didn't sing any songs. For lunch we had hamburgers but I didn't eat mine because it was gross so I traded it to Sarah for her peanut butter. Then we..." And on and on and on.

Even as kids, women communicate and men merely grunt out replies. Life really doesn't change much after that pattern is established. Many young male owners aren't comfortable managing women as employees, especially if a woman is older, so they continue to make the same mistake of hiring other young males just like themselves. This pattern is changing as the industry attracts more businesspeople and the percentage of female owners increases over time, but many owners would do well to consciously make an effort to hire outside their comfort zone.

Diversity is also a plus when building a sales force. A diversified staff has diversified solutions, and if your target market is mixed, then you're staff should reflect the people in your market and in your gym. If your business is in a market that has a mixture of races, sexual orientations, and cultures, then you send a very negative message to your community if you are a white owner who hires nothing but other young, white people on your team. Build a team that reflects your market and your sales will improve.

### Build the B-team model for success.

> When you analyze a club that is struggling with sales, you almost always find a common denominator: The sales team has one "A" sales dog or diva and a set of secondary players who are struggling.

When you analyze a club that is struggling with sales, you almost always find a common denominator: The sales team has one "A" sales dog or diva and a set of secondary players who are struggling. The model looks like this as follows:

| A |
|---|
| B, B, B, B, B, B |

If you don't have a sales system in place, then you make the mistake of shopping for someone who has sales experience and who can bring a system with him from where he last worked. The problem is that this person is a damaged good who probably exhibits many of the traits mentioned earlier in this chapter.

For example, he will need constant attention as a sales dog, he will threaten to leave if you don't give him what he wants, he can put numbers on the board but his losses are high, he can't train others to do what he does, and he ruins the rest of the staff because he won't support any effort you make to implement a system. In other words, he might write a few deals, but over time it isn't worth the pain.

This type of system is also characterized by a high turnover rate among the lower staff. In addition, the owner feels held hostage by the A player and the club is constantly short of sales staff that can produce, since the owner is only looking for someone who has a lot of club experience in someone else's system. A more efficient model looks as follows:

---

**Owners and sales managers manage/teach/develop systems**

**A solid team of B performers follow systems and are developed by the manager**

**A foundation of basic sales skills and a repeatable system increases effectiveness**

---

B players are those solid citizens that work as a team, produce numbers because they have mastered the basics and the steps of the sale, and who help others on the team become successful. These staff members flourish under a set system because, if given direction and structure, they work well within that structure. Contrast these folks with A players, who work hard to negate your structure even though they aren't usually capable of building any type of system of their own, or the system they do use is out of date and impractical for today's consumers.

In this model, the owner builds solid teams based upon starting everyone with the same training in the basic sales skills. These skills include shaking hands, greeting the person, handing off the guest from the counter person to the salesperson, using consistent sales materials to support the team, and explaining the prices the same way each and every time. These skills are the same for everyone, are taught the same way to each person, and become more effective more quickly because your team is mastering steps rather than trying to learn a variety of responses to endless sales situations.

Once the new salespeople master the basics, they become solid sales performers. Because they are all doing the same thing during each sale, it makes the sales manager's job much easier since he is correcting deviations from the system rather than trying to correct each person's individual style and approach. In football, for example, it is easier to correct a team that fails to

> **B players are those solid citizens that work as a team, produce numbers because they have mastered the basics and the steps of the sale, and who help others on the team become successful.**

**How can you truly manage a guy who uses a system only he knows?**

execute a play well, and a guy who misses a block on that play, than it is to correct a team that makes up their own plays every time. How can you truly manage a guy who uses a system only he knows?

This system is characterized by low turnover because it is a much truer team that features a diversity of team members. In addition, it is much easier for the owner to replace people who leave because he is just plugging bodies into a system rather than trying to hire the system. In other words, it's the system that makes people effective, not individuals who dominate the system. It is also easier to develop sales managers when you use a system-driven team of B players, because most of the job entails following the steps and teaching the steps rather than creating individual superstars.

# Key Points From This Chapter

- Sales were easier in the days of less competition and unsophisticated consumers.

- What worked then in sales, such as draw boxes, doesn't work with today's potential members.

- The glory days of club sales in the 1980s and early 1990s developed a generation of super sales dogs that went on to manage or own other clubs.

- Their systems are based upon star players that gather a great deal of combat experience and training over the years.

- These type of sales dogs, or A players, are very disruptive to most clubs and leave the owners feeling that they are held hostage in their own businesses.

- Club owners who build systems based upon a solid team of B players from a diversified group will do better with sales in the future.

# Slow down and speak easy.

Perhaps the best sales tip of all time is to slow the process down. The more you sell, the faster you go, and the more experience you gain, the more shortcuts you pick up. These habits are bad for your sales numbers.

After you've heard a few hundred guests tell you about their fat spots, cheating spouses, addiction to cheesecake, and the terror they are experiencing at being in someone's wedding, you become tempted to start finishing sentences for the person because you have truly, by this point in your career, heard it all. Once you get to this point, you can save your job, and the club's sales numbers, by simply taking a breath, slowing down the pace, and asking the leading questions that will get the person to talk a little. Once you get him to talk, sit back and listen and your sales will start to increase again.

Perhaps the biggest mistake an experienced salesperson makes is not in his technique, but in his timing. You know the material and the pace picks up. This routine, however, leaves the guest out of the process and, unless he gets to tell his story or get involved in the process, no sale will be made.

# 14

# The Numbers Never Lie

One of the most powerful, and disconcerting, questions you can ask a new fitness business owner or manager is: What percentage of your decision-making process is emotional and reactionary and what percent is based upon cold, hard facts? Most owners who don't really think about their decision-making processes operate by what is called situational management, which means that the owner doesn't have any base knowledge or plan to compare the decision he needs to make against, so he simply reacts to the problem in front of him at the time. One of the many problems with this system is that the solution for a problem that reoccurs is often different each time, since the owner is making that decision based upon what is happening in the business that day, how he feels, and who is in front of him at the time.

Owners and managers who rely on situational management often contradict decisions they made in the past, because the circumstances might be different this time compared to the last time this problem came up. This type of management drives your staff insane because of the inconsistency and can also cost you members if they realize that you treat each member differently depending on personality rather than on what is good for your business.

Leading a sales force is a perfect example of where many owners rely upon pure emotional responses rather than use objective methods to set goals and drive the team. For example, during the month of March, a salesperson does 22 new memberships and the owner tells her that she did a great job this month. During April, she again does 22 sales, but this time the owner is not happy with her and chews her out for a poor performance. Because the owner works off a totally subjective method, meaning that sales are either good or bad depending on the month at hand, the staff members never really know if their performance is good or bad until the owner counts the money at the end of the month.

An owner might feel that he is a little more sophisticated in business because he sits down each month and sets goals for each team member and for the entire team. But where did that goal come from and what is it based on? One owner trying to change her ways was asked why she had a sales goal of 100 new memberships for the month, especially since the club had been averaging 75 for the previous six months. Her reply was that she wanted to buy a new car and needed the extra sales to raise the down payment.

The staff in this club is doomed to get frustrated and fail, because the owner is basing her numbers upon arbitrary figures rather than setting goals and direction based upon actual performance of the business and reasonable potential sales. In this case, the owner didn't know how to project sales, sales income, or the total deposit because she was basing her numbers upon need and emotion rather than the performance of the business.

Problem solving also becomes an issue for managers who rely on emotional responses versus having any type of set system to work against. How does a manager solve the problem of low sales, for example, if he doesn't know how many true leads came through the club last month, what the team's closing percentage was, and what the individual closing rates were for each salesperson? More importantly, what if he doesn't have any standard against which to compare the numbers he does have available?

### You'll make better decisions, and more money, running your club off the numbers.

It's all in the numbers and the numbers don't lie. Master the numbers and you will know everything you need to run a better business. Understanding the numbers will tell you where to focus your training, your strengths and weaknesses, and whether the components of your business are working or need to be dropped.

Mastering the sales numbers will tell you how effective your team is and how effective the individuals on that team are. Getting control of the sales numbers will also give you the information you need to project reasonable numbers related to the current and past performance of your business.

Most importantly, gaining an understanding of the numbers will help you run a proactive business, rather than depend upon situational management. Projecting numbers for the coming month, and then building a plan to hit those numbers, is far more effective than waiting until the end of the month arrives to see what happened.

Far too many owners simply wait until the end of the month, hoping that the numbers will come together and that they will make a little profit. One of the most important things you can learn as a serious owner or manager is that *hope is not a business plan*. Put another way, you can get what you want or

> Master the numbers and you will know everything you need to run a better business. Understanding the numbers will tell you where to focus your training.

you can take what you get. Efficient owners who want to be financially successful are the ones that learn to make the numbers work for them.

# Lead Tracking

The most basic sales number to start with is how many actual leads you have coming through your door each month. Leads are defined as "butts in seats," or put another way, qualified buyers in front of a salesperson.

Even successful owners with experience often lose track of this number over time. You're hitting your sales goal and the club is running fine, so you lose a little incentive to stay on top of this number. It's easy to get sloppy, but even if you've been in business for a long period of time, sales leads are perhaps the most important number to track in your business.

A difference exists between total leads and qualified leads. Total leads vary from club to club and are dependent upon circumstances such as the number of tourists you might get in the summer, the number of hotels in your immediate market, and the number of professional businesses near your club that might have a lot of folks that pass through for a short period of time. In each of these examples, you might have a lot of total leads, but a much smaller number of qualified leads.

Also keep in mind that the goal of this sales system is to generate annual memberships rather than a lot of short-term memberships such as daily drop-ins or three-month options. Section 3 of this book details some basic pricing, and all of the books I have written for Healthy Learning have chapters that deal with building an effective price structure.

Another goal to keep in mind is that you want to sell annual memberships, since the long-term goal for any fitness facility is to build up a large receivable base that provides strong monthly cash flow from the member payments, as well as building a source of income that can be projected into the future. Short-term membership options don't accomplish this goal because they usually represent short-term cash compared to long-term income that arrives over time. For example, a club might sell a lot of three-month memberships and even one-month options, but not be strong at selling the members longer options such as the annual membership.

Such a club enjoys added cash flow each month from these shorter options, but remains vulnerable to competition or a decrease in traffic because it hasn't developed a stable cash flow from its combined monthly payments. The scenario a club owner should hope to achieve is reaching the point where his net membership payments each month, after collection expenses and losses, cover 70 percent of what it costs him to run his business. Consider the following example:

> The most basic sales number to start with is how many actual leads you have coming through your door each month.

### The club has an operating cost of $70,000 per month.

### The club's target net collected from all member payments each month should be: 70 percent of $70,000, or $49,000.

This number doesn't include any paid-in-full memberships or other short-term membership options. The $49,000 should represent only member payments made each month based upon some type of obligation, such as annual memberships. It is important to remember that no receivable base exists without some type of obligation. You might have cash flow from open-ended memberships—where everyone is just month-to-month—but this income could end in just 30 days because no contractual obligation exists to help you project income into the future.

## Who is a qualified lead?

Four factors
determine who is a
qualified lead.

Four factors determine who is a qualified lead. The team needs to track all leads from all sources each day, however, because if left to their own devices, a weak sales team will start reporting way more tourists or nonqualified leads to make their numbers look better than they really are. If a salesperson isn't closing well, then it is easy for him to simply tell the owner that a few more of his leads weren't really qualified, which makes his sales closing numbers look better than they really are. The four determining factors are as follows.

*Age.* You should have a minimum age that fits your target market. For example, if you own an upscale adult facility, then you would want the minimum age of your members to be 21. If you are a family club, then you would have an age requirement of 18, which is also the minimum age at which someone can enter into a contract on his own. Some clubs might also benefit from having a minimum age of 23 years old, especially if it is an upscale club in a college town and uses the trial membership. You wouldn't want to open up a trial membership to the entire student population. You set the age, but you should set one that builds more value into the trial membership.

*Local area.* If you offer a trial, then you only want to offer it to potential members who live in your market area. Verify this fact by asking for a valid local ID, such as a driver's license, at the time you set up the trial membership. When you ask for a driver's license, you are eliminating the need to offer the trial to people who should instead pay for short-term memberships, such as an engineer who is only in town for several weeks or someone who is visiting the area on vacation.

*Qualified to buy.* If you offer the trial, then you must make sure the person is qualified to buy at the end of that trial period. Many club owners balk at asking the guest to present a credit card, but keep in mind that you are offering the hospitality of the club free for 14 days in exchange for the person having an opportunity to experience the club and service before making a buying decision. You don't have to make a copy of the credit card or even touch it, but you should have the guest at least show it to make sure he is a real person who is able to buy at the end of the trial.

*May be used once a year.* If you offer a trial, then make it available to each person once a year. Maybe the person had a sick child, or maybe he had something come up at his job. that prevented him from trying the club during the trial. Always assume the best and let every person have a trial membership once a year.

If you don't offer trial memberships, then you can still use the first three points. An age restriction should be in place at every club, a person has to live in your market area to really be considered a qualified buyer, and if you offer any type of workout up front for free, then the person should present proof that he can buy later.

## Don't discriminate.

If you use any type of qualification system, then keep it consistent and make sure your rules are applied to each and every potential guest who comes through the door. Your sales staff can get lazy and feel the need to only apply the rules to those who they think need them. In other words, "I like the way this person looks, but I don't like the way that person looks." This discrimination, besides being bad business, is just plain bad living. Make sure your staff applies all rules equally to all races, colors, and orientations without exception.

# Use an Inquiry Sheet to Track Leads

Inquiry sheets are simple tools that your team can use to record each lead through the door, as well as to guide your staff's questions during every phone call or visit to the club. The best way to think about it is that every phone lead or actual visit to the club has to have a matching inquiry sheet at the end of the day.

An important point to remember is that your potential members are making a discretionary choice about a discretionary purchase. In other words, while a club membership is desirable in their lives, it is also something that they don't absolutely need to survive. They all need a place to live, food to eat, and perhaps a car to drive, but they do not have to have a membership at a fitness facility to survive in their world.

Keeping this thought in mind, look at the many barriers you create that work against turning a guest into a member. Clubs often use salespeople that are too young to communicate effectively with their target market. They force electronic funds transfers, rather than giving the person reasonable payment options. And they still use two-year and longer memberships in the southern

**Inquiry sheets are simple tools that your team can use to record each lead through the door, as well as to guide your staff's questions during every phone call or visit to the club.**

part of the country as the primary membership tools. Each of these barriers makes it harder for the salesperson to do his job and get the person into the system. Your goal should be to eliminate as many barriers as possible so the guest has fewer hurdles to overcome on his way to becoming a new member.

For example, how much information should the guest provide the club before he meets with a salesperson and tours the club? Several of the chains still ask the guest to fill out lengthy guest sheets detailing everything from medical conditions to current health habits. Some of these guest-participation sheets are actually several pages long and set up an adversarial relationship between the club and the guest before he even really gets started. "Hey, I just wanted to see your club. I really didn't want to apply for a bank loan or anything."

Scarier yet are the clubs that require the guest to fill out a liability waiver before touring the club. If the guest is going to work out, then he needs to fill out a liability waiver before he begins, but how dangerous does your club seem to a nervous guest when you ask him to fill out a waiver just to tour. "Yes, our club is so dangerous that you have to fill out a full liability waiver just for me to show it to you. If you think this is bad, you should see what you have to fill out when you actually join. Why, we had four members killed in here just last week, so you better believe that you have to sign all your rights away before you ever get in this place."

The rule is that you don't need the guest to fill out anything before he sees the club. It should be the salesperson's job, if done correctly and geared toward building a relationship, to gather information about your prospective member during the initial few minutes with the guest and not put the burden on him to fill out unnecessary and threatening forms.

## How to use inquiry sheets correctly

The inquiry sheet, or guest profile, is a tool to help keep the salesperson focused on the person in front of him at the time. If the guest fills out the sheet, the salesperson will often get in a rut and drop into old sales routines that are geared more toward presenting the stuff in the club rather than helping the guest get what he really wants from using this particular fitness facility.

If your salesperson fills out the slip as he goes along, he is more apt to stay focused on the client and the act of asking questions about who the person is, what he wants from a fitness program, and what kind of workout he is doing now. All of these questions help to develop that elusive relationship between a client and salesperson (Figure 14-1).

As a side note, it is recommended that you do away with sales offices. Taking someone into an office is intimidating, inefficient, and so 1960s. Today's more sophisticated consumer understands that an office is where the close is

> It should be the salesperson's job, if done correctly and geared toward building a relationship, to gather information about your prospective member during the initial few minutes with the guest and not put the burden on him to fill out unnecessary and threatening forms.

going to take place, and most consumers have that used-car-guy fear of offices that negates any possible good that could come from using one.

A good alternative to an old-style office is an information table. This table should be a high-top café table rather than a low table. When you sit with friends at a high table, most people lean in and put their arms on the table, which makes for a more intimate atmosphere. Low tables do just the opposite, in that most folks kick back in the chairs with their legs out in front of them and lean away from the conversation.

These tables are easy to work into the sales process. When someone comes to the club for information, the salesperson would spend a few minutes chatting up front and then let the person know that he has a lot more to show him if he would just like to step over to the club's information table for a few minutes.

This table should be near the sports bar/juice bar or on the edge of the workout floor. If you have a small pocket club, meaning 1500 square feet or so, this table will also work for you since you are in the intimate service business.

If you can't break the office habit, then try taking off the office door and replacing the desk with a round table. Round tables break the adversarial nature that comes from sitting across a desk from someone and also put your guest in a much less threatening mental position. Remember that you are much more likely to make that guest a member if he is relaxed and feeling good about the experience, as opposed to being closed up and nervous with his surroundings.

> **Round tables break the adversarial nature that comes from sitting across a desk from someone and also put your guest in a much less threatening mental position.**

The sample guest profile sheet shown in Figure 14-1 was designed as a front-and-back model. The questions don't have to be asked in the order listed. This form should merely serve as a reference to keep your staff focused on asking about the guest rather than spending all of the tour talking about all the cool toys that the club has to offer. Modify this form as you see fit for your club, but keep it classy by using quality paper and by printing out new sheets as needed rather than just running off a bunch of poor-quality copies.

## Simple rules for using the inquiry sheets

- The inquiry sheets are kept on the sales information table. Every guest that visits the club, whether qualified or not, should have a matching sheet at the end of the day.

- The salesperson fills out the slip. Once you get experience, you can probably ask the questions from memory and write the answers out on the sheet after the person has left the club. Do not let the guest fill out these sheets.

**Guest Profile**

Today's date _____    Date recorded by manager _____

Did the person:   ❏ Visit the club   or    ❏ Phone

**Guest's or inquiry's name:** _____

Have you heard about our trial membership? _____

Before we get started, may I offer you a gift from the club? _____

How did you hear about us? _____

Do you know any of our members? If so, who? _____

Have you ever been in the club before? _____

Do you work or live near the gym? _____

What type of workout are you doing now? _____

_____

**How would you classify yourself as an exerciser?**

**❏ I currently work out.**

What are you doing? _____

How long? _____

How many days a week? _____

How is it working? _____

What are you looking for that your current program doesn't provide? _____

_____

**❏ I used to work out.**

What did you do at that time? _____

Were you consistent? _____

How did it work? _____

Why did you stop? _____

How are you feeling since you stopped? _____

How long have you been thinking about getting back to a regular program?

What's kept you from getting back in the past? _____

Is that still a problem? _____

**❏ I don't work out.**

What has gotten you interested in working out? _____

How do you feel about your health and condition? _____

What was the best you ever felt? _____

What was different at that time? _____

How long have you been thinking about getting into a fitness program? __

_____

What's kept you from getting started in the past? _____

Is that still a problem? _____

_____

Figure 14-1. Inquiry sheet/guest profile

**We've found over the years people that who want to join a gym and begin a regular exercise program usually fall into one of three categories. Which one of these is your primary goal?**

❏ Improve your appearance

❏ Improve your health

❏ Improve things in your life, such as energy level, or reduce stress

**Keeping this goal in mind, what is the single most important thing you want to get out of a gym membership?**_____

_____

_____

**What are some other things you would like to accomplish with us?**

How would you like to change your body? _____

_____

Is your weight something you are concerned about? _____

What's the timeframe you've set for your fitness program? _____

On a scale of 1 to 10, how important is it for you to reach your personal fitness objective? _____

Is that enough to get you started and keep you coming to the gym on a regular basis? _____

**Now that I have a little information about you and what you're looking for in an exercise program, may I show you the club?**

Profile notes so we can best help our guest: _____

_____

**Most of our guests or phone inquiries want to know more about what we do here. May we have your email address so that we can send you ongoing information about the club as well as our electronic newsletter?**

Email address: _____

To thank you for taking the time to visit the club, we'd like to send you a gift. May we have your address? _____

_____

_____

What is the best phone number with which to reach you?_____

_____

Office use only:

Club representative _____

New member _____

Trial member _____

- You should also keep inquiry sheets near the phone at the main desk. Every incoming phone call to the club that is seeking membership information should have a matching sheet at the end of the day. These sheets help keep your team focused and guide them to ask the right questions despite how tired or busy they might be when that phone rings.

- Phone calls are extremely important to a club's business plan. If you spend a bunch of money each month on marketing, you obviously want the phone to ring. Your young staff, however, sometimes forgets or confuses the importance of that phone ringing with inquiries, especially when they are busy doing something else at the moment. This confusion often results in a dropped or poorly handled call that might have been very valuable to the club. Therefore, it is worth your time as a manager or owner to run several test (fake) calls a week through your front desk to make sure you are actually getting all your information calls and that each call is being handled properly.

- At the end of the day, all inquiry sheets are sent to the sales manager's office. In Chapter 21, exact procedures are detailed regarding how to do it and who is responsible for each step. The sales manager is responsible for keeping each sheet/prospect moving through the system. A simple, low-tech way to track these sheets is to have your sales manager keep them in a three-ring notebook for the month you are operating in at the time. Sometimes low-tech is still the best, especially if you are new and haven't built your first system yet.

## The 10 percent rule

One thing that every owner should come to realize is that your staff really never sees all the potential business in a club. "How was business Sunday morning Joey?" you ask. "Not much happening boss, just a couple of guys looking around who walked in from the coffee shop." Were these two guys randomly looking around or were two valid prospects really in the business and Joey was too busy hitting on the member of the hour to really take the time to tour them properly? This question also assumes that Joey actually tells you about these guys, something rare for the fabled "Sunday morning guy."

The 10 percent rule states that you add another 10 percent to your total inquiries for the month to determine how much real business came through the club. You have to assume, unless you were in the club yourself every hour it was open, that the staff just didn't see or report—or actually hid—the real amount of traffic you had through the club that month.

For example, if your inquiry sheets add up to 100 qualified leads through the door, add another 10 people to your total before you calculate closing percentages. More traffic exists than you realize in a business and certainly more traffic exists than your staff will actually report to you.

> One thing that every owner should come to realize is that your staff really never sees all the potential business in a club.

# Closing Percentages

Once you have accurate totals regarding the number of daily, weekly, and monthly guests, you can use this information to calculate closing percentages for your team. Closing percentages at first seem to be nothing more than a simple way to determine how effective someone is at getting his job done, but tracking closing percentages can actually give you much more information about how your business is performing and what you might need to fix.

For example, a low closing percentage might be a sign of poor sales training, a dirty club, lousy guest service at the front counter, or poor-quality leads generated by your marketing. By tracking leads correctly, an owner or manager can take the closing information about her team or individual salespeople and work backward to identify a host of problems that might be affecting her business.

The first step is to immediately start gathering inquiry sheets. You can't determine how many prospects you closed if you can't determine how many you talked to in any given time period.

Once you have a system in place to track all leads, you should begin to track individual closing rates for each salesperson daily, weekly, and monthly. You should also begin to track team totals for those same time periods.

## How good is good, and how good do you have to be?

The national average for closing sales is 38 percent, which means that a typical club converts 38 percent of its guests to an annual membership each month. Your goal is to convert a minimum of 55 percent of all qualified traffic to annual memberships over a monthly period. You track the total average over a full month because of the trial memberships, and you should use a gross average to track all sales, since a person may visit the club at the end of the month and then sign up during the next month, especially if you are offering trial memberships. Don't make things more difficult by trying to back a member into the month during which he first visited. Just use the new sale as a sales number during the month when he actually became a member and it will all average out over time.

The difference between the 38 percent a typical club does and the 55 percent a good club can do is the financial difference between breaking even and being very successful over time. The ability to close a minimum of 55 percent comes from:

- More and consistent sales training
- Better support materials
- Better tracking and follow-up
- An individualized sales tour

> Once you have a system in place to track all leads, you should begin to track individual closing rates for each salesperson daily, weekly, and monthly.

What happens if two clubs spend the same each month on marketing, but one of the clubs closes 38 percent of its qualified guests and the other closes 55 percent of its qualified traffic? Consider the following scenarios:

- Club Puppy and Club Big Dog both spend $5000 per month on marketing.
- Both clubs generate 150 leads per month from all sources.
- Club Puppy converts 38 percent of its guests to annual memberships each month.
- Club Big Dog converts 55 percent of its guests to annual memberships each month.
- Both clubs charge $59 down and $49 per month per member on an annual membership.
- Club Puppy—150 leads x 0.38 = 57 members per month
- Club Big Dog—150 leads x 0.55 = 82 members per month
- Club Big Dog has a 25-member edge each month

**The difference between the 38 percent a typical club does and the 55 percent a good club can do is the financial difference between breaking even and being very successful over time.**

Club Big Dog would have the following advantages per month and per year:

- 25 new sales per month = 300 more members per year
- 25 sales x $59 member fee = $1475 per month in new sales cash advantage monthly
- 300 new sales x $59 = $17,700 total new sales cash advantage annually
- $14,700 (300 x $49) per month difference in total member payments at the end of the first year
- $1225 per month difference added to the receivable base each month and compounding each month
- 300 more members in the system to use the club's profit centers and to refer friends and guests

Club Big Dog really doesn't have to be that much better to dominate its competitor. In this case, a mere 17-point difference in the closing percentage leads to a $14,700-per-month cash-flow advantage in the receivable base and another $1475 per month in immediate cash flow from new sales cash. Over time, Club Big Dog will simply run the competition into the ground with that much of a competitive edge and it all comes from the ability to close a reasonable number of new sales each month compared to the traffic each club has coming through the door.

## Closing on the first visit

So far, this section has covered overall closing percentages. The next step is to determine how many of your new sales should come from first-visit closes.

Closing on the first visit has been a status symbol for sales teams in the fitness business for years. One guy can close 60 percent on the first visit, this guy can close 80 percent, and that guy at the bar yells that he once closed 90 percent of all the people he talked to at this gym during their first visits. The sad thing is that some of these guys might have an unusually high closing percentage, but this personal success is often bad for the club owner's business over time.

Many salespeople get really good at slamming the client during the first visit, which means that they becomes competent at applying enough pressure to get someone to sign a contract even if that person still has doubts or concerns. This pressure, and this sale, then backfires on the club because many of these guests just sign anything to get out of the office and away from the salesperson. The salesperson is walking around the club talking about another great sales presentation and how he overcame a stream of objections, while the person who was coerced into signing something is now badmouthing the club to everyone who will listen and will punish the club by not making the first payment (called a first-payment default).

What are the chances you will get a referral from a person who was beaten senseless in a high-pressure sales encounter? How good does the person feel about what he just bought? And what type of buyer's regret will he show once he has time to think about how badly he was treated by a brutal sales terrorist?

The following very simple rule is key in the fitness business: The higher the pressure during the first visit, the worse the membership paper will be during the collection process. All those membership contracts that look so good going into the pile look a lot worse later when it becomes hard for the club owner to get his money. "Treat me wrong and I will punish you," is the thought process that many members who were pressured heavily carry with them daily.

The following rule also applies and is hard to overcome by applying extreme pressure during the first visit:

**Seventy percent of your guests need two or more visits to the club before they will buy if your monthly rate is $39 or higher.**

This rule is good to review in this context. If you remember from Chapter 13, this rule is the reason why you should use trial memberships to increase your overall sales.

When someone is shopping for a big-ticket item, defined as something priced at $500 or more, he will usually not buy it impulsively. The person might

**The following very simple rule is key in the fitness business: The higher the pressure during the first visit, the worse the membership paper will be during the collection process.**

shop a few stores, look online, and maybe discuss the purchase with his significant other. The only exception is probably golf clubs, when the guy buys a $500 driver and then puts the old cover on it and sticks it in the bag thinking he is hiding it from his wife. Then again, how many clubs did he try before buying that particular driver?

Salespeople often make the mistake of thinking that the membership is only $39 per month, but the guest is thinking about the $39 per month, plus the membership fee, meaning that he is now spending more than $500 and hasn't even bought new shoes and a gym bag yet. In his mind it is a major purchase, but salespeople attempt to sell it, and force it down his throat, as if it were a Diet Coke® and a munchie bar.

Somewhere in this process is a compromise between old-style sales dogs that want to beat guests into submission and a system that allows the club owner to close a reasonable amount of new business during the guests' first visit to the club. This compromise is 30 percent. Of the total sales closed for the month, your sales team should close a minimum of 30 percent of them during the guest's first visit to the club. Consider the following numbers, which tie together everything discussed so far in this chapter:

- 100 qualified guests come to the club

- 55 new annual memberships are sold (the club's sales team closes 55 percent of all qualified leads)

- 16 or 17 out of the 55 new sales are closed during the first visit (55 x 0.30 = 16.5)

In other words, this club writes approximately 16 new memberships out of the 55 total annual memberships for the month during the first visit. Keep in mind that 30 percent is the minimum acceptable number, but if someone on your team starts closing more than 50 percent of his guests during the first visit it is time to look for pressure tactics and first-visit defaults in his file.

# Projecting Revenue

**Projecting revenue and sales numbers should not be an arbitrary process.**

Projecting revenue and sales numbers should not be an arbitrary process. Arbitrary in this sense means that you make a wild guess or simply make up nonsense to show the staff that you have at least some idea of a target in mind. The problem with this technique is that you are either setting wildly high numbers that have no basis in reality and totally demoralize the staff, or you just base your numbers on trying to hit what you did last year, which artificially keeps your potential down and your numbers lower than they probably should be.

Learning to project numbers within a system that both drives revenue in your business and motivates staff is both a science and an art form. It is also one of the most important skills an owner should develop, because the ability to project revenue and sales is important for building business plans for yourself or a pro forma for your banker. If you want to be accurate with your projections, follow these basic rules:

- All projections are done during the last week of the month for the coming month. The samples presented in this section are for projecting the overall revenue for the club and your sales numbers for the coming month. Looking at both examples will give you an idea of how the overall system of projections works.

- Every dollar you project, and every sale you anticipate, has to be assigned to a team or department and then broken down to the individual level. No one on your staff should be allowed to work without an idea of what is expected of him for the coming month.

- Track your numbers daily and try to fix problems the day you aren't hitting your numbers. For example, if you are projecting three sales per day, then by the day 10 of the month you should be at 30 sales. If you are on track on day 9 but fall behind on day 10, then take action that day to catch up and do not, under any circumstances, wait until the end of the month to see if you can catch up. Remember, hope is not a business plan and you will only make money by taking action.

**No one on your staff should be allowed to work without an idea of what is expected of him for the coming month.**

## Start by projecting your target deposit.

Familiarize yourself with these key terms and then follow through the example. Using these numbers may seem strange at first, but a little practice over just one month will make them easy to calculate as a routine part of your business.

### Target deposit

The target deposit is the total amount of money—from all sources—that the club wants to deposit during a given month. The most common sources are as follows:

- Money from the sales department generated from new sales—This category includes down payments on memberships, paid-in-full memberships, short-term membership money, daily drop-in fees, and other funds from someone new joining the club. This entry does not include money from renewals, which is counted in the profit center area. Only count the actual money received and not future money that is expected.

- Money from the club's receivable base—This money is commonly referred to as the club's draft or EFT. This category includes the monthly income from the total of all member payments. This money is usually collected by a third-party financial-service company and then forwarded to the club, minus the collection fees. Only project portion that the club will actually receive and not the gross amount to be collected, since that amount will still have to be adjusted for collection fees.

- Money collected that is recurring—This money is collected each month through the club's profit centers, and also includes money from renewals.

- Additional revenue sources—This category includes items such as rent that add to the total amount of money that the club wants to target for the month. It is the owner's decision whether he wants to add this money to the target deposit or count it as separate income. Either method is correct, as long as you stay consistent.

*The net receivable check*

This income is usually the club's most consistent source of monthly revenue. The projected net receivable check can be calculated each month by averaging the last three net checks the club has received from whoever is handling the collection of the member payments. One of the most important decisions you can make is to let a strong third-party financial-service company handle the servicing and collection of your member payments. For example, a club's last three net checks after collection expenses have been:

- $39,000
- $42,000
- $43,000

Based on this example, the club has collected a total of $124,000 over the past three months ($39,000 + $42,000 + $43,000). The projected average for the coming month is $41,333 ($124,000/3). The club would use this number ($41,333) as the projected net receivable amount for the coming month. Once you calculate the projected receivable base, you can subtract it from the projected total deposit to determine your daily cash needs through the register.

### Target deposit (TD) – Projected receivable base (Rec) = Daily cash needs

For example, if the club was projecting a target deposit of $85,600 (as shown in the next example), and had a projected net receivable check of $41,333, then the club would need a specific amount of cash through the register from other sources, such as new membership sales money and profit center income, to meet its goal.

$$\$85,600 - \$41,333 = \$44,267$$

Divide this number by the number of days in the month (30 in this case) and you have the daily cash needs for your business. An easy way to think about the daily cash needs of your business is to remember that your

> The projected net receivable check can be calculated each month by averaging the last three net checks the club has received from whoever is handling the collection of the member payments.

membership money, in the form of the club's receivable base income, comes almost automatically through the sales process and that you are concentrating on money that has to be made each day from other sources, such as getting the most out of the club's profit centers.

$$\$44,267/30 = \$1475$$

This club owner has to generate $1475 a day on average through the register to meet the club's overall target deposit.

# Project Future Income

If you want to run a financially successful business, you must learn to project future income. Effective businesses set a target number that the team wants to hit before the month begins and then the owner or manager writes a plan for the coming month regarding how that number will be achieved. The best businesses project every dollar and then assign each dollar to an individual or team. That individual or team is then responsible for hitting the target share of the total projected target deposit.

**If you want to run a financially successful business, you must learn to project future income.**

An owner or manager can use several methods to project income. The most effective method is combining the historical prospective with a trend line analysis. This method is easier to use then it sounds. With a little experience, you will only need a few minutes each month to calculate these numbers.

## History

History is the comparison of the coming month with the same month during the previous year. For example, suppose a business had a total deposit of $80,000 during July of last year. A historical comparison would look at that month and build a projection for July of this year based on some type of relationship between the $80,000 the club brought in last July with what it is hoping to accomplish this July.

The weakness to this method is that a historical prospective is usually the least effective way to project future income. For example, in July of this year you might have an extra Monday, several new profit centers that you didn't have last year, and a new staff person who is more effective than the person you had last year. All of these factors make a difference in how the business might perform this year.

Historical prospective is a good reference point, but if used alone it is not an effective way to project how the business will do this year, and used incorrectly will actually pull your revenue potential downward. Owners stuck in the historical rut simply are happy beating last year's numbers, but if the market or the club has changed, then just beating a fixed number will lower your expectations and not really take into account the potential of your business at this point in time.

**Trend line**

Trend line looks at how the business is performing overall at the current point in time. This method compares the percentage difference in performance between the current time period and the same time period during the previous year. This method is more effective because it is based on the percentage of change over time rather than a single fixed point in time.

For example, a club owner wants to project the total deposit for the month of July this year. Using the trend line method, he first uses a historical perspective to compare the preceding three months of this year (the three months before the target month; in this case April, May, and June) against the same three months of the previous year.

The numbers from last year:

- July—$80,000
- June—$82,000
- May—$86,000
- April—$87,000

The numbers from this year:

- July—to be projected
- June—$84,000
- May—$92,000
- April—$98,000

Projecting the trend line requires that you compare the percentage of change for each month and then the average of the three months. Use the following formulas to calculate the percentage of change:

**This year − Last year = Difference**

**then**

**Difference/Last year = Percentage of change**

For example, use the June numbers from the previous lists:

**$84,000 − $82,000 = $2000**

**$2000/$82,000 = .025**

In other words, the club deposited $2000 more this June compared to June of last year, which is a 2.5 percent increase. Next, calculate the trend line using the numbers in the previous lists:

An owner or manager can use several methods to project income. The most effective method is combining the historical prospective with a trend line analysis.

|        | Last year | This year | % of change |
|--------|-----------|-----------|-------------|
| June   | $82,000   | $84,000   | 2.5         |
| May    | $86,000   | $92,000   | 7           |
| April  | $87,000   | $98,000   | 12          |

$$2.5 + 7 + 12 = 21.5$$

$$21.5/3 = 7.1 \text{ percent}$$

This club is averaging a 7 percent monthly increase in total deposits compared to the previous year. This average is the club's trend line for this year.

## How to use this information

Once you determine the trend line, you can then calculate your target projection for July of this year. July of last year saw $80,000 in total deposit from all sources. The projection for July of this year is as follows (using the 7 percent determined earlier):

$$\$80,000 \times 0.07 \ (7\%) = \$5600$$

$$\$80,000 + \$5600 = \$85,600 \text{ for July of this year}$$

Another way to look at this formula is that the club has been averaging 7 percent better over the same months from the previous year, which means that the club should be able to maintain that percentage (trend) in the coming month. In this calculation, you looked at July of last year (historical perspective) and applied the trend line (in this example, 7 percent). The total deposit from last July ($80,000) should increase by 7 percent, which is the club's trend in performance.

## Use the same system to project sales.

This same method will work to help you project sales on a monthly, and even annual, basis, as demonstrated by the following example. The goal is this case is to project total sales for the month of July this year:

Annual membership sales last year:

- July—46
- June—55
- May—59
- April—70

Annual membership sales this year:

- July—to be projected
- June—46

During your first year of business, it is recommended that you use a 3 to 5 percent increase in your numbers over the preceding month for your increase in revenue.

- May—62
- April—78

Comparison trend line:

|        | Last year | This year | % of change |
|--------|-----------|-----------|-------------|
| June   | 46        | 46        | 0           |
| May    | 55        | 62        | 12          |
| April  | 70        | 78        | 11          |

$$0 + 12 + 11 = 23$$

$$23/3 = 7.6 \text{ percent}$$

This club is beating the previous year's sales number by an average of 7.6 percent. In other words, this club's trend line is a 7.6 percent increase and the club is capable of beating last year's numbers by at least this amount.

This formula also could be used to project by department or even calculate an individual's performance. If you have history and you have a comparison, then you have the ability to do the projection.

As a side note, if you are a start-up business, you obviously won't have history until the end of the first year. During your first year of business, it is recommended that you use a 3 to 5 percent increase in your numbers over the preceding month for your increase in revenue. This number won't, however, work for sales, since you might have strong opening and then settle into a more normal sales routine. To get the most out of projecting at this stage of your business, adjust the numbers on your business plan against the actual numbers you are generating and then make your adjustments on the pattern. Always keep in mind the 1 per $1000 rule as the base number that you have to hit to keep the business growing.

## Other Numbers to Track

A few other numbers should be tracked the help make up the basis for a daily production report. The Thomas Plummer Company offers these reports in a kit form that helps owners focus on the key numbers that everyone managing a fitness business should look at each day.

**Everyone managing a fitness business should look at certain numbers each day.**

If you are building your own reporting system, include these numbers on your list. Each category that should be tracked is included along with a definition. A daily sales income projection system is also included at the end of this section.

You need to know the following terms to get the most out of sales management and tracking. These terms/numbers should also be part of your daily sales report:

- *Prospective members (first-time visitors to the club)*—Record new *potential* business for the day. The entries in this category are potential members who are visiting the club for the first time and seeking information about membership.

- *Prospective members (recurring prospects from trial memberships)*— This category pertains to clubs using some sort of trial system where the potential member may visit the club several times before deciding to buy. Please note that the potential member would be recorded as a *prospective member (first-time visitor to the club)* during his first visit and then recorded as a *prospective members (recurring prospect from trial memberships)* during each visit after the first.

As a side note, first-time visitors constitute the club's potential memberships for the month, while recurring visits constitute the number of chances the club had at signing memberships during the month. For example, during one month a club using a 14-day trial membership may record 80 first-time guests to the club, and those 80 potential members may visit the club a total of 232 times, which would be recorded in the recurring prospects category.

**First-time visitors constitute the club's potential memberships for the month, while recurring visits constitute the number of chances the club had at signing memberships during the month.**

You should also track your sales data according to these subgroups:

- *Today*—Record the day's business, or what happened yesterday through the close of business last night, if you are doing your reporting first thing in the morning.

- *Month-to-date*—Record the running total of business this month. Simply add today's business numbers from the category you are working with to the total of all the previous days that month.

- *Annual contracts*—Record new annual monthly-paying memberships that the club sold that day. Remember that the 1 per $1000 rule is based upon annual memberships, as are the closing percentages.

- *Annual PIF (paid-in-full)*—Record the paid-in-full annual memberships that the club sold for the day. They might be paid for with a credit card, check, or even cash. If a club is balanced correctly and is trying to build a receivable base, then members who elect to pay monthly should reflect 90 percent of all sales. The Plummer 90/10 Rule states that out of every 100 new memberships sold, 90 should choose to pay monthly and 10 percent or fewer should choose to pay in full. If your paid-in-full number is higher than 10 percent, your cash price, and overall price, might be too cheap for the market if it is so easy to pay for the membership all at once.

- *Month-to-month*—These memberships are pay-as-you-go or noncontractual memberships that the club sold that day.

- *Short-term*—These memberships are shorter than 12-months/annuals. These memberships are usually three months in length, but may reflect other options depending on the club's pricing structure. This entry would reflect how many short-term memberships the club sold that day.

- *Renewals*—These memberships, usually annuals, are from people who have already been a member once before in the club. Former members who have been gone for a while and who return and buy a new membership can be counted either as renewals or new members, as long as the club stays consistent in its counting and logging procedures for this category. This entry records how many renewals the club has done that day.

- *Membership fees*—Record all money taken in as down payments for annual memberships that day. For example, the club might sell a membership for $59 down (membership fee) and $49 a month for 12 months (monthly dues or monthly payment). This club would collect the $59 fee today, which is recorded as a membership fee, and the member would start paying the $49 per month the following month. If your club collects the membership fee and the first-month dues at the point of sale, then you would enter that total ($59 + $49) today in your tracking system.

- *Daily workout fees*—This line is used to record any monies collected that day for daily or one-day workouts. This line is also called the daily drop-in fee by some clubs.

## Phone Information Section

**You should have a section that is used to record the club's daily sales phone traffic, as well as the club's daily prospective members.**

You should have a section that is used to record the club's daily sales phone traffic, as well as the club's daily prospective members:

- *Information calls*—These calls are transferred from the club's inquiry sheets, or from the phone log if you are not yet using inquiry sheets.

- *Appointments scheduled*—These appointments are set from the information calls the club receives. Note that this number is always going to be smaller than the information calls entry.

- *Prospective members (first-time) and prospective members (recurring)*—These topics are discussed in the section preceding this one. These numbers should reflect the total potential membership the club has each day and for the month. If you are not using trial memberships, you will only use the first-time entry lines.

# Projections

Knowing where you are each day in your business is important and gives a manager or owner an edge when it comes to making important business decisions. An even more sophisticated tool is having the ability to project revenue, total sales, and profit-center income for the month during the first week of the month.

Once you master the concept, the projections are easy to calculate. The formula itself can be used to project almost anything in the business once you have a few days of numbers early in the month.

*Line 1: Total sales income month-to-date (a)*—This number is the total (running total) sales income for the month as of today.

*Line 2: Day of month*—Enter the day of the month (1–31) on this line (the day you are filling out the report).

**Knowing where you are each day in your business is important and gives a manager or owner an edge when it comes to making important business decisions.**

1.  Total sales income month-to-date (a)		$_____

2.  Day of month							$_____

3.  (a)/(day of month)
    = Daily average for the month			$_____

4.  Daily average							$_____

    x Total days in the current month			$_____

5.  = Projected total sales income for the month	$_____

*Line 3: (a)/(today's date) = Daily average for the month*—When you first use these formulas, they seem more complicated than they really are. On this line, simply divide the total sales money collected for the month (a) by the day of the month (the date you are filling out the report if it is the close of that business day or yesterday's date if you are filling it out on the following morning).

For example, assume you are filling out the report on May 14 (a 31 day month). Thus far, the club has collected a total of $7432 from the sales income section (Line 1). If you divide $7432 by 14, you get $530.85, which means that this club is averaging $530.85 each day from money generated from its sales department.

*Line 4: Daily average x Total days in the current month (days)*—On this line, you take the daily average number from Line 3 and multiply it times the number of days in the current month. By doing so, you can project the expected sales revenue for the month.

For example, so far you are averaging $530.85 per day in sales income through Day 14 of the month. Multiplying the $530.85 x 31 days in the current month gives you $16,456.35. In other words, this club is projecting $16,456.35 in sales revenue for the month if it can hold its average, which is pretty likely since it has averaged this number for 14 days already.

*Line 5: Projected total sales income for the month*—Use this line to record the final calculation from Line 4.

All of these categories should be accounted for in your daily sales report. It is important to begin tracking these numbers daily instead of waiting a week or longer and then trying to sit down and figure out where you stand in your business.

**If you learn to run your business by the numbers, you will learn to make better business decisions, because you are eliminating much of the subjectivity and replacing it with a more objective thought process.**

In summary, if you learn to run your business by the numbers, you will learn to make better business decisions, because you are eliminating much of the subjectivity and replacing it with a more objective thought process. Your staff might lie, your spouse might lie, and the members will assuredly lie if they think they can get free stuff, but the numbers never do. If you get control of them, they will lead you to where you need to be in your business.

## Key Points From This Chapter

- Most owners make emotional decisions in their businesses because they don't understand how to track and manage the important numbers.

- Get control of the leads first.

- Qualify the leads you do get, but only at the management level.

- Sales offices and guest paperwork hinder the sales process.

- You should be closing 55 percent of all leads as annual memberships and 30 percent of that number should be first-visit closes.

- You need to have a systematic method, based upon history and trend lines, of projecting your business forward.

- Get involved in your business the first day you fall behind in your projections in any area of your business. Do not wait until the end of the month to see if you will catch up.

**Tip of the Day**

# Find a mentor.

Find someone who has gone before you and isn't afraid to show you the way. As you become more successful in your life, you may find that your current set of friends tends to pull you back to your old habits. If they're not as successful as you, many might resent the fact that you're moving past them at a quick pace.

Always find someone you respect that is at a higher level of success to lend you a hand. These mentors come in all shapes and sizes and might be someone you already know, such as a boss or parent, or someone you respect and know you could learn from over time. Don't be afraid to ask for help. People who are successful in some aspect of their lives are usually willing to help others grow, especially since they remember that someone probably helped them on the way up as well.

Mentors are powerful tools in your life and can open doors that you might not yet have the keys for. As you grow, surround yourself with people who are also on the road to the success you are seeking and ask them what they are doing in their lives to continue to grow. Always remember that as you become more successful someone will always be a little further down the road who can help you take the next step.

# 15

# You Always Enhance and Never Discount

What would you do for $50? Would you throw a big party on the weekend for all your friends for $50? Would you get naked and run through the local mall with the 50 in your teeth and sing "God Bless America"? Put another way, would you call the local police and tell them you found a stray $50 bill on the sidewalk and it is so much money that you want to turn it in at the station?

Fifty dollars just isn't the big motivator it used to be. It is not enough to excite most people, and in most parts of the country it's not even enough to buy a good meal, play a round of golf, or take your family to a movie.

To make matters worse, assume that the $50 bill isn't even real. It's just an illusion cooked up by a desperate salesperson working off of 55 years of bad habits. Then what would you do for this $50, considering that it might not have even been real in the first place?

This mysterious $50 comes up every day in fitness centers and clubs all across the country, and the idea behind it is so old that most people don't even really question it anymore. Of course, this $50 comes in the form of the drop close sales technique still used by way too many fitness businesses.

Drop closing is a technique used by a salesperson to apply high pressure at the point of sale with the expected outcome of leveraging the person to make the buying decision immediately. For example, a nervous buyer is almost ready to sign up but just can't quite commit. The salesperson leans in and states: "Normally our membership fee is $100, but if you're ready to make up your mind today to get started, we will cut that fee to only $50, and of course that's good for today only. Joe, I know you're serious about getting started or you wouldn't have come in here today, but you seem to have a little problem with making the decision. I can't offer this $50 discount to everyone, and I definitely can't offer it beyond today, but if you're willing to stand up and make the right decision then we can get this done today. So come on Joe, let's get you signed up."

This technique may seem harsh, or perhaps soft if you have been selling memberships in clubs for a long time, but some form of this close is happening all day long in clubs everywhere in this country. The drop close itself may be the oldest technique still in existence from the old days of fitness, and probably is the most outdated and abused as well.

Drop closing actually predates the fitness business and goes all the way back to life insurance and dance studios in the late 1940s and 1950s. In those days, the dance instructors/salespeople were selling three-year and even lifetime dance lessons that were paid for over time. At that time, getting someone to commit to something that was such a major commitment required a lot of pressure being applied at the point of sale.

Visualize the situation and you can see how the salesperson made his move. Imagine a nice dance studio with great music and other couples swirling around the room. You just finished your trial lesson with a skilled dance partner and she whispers in your ear that you have talent and with a few lessons you might turn out to be one of the great ones. Just imagine how exciting it would be to grab a woman at a dance and dazzle her with your technique.

Now you're sitting in the office with the salesperson, who can't believe all the great things your dance partner had to say about you. In fact, she thinks you might be too advanced for the regular dance lessons and should be invited to join the instructor's program, where for just a little more money each month you can learn what it takes to be a dance instructor and join the staff once you finish your program.

Your salesperson lays out your three-year deal, with the lifetime option of course, which costs only a small fee of $69 per year after the first three years. You're really excited to get started, but that down payment is just too much for your budget. But the salesperson leans in and points out the window and says, "See that instructor over there dancing with the beautiful girl? Well he sat right there in that chair just a year ago and look where he is now. I know you really want to do this Fred, so here is what I'm going to do for you today to help you get started. Normally, it's $1500 to get started, but we would really like to have you as part of this program so I'll knock off $1000 if you're willing to sign the paperwork and get started with us today. Come on, let's get you signed up today and dancing tomorrow."

This conversation probably took place in 1946, which is about the same time the fitness industry got underway in this country. In fact, a lot of the techniques, and even some of the same salespeople, were the foundation for a lot of the membership sales programs in the early days of fitness. Many of these guys went on to be part of some of the first big chains, such as European

> The drop close itself may be the oldest technique still in existence from the old days of fitness, and probably is the most outdated and abused as well.

Health Spas, and they brought their knowledge base with them. Two-year and longer contracts, high-pressure first-visit closing, 10-page closes for the salesperson to memorize, and double-teaming were all techniques brought to this industry from other businesses.

The insurance industry also contributed its share of training. Jobs were scarce in the 1940s and 1950s and selling insurance door-to-door was how a lot of unemployed guys kept busy. The sales techniques for these companies were ahead of their time and the sales guys had great training on how to close long-term deals at someone's dinner table. In fact, one of the most famous sales lines ever came from this era.

Life insurance guys needed a strong close since, in essence, they were selling something that didn't pay unless you died. Imagine a family, crowded around a dinner table, listening to the sales guy make his pitch. Yes, people actually let salespeople in their homes in those days, because the art form was new and actually doubled as entertainment for some families. Now imagine the salesperson seeing the family picture on the mantle, getting up during his pitch, and laying the picture on the table. "Sir, you have a beautiful family here and I know you want to do the right thing for them. What I want to ask you sir, and I want you to think about it carefully, is what happens if for some reason you step out of the picture? What happens to them at that point without you?"

This classic close, done in front of his family and not using the word "dying," was very powerful and sold a lot of insurance in those days. Those guys were tough, hard workers and eventually found their way to the fledgling fitness industry. Hey, if it worked at the dining room table, then it must work at a desk in a sales office in one of these new gym things.

## Why Those Techniques Worked Then and Don't Work Now

These techniques worked then because they were new and fresh and because the buyer didn't have a lot of sales experience. These same techniques don't work now because the buyer is older in years, wiser, and jaded when it comes to anyone selling him anything.

In the 1960s, when the fitness industry was just picking up speed, the buyer wasn't very sophisticated. He might have been in his mid-20s and probably had never really been pitched by anyone.

**In today's market, if you're over 15, you have probably heard just about every sales pitch in existence.**

In today's market, if you're over 15, you have probably heard just about every sales pitch in existence. People get hit at a younger age, and from more sources, including places such as the mall for clothes, electronics, and music, when they buy fast food ("Super-size you, dude?"), and even for big-ticket items such as phone plans and cars. People in their 20s today might have heard more sales pitches already than their parents did their entire lives.

Money also seems to have a different perceived value today. Knocking off $50 in a sales pitch in the 1960s and 1970s had more value than knocking off $50 now, especially when the guy at the desk has a $400 Ipod® around his neck with $100 upgraded headphones.

Some chains try to compensate for the difference in money value by just raising the total and knocking off more, hoping that a big slash will startle the consumer into buying. It seems, however, that it accomplishes just the opposite.

One particular chain currently shows the consumer a down payment of $350 and then slashes the joining fee down to $50. Therefore, the buyer saves $300. At what point is the number so big it becomes stupid money? "Well, it is normally $1 million to get started, but I know you're serious, so today, and today only, I am going to lower that to just $50. Now, I have to approve this with my boss, but if you tell me you're going to sign today then I think I can talk him into letting you have this deal. Come on, just think, you can save $999,950 if you're willing to make that decision today."

At some point, the money stopped being leverage for the consumer and became like it is in a furniture store, where everyone knows that they mark everything up so they can have a sale and mark everything down. Consumers today know that if you offer something for $350 and then offer it for $50, no one has ever really purchased it for $350 and all it is worth is $50.

The other reason drop closing fails with a sophisticated buyer is that everyone but idiots knows that if they come back the next day the price isn't going back up to $350. You've established the price, or value, at $50 and that is what the customer will pay tomorrow, and the next day, and the day after that one.

Drop closing is based upon fear of loss and only works if the consumer really believes that by not making a decision today, he will lose the $50 knockdown on the price. When you lose that fear, the system fails, and unless you are a very naïve person living in a very sophisticated world, no one has that strong fear of loss anymore, especially over a small amount of money.

Another reason drop closing has failed as a tool is that a more educated consumer started feeling bad about his purchase. "If he knocked off $50, maybe I should have held out and got him down to just $25."

**Drop closing makes most people feel like they have been violated somehow.**

Drop closing makes most people feel like they have been violated somehow. "Everyone wants a deal, but what if my deal isn't as good as someone else's or isn't the best I could have gotten if I had just been tougher," the frustrated buyer says to himself on the way home.

# You Still Can Buy the Deal, but the Techniques Have Changed

More sophisticated clients demand a more sophisticated approach. In other words, as a salesperson you still have to buy the deal but how we do it has changed.

The consumer still wants a deal, and still needs that little push, but doesn't want to be insulted by your sales pitch. He wants to buy, but just doesn't want to look stupid, cheap, or easy.

You also need a system that closes a high percentage of your guests today, but still makes them feel good about coming back tomorrow. Remember, 70 percent of your guests will need two or more visits before they can make the decision to join if your price is $39 per month or higher. The question is: "How can you get a high number of first-visit closes without insulting the rest of them to the point they won't come back at all?"

## Validating the buying decision

As a salesperson, you still have to buy the sale, and you still have to validate the buying decision. Validating the buying decision means that you prove to the person who just bought that he is the smartest person in the world and that buying a membership from you was not only a good thing to do, but also something he wants to share with his friends. If a person feels good about what he bought, and has a good experience in the process, then he will share that experience with his friends, because everyone likes to look smart to his buddies.

> Validating the buying decision means that you prove to the person who just bought that he is the smartest person in the world and that buying a membership from you was not only a good thing to do, but also something he wants to share with his friends.

You're probably asking why this validation doesn't occur with a drop close, since in essence the person got a deal. The key is that he didn't really get a deal and he knows it. More importantly, he is not likely to refer his friends to a public beating in an office by an overly aggressive salesperson. "Kirk, you just have to visit that gym. I guarantee that the salesperson will take you into an office and pound the snot out of you—and then it really gets good. At the end, he will insult your intelligence by doing some fake drop close to pressure you to join. If you live past the office part, it is a decent gym, but everyone has to take the beating first before they let you in. Sorry dude."

## Buying the sale with class

People like to be appreciated, especially when they spend money with you, but sadly this is a lost art in most businesses. On a lower level, look at how a typical clerk treats you in a coffee shop. You just spent $6 for coffee and a bagel, which is expensive, but remember that you're buying the experience. Then the person behind the counter slides your change back and says, "There you go, man."

The urge is to stick that bagel up his nose and scream, "No, there you go, scum boy." Even at just $6, you want to be appreciated for what you just spent. You work hard for your money and someone should appreciate it when you choose to spend it with his business.

**People like to be appreciated, especially when they spend money with you, but sadly this is a lost art in most businesses.**

Now think about buying a car. You just signed your life away for the next five years by buying a $35,000 automobile, a big purchase for most people, and you drive home with nothing but that wad of paperwork on the seat next to you. And then nothing. No gift in the mail, no flowers to the office, no bottle of wine, just nothing from the company and salesperson that you just spent $35,000 with last week. In fact, the only thing you heard from the salesperson was a phone call asking for a referral to your friends.

---

**If you spend $35,000, you deserve something.**

---

It is the same in the fitness business. You order $50,000 worth of equipment and all you get is a free T-shirt and a few water bottles—and don't forget the banner with the company name that you can hang in your club to further promote their brand.

The industry needs to change that thought process and it begins with your memberships. If the consumer spends $500 for a membership, or anything at all actually, then he needs to go home with a gift that cements the relationship and makes him feel good about what he just bought.

You can make the customer feel good by offering what is called the Trial Gift Certificate, which is nothing more than a leverage tool for the salesperson to use with a more sophisticated buyer. This tool uses gifts and club services as incentives, and most importantly, provides a way to say, "Thank you for choosing our business." For example, the salesperson might say the following: "One further benefit of our club is our gift packs. We truly appreciate your business and we realize that you have other choices in the area. We really do want to thank you for deciding to become a member here."

The gift pack listed on the Trial Gift Certificate can include bonus months, a gym bag (always the most popular part of most surveys), small things such as munchie bars, sports drinks, and a water bottle, and club services, such as training packages or tanning. The idea is to build value into the pack and then use it as a means of closing the deal.

Review Figure 15-1 to get an idea how much one owner is willing to put up to sell the membership. Keep in mind that if you have competition, you are probably offering something that they won't, which further differentiates you from everyone else in your market.

# *Workout America*

*We realize you have choices when it comes to joining a fitness facility,*
*and as a way of saying thank you for selecting us as your gym,*
*we'd like to start you off with some special gifts.*

*If you are already comfortable with the club and are planning to join during your first visit, we'd like to offer you our special premiere package of gifts and incentives.*

- TWO MONTHS ADDED TO YOUR MEMBERSHIP, GIVING YOU 14 FOR THE PRICE OF 12
- $50 IN CLUB BUCKS THAT CAN BE SPENT ON ANYTHING IN THE GYM
- THREE PERSONAL TRAINING SESSIONS VALUED AT $150
- A FREE GYM BAG VALUED AT $49
- A FREE T-SHIRT VALUED AT $19
- A 30-DAY GIFT CERTIFICATE FOR A FRIEND OR RELATIVE, GIVING THAT PERSON UNLIMITED USE OF THE GYM FOR 30 DAYS, A T-SHIRT, AND A PERSONAL TRAINING SESSION, ALL VALUED AT $118

**Total Value $444**

*If you need time to experience the club before you commit to a membership, we'd like to offer you the following package, which is yours anytime during the first seven days of your trial membership.*

- ONE FREE MONTH ADDED TO YOUR MEMBERSHIP
- $10 IN CLUB BUCKS
- ONE PERSONAL TRAINING SESSION VALUED AT $50
- A FREE GYM BAG VALUED AT $49
- A FREE WATER BOTTLE, T-SHIRT, AND KEY CHAIN VALUED AT $23
- THREE FREE TANS VALUED AT $21
- ONE FREE COOLER DRINK VALUED AT $1 & FREE MUNCHIE BAR VALUED AT $2
- 20% OFF OF YOUR FIRST SPA SERVICE
- ONE FREE SHAKE VALUED AT $5
- A 30-DAY GIFT CERTIFICATE FOR A FRIEND OR RELATIVE, GIVING THAT PERSON UNLIMITED USE OF THE GYM FOR 30 DAYS, A T-SHIRT, AND A PERSONAL TRAINING SESSION, ALL VALUED AT $118

**Total Value $328**

*If you don't become a member during the first seven days of your trial membership, but decide to join the club* | *you will still receive a club gym bag valued at*

**$49**

Member Name _____    Expiration Date _____

Club Representative _____    Today's Date _____

Figure 15-1. Sample gift certificate

This certificate would be presented at the end of the sales close, just after the salesperson gives the price: "Joe, these are our prices, but before you make up your mind about which one of these is best for you, I'd like to show you something we feel makes our club special."

This certificate should be the nicest thing in the club. It should be printed on high-quality paper and be handed to the guest at the appropriate moment. Think of this certificate as a leverage tool that helps you stand out from your competition. The guy down the street drop closed this guy, which probably insulted him somewhat, and now you are offering him free gifts and a big thank you for considering your club.

Do not think of these certificates as closing incentives and don't use that language with your guests. The key is that these gifts are your way of saying thank you for the business and that you really do appreciate the person spending money with you.

This strategy not only validates the buying decision ("Wow, am I smart to buy from this guy"), but also makes the person feel good about what he just bought from you over time. His friend at work, for example, joined a gym last week and didn't get anything to take home but the pink copy of the contract, an aerobics schedule, and a cheap brochure. I bet he feels really good about that purchase. Your guy, on the other hand, left with a gym bag full of goodies, proving that he not only bought from the right guys who appreciate his business, but also that he is a lot smarter than the guy he works with every day.

Notice in Figure 15-1 that the incentives are stronger on the first visit and then are reduced during the first seven days of the trial (if you are using a 14-day trial, then offer the reduced incentives to anyone who joins by the end of the seventh day). The price, however, does not change and the drop-close discount is replaced by the different values of the loot package, as many clubs call it. This difference is important to note, since this method allows you to get people to sign up today but feel good about coming back tomorrow. You are telling the prospect, "You may get more stuff today, but we won't change the price if you come back tomorrow."

> **Most of your first-visit closes will probably be people who have some type of experience with your club anyway, such as buddy referrals or someone who has seen your marketing over time.**

It is worth noting that most of your first-visit closes will probably be people who have some type of experience with your club anyway, such as buddy referrals or someone who has seen your marketing over time. Most of these people come ready to become members and the gift packs help make the decision easier while still validating the decision and creating goodwill.

### Buyer's regret

Buyer's regret has been vaguely alluded to throughout this chapter. Buyer's regret is the classic feeling of, "What in the name of my youngest child did I buy this time?" It's that feeling you get when you go to the mall to buy a pair of shoes and come home with three new outfits and a belt and forgot the shoes.

In the fitness world, it's the feeling a person gets when he leaves your club and has nothing to show for the money he spent except a pink sheet of paper and a business card lying on the seat. As he drives, he thinks, "What did I waste my money on this time? Will I even stick with this? My wife is going to kill me for wasting money for a gym membership."

This same guy driving home with a gym bag full of goodies on his seat, munching on his free snack bar and drinking his free drinks, while wearing his new free T-shirt, is much less likely to complain much to himself. He is, as you proved by giving him this stuff, a very astute buyer who bought from people who appreciate his time and money—and he really doesn't care about what his wife thinks because he now has cool stuff.

## How much to spend

Keep your hard costs, without labor, to the equivalent of one month's dues. For example, if your monthly fee is $49, then your hard cost for everything in the gift pack should be $49 or less. Don't forget that your closing rate should increase and your cost of marketing should come down slightly with this system, since you are probably offering something that no one else in your market can match.

> Buyer's regret is the classic feeling of, "What in the name of my youngest child did I buy this time?"

Don't count labor in this cost, since you would have to spend something to get the new member going anyway and you also have the opportunity to sell training and other services if the person is exposed to everything you have to offer. Review the basics of the certificate:

- Use it at the close after the price presentation.
- Keep the hard cost to one month's membership or less.
- Make it a quality piece.
- If you can't start with a full package, then at least start with an inexpensive gym bag and a T-shirt.
- Use the gifts as incentives, with a stronger package for first-visit closes and a reduced package later.
- If you are offering a 14-day trial, use the secondary package if they join by the end of the seventh day.
- If you are offering the seven-day trial instead of the 14-day trial, use the secondary package if they join by the end of the seventh day.
- Stuff it full of little things, such as bars and drinks that don't cost a lot but add value to the presentation.
- Use the gift strategy and say, "Thank you for your business. We do

appreciate you spending money with us." People like to feel appreciated for money they spend and this technique was designed to enhance that feeling in the club.

- Rotate your gifts and experiment until you find the right combination that really turns people on.

### Always give the person at least the secondary package.

If you notice in Figure 15-1, the certificate is divided into three different segments. The first segment is heavily weighted to help close first-visit people. The second level is for people who don't buy today, but who buy in a designated trial period. The third level is for people who finish their trial and join at the end.

If you notice on the example, the third level is just a gym bag. It is important to note that if someone finished a full trial with you and is trying to join, you should take the money you fool!

You must give any person trying to give you money and join your club at least the secondary level and do not punish them for waiting. For example, "So you want to get started Kristen. Let's see, you're at the end of the 14 days and have a gym bag coming. You know what, thank you for sticking with us and for joining our gym. We really appreciate your business and I'm going to give you the next package up on the certificate."

Yes, the members might figure you out, but so what? If someone is trying to give you money and join your facility, then give her some cool stuff and get over your silly self and take the money.

> If someone is trying to give you money and join your facility, then give her some cool stuff and get over your silly self and take the money.

# Key Points From This Chapter

- The drop close that so many clubs still use is an old technology that needs to go.
- Your clients are more sophisticated now than they were just a few years ago when it comes to sales, and they need to be treated differently.
- You have to learn to validate the sale in the consumer's head.
- Trial certificates are a way of saying, "Thank you, we truly appreciate your business and the money you spend with us."
- Gift packs kill buyer's regret.
- Keep your cost down to one month's membership.
- Strong trial certificates will increase your closing rate.
- Gift packs are a strong differentiator in most markets.

# Bring it all every day.

At the end of the day, can you honestly say that everything you did at work was truly the best effort you had in you? Two types of people go to work for a living. The first group consists of people who bring it all every day and then say to the owner, "I am making money here and giving you my best work. Let's talk about money and my future here." They take responsibility at work, look for things to do to help the company, show leadership by stepping up when needed, and give whomever they work for the best they are capable of every single hour they work.

The second group consists of those people who withhold their talent because they don't feel like they are being appreciated and then spend the day crying, "If only I was paid more or had that particular job, then I would show these people how it is done." These people withhold their work, put in their hours doing the least amount possible, and hit the door running five minutes before their shift is over.

The first group makes money, manages or owns clubs, and will often lead rich and rewarding lives. The second group will never amount to much of anything because the money is never enough and they can't find the right job to please them.

Once you start withholding your talent, it becomes hard to ever deliver it again. Bring it all every day, and if you are doing your best work and not getting paid, then take your services somewhere else, because people who deliver their best work time after time will always have a place to work and the ability to make some real money.

# 16

# The Welcome Guide

So this guy is sitting at home—a kind of fat guy—and gets this cool direct-mail piece delivered to his house. His wife says, "Go check this out. You're fat, and I'm kind of fat too, so maybe we both need to join a gym."

This guy, whose name is Billy, sets off on the road Saturday morning to visit the fitness facility, along with several other gyms and fitness businesses in the neighborhood. He suffers through four different salespeople and ends up back on the couch Saturday afternoon, drinking a beer and explaining his day to his wife. Don't forget that they are both kind of fat and need a gym.

*"Well, what did you find out honey?" she asks.*

*"I visited four different clubs and here is what I got," he replies. "First of all, here is the price sheet, a business card, and an aerobic schedule from the club on the mailer. Then I visited that old chain club on the same street and their guy gave me this cheap, six-cent, threefold brochure with a business card and an aerobic schedule, but he wouldn't give me a price for you unless you came down too, so he could talk to us together. I had to sit in that office for almost an hour because he just kept pounding me about getting started today and I finally just had to walk out."*

*"After that, I visited the big recreation center and they gave me a price sheet and an aerobic schedule and a flyer about raising money for their new addition. And finally, I visited that new place by the mall and they gave me this 70-page, three-ring binder with pictures of the club, testimonials from their members, including our insurance agent, pictures from their last party, and all their services and prices. The salesperson also said that I can try the club absolutely free for 14 days with no risk and I don't have to give them any money up front. And I mentioned you and she also gave me a 14-day pass for you to use. I don't know honey, which club do you think we ought to try?"*

### What do you want in front of the person when he decides which gym to try?

The club industry has a reputation of having an "all-or-nothing" approach to getting someone to sign a membership during their first visit. After more than 30 years, this attitude of, "Don't let them leave without a membership," has done extensive damage to the growth of the club market. Consumers are wary and some won't even try, knowing the horror stories their friends have suffered by walking into the wrong club and meeting the wrong salesperson who is desperate to sell a membership and desperate to keep his job.

If you have confidence in your business and your staff, then let the guest walk and remember that 70 percent of your guests will need two or more visits to your club before they will commit to a membership if the monthly price is $39 or higher. Owners will spend thousands of dollars each month trying to attract new members and then gamble that all that money will pay off in a 30-minute encounter between the guest and the salesperson. The point is, why risk it all on just one shot if you know that the higher the price and the more sophisticated the potential member, the more likely he is to gather information and then go home to think about it overnight?

The risk is just too high in this scenario, especially when someone on your sales team might be having a bad-breath, bad-hair, just-broke-up-with-my-significant-other kind of day. People are going to shop and they are going to walk. It's just the nature of today's market. The key point is that you have to break away from the traditional take-home packages that have become so obsolete and ineffective over time. The standard take-home fare, as detailed in the earlier conversation between the spouses, is composed of an aerobics schedule (when will the old-style guys begin to call it group exercise?), a business card, a cheap brochure, and a price sheet, which is often handwritten on a yellow pad.

Some of you are so proud of yourselves as you read this section, thinking about how nice your stack folder is and how you're really ahead of those cheap, threefold brochure people. Bad news: You're not ahead. You're just sort of ugly in a land of ugly people, and being the best of the worst is still not a viable business plan.

### All they are really taking home is the price.

The last thing you want Billy and his wife to sit and think about over their cheap beer is the price. When you send someone home with just a few scraps of worthless paper, you're forcing the person to sit and compare you price alone, since that information is all he really has in front of him from most facilities.

The goal is to practice behavior modification. In other words, you want to change and guide what they are thinking about when they are not in front of a salesperson.

If the last thing you want the person to think about is price, then the first thing he should be thinking about is how the club is different from others in the area and what your club can really do for him as an individual. You initiate this control be making sure your guest leaves with a carefully prepared package that guides him through all of the important points you want him to see and remember about your business, especially when he is kicked back on his couch trying to decide which club is for him.

# The Welcome Guide

The Welcome Guide is the tool you need to begin this process. It is a three-ring binder with a nice cover and approximately 70 pages of club information that helps keep your potential member focused on the important aspects of your business. The Welcome Guide should hold the following components:

- A letter from the owner or manager positioning the club in the market

- A list of all the services, and appropriate prices, that the club offers

- At least four, full-page testimonials (more if desired)

- Motivating articles about fitness (some clubs have separate articles for men, women, and special populations)

- A first-time experience section (don't call anyone a beginner). Tell them how to get started, what to wear, suggestions about how to get the most out of their program in the shortest period of time, and articles about getting started with their first fitness program.

- The club layout, even if the club is small

- The staff team picture

- Club rules presented in a positive manner

- The management-team information

- Important phone numbers, such as your third-party financial company

- Pictures from the last member party or event

- All membership prices

- Any other fun articles, cartoons, or success stories that help a person sitting on a couch at home get more involved with your business

The three-ring binder is recommended because any other system quickly becomes stagnant. If you print something more cheaply, such as a bound book from a copy center, it will be out of date in a week, because something in your business will undoubtedly change. The bad news is that since you have a few boxes of printed books, you feel obligated to keep handing out the out-of-date copies.

Binders should be made on demand, meaning that once a week or so you might want to create a new batch. Some sheets, such as the club layout for

**If the last thing you want the person to think about is price, then the first thing he should be thinking about is how the club is different from others in the area and what your club can really do for him as an individual.**

example, don't change often, but other things, such as the pictures from the last event or a notice of a party or coming event, need to be updated often.

Done correctly, these guides should cost you somewhere between $2.50 and $3.00 per binder when complete. It is easy to be cheap, but you need to ask yourself the following question: If you are willing to spend thousands of dollars a month to market your club, would you not be willing to spend a few bucks to close more people and extend your brand into the community?

Remember, you built or manage a facility that was probably expensive to build. Some owners spend $10 million or more to build a facility for their community, while others put their whole lives and all of their money into smaller clubs. The issue is, no matter what you own or how much you spent, do you really want the image of your club to be a few pieces of cheap paper and prices presented on yellow pads?

Everything you do affects your brand, but some owners forget that the brand often extends beyond the walls. When Billy and his wife are sitting on their couch looking at the Welcome Guide from your club, they are in essence holding an extension of your business in their hands. Spend the few extra bucks per potential member to really make sure your brand has the best reputation it can have, even when people aren't within your walls.

> **Everything you do affects your brand, but some owners forget that the brand often extends beyond the walls.**

## How to use Welcome Guides

Welcome Guides are given as a gift to the guest somewhere very early in your tour. Do not wait and give the guides out at the end. Many new owners and managers fear that if they give these books out early, the guest will spend his time looking at them and not listen to the salesperson. For example, after spending a few minutes getting to know the person and before you ask him if he would like to step over to the information table, say the following:

*"Well Billy, if you'd like to step over to our information table, I think I have some stuff that might help answer a few of your questions about our gym. First of all, I'd like to start you out with a gift from the club. The book is called our Welcome Guide and it has just about everything you need to know about our club. We just know from experience that you'll get home tonight and say to yourself, "What did he say about those classes?" This book also has some articles about working out, what we believe fitness should be, some pictures from our last party, and a lot of other things that you might find interesting about what we do here. Keep it as a gift from the club and, with your permission, I would love to show you around while you're here."*

Consider the following additional tips for using the guides:

- Don't be afraid to send the person home with an extra book if he has a friend or relative who might need one.

- Let the person carry his new book on the tour. The guides act as a focus beacon for the rest of the staff that you have guest in the club and everyone should be introducing themselves as the salesperson makes the rounds with the guest in tow.

- You can make these books yourself by buying quarter-inch view binders at one of the wholesale clubs or you can buy them with generic or customer covers from the Thomas Plummer Company.

- If you're in a college town, save a little money by having a lighter version of your guide with fewer pages for the students.

## Everyone should leave the gym as a member.

This statement seems like a contradiction from earlier discussions, but when you use the trial membership, you have other options that are less threatening to the consumer. In this case, your guest either leaves as a regular member with his loot bag and membership papers, or he leaves as a trial member with a temporary membership card. In either case, he is a member and has a reason to come back to the club without feeling pressured.

If someone joins the club during his first visit, the guide serves as starting point for the member once he gets home. After reading your guide, he should feel comfortable about how your business works, including club rules, times, and services.

Fear of the unknown is a big killer for new members, and without information to help guide them through their first workouts, you will lose more people than you realize. You might like to think that you can create systems with which you can verbally talk everyone through the first stages of a new membership, but this system fails for many reasons. The salesperson might forget a few key points. He might have been rushed or overloaded during that guest's visit. Or the prospect might just be a visual learner who simply needs to sit and read about things rather than listening to a salesperson. The Welcome Guide should be the tool that gives hope and inspires the person to get involved and stay involved.

The guide also serves as a connective bridge between your club and the new trial member. In most clubs, if a person doesn't sign up, very little really draws that person back to the business. Remember, all he has in front of him at home in most cases is a class schedule and a price sheet, neither of which inspires action.

Your Welcome Guide should be filled with the kind of information and articles about fitness that make the person want to come back and get involved with you and your business. This content is especially important if the person has visited several clubs and is looking at all the material he has gathered during his trek. Remember Billy and what he brought home to share with his

**Fear of the unknown is a big killer for new members, and without information to help guide them through their first workouts, you will lose more people than you realize.**

wife? Which club will be the one that has information to motivate him and his spouse to take action?

## Another use for the Welcome Guides

Your sales manager can also use the Welcome Guides as part of the club's marketing plan. In a perfect sales world, your sales manager would visit five small businesses a day during the slower afternoon hours. He will have better success if he concentrates on businesses with fewer than 30 employees that are within three miles of the club.

A politician once famously said that one handshake is worth 250 votes. The same holds true in your business. One visit by a representative from your club is worth many memberships over time, since the folks at that business will then have a personal connection to your club. This personal connection breaks down one of the biggest barriers, which is not knowing anyone at the club. Visiting smaller businesses also usually means that you can get through and actually meet someone who is in charge.

Your sales manager should bring along Welcome Guides and a special 21-day trial guest pass (assuming that you are using the 14-day trial in your regular marketing). This pass should be on a 4 x 5 card, *not on a business card.* Business-card-size passes have no perceived value and they look like you just hand them out to anyone walking by. Sample copy on one these cards might look as follows:

> One visit by a representative from your club is worth many memberships over time, since the folks at that business will then have a personal connection to your club.

---

Presented to
_____

By
_____

This card entitles the bearer to 21 days of unlimited fitness at (your club), including participation in our group orientation sessions, a personal coach, and group nutritional guidance. This offer also includes a free club T-shirt and water bottle.

_____
Authorized by

_____
Date

First workout must be taken by:_____

---

Your sales manager should make a big deal out of getting a pass for each employee, along with a Welcome Guide, and for setting a time when the whole group might come in as a team for their first workout. Keep in mind that these prospects are qualified people you solicited, so giving out T-shirts and some group training is a small investment to attract a large number of new prospects.

## Sample Welcome Guide Components

### Letter from the owner or manager

*Welcome to our club!*

We realize that you have other choices when it comes to fitness and we'd like to thank you for choosing our business as your place to explore acquiring a gym membership. We believe that we have the best club in the area, with the most attentive and knowledgeable staff, great members, equipment that sets us apart from all the other fitness businesses, and a club that is truly a clean and comfortable place to work out. Talk is cheap, however, and all owners in the area are equally proud of their businesses.

What sets us apart from our competitors is that we are the only (first) fitness business in the area that will let you try before you buy with no risk, no obligation, and absolutely no money up front. Come meet our staff, hang out with our members, try a few workouts, and evaluate our service. At the end of your 14-day trial membership, if we don't earn your business, then we don't deserve to have you as a member. It's that simple, with no strings attached and fine print. If you live in our market area, then we will stand behind our business by letting you try us absolutely free for 14 days with no risk to you, except for the fact you might actually get into a little better shape during your trial membership.

**Visiting smaller businesses also usually means that you can get through and actually meet someone who is in charge.**

Our club has been in business for (years) and we understand that making a decision to commit to working out is difficult and that picking the right club for you is even harder. Will I like the gym? Will I like the other members? Am I going to get service in this business after I become a member? Will I be able to get any help? These fair questions can only be answered by trying our business before you become a member. Remember, it isn't hard to hide the flaws during a single visit, but it's impossible to hide bad service and a poor business over an extended trial membership. We feel that we can stand up to this test and we invite you to take the trial and see what we are really all about.

One of the most important things we want you to know about our business is that we are solution-based, which means that we only need to ask you one really important question: What's the single most important thing that you want from your fitness experience? Based upon your answer, we will recommend anything from a full membership to a simple weight-management program. Think of us as your fitness resource. If you know what you want to accomplish we can help find a solution tailored just for you.

Another thing that makes us unique is that we treat every member in this club in the same way every single day, which means that we don't make deals with one person and not offer our other members the same thing. We also understand that you have choices when it comes to fitness, and as a way of saying thank you for choosing us, we offer substantial gift incentive packages with our trial certificate to every new person who is considering becoming a part of our business. If you have any questions about our gift incentives, please call us immediately.

If you have shopped other businesses in the area, you will note that we are one of the more expensive gyms in town. We do this by choice. To us, poor service, unclean facilities, and lack of service all go hand-in-hand with being the cheapest price in town. You simply can't be the best and the cheapest at the same time in any service business. This pricing structure also means that our gym is not for everyone. If you appreciate quality, then we're the club for you. If price is your deciding factor, then you won't be happy with us and won't get the most out your fitness experience.

> **To us, poor service, unclean facilities, and lack of service all go hand-in-hand with being the cheapest price in town.**

Thank you again for your trust and we look forward to serving you as a member in the future.

Yours in fitness,
*Manager or Owner*

## Club policies and membership guidelines

*Note:* These policies should be reviewed by your attorney and insurance company.

Some suggestions for member etiquette are covered later in our club guide, but we also want to make our new members aware that we do have guidelines in place that ensure the safety and comfort of all members at all times. If you have any questions about these guidelines, please see a staff member before you begin your workout.

As a member or guest, you acknowledge that you are physically able to engage in any activity, program, or training provided and agree that all exercises and use of this facility are undertaken at your sole risk. You also agree to accept full responsibility for all personal belongings. Derogatory remarks involving any other member or club personnel will not be permitted.

*Proper clothing and hygiene:*

- Wear appropriate athletic shoes only. No street shoes, boots, or sandals are allowed in the workout areas.
- Shorts, sweat pants, T-shirts, tank tops, and spandex accessories may be worn if deemed appropriate by the club management.
- Clean workout clothing is required. Any unsatisfactory hygiene condition will be addressed by the management and corrective action may be required.

- All other clothing and shoes must be kept in lockers. Please keep all valuables at home. Again, we are not responsible for any lost or stolen items.
- Please avoid the use of heavy perfume or cologne.
- No belt buckles, blue jeans, or loose jewelry may be worn in the workout area.

*Equipment and cardiovascular areas:*

- Please be courteous at all times.
- Allow others to work in during your rest periods.
- Keep your hands and feet away from all moving parts and weight stacks.
- Do not attempt to repair or adjust any equipment that has malfunctioned.
- Immediately report any equipment problem to the staff.
- Use your workout towel to wipe off equipment and benches after each use.
- If you are unfamiliar with the use of any equipment, please ask a staff member for assistance.
- Children under the age of 16 are not allowed in any of the weight or cardiovascular areas.

*Weight room areas:*

- Again, be courteous at all times.
- Allow others to work in during rest periods.
- Rack all weights after each use.
- If dumbbells appear loose or cracked, report the item to the staff immediately.
- Always use a spotter when attempting to lift maximum weight.
- Collars and clips must be used for free-bar lifting.

*Food and drink in the club:*

- Water bottles with spill-proof lids are allowed in all areas of the club.
- Please consume all food items, shakes, and supplements at the juice bar.

*Club decree:*

All members and guests are required to have fun. We are here to help you reach your fitness goals and provide you with a safe workout environment.

Please let us know if you have any questions or recommendations on how we can best serve your needs.

**You have questions. We have the answers you need to get the most out of your membership with the club.**

### About getting started:

*Can I try the club before I become a member?*

Yes. Our 14-day "try before you buy" trial membership lets you try the club absolutely free, with no risk or obligation, before you decide to become a member. We want you to meet our staff, meet the other members, and give us a chance to earn your business. If we haven't earned your business at the end of 14 days, then we don't deserve to have you as a member.

*Do I have to sign a contract?*

No, we offer a month-to-month membership along with our annual agreements. If you anticipate traveling or just don't feel that you are ready to get involved in an annual fitness program, then our month-to-month option is for you. If you are committed to fitness and want to save money too, then our regular annual membership is the tool for you.

*Can I get a deal of any type?*

We pride ourselves on treating every single member in the same way every single time. Therefore, we don't make individual deals with new members. We also guarantee that any new member who signs up after you will never pay a lower price than you did when you joined.

> We pride ourselves on treating every single member in the same way every single time.

*What are the incentive gift packages about?*

We understand that we have competition and use the gift packages as a way of saying thank you for choosing us. We appreciate your business, and we use these opening gifts as a way of showing this appreciation. Most new members are also looking for that little extra incentive that will help them make that final decision to get started on a fitness program. The gift incentive packages, which include a gym bag or backpack, training sessions, a gift membership for a friend or relative, and other cool perks are often just enough to help that member on the fence take that final step and join. Hey, we understand that getting started is not the easiest thing in the world, and if we can offer you some gifts to help get you going, as well as show our appreciation for your business, then everyone wins.

*How do I get started?*

It's simple. Call the club or stop by and any of our membership folks can help you choose the right membership for you. The paperwork only takes about 15 minutes.

*Do I have any other payment options?*

You may pay monthly with an annual membership, take advantage of our no-commitment membership, sign up with a short-term membership good for up to three months, or use the club on a daily or short-term limited basis. We also offer several methods of payments, including EFT and good old check or credit card. The club also offers a number of solution-based programs, such as our weight-management department, where you do not have to be a member to take part.

## Club questions:

*How's the parking?*

Parking is easy at the club. We have plenty of spaces directly in front of the club, overflow spaces on the side, and during busy times we also use the additional parking in the back of the club.

*Do you have lockers and towel service?*

We have a large number of free day-use lockers, a limited amount of rental lockers for those people who like to keep their workout stuff at the gym, and we offer a rental towel service for $1 per towel. Small workout towels are free and are available at the desk.

*Do I have to have a card to check in?*

We will issue you a membership card that makes checking in much easier and faster, but if you forget your card you can simply stop by the desk and we will make sure you get your workout.

*Do I have to register for group classes?*

Some of our most popular classes, such as Body Pump™, are limited to a certain number of students. We do not accept advanced registrations, but we do offer a simple system that will hold your place in class once you arrive at the gym.

*Can I book training or other club stuff by phone?*

Almost everything we offer, beyond those things included as part of everyone's base membership, such as group, can be booked by calling the front desk at 555-1234. Members can also book services on their own by using the club's website: www.theclub.com.

*How do I bring a guest?*

Guests are always welcome at the club. If your guest lives in the club's marketing area and qualifies for our trial membership, we will be happy to extend the courtesy. If your guest is from out of our club's area, we offer a 50 percent discount off of our daily drop-in fee for your friends or relatives.

**The club also offers a number of solution-based programs, such as our weight-management department, where you do not have to be a member to take part.**

**Guests are always
welcome at the club.**

*Can I make my payments for my membership at the club?*

If you are on any type of membership plan, we cannot accept payments at the club. ABC Financial Services, a company that specializes in helping fitness businesses service their memberships, is our company of choice and handles all membership payments for us. They can be reached at 800-000-0000. Money for services rendered within the club can be paid at the desk. Please keep in mind that any service over $100 can usually be financed at no cost over 90 days.

## Member etiquette

If you are new to fitness, or worked out in a fitness facility that didn't establish guidelines to help keep the members safe, we have a few suggestions in this section that will keep the gym moving and safe for all members. We also included a separate section earlier in this guide covering club rules. Please adhere to the following etiquette guidelines:

- Always carry a workout towel and clean up after yourself on each piece of equipment you use. The club furnishes spray cleaner throughout the club and we suggest that you use it after using any piece of equipment that your body comes in contact with, such as a bench, or anything else you might sweat on, such as a piece of cardio equipment.

- Allow others to work in between sets. If you are using a piece of equipment for multiple sets, please allow other members to share with you while you are resting.

- Please wear clean outfits. Wearing that favorite T-shirt that has aged in the trunk of your car since your last workout is not acceptable to the other members.

- Be safe at all times. Use the collars on the weights, be aware of where other members are working out, replace all weights after each use, and do not do any exercises or movements that may endanger yourself or other members.

- Watch your language. Questionable language offends many of our members and will not be tolerated.

- Keep your personal things off the workout floors. Gym bags and other personal workout aides are not allowed on the floor due to the hazard they create for other members.

- Please help keep the restrooms and locker rooms safe and clean by cleaning up after yourself. Wipe the counters, flush the toilets, use the urinals, and please shut your lockers after each use.

- Heavy perfumes and colognes are not recommended.

- We ask that all members are left to enjoy their privacy and peace and that no one solicits or bothers other members when they are in the facility

## The first 30 days

Many of our members start their fitness program with their own agenda and simply want to know how they can get the most out of their fitness experience in the shortest period of time. Keeping this in mind, we asked the National Academy of Sports Medicine (NASM), one of the industry's premier certification companies for fitness professionals, to offer their suggestions regarding how members can get the most from their memberships in the shortest period of time. The following list presents their suggestions for how you can be more successful in your personal search for fitness:

*Know your club:*

- Make sure that you know and understand all the services and amenities that your club offers so that you can work with the staff to create a map to success. Many members start first and find out later that the club offers support and guidance in areas that will help them reach their goals that much quicker.

- Have your membership advisor or manager introduce you to someone in the fitness department so you have a point of contact for questions related to your goals. Book your first orientation appointment upon joining the club.

- Explore the facility and acquaint yourself with all the programs and equipment available. Look for your favorites and try something new.

*Know yourself:*

- Work with the fitness staff to complete a comprehensive assessment of your current fitness levels, including movement, general health, and fitness history. These factors are critical in building a successful plan for reaching your goals.

- Create a realistic schedule that is fun and empowering. Many new members dive in too fast and overcommit their time and energy. Build a plan that fits into your current lifestyle and then increase your commitment a little at a time. Schedule your time at the club and book it in advance.

**Build a plan that fits into your current lifestyle and then increase your commitment a little at a time.**

- Hiring a personal trainer short-term or long-term is a great way to make sure you can get the most out of your membership. A qualified trainer will save you tremendous time and focus you on your goals by creating a concise individualized plan. Working with a personal trainer also creates accountability for your time and keeps you motivated.

- Utilize both the fitness and nutrition services that your club provides to maximize your efforts and achieve your goals. Your club provides several options, from specific nutritional guidance and programs to convenient supplements and snacks. Use this expertise and these tools to accelerate your success.

- Take advantage of the floor trainers. Use them to help you learn new equipment that you may have never used before and build rapport with them to help you create accountability and adherence to your goals.

- Leverage the variety your club offers. For example, incorporate group exercise into your program for variation and motivation. By incorporating new activities and exploring other areas of the club, you will truly maximize your membership and your outcomes.

*Fitness and nutrition tips:*

- Work with a professional to assess your current level of fitness, outline an individualized fitness and nutrition program, and follow up every four to six weeks to evaluate progress.

- Your complete fitness plan must include flexibility, core, balance, strength, and power training, combined with a well-rounded nutrition and cardiovascular program. All of these elements are crucial to the overall success of your plan.

- Monitor your fitness and nutrition plan as you progress. Training and nutrition programs should energize you and leave you feeling relaxed. Be cautious not to overtrain or modify your diet too severely, as doing so will cause soreness, fatigue, and discomfort.

- Work to spread your meals throughout the day. Four to six smaller meals will tend to help you curb your appetite and provide sustained energy throughout the day. Utilize your club's nutritional programs and tools to track calorie intake and calories burned.

- Hydration is critical to the overall success of your fitness and nutrition program. On average, a person should consume at least 64 ounces of water per day. It should be noted that strenuous exercise that results in a heavy level of perspiration may further increase an individual's need for water intake.

- Work with a fitness professional to implement an individualized, progressive fitness plan. Reaching your goals faster and more effectively relies on sticking to your plan and progressively increasing your activity and intensity. Minutes, hours, days, and weeks are wasted in the gym without a plan to succeed. The right plan will help you achieve results faster than you ever imagined.

> Your complete fitness plan must include flexibility, core, balance, strength, and power training, combined with a well-rounded nutrition and cardiovascular program.

# Additional Welcome Guide Components

### Using testimonials in your Welcome Guide

You should include at least four full-page testimonials in your Welcome Guide, but don't hesitate to add as many as 10. Testimonials solve one of the most common barriers to joining a fitness facility: Will I fit in as a new member and do other people like me use this business?

To get the most out of your testimonials, use real people who are in your club's target market. Stay away from extreme cases of people who have lost an enormous amount of weight or are too rare in your membership, because the average person can't really relate to these stories. Focus instead on the average people who fit into one of these categories:

**To get the most out of your testimonials, use real people who are in your club's target market.**

- The average person who has lost 20 pounds or so in a reasonable amount of time.

- A person who had a bad experience at another facility and who is now a fan of your business.

- A couple who works out together.

- Someone who feels safe in your business and didn't realize that he would fit in at a gym because he had a bad image of what a fitness business really is.

- An athletic person who is successful in a sport outside of your business.

- A successful businessperson who represents someone in your club's target market.

This list presents just a few examples of the type of person who makes for a good testimonial ad. Plenty of others are out there, but these types are a good place to start. The person will often ask what he should say and you can gently guide him to the point you need to make.

Get the best picture you can and concentrate on how the person looks now. Not many of your members like "before" shots, but if someone is willing and you have quality pictures, you may consider using them.

Be sure to tell the member's story. Who is the member? Does he have kids (put the kids in the picture)? What kind of business does he own or where does he work? The point is to make the member as real as possible to your potential members, since a successful member makes new members feel that they too can succeed at your business.

## Summary

Welcome Guides are great tools to differentiate you from your competitors. The most important question you can ask yourself is: What do I want in front of my potential member when he is sitting at home thinking about my club? You don't want senseless scraps of paper, and you definitely don't want him sitting there with nothing but your price to mull over between beers.

You spend a lot to build your club, and you should remember that whatever someone has in front of them outside your business is also part of your brand.

Welcome Guides also extend your brand beyond your walls. You spend a lot to build your club, and you should remember that whatever someone has in front of them outside your business is also part of your brand. If it looks cheap, it reflects on you and your business.

## Key Points From This Chapter

- Most clubs send guests who don't join immediately home with nothing more than a class schedule and a price sheet.

- If your price is $39 per month or higher, 70 percent of your guests will need two or more visits before they will buy.

- The last thing you want to send the person home to think about is price alone.

- Everyone leaves as a member—either a full member or a trial member. The Welcome Guide is important for both of these groups

- Don't be cheap. Use a three-ring binder with a nice cover that you will change weekly to keep it fresh and exciting.

- If your competition just sends people home with junk, why not be different and give the guest a whole different idea of what service can be even before the sale?

**Tip of the Day**

## Become an expert.

Find something you love and learn more about it than any other person and you'll always find a way to make money. An old adage states that if you read 10 books about something, you will know more about that subject than 90 percent of the people in the world. That statement rings true, especially in the business world.

Find something you are truly passionate about and then learn as much about it as you can. Take classes, read books, ask the experts, and do what it takes to be that one person who knows the most about that subject.

Much of higher education is based upon this premise. Experts focus on certain birds, cultures, countries, types of cars, specific periods of history, and thousands of other topics too numerous to mention. Each is an expert and each has a passion for his area of expertise.

If you want to be a great salesperson, then master the subject. If you want to be a great fitness business owner, then learn more about the industry. The world is wide open to people who have passion and are willing to learn.

# 17

# The Simpler the Price Structure, the Easier the Sale

Even if everything else in your club is right in terms of sales, you still might fail to turn the guest into a new member if your pricing structure is too complicated or confusing. Complicated price structures, which are often the result of a club that has been in business for a long time or of an owner who thinks that he needs something for everyone, can often shut down the sales process, because too many options or choices are available for the consumer to choose from without taking more time to think it over.

Consider the following story of a young couple. The man and woman have been out on a few dates, find each other attractive, and each considers the other to be someone worth spending time with in the future. After a nice evening with dinner, wine, and a little dancing, the guy asks, "Would you like to come to my place for a drink?" This approach is simple yet bold and right to the point.

If he was a club owner, the story would be different. It might be the same dinner, the same wine, and even dancing at the same place, but the question would be different because club people almost always have to do things the hardest way possible.

*"So, let me tell you about the plans you have available with me tonight. First of all, we have the basic plan where you just come to my place, we drink cheap beer, and I hope we get naked somewhere in the process."*

*"The second option, and this offer is for that person who is a little more serious about a long-term relationship, includes a bottle of nice wine, a movie, and, as an extra incentive, if you're willing right now to make up your mind that we should mess around this evening, I'll call ahead and tell my roommate to clean up the place a little and disappear. Of course, the third plan is the one that most women take when they date me. This plan includes*

*really nice wine and breakfast tomorrow, with a personal guarantee that if you don't get the results you want from this evening then all your money will be refunded and you'll be under no further obligation to ever see me again. So, which one of these options is best for you?"*

Club people just make things a little more difficult than regular people, and much of what they stems from old habits from the good old days of fitness. Keeping this fact in mind, this chapter presents the seven deadly sins of membership structures—things that owners do that sabotage their membership structures and kill the sales efforts at the last minute. Closing is not discussed here but is covered in detail in Chapter 18.

# The Seven Deadly Sins of Membership Structures

### Sin #1: Offering way too many options

**Keep it simple by never offering more than three choices to any person at the point of sale.**

Keep it simple by never offering more than three choices to any person at the point of sale. If you focus on just two or three options, you'll gain more confidence in presenting those options and the client will have fewer choices to mull over. It is important to note that any more than three options causes their little heads to shut down and they have to go home to think about it. In other words, too many choices kill the impulse sale.

The alternative close is the tool you want to strive for with your sales team: "So John, which one of these options is best for you?" Car salespeople, while universally hated as the stereotypical hardcore sales dogs, still do practice some solid sales techniques if they are any good. One of the classic sales techniques from their industry is to help the buyer get his choices down to just two automobiles and then say: "Well, John, which one of these two is it going to be today—the red one or the blue one?"

Obviously, what is going on in this situation is that the buyer is no longer considering whether he should buy at all, but rather which one is he going to buy. This simple tool accelerates the sales process because it takes the person out of the realm of tourist and into the reality of actually buying something that day.

Club owners usually get to the "too many options" phase because of that dreaded feeling of trying to have a membership that fits everyone. When you are on trying to build a successful sales program, or improve the existing sales program in your club, start by cleaning up the endless membership choices you present your guests.

The key point is that multiple choices don't individualize the sales process. Instead, this endless array of options just confuses the issue. Another way to view this situation is that offering multiple membership options is really nothing more than throwing a lot of different versions of the same thing at the person without trying to address his individual needs or wants.

Solution-based selling, on the other hand, attempts to build a personalized membership plan based upon a menu system that allows the guest to pick and choose options that he thinks will help him meet his needs. Traditional membership lists merely offer different versions of how long the person can join for, with perhaps a training package tacked on somewhere in the pitch.

*Review the membership tools and what losses mean.*

Annual memberships, because of their collectability and ease of sale compared to longer-term memberships, should be the tool of choice for most club owners. The word "collectable" is another way of describing the loss rates associated with this membership tool. Annual memberships are the most collectable out of all the membership options, which means that you'll collect the most money from the most members over time.

Annual memberships, if handled by a strong third-part financial-services company, traditionally have losses of less than 1 percent per month. It is important to know that losses are calculated monthly but compounded annually. In this case, annual losses for a yearly membership should be less than 10 percent, or put another way, you should collect about $0.90 per dollar of each membership you write over a year's time.

Other popular membership options also have associated loss rates. Review these choices, which you'll find in many facilities, and the loss rates that go with each:

- 24-month memberships and longer—losses of 35 percent and higher
- 12-month memberships—losses of about 10 percent annually
- Open-ended, pay-as-you-go memberships (no contracts)—losses of approximately 48 to 60 percent annually
- 18-month memberships—losses of approximately 12 percent annually

The basic rule to remember when you build your membership plan is as follows: He who collects the most money from the most members will win the fitness business game. In other words, you as an owner or manager have to create a system with which you can sell the highest number of memberships possible from your lead base while using a tool that has the highest probability of collecting the most money from those memberships on the back end using your third-party financial-service company.

*The right tool builds the strongest receivable base.*

If you have the right tool, meaning the one that allows you to collect the most money from the most members, then you will build the strongest

**Annual memberships, because of their collectability and ease of sale compared to longer-term memberships, should be the tool of choice for most club owners.**

receivable base. Receivable base is defined as the combination of all of your members' monthly payments, collected each month in your name by your third-party financial-service company, and then forwarded to the club.

The mistake most rookie owners make when they open their first club is to assume that everyone who buys a membership pays. These owners build business plans that show 1200 members all happily paying their $49 monthly payments—and the gym owner is rich after a year of being in business.

**The trick in the real world is to collect the most money from the most members.**

The trick in the real world, however, is to collect the most money from the most members. Some people just refuse to pay, some get divorced, some lose their jobs, and at least 1 percent of your file moves more than 25 miles from the club each month. In most states, a move of this distance means that you have to cancel the membership. Look at the following example, which shows numbers from a good club:

100 members join your gym on an annual membership
– 10 lost through normal losses (closed accounts, divorce, lost job, etc.)
– 12 lost who move over 25 miles (about 1 percent per month for most clubs)
 78 pay through the end of their year

Using these numbers, if the club owner signs up 1200 members, after adjusting for losses, only approximately 936 will be paying at any one time, (1200 x .78 = 936). The thing to remember is that the receivable base, again the accumulation of all member payments, is the most important asset a club owner owns, because with a receivable base you have the ability to project your revenue into the future. This stable income allows an owner to build a business, acquire debt, and take risk, because once you get a certain amount of members paying each month that money usually stay consistent over time.

Note, however, that no receivable base exists without obligation. Obligation means that the club member has some type of commitment to pay over time, usually in the form of a 12-month membership agreement.

Without obligation, the club may have a lot of members paying each month, but as noted earlier, open-ended, pay-as-you-go memberships have losses of approximately 4 to 5 percent per month, or 48 to 60 percent annually. With these types of memberships, the club has cash flow, but doesn't have the stability that comes from having an actual receivable base. Clubs that use exclusively open-ended, pay-as-you-go memberships, for example, might lose as much as 40 percent of their memberships to a new competitor in the first 90 days that new club is open, because no obligation tool is in place to keep the members from leaving en masse.

*Back to the simple choices*

Assume a club owner is operating in a competitive market that has his prime opponent using nothing but open-ended memberships. The owner wants to compete, but doesn't want to lose the power of building a receivable base. The following plan is both simple and effective at protecting this owner's business:

- $59 one-time membership fee—$59 per month open-ended
- $59 one-time membership fee—$49 per month x 12 months

Both of these options would be presented at the point of sale and the club's sales team could still use the alternative close: "Well John, which one of these options is best for you." The owner is this example can still show an open-ended membership that matches his competitor's price strategy, but also build up his receivable base with the 12-month core membership. Research shows that if you offer an annual membership that is between $8 and $10 cheaper than the open-ended option you will get about 80 percent of your new members to pick the annual option. You might explain the options to your prospects as follows:

*"Well, John, we have two membership plans available. The first is our month-to-month, pay-as- you-go membership and it is designed for members who like the freedom to come and go as they please. We have, for example, a lot of members who only spend part of the year here and like to have a membership only while they are in town.*

*If, on the other hand, you are a local who is here year-round, then you might want to look at the annual membership plan, with which you can save $120 per year. This plan is our most popular, as it is designed for folks who plan to work out on a regular basis and want to save a little money.*

*So John, which one of these plans is best for you?"*

In this example, the member was given two options to choose from at the point of sale, again based upon the club owner's desire to be competitive. The owner will also build his membership receivable base by selling a large number of annual plans.

*Don't forget the method of payment.*

Annual memberships, based upon a contractual agreement, establish the obligation between the club and the member. If you have an obligation from the member, which provides the club owner with the ability to project income into the future—and a high percentage of members will fulfill that obligation by paying to term—you then have one of the two components in place to build a strong receivable base.

The second component is securing the method of payment by the member. Method of payment is how the new member elects to make his payment each month. The trend is to force electronic funds transfers (EFT) from the members. EFT means that the new member gives the club

If you have an obligation from the member, which provides the club owner with the ability to project income into the future—and a high percentage of members will fulfill that obligation by paying to term—you then have one of the two components in place to build a strong receivable base.

permission to automatically take his payment each month on a certain date from his checking account, savings account, or a credit card.

However, a large percentage of your members still won't embrace the idea of giving a young salesperson at a fitness center—not always thought of as a stable business anyway—access to their personal finances. Most owners who defend EFT as the only option claim that they never have any problem getting their new members to take EFT, so it isn't a problem in their area. This defense is like a Honda® salesperson stating that he had no trouble selling Hondas to his customers who bought Hondas. The person came in for a Honda, bought a Honda, and is probably happy with his Honda.

If someone is in your gym to buy a membership, then he is probably already comfortable with what you do and how you charge, meaning that he is also the wrong person to ask about your pricing structures and method of payment. Yes, you probably had no problem selling EFT to your new members, but the big question, and it would be the same question to ask the Honda salesman, is what is the perception of your product or method of payment to someone who is not already standing in your business buying?

Forced EFT can be a barrier to someone even inquiring about a membership, especially if he believes that it is his only payment method. What owners forget is that joining a fitness facility of any type is a decision made based upon the discretionary money a person has available. If any money is left after his primary expenses are paid, then he might decide to spend a little on a membership at a fitness business. As an owner, you have to remember that he doesn't need you to survive; so forcing him to take EFT might be a good thing for the club, but is not necessarily a good thing for the potential member.

The theory behind EFT is that you will collect more money from more members. In fact, an EFT company in the fitness business years ago did quite well with an ad campaign that stated that you could now collect all the money from all of your members every single month. When EFT first came out, this new system of getting a member's payment seemed like a source of magic that would solve every collection issue in existence. It didn't, but it did make for a good ad.

Owners have to stop obsessing about collecting every payment from every member, and they have to get over the feeling that if a member stiffs them for a payment, it is something personal against them or their club. Remember, he who collects the most money from the most members will win the fitness business game. Your goal then is not to collect every payment, but to collect the most money you can from the most people.

A prime example is a club owner who forces EFT and won't let someone become a member who doesn't have a checking account or credit card, or just

> **Owners have to stop obsessing about collecting every payment from every member, and they have to get over the feeling that if a member stiffs them for a payment, it is something personal against them or their club.**

doesn't want to give the club access to his accounts. Many owners refuse to accept this person as a member because of fear that he will sign up and then not make all of his payments as promised. So what if he doesn't? Assume that the club has the following pricing strategy:

- $59 one-time membership fee—$49 per month on an annual basis (EFT)
- $59 one-time membership fee—$54 per month on an annual basis (coupon/check)

Coupon/check means that the person pays just as you probably pay most of your personal bills: You get a statement or coupon book from the company you owe money to and then you write check each month and mail it to them. EFT is cheaper to process and most third-party financial-service companies charge the clubs less for EFT per member than they do for manually collecting checks each month. It is cheaper for them to service EFT and they pass that savings along to the club, so it is cheaper for you to have your members serviced via EFT. You should in turn pass that savings along to those clients who choose that method of payment as illustrated in the previous pricing example.

But you should always offer both options of payment. As mentioned earlier, the owner who won't let anyone pay without EFT is actually losing money. Would you rather have six payments from someone and then have him go bad, or not take any payments and force that person to join another gym, where he will make those six payments? The owner was so worried about getting stiffed, which he did, that he actually turned down six payments from a member. Again, don't worry about collecting all the money from all the members. Instead, worry about collecting the most money from the most members.

> **The owner who won't let anyone pay without EFT is actually losing money.**

Continuing with this example, this club owner offered a $5 discount for the new member who is willing to set up EFT with his accounts. You might present this option as follows:

*As you can see John, we have a one-time membership fee of $59 and our monthly dues are $49 per month based upon an annual membership. This payment is based upon our Easy Pay program, which allows the club to automatically draft the payment each month from either your checking account or credit card, saving both the club and you time and money.*

*If you'd like to write a check each month for your payment, that is fine with us too, but we charge $5 more for that option since it does cost the club a little more to process those payments each month.*

*So, John, which one of these options is best for you?*

The difference in price should at least be $5 and some owners have gone as far as a $10 difference. The choice is yours as an owner, but you should offer both options at the point of sale and let the member decide which method of payment is best for him.

*Alternatives to the annual membership*

Sometimes a person trying to join your club might have a legitimate reason why he doesn't want any type of annual, or even month-to-month, membership. He might be, for example, a professional of some sort who is only in the area doing consulting for a month or two, or he might have just sold his house and will be moving in a few months.

You should, in this case, have a backup to the primary two or three choices that you offer to everyone else. These alternatives to your regular memberships should also be kept as simple as possible. Avoid adding more layers as you get more experience and as the club ages.

You should think about your membership structure as being similar to having to clean out your garage every year or so. Once a year, you should go back and review your entire membership offering and see if it can be simplified or restructured to lower any possible barriers for your sales team.

> **Once a year, you should go back and review your entire membership offering and see if it can be simplified or restructured to lower any possible barriers for your sales team.**

❑ *The short-term membership.* This membership is good for up to three months, but *do not call it a three-month membership.* This tool helps you avoid adding a one-month and six-month option, both of which clutter your offerings and confuse the potential member. "Do you have a one-month membership?" "Well, yes we do. It's called our short-term membership and it's actually good for up to three months."

❑ *Two adults living at the same address.* You can't, and shouldn't, list membership options as "couples." Two adults living at the same household is a better way, and a legal way, of handling married couples and couples of the same sex. The short recommendation, which most owners don't really follow, but it bears mentioning anyway, is that you should drop many of the archaic ways you may be tempted to use to identify what a couple really looks like.

The old standard was to restrict your couples membership to two people who are married and share the same last name and the same bank account. Those of you who think this scenario is still relevant need to crawl out from under that time rock. For those of you who still think Elvis is alive, it is time to consider that one half of a married couple may keep his or her own last name for business, professional, or personal reasons. Many people manage their own money, especially in couples that both work, and maintain separate checking accounts. And as shocking as it is to you ultraconservatives, people of the same sex often get married and are protected by the law in many states as a legal union, even if the state doesn't consider the union to be a "marriage."

What does all this mean to you as an owner or manager? Keep it simple and lower the barrier to sales. You can do this by using "two adults living at the same address" as your category head and then accepting any two people who ask for that membership without wasting a lot of time trying to determine if indeed they are a couple. Why would you care? Take the money and take the membership and avoid the appearance of discrimination.

You should also try to maintain a higher return-per-member by limiting the discount you offer through this category anyway. For example, review this recommended two-person membership:

- One person:$59—$49 x 12 months
- Two adults living at the same address:$89—$89 x 12 months

In this example, the owner is offering his version of the couples membership at only a slightly reduced price. Note that the membership fee is $89 for the two people and the monthly fee is only $89, which represents a $9 dollar discount from the full price.

If you want to collect the most money from the most members, you should write each couple as two separate memberships by dividing the monthly fee by two. Over a year's time, and due to things out of your control as an owner, such as divorce, you will collect a higher percentage of total money from the file by using this technique. The obvious reason is that when a couple breaks up and they are on the same contract you probably won't get paid by either one, but if each person in the couple has his or her own membership agreement you will have a better chance of collecting from at least one of them.

❏ *The daily drop-in fee.* You should charge at least $15 per visit for your daily fee. Some small-town owners and managers are currently charging $5, so $15 seems outrageous, but you have to establish a solid minimum somewhere. In this case, you should show the higher daily fee because of the member/guest scenario that eats many owners alive. This situation occurs when a member walks in with his friend, often from out of town, and says, "This is Jimmy, and he is my brother from out of state. You don't mind if he works out today for free, do you?"

**You should charge at least $15 per visit for your daily fee.**

Yes, you do mind but you're stuck due to the limitations of your membership options. If you state a higher daily fee, however, you can offer a member guest option:

- Daily fee—$15
- Guest of a member (who does not qualify for a trial membership)—$7.50

If you offer a 50 percent discount to your member's guest, everyone wins. Your member feels that he got his brother a deal, the brother did get a deal, and you didn't have to give away a free workout.

❑ *Punch cards.* Using punch cards also simplifies the system. Using the $15 daily fee, your punch-card option would be 10 workouts at $120 (member saves $30). You not-so-brave people can go down to $99, but that's the bottom limit. Be sure to put a two-month expiration on the back.

❑ *VIP memberships.* If you are operating in any type of resort or tourist area, consider a VIP Week option at approximately $69 for the week. Owners give away too much with a traditional one-week membership option by undercharging at approximately $29 for the entire week. Throw in a T-shirt, because nothing says vacation like "World Gym®, San Diego," or any other cool town or area, and add a few bottles of water and maybe some tanning if you have it. In other words, jack up the price and throw in a lot of stuff that doesn't cost you much. Remember, it is all about the T-shirt with the name of some cool place on it that the guy can wear at home.

In summary, keep your options simple. Your offering at the point of sale should be limited to two or three choices, but have backups for the legitimate person who doesn't fit a regular membership.

## Sin #2: Trying to collect too much money "today"

Exceptions exist for every rule, and you may own one of those clubs in such a high-end area that this rule doesn't really apply to you, but the other 99 percent of owners and managers would make their sales process easier by limiting the total amount of money you collect from a new person for a membership (paid-in-full memberships don't count in this context) to $89 or less on the day he signs up. A lot of research has been done on this topic by various consumer groups, but the bottom line is that any combination of money due from someone trying to join your facility that is over $89 limits the impulse nature of the sale, turning it into a family decision, or at the very least something a single person needs to walk away from so he can think about it overnight.

*The one-time membership fee*

Through the years, this fee has been called an initiation fee, a down payment, commitment money, or the initial investment. The term that makes sense to most members, however, is a "one-time membership fee."

You need to collect this fee to offset the various costs of getting a new person started. This fee should cover at least the cost of marketing and the commission for the person making the sale.

The cost of marketing is really the cost per lead. All owners and managers should calculate their cost per lead once each month. The cost per lead is determined as follows:

> Any combination of money due from someone trying to join your facility that is over $89 limits the impulse nature of the sale, turning it into a family decision, or at the very least something a single person needs to walk away from so he can think about it overnight

Total cost of marketing for the month/total leads from all sources = cost per lead

For example:

**$4000 marketing cost/100 leads = $40 per lead**

In this example, the club owner had a $40 cost per lead to generate 100 leads from for the month. Count all leads from all sources and work from the gross average, because you don't always know the exact source of each prospect.

The cost per lead has risen in recent years, but you should try to keep your number in the $35 to $50 range. This number only includes money spent on external marketing and does not include fixed advertising costs, such as the Yellow Pages.

If your number is over $50, then you probably need to reevaluate your marketing sources. You may be below that range and still be able to write enough business for your club if you have a high referral number or strong referral program.

Commissions are mentioned throughout this book, but are worth mentioning in this context as well. You should pay salespeople a flat hourly rate and a flat fee per sale. You should not pay any percentages, which tend to get your salespeople thinking like car guys and also drive your cost of sale too high.

It is hard to give exact numbers due to the variations in what it costs to hire someone in various parts of the country, but you can use a few safe rules as guidelines. Your salespeople might make two or three dollars more per hour than a front-counter person in your market. The cost of a front-counter person usually reflects what is called "local minimum wage," which is not the actual federal minimum wage. What it takes for you to get someone to show up and work your counter is approximately the same amount it takes in your market for other businesses to get entry-level workers.

Salespeople are usually front-counter people, or other entry-level people, who have proven themselves and are moving up. They might also be people from the outside world with the traits and skills you need. In either case, that person is probably a more qualified employee and worth the extra two or three dollars it takes to hire talent in your market.

Commissions also vary around the country, but you can use the following general guideline to build your system. Owners and managers in most Southern and Midwestern states start commissions at approximately $10 to $15 for each new annual membership sold. Other markets are in the $15 to $40 range, with the upper dollars being paid in major metro markets that can generate a higher monthly fee, such as New York and its $89-per-month memberships.

> The cost per lead has risen in recent years, but you should try to keep your number in the $35 to $50 range.

Putting these numbers together, your one-time membership fee should at least cover the cost per lead and the commission to your salesperson. For example, if you charged a one-time fee of $59, this fee would easily cover a $15 commission and a $40 cost per lead.

*Don't collect the membership fee and the first month's dues together.*

It is not unusual for an owner who panics in a price-sensitive market to drop the membership fee altogether and just charge one month's dues up front and write a membership for 11 months. But this owner is still collecting a chunk of money up front and is still writing a membership paid out over time. In other words, by asking for money up front from the person buying the new membership, the owner still collected a membership fee—he just didn't call it a membership fee.

If you are good enough to get a large chunk of money up front, which might be the combination of a membership fee and the first month's dues, then simply restructure your program slightly, and you will make more money. For example, consider a membership with a $59 membership fee and monthly dues of $49 per month based upon an annual membership:

- Possibility 1: $59 and $49 ($108) collected today and the owner writes a membership for 11 months, creating a total of $647 for this membership.

- Possibility 2 (Modifying the membership slightly): $69 collected today and the owner writes a membership for 12 months, creating a total of $657 for this membership.

In the second possibility, the owner makes more money overall but has an easier membership to sell because he is asking for less money up front. Most importantly, he is adding a twelfth payment from each member to his receivable base. Over one year, his entire outstanding membership base will increase by 8.3 percent, which is quite substantial for most clubs.

*How to determine your membership fee*

Your one-time membership fee should be at least equivalent to your monthly dues but no more than $89. For example, if your dues were $49 per month per member, then your membership fee range would be $49-89, again without collecting the first month's dues.

## Sin#3: Forcing a specific payment date

**Always remember that you need customers more than they need you.**

Always remember that you need customers more than they need you. This thought should be obvious to any business owner, but over the years, as you become mired in your own systems and bureaucracy, you may tend to lose

254

sight of the fact that when someone signs up as a member at your club, he is actually doing you a favor and not the other way around.

Small-business owners tend to build or acquire systems over time that they think will help their businesses grow. Sometimes, however, those systems become barriers to the customer and can actually start to work against the business.

In the real world, defined as anything out there beyond the fitness realm, no better example exists than the American Express® card. Many small businesses, because of the slightly higher cost of the card versus MasterCard® or Visa®, won't take American Express for any purchases.

Think about that decision from the customer's viewpoint for a minute or two. The customer picked a restaurant out of a whole street of choices, brought his business associates, spent several hundred dollars or more on a meal and wine, and now the owner of that restaurant informs the meal's host that he doesn't take American Express, which is the guest's primary business card.

The restaurant needs the customer much more than the customer needs the restaurant, especially when a dozen other places to eat are within a few minutes walking distance. The owner should take the card, be thankful that someone is trying to spend money in his business, and get over it. If he is that worried about the extra dollar or so per $100, which is the difference between that card and the others, then he should adjust his prices by a few cents and take the card.

In fact, the most important thing this owner needs to learn is that if someone is trying to give you money you should consider taking it, especially when the person spending the money walked by other businesses just like yours to get to you. "Take the money and be grateful" is not a bad business plan.

Many owners suffer from this same mentality in the fitness business, and it is often due to their systems. For example, a club owner tries to falsely save money by collecting his own memberships. He buys some software, hires a woman he knew from high school who is sort of a bookkeeper, and sets up his own service office in his club. The flaw to his thinking, besides giving his most valuable asset to someone who is not skilled enough to handle the job, is that his bank, which is handling the monthly draft of member payments on EFT, only allows the club to use one payment date per month.

The club's sales team now has to make sure that every EFT payment they set up with the new members falls on the fifth of the month, which again is the only day the bank will allow the club to use as a payment date. The problem arises, of course, when a person trying to become a member requests any other day of the month but the fifth.

> **When someone signs up as a member at your club, he is actually doing you a favor and not the other way around.**

*"Well, I think I will get signed up today, but could you change that payment date to the fifteenth of the month, which is my payday."*

*"No."*

*"Well, I do get paid twice a month, so just go ahead and make it the first."*

*"No."*

We know that the salesperson goes through all of the practiced cover-ups at this point, because this conversation is definitely not the first time this scenario has happened in the sales process, but the answer, no matter how he sweetens it, is always "no." And "no" is not a word you want to use often if you are trying to learn customer service.

First, the system itself is wrong, but instead of listening to the guests and their complaints and then changing the system, the club owner just keeps forcing the issue because that's what his bank told him to do. Second, the club needs the new member more than the new member needs the club, which begs the question of why an owner who is trying to make money would put up a barrier that makes the sale harder for his staff. The answer to the customer's request should be as follows:

*"Of course we can change that date to the fifteenth for you. We appreciate your business and we try to do anything we can to make sure you're going to enjoy this club."*

Set the payment date on any day the person wants. If your system can't handle that option, then change systems. Also, don't forget to take the money if someone is trying to give it to you, even though it may not be the most convenient form for you. Remember, the person did have other options and decided to help you feed your family this week.

## Sin #4: Not having quality closing tools

Nothing says "cheap" and "low-rent" to your potential members more clearly than writing your prices out during your close on a yellow pad or plain paper. Another common mistake, especially in clubs that have been around for a few years, is that over time the club accumulates a variety of forms that have been added by different managers or employees or during different phases of the club's history.

*"Oh, that sea green brochure with the Oriental lettering. That is from our mind/body days when we were really into meditation and yoga, man. We had mats, candles, and this really cool tinkling music. Yeah, and that threefold brochure is from our franchise days. We started out as a franchise and left, but we really like the brochure and that big furry animal on the cover is my favorite. And that group schedule—just copy the copy because I lost the*

> Nothing says "cheap" and "low-rent" to your potential members more clearly than writing your prices out during your close on a yellow pad or plain paper.

*original last year but we haven't really changed the classes much, so we just copy the copies when we get low."*

The key to remember is that everything has to match if you're trying to build the image of a quality brand—and to sell your club memberships for a higher dollar. At least once a year, you should lay all of your forms and handouts on a table and make sure that they present a common image when shown together. What happens is that you never really see all of your materials together, so most owners aren't really aware of how old and dated some of the forms are or how cheap they look when displayed together.

One of the most important forms in the overall scheme of things is the closing sheet, which is the tool you use to present the prices toward the end of the sales tour. For a closing sheet to be effective, it should have the following characteristics:

- It should be one page front and back.

- It must clearly state your two or three primary membership options on the front.

- The front should also list everything that is included with your base memberships.

- The prices should be printed on the closing sheet and not written as you present.

- The back should clearly state, with prices, options related to the annual or main membership you offer.

- Other options in the club, such as personal training or weight management, should be listed and detailed on a separate sheet, including the prices and financing options. Do not list these items on the regular price sheet. Sell the membership first, fill out the membership agreement, and then move on to other options in the club. If the client signs up for other options and is financing, use a separate membership agreement with a separate payment schedule. This system is detailed later in this chapter

- Have a line on the bottom where the club's salesperson can sign and date it so you know who presented the prices to that guest.

- Print the closing sheets on heavy cardstock and use a professional designer to give this tool a professional look. Remember that you are asking for money at this point.

## Sin #5: Offering deals (and dancing with the devil)

If you have to make deals to close someone, then you are not a salesperson. You are a discounter, and a difference exists between the two. Salespeople learn to present the service, and learn to close, by using added value. Chapter

> One of the most important forms in the overall scheme of things is the closing sheet, which is the tool you use to present the prices toward the end of the sales tour.

15 covered the concept of enhancing rather than discounting, and while this technique is very strong and effective, many of the old sales guys just can't make the transition. This resistance, or inability, to change stems from the fact that a lot of these old sales dogs never really learned to sell in the first place.

In real-world sales, those salespeople at the top who sell for companies such as Xerox® learn how to master their product, present for value, and add value to drive the sale. Other salespeople on the lower end of the sales spectrum only move product or make sales by learning to cut the price of what they are selling. Anybody can sell a Mercedes® for half price, for example, but what kind of salesperson do those dealerships attract that they can sell an expensive item for full price?

**The fitness industry has a history of whacking the price to get the deal done.**

The fitness industry has a history of whacking the price to get the deal done. This system of pressure selling has built a large amount of distrust and fear regarding how the industry operates. Who looks forward to buying a new car when you know that the beating in the office, the cheap décor, the salesman leaving the office to see the closer, and mind-numbing rudeness are all part of the process?

The negative perception of how people are going to be treated in a fitness center when they visit is the same, and the primary villain in this process is the technique used to make deals. For example, two friends come in together and are sitting across from the salesperson after a brief tour. The sales guy presents the $59 membership fee and monthly dues of $49 per month. The two guys balk and the salesperson comes back immediately with the classic, "If you're willing to get this done today, I'll let both of you in for just one membership fee so you can split the $59 instead of both paying."

Some salespeople say such things out of habit and have been doing so since the dawn of modern fitness, but the industry as a whole seldom stops to think about how this technique is perceived by the consumer. These two guys might buy, for example, but how good do they feel about what they bought?

*"Well, we beat that guy up on that one didn't we?"* says the first one.

*"I don't know. I think we should have held out a little and he might have dropped the $59 completely,"* replies the second guy.

*"Come on, we got a good deal and you know it,"* says the first.

*"Yeah? I'm not so sure. My buddy from work, Kenny, was in there last week and he said the guy threw him some personal training and let him in without any money up front. I don't know, man, I think we're the ones who got hammered here."*

These two guys just joined a new club and feel, at best, questionable about the experience. Did the guy treat us right? Should we have asked for more? Did someone else get something we didn't? Consumers ask all of these legitimate questions every day about this type of fitness business and this type of sales practice.

Your brand is more than just ads and signage. It's also about word of mouth and your image in the community. In this example, the salesperson did his job as he was taught and sold two memberships, but how much damage does he do to this business in the long run?

It's hard to imagine that this club would get many buddy referrals, because who—especially among women—is going to want to put their friends into a situation where they know they are going to feel like they were taken advantage of by the salesperson? It is also hard to imagine that many new members are going to want to buy other products and services from that club, since they would have to question if they were being cheated on those prices too. Club owners that use this deal-making process will have trouble selling almost everything else because the members are trained, by the owner's own staff through the initial sales process, to try to beat down the price on everything. The stated price is no longer the real price to the member, but simply a starting point to let the negotiation games begin.

Remember, close the deal with services and enhancements, but never come off the price. The old adage that states, "The price is the price is the price," is a good model to follow. Deal making at the point of sale kills your integrity, and once you lose that value it's hard to regain a positive image in your community.

## Sin #6: Asking for real money in a T-shirt

As a group, club employees often resemble homeless people without the shopping cart or the puppy. Owners buy cheap T-shirts for their staff members and call them uniforms. They don't set, or enforce, dress codes and details such as decent shoes and real pants escape them.

The trainers are an entirely other story: work boots, skin-tight shirts actually designed to be worn under other clothing, baggy shorts, ponytails on the guys, and the apparent need for tattoos. Are they hip and trendy, or are they just being the stereotypical dumb trainers who don't know how to dress enough to show any respect for their clients?

The rule in sales states that it is harder to get full price from someone when you're dressed in a T-shirt and jeans. The consumer just stares and wonders what he is missing when someone so young and dressed so poorly talks about the benefits of the club and says that it is only $49 per month, which is obviously more than the salesperson spent on his entire outfit.

The old "dress for success" theory does still apply to making money in sales. If you want to get $49 from someone, then you should at least look like

**The rule in sales states that it is harder to get full price from someone when you're dressed in a T-shirt and jeans.**

you're worth $59. Another way to look at "dress for success" is that your uniforms should be at least one step above the image of your club if the plan is to present your business as professionally as possible.

Many male owners get lazy and start drifting into the club in old jeans or khakis and a slightly worn golf shirt. Female owners sometimes wear their workout clothes all day long. Your staff then matches your standard and the entire business gets that lazy, much-too-casual look that will hurt your sales efforts.

You have to remember that a sale is still taking place and that someone from your side is going to ask someone from the other side for money. With this fact in mind, shouldn't you at least show the person you are asking to support your business a little respect by dressing your staff in decent business clothes?

**It is just good business to do everything you can do to present your business in the best light possible, and that effort begins with something every owner can do: Make your people dress as well as possible.**

It is just good business to do everything you can do to present your business in the best light possible, and that effort begins with something every owner can do: Make your people dress as well as possible. Adhere to the following simple rules regarding uniforms:

- Don't buy uniforms—Don't spend the money as an owner or manager on uniforms. They are a waste of money, and since you probably try to save a little cash whenever you can, you end up buying the cheapest things imaginable, such as golf shirts and T-shirts. Golf shirts or T-shirts with your logo on them are not great uniforms. They are just what you do when you don't know what else to do.

- Start with black—Ask your staff to wear black to work with no T-shirts or golf shirts. If they have a question about how something looks, you, as the owner or manager, have the right to say no. Labor boards won't make you pay if you ask your staff to wear black, because it is a color most people own and would wear anyway. Your sales team, for example, could wear black pants or black skirts, a nice black top, such as a mock turtleneck for the guys and even black jackets if it's that type of club. The newer-style shirts, which are made to be worn outside and not tucked in, would also be a great choice for a salesperson or even a trainer. Trainers could also wear black shorts, black shoes, and a mock turtleneck in the cooler months or an open-neck shirt with long sleeves—anything except cheap T-shirts and worn-out golf shirts. Golf shirts, as a note to you male owners, are not very flattering for your female staff members and seldom fit well.

- Avoid the killer logo—Don't put your logo on their stuff. First of all, if you require a logo, then you have to pay for the clothes. Secondly, it doesn't really add anything anyway. If the guest doesn't know he is in your club, then a logo on the salesperson's shirt probably won't really help matters much anyway.

- Require owners and managers to dress well—If you work in the club, even if you own it or manage it, then you must dress like everyone else. Let members know that you're all on the same team. ""If you need help, look for anyone wearing black."

- Replace your name badges—Replace the old-style name tags with neck lanyards. The employee walks in feeling good because he is wearing nice, black clothes that look a little stylish, takes his lanyard off the hook, slips it around his neck, and he is ready to go to work. When he takes it off and goes to lunch, he still feels good because he is not a human billboard for your business. You might consider using round plastic disks attached to the lanyards with the person's first name on both sides. The first name is all you need—no titles and no name of the club. It makes it easy for the member to see your name without having to get too close to someone's chest to read the fine print.

- Make exceptions—You will save a lot of money by not buying uniforms, but once in a while you might want to splurge for a special occasion. For example, if you've had a long winter, you might want to buy some bright, special-colored shirts for the spring to get some energy in the place. You might try purple or bright gold, which looks good with the black pants. In the summer, you could switch to shorts and fun shirts. You must pay for any special clothing requirements, but you can use uniforms as a way to infuse energy into your business.

Uniforms are a sales tool, just like a sales close or a free gym bag. Many owners spend more time in their clubs than they do at home and they become too casual over time. The club is a place of business, and you have to remember that you are asking for money, so dress for success and give yourself the best chance possible to score the sale.

## Sin #7: Using traditional upselling, which lowers your overall sales

Traditional upselling means that a potential member comes into the club to buy a simple membership, and 20 minutes later, he is getting pitched on a much higher-priced package that includes training, childcare, tanning, and whatever else the salesperson can throw into the deal. This process can be somewhat successful with the right salesperson, but is it effective when compared to your overall sales numbers?

Owners sometimes forget the emotional aspect of getting yourself into a club and signing up for a membership. They also forget that the person probably has some type of vague idea of what the club charges for a membership.

Emotionally, the person is ready to get going or he wouldn't be in club, but don't think that he is such a wreck that he will do stupid things, such as sign up for everything you have available. Most importantly, he probably came in

> The club is a place of business, and you have to remember that you are asking for money, so dress for success and give yourself the best chance possible to score the sale.

with an idea of what he has to pay for a membership, and if you're too far outside that range you shut him down when you hit him with the big numbers.

For example, he knows from the guys at work that you cost about $50 per month, which he also knows is within his budget. He also realizes that he is fat, disgusting, hasn't had a date in two years, and needs to lose 20 pounds. The salesperson smells a weak fish in the water and strikes. The guy is a mess and the salesperson tries to sell the full package, including training, at the point of sale. Instead of hearing the $49 he was expecting, along with about $75 to join, the potential member hears $150 to get started and learns that he will need to come up with another $400 to get started on that training package. The salesperson offers to finance it, but the guy's monthly dues go from $49 to $89, which is more than he had in the budget in his head.

The sales guy might get this sale, but the important question when it comes to building a successful sales system is, how many people does he lose because the guest simply became overloaded at the thought of the bigger price and walked out of the club? It is almost like an old bait and switch that car guys use, where they advertise a car at an unbelievable price but when you get to the dealership that particular one is gone. They do, however, happen to have another car that costs slightly more money. The bait was the cheap car and the switch was the move to the higher-priced model. In many ways, you are doing the same thing to your guests by saying, "Here is the price, but by the time we're finished with you that price will be gone."

A pricing model was used in the fitness industry not too many years ago, for example, that had a price sheet showing the base membership as advanced, using the explanation that since you didn't get any help with this program then you must be an advanced exerciser. The basic program was much more money, but you actually got help from the club, including the club's weight-management program and training. This type of sale actually shut down the consumer, since he was obviously new to the club, didn't fit the advanced membership description, and couldn't afford the basic program. This all-or-nothing approach by the club forced the prospect to buy more. It backfires if he doesn't want to, or simply can't, spend more money. He has to walk out because he doesn't fit the other category left open to him, which is the advanced membership.

**If you want to build an effective sales program, you don't build with the thought of making people feel stupid in the process.**

If you want to build an effective sales program, you don't build with the thought of making people feel stupid in the process. In the previous example, the guest has nowhere to go but out the door. The membership he wants and can afford is taken away from him by a strategy that makes him feel really stupid about fitness, while the one that might help him the most is too expensive and was forced on him when he came in looking for something else.

*Try the sales two-step and everyone is happy.*

A bird in the hand is worth two in the bush. You heard old people say nonsense like that for years when you were growing up, but what does it really mean and does it apply to you?

Put in other terms, you are sitting in a bar talking to a 7 when two 10s walk in the door. Do you risk losing the 7, who is a sure thing, and take a chance on a clearly better option, or do you hold onto your 7 and be happy with what you have? The old adage suggests that you would be wiser holding on to what you already have rather than risking it all and coming up with nothing later.

This saying also applies to selling memberships in a club. If someone is trying to give you money for a basic membership, take the money first and then risk going for extra money later, after the potential member has signed the paperwork and joined the club. The system for getting this sale done is called the sales two-step, which simply means that you should still upsell and go for more money, but you should use a two-step process that ensures that you will get the membership first before you risk going for the extra money and total rejection.

**If someone is trying to give you money for a basic membership, take the money first and then risk going for extra money later, after the potential member has signed the paperwork and joined the club.**

When the guest comes in and is sitting at the table, get the basic membership out of the way first before you attempt to sell him anything else. The sales two-step might look as follows. John has been shown the following membership options:

- $59–$49 per month for 12 months (EFT)
- $59–$54 per month for 12 months (coupon/check)

*"Well John, pick out the best option for you and let's get you signed up today…*

*Okay, you've picked the $49 per month EFT option. Let's get that membership agreement filled out and get you started today…*

*Good, now that the paperwork is done, John, let me show you a little more about that personal training option we were discussing. The package I would recommend to you is this one for $500 for 10 sessions, which would get you through a full month of training here at the club. You were worried about doing the right things this time and a full month of working with one of our personal coaches would definitely get you set up correctly and help you get the most out of your membership…*

*We also will finance that training if you like. Simply put down one-fourth and we'll finance the rest over 90 days.*

If John can afford this extra money, then the club will win by getting a second membership agreement to collect in addition to John's original membership. More importantly, if he balks at the training, the club still has John's basic membership, he is in the system, and he might buy the training in the future when he has more money. Either way, the club wins, as opposed to the earlier example.

The sales two-step is an easy way to work through the upsell process without hurting the client or the club's overall sales numbers. The client came in expecting to buy a membership and that is what he was sold. He also was pleasantly surprised at the other options that were explained to him, but he didn't feel the pressure to take it if he couldn't afford it. Again, he still got what he wanted and the club still made money that day.

## A bonus sin: Sitting in the office

You don't make money in an office; you make money on the floor. As stated in Chapter 2, 95 percent of what you do is sell somebody something every day, and most of that selling isn't done in an office.

You make friends, build contacts, get referrals, and drive business by staying behind the counter or on the floor, especially during prime time. The last place you need to be if you're serious about making more money is in an office sitting and staring at a computer.

> Concentrate on making money by being where the money is made, which is where the people are.

Concentrate on making money by being where the money is made, which is where the people are. "Thank you for coming in today," "Thank you for your business," and "Hey, you brought a guest. My name is Mike and I'm the owner. Welcome to the club," are all comments that drive the numbers, but they can only be made when you're in front of your customers on the floor.

If it is prime time, get on the floor. Develop this discipline by setting a fixed time every day when you and the managers shut your doors and are banned from going back into those offices until the club is through its prime hours. When you're consistently on the floor, you'll start to see money you didn't notice before and you'll start to make more money from a lot more people.

# Key Points From This Chapter

- The simpler the price structure, the easier the sales process.
- Most clubs have way too many membership options due to years of adding as they go in an effort to find something for everybody.
- The right membership tools will build a strong receivable base for the cub.
- You never collect all the money from all the members: He who collects the most money from the most members will win.
- Keep your choices at point of sale to no more than two or three options.

- Keep the total upfront money to less than $89.

- Don't force a specific payment date. If your system can't handle random dates, then change your system.

- Use quality closing tools, such as printed closing sheets.

- If you make deals, you lower the perceived value of your business and make it harder for your salespeople to do their jobs over time.

- Dress for success, especially when it comes to your sales team.

- Traditional upselling will hurt your overall sales numbers over time.

- Stay out of the offices. You don't make money sitting in front of a computer.

---

**Tip of the Day**

# Learn to work.

Many fitness business owners lament about the good old days and how the work ethic of their employees used to be so much better than it is with today's work force. These owners are not crazy old men lost in the past, but frustrated employers who have a hard time finding good employees who display any type of work ethic.

One owner was particularly upset that he had to fire a young female desk person who just couldn't understand why she couldn't text message her friends from work if she wasn't busy. Another was equally frustrated over employees that take the maximum sick days every time they want to hang at the beach with their friends.

Do people have different expectations about work today compared to the past? Yes, but at some point you still have to make a living and you still are taking someone else's money. Work ethic is just another way of being professional and having pride in who you are and how you work.

Coming in late, not being properly dressed, wasting the day on the Internet or your cell phone, or calling in sick when you know people are counting on you isn't cool, hip, or trendy. It's rude and the first step toward unemployment.

Some employees wake up too late after wasting a lot of years bouncing from job to job trying to do it their way. Do things this way and you end up broke and with no references, because you either quit or were fired from every job you had. It may sound old, but working is a privilege and sooner or later you're going to need to understand what the term "work ethic" really means.

# 18

# The Steps of the Sale

The goal of building an effective sales system in your club should have the expected outcome of ending up with a repeatable, structured system that can be used by seasoned veterans and rookies alike to drive memberships in your business. "Repeatable" is defined as a structure that uses the same steps and processes each and every time without a lot of variation. This structure, or set plan of attack, gives you, as the owner or manager, the highest probability of closing the sale each and every time, no matter who is doing the tour or how much experience he might have. In other words, whoever is doing the sales tour has the highest chance of getting the job done despite his level of training or experience in the field.

This structure is developed by breaking the tour into steps that are taught and practiced in order and then carried out during an actual tour in that same order. As an owner, using a step-progression method allows you to get your rookies up and running much more quickly than trying to get them to think their way through the sales tour.

Rather than learning endless and often too-advanced techniques too soon, your new salesperson concentrates on learning to present your business in a set way each time. This technique ensures that your guests see what you want them to see and they are presented the true benefits of what your business has to offer.

This structure also prevents your experienced employees from slowly developing unproductive habits that stem from doing it on their own for too long. Each salesperson either follows the steps or he doesn't, and the manager or owner has an exact map that identifies when the person left the structured tour and began to use techniques that aren't part of the club's sales philosophy.

As a salesperson, you can make more money, since no matter how tired you are or how many tours you do, you have fewer moving parts to worry about, which keeps you more focused and more effective during the busy times. Structure and steps allow you to master fewer components. Therefore, you gain more confidence in the material you use each day. In other words, it is easier to master a few set lines as opposed to learning endless sales babble that doesn't always work in this business.

The steps presented in this chapter are based upon the use of a trial membership, but can easily be adapted to other systems. The important thing to remember is that you must establish a set system that each salesperson uses each time. This consistency will translate into more money for the owner or manager and more commissions over time for the salesperson. The steps that have to be followed in every sale are as follows:

- Greet the prospect
- Use the salesperson's standard first greeting
- Meet and greet
- Offer the Welcome Guide as a gift
- Preview the club using the Welcome Guide
- Individualize the coming tour with one last question
- Tour the guest
- Review at the table
- Present the prices
- Buy the sale
- Ask for the sale
- Make sure no one leaves without a membership

# Step 1: Greet the Prospect

**How the person inquiring about a membership is greeted sets the tone for the rest of the sales tour.**

How the person inquiring about a membership is greeted sets the tone for the rest of the sales tour. Most club owners neglect this step or don't realize the importance of it and how it affects the bottom line.

In typical clubs, the front-counter person is often too young and undertrained for the role he plays in the sales process. The guest is handed a few sheets of paper and told to take his own tour and stop by on the way out if he needs anything else.

Other owners, believing they have superior sales systems, hire the same young dummy up front but try to compensate by loading up with salespeople. The counter kid is rude, too busy, or poorly trained to deliver any kind of service and the club's salesperson now has to spend the rest of the tour trying to overcome the damage done up front at the counter. Remember that everything counts in the sales process and that the guest will decide to buy based upon the entire experience, not just a few well-chosen sales phrases used during the close.

## The club's welcome statement

Every person who walks through your front door during business hours should be greeted with a strong welcoming statement. In smaller to moderate-sized clubs, this greeting should be shouted out by the front-counter people, strongly and with enthusiasm. For example:

> *Hi, we're having a great day at the Workout Company.*

Larger clubs that have a lot of traffic through their main door might not be able to keep up, or even be heard, due to the volume of guests during the busy times, but they should still have a welcoming statement that is used at the front desk and done individually as people check in for their workouts. For example:

> *Hi, thank you for working out with us today.*

Some of you are thinking that this strategy might be goofy and repetitious. You're right, but it doesn't matter. The members love it and the guests find it a nice touch of customer service. Remember that it is not what you want that often makes money; it's giving the guests what they want, and your members want to be greeted energetically each time they come to spend money with you. Your guests also want to know that you value customer service and that your staff is trained to appreciate your customers.

You also might be thinking that your current staff just won't be comfortable shouting out a welcome statement when the door opens. Get new counter people. Customer service is part of the revenue stream and if your current counter help can't participate, they need to go home. Customer service is delivered one member at a time and starts when the front door opens.

## Greeting guests

A guest is usually easy to spot among the trafficking hordes. He steps in, hesitates, and slowly finds his way to the counter. This person must be acknowledged within four seconds—not five, not 10, and not ignored because the counter people are busy. If your counter person is not busy, she says:

> *Hi, welcome to the club. How may I help you?*

If she is busy answering questions or making a shake, she still has to say the following in four seconds or less:

> *Hi, come on over (or in). I'll be with you in just a second.*

**Every person who walks through your front door during business hours should be greeted with a strong welcoming statement.**

The four-second rule comes from the restaurant business, where a good restaurant person prides herself in greeting customers as they enter the business with grace and respect. Anything longer than four seconds feels like an eternity to the guest. Test this theory yourself by walking in the front door of your business with a watch in hand and just stopping and staring at the front counter for about 10 seconds. It will feel like a much longer time, and leaving a new guest, who might already be nervous anyway, standing in the doorway feeling like a fool won't make the sale any easier later on.

## The handoff or transfer from the counter person to the salesperson

Never forget that everything counts when it comes to raising your sales effectiveness.

Never forget that everything counts when it comes to raising your sales effectiveness. Also remember that very little should be random in your world if you want to squeeze every last sale you can out of the traffic you generate.

Keeping these points in mind, you have to become anal enough to practice the small things that are often overlooked, such as how a front-counter person would hand a guest over to the salesperson. This small act, as one of a dozen that makes up a great experience for the prospective member, is better and more effective when it is practiced by anyone on your staff who might be involved.

Once the front-counter person greets the guest, one of two things might happen. The salesperson is busy and the guest has to wait, or the salesperson is free and can take care of the guest immediately.

In the first scenario, the club should have a waiting strategy in place. The waiting strategy is an automatic plan that kicks in whenever the front-counter person is facing a guest who has to wait for a salesperson to be available. It is important to note that a guest should never experience a time in the club when he cannot get information.

If a prospective member stops by the club in the morning, for example, and a salesperson is not yet on duty, the morning person should have enough sales training to give a reasonable tour and at least get the person on a trial membership. You are better off as an owner or manager getting the guest as a trial member than you are trying to get the person to come back later when the salesperson is working.

Don't forget that you are trying to develop systems that make your rookies more effective and that give everyone a chance to become a decent salesperson in a very short period of time. Your morning person, by following the steps of the sale, should be able to have a reasonable chance of getting the sale and ensuring that the guest at least leaves with a trial membership and an appointment to get started.

If a guest has to wait for a minimum amount of time, then the front-counter person has to be trained to automatically use the wait policy. This simple strategy involves nothing more than stating the following:

> *I apologize, John, but the person you need to see will be*
> *about five more minutes. May I buy you a bottle of water*
> *(or smoothie/soft drink, etc.) while you wait?*

Keep your wait strategy simple, but state it clearly so that any counter person can follow it with a minimum of training:

- If the guest has to wait for more than five minutes, the front-counter person may buy the guest a drink.

- Put the charge on the manager's account so the club may track it.

- Always be courteous and apologize for the wait and the inconvenience.

- Use the Welcome Guide as a tool to keep the person busy at the counter.

If the salesperson is not busy, or becomes available after the guest has been waiting, then the handoff needs to take place. The handoff should also be simple and scripted. These scripts should be stated clearly in your club's procedure manual and practiced weekly with the entire front-counter staff. In the following example, the club's salesperson, Sarah, approaches the front desk and the counter person, Kristen, does the handoff:

**If the salesperson is not busy, or becomes available after the guest has been waiting, then the handoff needs to take place. The handoff should also be simple and scripted.**

> *Hi Sarah, I would like to introduce John to you. He is here to get some*
> *information about the club. John, this is Sarah. She is the best person in the*
> *club to help you with that membership information. By the way John, it was*
> *a pleasure to meet you. Again, my name is Kristen and if you need any*
> *help in the club please come find me. I am usually here during the evenings*
> *and you can almost always find me here at the front counter. Thank you for*
> *coming in and we look forward to having you as a member.*

The statement should be simple and no more than four or five sentences that can be memorized and practiced by any entry-level employee. It's all in the training and you get what you put into it, so be sure to practice this statement at least weekly with the entire staff.

# Step 2: Use the Salesperson's Standard First Greeting

The salesperson's greeting is also not a random act and should be very structured and practiced. This greeting sets the tone for the entire sales encounter and has to be a professional technique that differentiates the club from any other place the guest might have stopped before visiting your club.

Left to their own devices, many salespeople start their first encounter with the guest in a less than professional manner, especially younger, male salespeople who usually just work with other young males. "How ya doin' man?" is not the professional greeting of choice and lowers the expected service and image of your business. First impressions do count more than you think and the salesperson's communication skills, dress, and professional image are all on display at this moment. Set the tone well at this point and the sale will be easier later on. Start off with a poor first impression, though, and it will be harder to get the guest to join down the line.

Structure rules at this point of the sale so that salesperson is limited to just one set greeting that can be practiced over and over, which will lead to mastery by the salesperson. Another way to think about structure is that you limit the things that can go wrong by restricting what the person can say to just that one set line. This structure makes your job as an owner or sales manager much easier, since you are not trying to correct every salesperson's individual style, but instead just coaching each person on his standardized greeting.

**The greeting of choice is simple, yet professional and takes a leadership position from the beginning.**

The greeting of choice is simple, yet professional and takes a leadership position from the beginning. In this context, leadership position means that the club's salesperson demonstrates leadership by taking control in the conversation. Remember that the guest is coming to you for help and is looking for answers, so it behooves you to be the professional and answer those questions as any other professional might, such as your accountant or lawyer. Consider this recommended greeting:

*Salesperson:* Hello, welcome to the club. My name is Sarah, and you are? (Pause/get name)

*Guest:* My name is John

*Salesperson:* John, what brought you into the club today?

If Sarah says anything else, drag her out the door and toss her into the club's dumpster, because she will end up killing your sales over time. When people get tired, especially after five tours on a Monday night during a busy month, they get stupid—and stupidity costs you money. Stupid means that as the night progresses the salesperson wears down and gets sloppier during each tour. Memorizing a standardized greeting eliminates much of this stupidity because at some point the automatic response kicks in and the person relies on his training, rather than just making something up or mumbling because they are tired.

The best analogy to this type of training involves U.S. soldiers. Many countries believe that this country has the best soldiers in the world because they are the best trained. When a young soldier gets into a combat role for the first time, he is successful because his training takes over, which is the product of countless role-playing exercises and practice sessions. This automatic response overcomes his fear and nervousness.

In your case, practice fewer things, but practice them often. When Sarah is tired, cranky, and hungry on a busy Monday night, she is still likely to be effective because her training will overcome the exhaustion. "Hello, welcome to the club. My name is Sarah, and you are…" just comes out of her mouth because she has said it so many times before in her practice sessions.

This automatic response ensures that your business is presented in the same way each and every time and that the greeting from each salesperson is a professional, polished statement that sets the tone for the sales encounter. Consistency builds effectiveness and over time you will get more memberships.

# Step 3: The Meet and Greet

The first two to four minutes of the sales encounter is the most important part of getting the sale. If this period goes right, the rest is easy, but if you get it wrong, then you will spend a lot of time trying to close someone who was lost much earlier in the process.

> The first two to four minutes of the sales encounter is the most important part of getting the sale.

You do not sell during the first two to four minutes. Your goal is to get to know the person, make him feel comfortable in the club, and start to build the foundation of a solid relationship that should last beyond the sale itself. Several different parts comprise the meet and greet. These things should be done in the following order whenever possible:

- Transition to the table
- Use the five Ws, how, and have as your tools
- Work in the trial membership
- Fill out the inquiry sheet as you go

## Transition to the table

The guest is usually greeted at the front desk directly in the traffic flow, which is at best an awkward place to discuss memberships. Your goal is to spend a quick minute at this location and then transition to the information table. The following example picks up where the salesperson greeting leaves off:

*Salesperson:* Hello, welcome to the club. My name is Sarah, and you are?

*Guest:* My name is John.

*Salesperson:* John, what brought you into the club today?

*Guest:* Well, I'd like to get some information about your prices.

*Salesperson:* Of course, I'd be happy to help you with that. By the way, have you ever been in the club before?

*Guest:* No, this is my first time. I received your mailer this week and I just wanted to check it out.

*Salesperson:* John, if you have a minute or two I have some material that you can take home with you over at the information table. Please come on over and I'll get you everything you need.

Before you analyze this scene, you need to understand the Plummer 99/1 Rule, which states the following:

---

### The Plummer 99/1Rule:

### Ninety-nine out of every 100 times, this stuff works.

---

The other 1 percent of these situations are called war stories, and while fun to talk about, should be downplayed in your training. The distraction comes when you are training for this scenario and a staff person brings up the exception. "Hey, what about the guy who just comes in and is all pissed off about the last gym he visited and he wants to take it out on us? I tried this stuff and he just yelled at me more."

Yes, this strategy didn't work for that guy, but just how many of those people did you have in the club last year? Maybe you had one, two, or at most three, but now you have a distraction in your training because this salesperson is focused on the 1 percent exception and not the 99 percent of the people who do talk and respond like normal human beings.

**Exceptions exist for every rule, but you should train for the norm.**

Exceptions exist for every rule, but you should train for the norm. Your training sessions can become totally meaningless if all you do is come up with solutions for the guy who doesn't talk or the woman who cries the entire time. Those situations happen, but not as often as your staff believes.

On the other hand, when a staff person does find that exception, write it down and give a team solution after the regular training is completed for that session. In this way, you stay focused but still arm your team for the occasional exception that does come through the door.

Returning to the discussion between John and Sarah, several good things are happening. Sarah is showing great customer service by using the words, "Of course, I'd be happy to help you..." These positive words let the guest know that he is going to be helped and that he is going to get some good service in the process.

The salesperson also leads with a strong opening question, which seems obvious but is one that salespeople often forget to ask: Have you ever been in the club before? Many rookie salespeople have started on their pitch only to find out 15 minutes later that the guest was in last week and talked to Carl, another salesperson, about getting a membership. If he has talked to another salesperson, and that person is in the club, the guest should be turned over to him. If the other salesperson is not in the club, then Sarah should proceed and finish the sale. Most clubs split the commission in this case, putting the emphasis on teamwork and getting the sale done while the guest is in the club. Besides being a solid opening question that determines if indeed Sarah should be working with the guest, the question, "Have you ever been in the club before?" takes the lead and starts to guide John into the sales process.

Most importantly, Sarah transitions her guest to the table using courtesy. Courtesy sells, but is not something most staff people are taught much anymore. You need to establish what courtesy is and what it looks like when it is delivered properly.

In this example, Sarah shows respect for John's time by asking if he has a minute or two so she can give him some information. She then uses "please" when asking him to step over to the information table. Showing respect for someone's time and being courteous are fundamental parts of any type of sales, but again, these components can be scripted and practiced along with the rest of the sales process.

*Keep the guest in the right atmosphere.*

Getting the guest to step to the information table to get some materials he can take home is so much easier than trying to get someone into a sales office. Remember from previous chapters that an office sets up an adversarial barrier that is hard to overcome, while the information table is viewed as something harmless that makes the sale easier.

**Getting the guest to step to the information table to get some materials he can take home is so much easier than trying to get someone into a sales office.**

It is also important to keep the guest in the club's energy zone. People are walking by, the club has energy and music, your cardio deck is full and happening, and the overall excitement in the club is working in your favor. Why would you ever want to take a guest out of that atmosphere and try and close him in an office? Keep him in the midst of the energy that is getting him excited and away from the black holes, such as an office, that suck the life and energy out of the sales encounter.

This table should be a high, café-style table somewhere near the front counter or off to the side of the workout floor. The high table is preferred because people tend to lean forward on this table and not lean back as they do at a regular table.

Keep a reserved sign on your information table to keep the members away and keep it ready at all times for your guests. It should have inquiry sheets, a Welcome Guide, and the gym bag and closing loot neatly arranged on the top. This table is where the sale starts and ends, and this space should be treated accordingly.

## Use the five Ws, how, and have.

Who, what, where, when, why, how, and have are the key words that start great discussions and demonstrate true interest in your guests.

Who, what, where, when, why, how, and have are the key words that start great discussions and demonstrate true interest in your guests. Learn these terms and your ability to communicate gets a lot stronger.

These key words are used by the salesperson to string together a number of guiding questions that not only lead the conversation, but also help the guest feel that he is being treated as an individual. Most importantly, these questions demonstrate sincere interest, which is not something most of your other competitors will bring to the sales process.

Remember, you do not sell during the first two to four minutes of the meet and greet. You ask questions, you listen, and you get to know your guest as an individual. Slow down at this point and avoid selling the club or pitching and the actual sale will be much easier later. Review the following scene—which takes place at the information table—and note how the questions and the key words are used by the salesperson. Again, note that no selling is taking place just yet:

*Salesperson:* John, please sit down and I'll get you some information. So you said you received our mailer. *What* caught your attention about that piece?

*Guest:* I just moved here and I like working out and you saved me the trouble of looking for a gym.

*Salesperson:* Well, it's probably a good start for us by making your life easier from the beginning. *Where* did you move from by the way?

*Guest:* I just left Chicago to take a job here in Denver. I always wanted to live out here and this was my chance.

*Salesperson: What* kind of work do you do?

*Guest:* I am a software engineer and I took a job at Tech South just down the street.

*Salesperson:* Yeah, we get a lot of folks from there in here. We must have a 100 or so of their staff as members. So, *where* were you working out before the move?

*Guest:* I belonged to a World Gym® there and just do basic cardio and strength training. I'm an outdoor person and I just do enough to keep me in shape to hike and ski.

*Salesperson:* Hey, you're in the right town now for those things. You'll meet very few people in this gym who aren't doing something outside whenever they can escape. I'm a skier myself and we're only a couple of hours away from the slopes. I'm gone every chance I get. You know, you didn't mention it yet, but *have* you heard about our trial membership or did you notice it on your mail piece?

*Guest:* Yeah, I did notice something about a 14-day trial. How does that work?

*Salesperson:* Well John, we're very proud of our club and feel that we have the best one in the area, but talk is cheap. We'll let you try this place before you buy absolutely free for 14-days with no risk or obligation and no money up front. We want you to come meet the staff and the other members, and if we haven't earned your business at the end of 14 days then we don't deserve to have you as a member.

*Guest:* That sounds interesting. Can you tell me a little more about the club?

*Salesperson:* Of course. Now tell me, *what* kind of workout are you are interested in doing with us?

The important thing to note is that Sarah, the club's salesperson, has spent a few minutes sitting at the table gently getting to know John, but she still hasn't gone into any type of sales presentation yet. It is much more important to get to know the guest at this point than it is to try and shove the club down his throat too quickly. He is in a fitness facility. He is probably making the leap of faith that all fitness centers have fitness equipment of some type and that the salesperson will get to those things eventually.

What will make your sales efforts more effective than your competitor's is taking the time to get to know the person as an individual. "Yeah, we have everything you need to get in shape here just like any other good facility, but before I show you this stuff let's spend a few minutes focusing on you and what you want from us and out of your workout." This statement isn't often spoken, but it should be the underlying thought process beneath all of your sales.

Several other important things are going on in this scene. First of all, the salesperson has effectively worked in some of the guiding questions by using the key words:

- What caught your attention?
- Where did you move from?
- What kind of work do you do?
- Where were you working out before?
- Have you heard about our trial membership?
- What kind of workout are you interested in doing?

These leading questions are just a few examples of how the five Ws, have, and how can be applied to any sales situation. Salespeople need to master a limited number of these questions, and each salesperson should write out the

**What will make your sales efforts more effective than your competitor's is taking the time to get to know the person as an individual.**

most common ones in his training notebook. The following lists present some of the most common options, although others may be useful in your sales process:

Who:

- Who referred you to us?
- Who do you know that might be a member here?

What:

- What kind of workout are you doing now?
- What are you looking for in a fitness center?
- What kind of work do you do? Are you up and moving or at a desk all day?
- What is the single most important thing you want from a membership at this gym and why is that important to you?

Where:

- Where are you working out now?
- Where do you live?
- Where do you work?

When:

- When are you planning to get started?
- When was the last time you worked out?
- When was the last time you really felt like you were in shape?

Why:

- Why now? (You haven't been working out for four years. Why are you interested in getting going again now?)

How:

- How long has it been since your last workout?
- How did you hear about us?
- How long have you been thinking about getting back into the gym?

Have:

- Have you ever been in our club before?
- Have you ever heard about our trial membership?

All of these questions elicit answers from the guest, and all keep the conversation going. The key, though, is to listen and respond. Rookie

**Salespeople need to master a limited number of these questions, and each salesperson should write out the most common ones in his training notebook.**

salespeople sometimes get so excited about the questions that they forget to listen to the answers that the guest is giving before they move on to the next question. It can be helpful if the salespeople think of the conversational cycle as follows:

Ask—listen—respond—listen—ask another

For example:

*Ask:* Have you ever been in the club before?

*Listen:* No, this is my first time. I was driving by and saw your sign

*Respond (to the answer):* Oh, were you on your way home from work or do you live in the area?

*Listen:* I actually just moved here and I live in those condos just down the street.

*Ask another:* Yeah, I am familiar with those. A number of our members live there. Where did you move from John?

In summary, you're spending the first two to four minutes getting to know the person without selling. For just a few minutes you have to learn to make it all about them and what they really want from us. This individualization of the sales process will build that relationship that is so important, and such a strong part of a more sophisticated sales process, leading to more sales over time.

## Work in the trial membership.

The temptation among all salespeople who are making the transition from the older, high-pressure system to using trial memberships is to hide the trial until after they give the hard pitch first. When that pitch fails, the salesperson then pulls the trial out as a last-ditch effort to keep the person from walking out with nothing. This all-or-nothing approach really makes the guest angry. "If you had this trial all along, then why didn't you show me this up front?"

The thought process is that if you tell the person up front about the trial you blow any chance you might have to get the sale that day. In reality, just the opposite is true. If you use the trial up front, you disarm the person, thereby making the sale easier later on and increasing the chances of getting the sale that day.

People who visit your business looking for a membership are nervous, and if they have visited other clubs with pressure systems in place they might well be damaged goods. Combine this fact with what they think they know about how badly you are going to beat them to get that membership today and you end up touring a very closed-up guest who is on the defensive the entire time he is in the club.

The temptation among all salespeople who are making the transition from the older, high-pressure system to using trial memberships is to hide the trial until after they give the hard pitch first.

If this person is closed-up enough, he will hardly even hear what you have to say during the tour. He knows the office is coming and he knows the pressure will surface in the end. It is the same feeling many people have about car guys. Looking at new cars should be fun, but most people hate the process because they know that once they find a car they like they will have to deal with a salesperson who will make them feel stupid and angry. If you introduce the trial membership up front, most of this defensiveness vanishes because the pressure is off the guest once he knows in the back of his mind that the worst thing that can happen to him today is that he will walk out with a trial membership.

Review the scene between John and Sarah. Sarah worked the trial membership into the meet and greet before she showed John the club. Her goal is to relax him before he leaves the table so that he will be more open to her questions and information. The pressure is off John because he has the trial to use if he likes, but more importantly he knows that the club will stand behind its product by letting him try before he buys.

Sarah will still try her best to get the sale today by using the Trial Gift Certificate. Your club should still close a minimum of 30 percent of all of its sales during the first visit, and working the trial in before the tour will help you drive that number even higher.

## Fill out the inquiry sheet as you go.

The inquiry sheets are important as lead trackers and should be filled out by the salesperson—never the guest—during the meet-and-greet phase of the sale. If you look back to Chapter 14, you will see that most of the five Ws are actually worked into the inquiry sheet itself. Once you gain a little experience asking these questions and filling out the inquiry sheet, you'll find that you can almost memorize the questions and work through the sheet without looking at it.

> The inquiry sheet is nothing more than a tool to track all leads and to ensure that any brain-dead salesperson or counter kid can focus enough to simply read the questions to the guest or phone inquiry when all else fails.

The inquiry sheet is nothing more than a tool to track all leads and to ensure that any brain-dead salesperson or counter kid can focus enough to simply read the questions to the guest or phone inquiry when all else fails. In this case, Sarah might fill out the questions as she spends her first two to four minutes with John or, if she is experienced, she might wait until he leaves to fill out the sheet. Either way, you must have a matching sheet at the end of the day for John's tour, or Sarah will be in big trouble.

In summary, the meet-and-greet phase of the tour is a lot like making small talk at a party. You meet someone, ask a few leading questions to make conversation, and then move along to the next person or group. In other words, you are simply getting to know someone at a very base level through a series of harmless questions everyone has answered a 100 times before.

During the meet and greet, you need to stay on track by making a smooth transition to the information table; using the five Ws, have, and how; working in the trial membership; presenting the Welcome Guide as a gift; and making sure you end up with a completed inquiry sheet. All of these things can be done in about two to four minutes with a little practice, and all of it can be repeated time after time by anyone on your sales staff.

## Step 4: Offer the Welcome Guide as a Gift

Sarah, the club's salesperson, also needs to do some behavioral modification with John before she tours him. Most guests come in with the same expectations: I'll tour for 10 minutes, get pounded in an office for 20, and get sent home with a price sheet.

If he is touring a typical non-profit facility, his expectations are even lower. He'll check in at the desk, be handed a wad of paper, and be told to tour the facility himself. Once back at the front desk, he can pick from the endless supply of membership options and sign himself up. Either way, his expectations are low and he is expecting a negative experience.

Increase your sales by messing with his little head, which is a low-tech way of doing behavioral modification. He expects the worst, so change his expectations early by giving him a gift from the club before he tours the facility. The following is a continuation of the ongoing sales scene:

*Salesperson:* Of course, now tell me *what* kind of workout you are interested in doing with us?

*Guest:* I was working with a trainer at my other gym that set me up on my program, but living out here is going to be different. I'd like to get some more help, so I guess you can say I am going to do a workout that will make me a better skier and more versatile outdoors.

*Salesperson:* We can help you with that. In addition to a trainer, we also offer a number of conditioning classes depending on the time of year that will get you ready for some of the sports you might be doing here. You know John, you seem to know what you're looking for, so the best thing I can do is show you our club. But before I do, I would like to give you a little gift. This book is called our Welcome Guide and it covers everything in the gym. It has information about all of our programs and services, general information about the business, some great articles about working out that will apply to what you're trying to accomplish, a letter from the owner introducing what we do here, some testimonials from some of our regulars, and lots of other information, including the prices. I know you'll get home and say, "What did Sarah say about that?" and I guarantee the answer is in here. It's a gift from us and it should help finding a gym easier for you.

He came in expecting to get a little information and maybe a small brochure, but before he even tours he is given a full three-ring booklet with fun

**During the meet and greet, you need to stay on track by making a smooth transition to the information table; using the five Ws, have, and how; working in the trial membership; presenting the Welcome Guide as a gift; and making sure you end up with a completed inquiry sheet.**

articles and information that he may keep as a gift from the club. This gift changes his perception, and subsequently his behavior through the tour, since he expected the worse and received a free gift instead. More information about using this tool during the tour is presented later in this chapter.

# Step 5: Preview the Club Using the Welcome Guide

**The salesperson should be sitting almost next to the guest if possible.**

The salesperson should be sitting almost next to the guest if possible. In this example, when Sarah hands John the Welcome Guide, she should slowly page through it with him, pointing out the key sections and what's in each. The important thing to understand is that the salesperson is trying to preview the club before she shows it to the guest. In other words, she wants to tell him what he is going to see before he sees it. Consider this example:

*Salesperson:* John, let me show you a few things in your Welcome Guide. Here is the section on club services. Each is listed in here and I'll show you each one as we walk through. Here is a map of the club and I will also point out the highlights during our tour so you can become more familiar with our layout (important even if you have a very small club). Listed back here are our club managers. I'll introduce you to most of them, since everyone is usually here at this time of day, etc.

Remember this important rule for making any type of presentation. It applies to what the salesperson is trying to do during the sales process, with the first step taking place as he flips through the Welcome Guide:

- Tell me what I am going to see (preview)
- Tell me what I am seeing (tour)
- Tell me what I saw (review)

If you want to make the strongest presentation you can for your business, always come back to this simple rule. Part 2 of this process, tell me what I am seeing, is covered during the actual tour and step 3, tell me what I saw, is done after the tour.

# Step 6: Individualize the Coming Tour With One Last Question

Guests are all different, but in many ways they are all the same. One of the hardest parts about being a club salesperson is that after a while, all the guests start sounding the same, with the same stories and same flabby body parts. Despite this repetition, the guest still demands that he or she be treated as an individual, and rightly so, since they are spending money with your business.

So the question is: How do you listen to 100 prospective members a month and still be able to individualize the process? The tool you use is a simple question, coupled with a simple follow-up that brings out the layer under the layer:

- What is the single most important thing you want from a membership at this gym?
- Why is that important to you?

When you ask someone what he wants from a membership to a fitness facility, he usually pats someplace on his body and tells you how he wants to shrink or change that part. This response is the first layer, and while important, is nothing more than a start to uncover the layer beneath, which is important for the sale.

**Guests are all different, but in many ways they are all the same.**

The second question frees the hidden agenda and, if used properly, is the first step toward building that emotional connection between the guest and the club that is so important to the outcome of the sale. Consider the following sequence, which is typical if a club sale:

*Salesperson:* Well Debbie, you seem to have put a lot of thought into joining a gym and you have some pretty good questions. With your permission, I'd love to show you around, but first let me start you with a little present from the club.

This book is called our Welcome Guide and it covers everything in the gym. It has information about all of our programs and services, general information about the business, some great articles about working out that will apply to what you're trying to accomplish, a letter from the owner introducing what we do here, some testimonials from some of our regulars, and lots of other information, including the prices. I know you'll get home and say, "What did Sarah say about that?" and I guarantee the answer is in here. It's a gift from us and it should make finding a gym easier for you.

*Guest:* Thank you, that is very generous. I'd have to say that I didn't get anything like this from the club I visited down the street.

*Salesperson:* Yes, we've found that our guests do a lot of thinking and comparing at home and we want you to have all the information you need right in front of you when you're trying to decide how to get started. But before I show you around, I do have one more question I'd like to ask you Debbie. What is the single most important thing you want from a membership at this gym?

*Guest:* Well, I'd have to say that I'd like to lose some of this from around my waist. I'm at the biggest size I've been since I was in high school.

*Salesperson:* Why is this important to you?

*Guest:* I guess I'd have to admit that my class reunion coming up in a few months is really depressing me. It's my tenth year and I just don't want to go back carrying all this extra weight when I know everyone else is going to be in shape. Besides, I used to be in great shape and I was actually a cheerleader, although you couldn't tell that from the shape I'm in now.

*Salesperson:* Well, from my experience here working with so many different people, I doubt that everyone is going to be in shape, but I also know that if you don't feel good about the way you look you probably won't have as much fun. Just keep in mind as I show you the club that we can get quite a bit done in just a few months if you're willing to get started soon. With just a few months to go, every day at this stage is important. Well Debbie, with your permission, may I show you our club?

In this example, admitting she needed to lose weight was probably the easy part for the guest, compared to telling the salesperson that the thought of her class reunion is depressing her and that she used to be in much better shape. Also note that the salesperson is gently guiding the guest along the fitness path without selling. The guest is looking for answers and leadership and the salesperson is providing both in the form of her suggestion that with just a few months remaining Debbie might want to get moving, since every day could make a difference in the outcome.

**Even experienced salespeople often confuse sales techniques with quiet leadership.**

Even experienced salespeople often confuse sales techniques with quiet leadership. In this example, the salesperson hasn't sold at all; she merely suggested that Debbie get started immediately due to the time constraint.

This suggestion is actually a much more sophisticated approach to sales, although it is much easier for a fitness salesperson to naturally grasp. Instinctively, most people who work in gyms want to help other people and the act of providing direction and leadership to someone who is inexperienced is more of a natural act for most salespeople compared to learning outdated sales techniques that sound artificial.

## Step 7: Tour the Guest

The last thing the salesperson asked for in this scene was permission to tour. This question marks the transition point between the table and the tour. The salesperson spends the two to four minutes getting to know the guest and then looks for the point at which it makes sense to say the following:

*You have some really good questions. I think I can best answer those questions by actually showing you around. With your permission, may I show you our club?*

Asking permission lowers the perceived pressure because you are doing nothing without the person's prior okay. Again, this technique lowers the adversarial nature of a typical sales tour in a club.

Remember, the foundation of a good presentation of any type is to tell the guest what you are going to show him, show him, and then tell him what he just saw. The tour represents the second step in this sequence. Salespeople need to keep two important concepts in mind as they learn the tour:

- Everyone sees everything every time.
- Tour using the mall concept.

## Everyone sees everything every time.

Besides being a mouthful to say, this statement is also one of the most important rules to emphasize when you are training new salespeople. One of the ineffective processes—meaning that the staff person must make a thinking or judgment decision—that is embedded in a traditional, old-style sales approach is that you only take the guest to the parts of the club that he wants to see and skip the parts you don't think would be relevant and are therefore a waste of the guest's time.

For example, a hardcore salesperson might take a single male with big arms and that almost-bodybuilder look directly to the free-weight area and skip the softer areas of the club, such as the spa and childcare room. This decision was a supposedly educated guess made by the salesperson about what the guest really wants to see. What if the guest has a significant other who is into spa services or is dating someone who has kids? When he leaves the club after this tour, he will be loaded up on the free-weight area and be totally unaware of anything else the club has to offer.

This type of tour actually works against both the club and the guest. The club is presented poorly in that the owner has spent a considerable amount of money in those areas and feels that every area of the business should be represented during any tour. On the practical side, leaving areas out of the tour makes the club feel smaller than it really is, since the guest will leave with only a service or two in his head.

The guest leaves without a true feel for what the business offers because he only really saw a small portion of the business. When he is sitting at home with his girlfriend he won't be able to tell her if the club has childcare or not, since he wasn't really shown that area of the club. Welcome Guides overcome this obstacle of course, but clubs that use the old-style presentation probably aren't using that tool either.

Probably the biggest reason club salespeople stopped showing the entire facility is just plain laziness. Cut to the interesting part, make it short, and justify it later to the owner. "He was single and only wanted to see the weights anyway."

If everyone sees everything every time, the tour develops a set pattern that makes the management of a sales team that much easier. As stated repeatedly

> The foundation of a good presentation of any type is to tell the guest what you are going to show him, show him, and then tell him what he just saw.

in this book, it is easier to teach steps than it is to teach thinking. In this case, don't try to guess what the person wants to see; simply show him everything. You might spend more time in some areas, but the tour is a set pattern that can be taught in a repeatable format.

The guest who sees everything leaves with many more snapshots of the gym in his head and gets to see the gym from many different angles. This type of touring sends the person home with a feeling that this club had a lot of different things to offer, versus a club that feels smaller because that club's salesperson took a shortcut, even if it might have more services and offerings.

## Tour using the mall concept.

When you go to a super mall, are you sometimes overwhelmed by the shear number of stores that mall has to offer? Many people can spend an entire Saturday just wandering from store to store, with a stop for lunch along the way. Touring your business should be much the same experience since most clubs do offer many different stores in their mall, though the owners seldom think of it that way.

Your mall, of course, is the total business and the stores in your mall are the individual components you offer. When you tour a guest, tour from store to store to create an illusion, no matter how big or how small your club is, that you have everything the person needs to be successful in reaching his goals. For example, the salesperson might say:

> *Here we have our Shake This Sports Bar and over here is our Endless Summer Spray Tan Center. We'll also stop by our Lifestyle Enhancement Department and our Apex Weight Management retail area.*

Obviously, these areas would be spread out over the entire tour, but you present the club as a series of different businesses, each designed to enhance the fitness experience. Each one of these areas should have its own branding, with signs and appropriate identification, so these components truly exist as stand-alone parts of your business.

By using this method, you're showing a lot more depth in your business, which means that you're showing the guest many more ways in which you can help him get it done. Compare this method to the one used in a typical club, which might have tanning and training, but presents the club as a just a fitness business with a bunch of different rooms where it offers some services.

## The key to the tour is the yellow brick road.

Not too many people in this country haven't seen the "Wizard of Oz" and aren't familiar with the yellow brick road. For those of you who haven't seen the movie in a few years, the yellow brick road was the central path through Oz

The guest who sees everything leaves with many more snapshots of the gym in his head and gets to see the gym from many different angles.

that you had to follow if you wanted to get to the Emerald City and meet the Wizard himself. Stay on the yellow brick road and you would find your way from the start to the finish and have great adventures along the way.

Your version of the yellow brick road consists of selling stations, which are laid along a set path throughout the club, leading the salesperson and the guest from the start of the fitness adventure along a set path and back home safely. Each station identifies a part of the club and explains the benefits of using that station or taking part in that program. As the salesperson tours, he stops at each of the stations—which are usually marked by 2- x 3-foot signs mounted on a wall, mirror, or easel—points out the component, and explains that area to the guest.

Selling stations should be of a very high quality, done by a real artist and printer, with the club's logo screened in the background. They should also be framed and professionally hung throughout the club. Use as many as you need. Even small clubs will benefit from this technique, since the goal is to highlight everything you offer and make you look more like a full-service business than a simple workout place.

Most sales trainers like to put a mini-logo, small star, or a simple "X" on the floor in front of the station. Doing so creates another focus tool to help new salespeople become more effective more quickly, since their training includes the instructions: Go stand on the mark on the floor, paraphrase the selling station, and relate it to the guest. A sample selling station is shown in Figure 18-1.

This station would be hung near the counter/bar area and would most likely be stopped at early in the tour as the salesperson and the guest leave the information table, which is also near the front of most clubs. The salesperson would approach this station, find his mark, and then paraphrase what is written. Reading the sign word-for-word is lethal and not necessary, but the salesperson does need to be able to present the main points to the guest. Study the following scene and see how the salesperson relates this service to the guest:

*Salesperson:* Okay John, this is our Shake This Sports Bar. Shake This is a national brand that specializes in making healthy shakes and snacks for workout people and is in hundreds of clubs around the country.

Many of our members are on very tight schedules and stop here to get a meal-replacement shake to take back to work or to eat on the ride home. We also have a large number of people who are watching their weight, so we get a lot of folks who want the lower-calorie shakes to substitute for their morning snack at work or even for their lunch.

And as you can see, we have quite a few televisions at the bar. We also have our share of sports nuts, so we get all the major games here during the year and this is a great place to watch Monday Night Football or baseball during

**Selling stations should be of a very high quality, done by a real artist and printer, with the club's logo screened in the background.**

**[Your Club Name Here]**
**Our Shake This Sports Bar**

The best part of working out are the relaxing moments afterward, when you have a chance to enjoy a few minutes of the day just for yourself. Our Shake This Sports Bar provides you with an opportunity to sit and decompress before your workout, or take that much-needed break before heading home or to work after your workout.

Shake This offers:

- 26 different shake combinations for energy, weight loss, gaining mass and muscle, or a simple low-calorie snack or meal replacement

- 8 televisions at the Shake This Sports Bar that feature all sporting events, the local and national news, and other programming of interest to our members

- A full coffee bar with specialty snacks

- The chance to open a credit account with the club so you can enjoy all of the club's services without carrying cash

- A full line of meal-replacement snack bars, powders, and other nutritional products that can be purchased individually or discounted by the box

**[Your Logo Here]**

Figure 18-1. Shake This Sports Bar

the week. During the World Series last year, our staff members wore jerseys from their favorite teams and we had a number of parties here during those two weeks.

John, have you ever had a healthy, but tasty smoothie?

*Guest:* Not really, just the ones you get at the mall.

*Salesperson:* May I buy you one? Nothing is better than a tasty shake that also happens to be free.

*Guest:* Yes, thank you.

*Salesperson:* Let's grab you one while we're passing by and introduce you to something new today. By the way, you said you are trying to lose 10 pounds. Are you using shakes as meal replacements yet?

*Guest:* Not really, just that stuff you get in the cans and just once in awhile.

*Salesperson:* Have a seat and welcome to our sports bar. Great spot to watch a game on Saturday, isn't it?

*Guest:* Yeah, this is a nice part of the club. I didn't realize you have so many televisions at the bar…

A lot of things happened in this short encounter. Most importantly, the guest was introduced to another service the club offers, but it isn't just a homemade juice bar; it's a national brand that specializes in fitness people.

The salesperson also casually worked in a few ways that the shakes might benefit John, such as a meal replacement, a snack to take along to work, or as an option for someone trying to lose weight. The salesperson also took the initiative to get John a shake so he could taste one for himself. This move is something that few competitors would copy, and John is now more relaxed and feels a little more like part of the club, since he is sitting for a few minutes at the bar having a shake and watching people. The salesperson would have to be careful not to sit too long. The goal is to expose John to the bar, give him one more small gift, and then keep the tour moving.

The club's salesperson also did a good job of letting John know about the social aspect of the bar. People who join fitness clubs often want more from the business than most owners are prepared to offer. In many ways, the club becomes the social outlet for people who would enjoy watching a game with a lot of people, but not in a bar with a bunch of drunks. Juice bars/sports bars, done correctly, can become the social center for the members, and the salesperson did a nice job of painting that picture for the guest.

**People who join fitness clubs often want more from the business than most owners are prepared to offer.**

## Green lights, red lights

The final point to note from this scene is how the salesperson looked for the connection between the guest and what he is seeing or experiencing. In this case, the salesperson referenced the fact that John stated that he would like to lose weight, which probably came up during the first two to four minutes, by asking if he was doing anything yet to lose those 10 pounds, such as drinking some simple meal-replacement shakes.

**The goal for the salesperson is to look for the green light/red light at each station.**

The goal for the salesperson is to look for the green light/red light at each station. Green light means that the guest has some connection point to that particular station, while red light means the opposite. Salespeople should try to spend a few extra minutes at the green-light stations and move on quickly from those stations that generate red lights.

For example, the salesperson had a green light at the juice bar. John was willing to try a shake, he is sitting at the bar, and the salesperson has worked in the trial green-light question: Great place to watch a football game, isn't it? The salesperson should spend an extra minute or two here because John is enjoying this aspect of the club, which is another connection point that will help make the sale easier later on.

Red lights are easy to spot. For example, you are touring the classic bodybuilder type in his late 20s who is single and lives for the gym. During the tour, the salesperson stops at the station for childcare and says:

*"Eddie, this is our childcare area. It's open 32 hours per week and is only $5 per child per session. As you can see, we have some unusual features in this room, including three game stations, an infants-only area, security cameras, and scheduled activities. Eddie, is childcare something you, or perhaps one of your guests, would anticipate using as a member here?"*

*Eddie replies, "I hate kids and probably wouldn't step foot near this room as a member."*

Red light… move on, but the salesperson did his job by stopping at this station. Your job is to search for the green lights. A couple of easy questions can be memorized and added to your training that uncover the green lights at each station. Others exist, of course, and you will add more as you practice and learn the system, but consider the following examples to start with:

*Is this something you can see yourself doing?* The salesperson might be talking to a runner in a northern state where it is hard to run in the winter. This question might be used at the cardio station, where the salesperson asks: "It must be tough running outside all winter. Is running in here on one of our treadmills something that you can see yourself doing this winter?"

*Would this feature be something you would anticipate using?* This question applies more to services. Variations might include the following: Are you a tanning person? Is childcare something you might anticipate using?

*Is this a service you normally use?* This one might be a good spa question, and remember that a significant number of men now use a variety of spa services and this question works for anyone you are talking to at the time, not just women. If the person uses the service outside the club, it might be an added benefit to have that same service where he or she works out.

*Feels good, doesn't it?* Is this feature something your last club had? This question might be applied to amenities, such as massage, or it could also apply to some type of workout or class unique to your club, such as specialty group classes or functional group training.

*How does that feel?* This question is one of the most powerful questions you can ask someone in any type of sales situation. "How does it feel?" taps the emotional base in the person, as opposed to asking, "What do you think?" Never ask the thinking question because intellectually no one wants to spend money or take the risk of doing something new. Emotionally, however, people know that they need to lose weight or get into better shape. When a guest walks out of a good group class with a smile on his flushed face, for example, the question to ask is how he feels at that moment. You know you're going to get the right answer and the emotional connection between the guest and the club is cemented. Ask what that same person thinks, however, and you might hear, "That class is too damn hard and I am too out of shape to do this," which is not what a salesperson wants to hear from a guest.

The final point to consider about selling stations is that your goal is to keep everything benefits-driven and avoid the feature trap. Features are the components that make up the club, such as 80 pieces of cardio equipment or 40 classes a week, while benefits answer the question, "What's in it for me as the consumer?" Answer that question, and you will sell more memberships.

The following sample stations shown in Figures 18-2 through 18-13 can be adapted for your club. Remember, selling stations are effective no matter what size club you are selling.

## A summary of the selling-station concept

How do you tour if you don't use a set path in your club? Most sales tours are simply based upon the salesperson walking through the club and pointing out the equipment, group rooms, and locker rooms. The salespeople on these tours spend the majority of their time showing the person what the club has instead of what they should be doing, which is spending all of their time helping the person see what the club can do for him.

The final point to consider about selling stations is that your goal is to keep everything benefits-driven and avoid the feature trap.

# [Your Club Name Here]
### Club Hours

The club is open the following hours from
## September 1 to May 31
**Monday through Friday**

**5:00 a.m.–10:00 p.m.**

**Saturday & Sunday**

**8:00 a.m.–8:00 p.m.**

Summer hours are in effect from
## June 1 to August 31
**Monday through Friday**

**5:00 a.m.–10:00 p.m.**

**Saturday & Sunday**

**8:00 a.m.–4:00 p.m.**

The club closes on Thanksgiving, Easter, and Christmas so that the staff can be with their families. On other holidays, the club posts the changes to normal hours for that specific day.

# [Your Logo Here]

Figure 18-2. Club hours

# [Your Club Name Here]
## Our Apex Weight-Management Program

Are you tired of exercising without getting the results you expect?

Are you fed up with trendy diets that only give you short-term results?

The answer is simple: Diets don't work and never will.

Our Apex program offers you:

- A guided weight-management program designed specifically for you and your lifestyle.

- Online support tools with which you can take control and monitor your progress on a daily basis.

- Your own monitor that tracks all of your daily activity.

- Weekly support from a trained professional who will help you accomplish your goals.

- The option of bringing a friend who can share the program with you for a substantial savings.

And don't forget our Apex Nutritional Products.

We carry only Apex Nutritional Products designed exclusively for Fitness-club members who are seeking a healthy lifestyle through fitness and advanced nutritional products.

# [Your Logo Here]

Figure 18-3. Apex weight-management program

# [Your Club Name Here]

## Our Group Exercise Program

[Your Club Name] features Body Training Systems™, known worldwide for Group Power. Group exercise can offer many advantages that working out on your own just can't match.

Why group exercise can work for you:

- Group exercise offers the motivation of being part of a large, enthusiastic, and sometimes rowdy class of people who want their fitness in a class setting.

- Group exercise allows you explore the mind/body aspects of fitness in a safe and controlled atmosphere as part of your membership.

- Group exercise can keep your personal schedule on track with workouts that don't run over, meet at regular times, and that get you in, done, and out while still feeling that you had a great workout that day.

- Group offers variety for those who want to mix things up each week to keep their workouts fresh and exciting.

# [Your Logo Here]

Figure 18-4. Group-exercise program

# [Your Club Name Here]
## The Spa at [Your Club Name]

The Spa is a separate business within our gym. It is open by appointment seven days a week. The following menu offers just a few of The Spa's services. Members at [Your Club Name] receive a 10 percent discount and receive priority offerings and other discounts throughout the year.

- Essential aromatherapy facial (1 hour) $40

- Mini-aromatherapy facial (30 minutes) $25

- Firmative action facial (1 hour) $55

- Eye zone wrap treatment (30 minutes) $20

- Gentle mist spray tan (20 minutes) $45

- Body polish (45 minutes) $40

- Aveda® aroma body wrap (1 hour) $50

- Pedicure and nails (1 hour) $45

- Custom nail packages (1 hour) $40-60

- Deep-tissue massage (30 minutes–1 hour) $30-75

## [Your Logo Here]

Figure 18-5. The spa

# [Your Club Name Here]
## Our Endless Summer Tan Center

[Your Club Name] features our own in-house tanning center specializing in meeting all of your tanning needs. Our Endless Summer Tan Center offers 15 beds exclusively for use by our members.

The tanning center is available by appointment only, which may be made online, by stopping at the central check-in desk, or by calling the club. Prices vary according to the time of year, and we also offer separate memberships for those who make tanning a part of their daily schedule.

Some things you should know about our tanning center:

- We feature Sun Ergo beds, the safest beds in the industry.

- We guarantee that the bulbs are changed every 500 hours.

- The rooms are thoroughly serviced after each visit.

- Endless Summer is exclusively for our members.

- Discounts and specials are offered throughout the year for our regular tanning customers.

# [Your Logo Here]

Figure 18-6. Endless Summer tan center

**[Your Club Name Here]**
**We're proud of our business, and we'd like you
to know several things about us:**

- We are the only fitness business in [Town Name] that will let you try before you buy—not for just a single workout, but for a full 14 days with no risk, no obligation, and no money up front. Try us free for 14 days, meet our staff and other members, and then make up your mind. If we don't earn your business, then we don't deserve to have you as a member.

- We have been in the fitness business in [Town Name] for more than [#] years under the same ownership and management.

- We have never had a price special. No one who signs up in the future will ever pay less than you do today.

**[Your Logo Here]**

Figure 18-7. Things we're proud of at our club

# [Your Club Name Here]

Maybe you've always wanted to try working with your own trainer, but you just don't know how to get started or you've been a little too nervous to try it out. Never fear, we have the solution for you!

**[Your Club Name's] trial training offer:**
**3 sessions with a trainer for only $99**

Who the trial is for?

- This trial offer is for anyone who has not been involved in our training program in the past.

What is the trial offer?

- We know that many of our members could benefit from working with a trainer, but they're a little too nervous to try or don't know how to get started. This trial is a low-risk way to experience the benefits of a trainer and explore new ways to reach your goals.

You might have the wrong impression of what a trainer does (they are not gym drill sergeants), don't know how to get started, or simply don't understand what a trainer can do for you. This program is your introduction to how we can help you reach your goals beyond just having a membership.

# [Your Logo Here]

Figure 18-8. Trial training offer

# [Your Club Name Here]

Want to find out where you are on your path to fitness and the next step to take to reach your goal?

If you're a seasoned fitness person with training experience and want to know exactly where you are in your fitness training, then we have a specific program just for you.

**The Eval**
**$189 for a 90-minute assessment and training session**

Who is the Eval for?

- The Eval is for anyone with training experience who has reached a plateau in his or her workouts. Signs of a plateau are boredom, lack of results, a lack of new training ideas, or a frustration that you simply don't know what kind of shape you're really in and what to do next.

What is the Eval?

- The Eval is 90 minutes with one of our senior trainers. The trainer will do a full assessment to find out where you stand today and where you want to be in the future. Based upon the assessment and your personal goals, the trainer will design an individualized program just for you. To schedule an Eval, contact the front desk or talk to any trainer.

# [Your Logo Here]

Figure 18-9. The Eval

# [Your Club Name Here]

Are you the type that needs extra personal motivation to get to the gym? Would you get more from your workouts if someone took you through every exercise every time you came to work out? And are you the type that just doesn't want to think when you're at the gym and would do better if someone held your hand and guided you from the time you got here until the time you went home? If you answered yes to any of these questions, we have a program for you.

**[Your Club Name] Personal Training Program**
**A single session with a trainer @ $75**
**10 sessions @ $500**

Who is personal training for?

- Personal training is for anyone who struggles with his or her motivation when it comes to fitness. Book a trainer and he or she will be waiting for you to arrive. Your trainer will then take you through every step every time you're in the gym to make sure that you get the most out of each workout with the least amount of hassle or thinking involved. Our trainers act as your personal coach and motivator to keep you on track in your workouts.

# [Your Logo Here]

Figure 18-10. Personal-training program

# [Your Club Name Here]

**Does the thought of working out with a group of motivated people doing new and exciting exercises inspire you?**

We have a group experience that is guaranteed to raise your level of training while offering a different approach to fitness. Lifestyle-enhancement training, which works on your core strength, affects everything you do in your life. Our goal with lifestyle enhancement is to help improve your life!!

**[Your Club Name] Semi-Private Group Experience**
**1 session @ $50**
**10 sessions @ $500**

Who is semi-private group for?

• This type of training, which focuses on lifestyle-enhancement training, or functional training, is offered for people who like the group dynamic and who are driven to new heights when surrounded by a group of motivated training partners.

# [Your Logo Here]

Figure 18-11. Semi-private group experience

# [Your Club Name Here]
## Some of the best excuses we've ever heard in the fitness business:

### I don't have time to get in shape!

You had time to get out of shape. Why can't you make the time to get in shape? Fitness is as simple as just moving every day, whether you are enjoying the motivation of a gym membership or simply spending 30 minutes walking the dog. Everyone can experience fitness at some level and everyone has the time. Keep in mind that the average television is on 7½ hours per day, 60 percent of all kids in the country are overweight, and more than 30 percent of all adults are considered seriously overweight. Less than one hour a day, three days a week or so, will change your life if you can let yourself make the time.

### My spouse might not want me to join a gym!

We know that your spouse truly wants you to be out of shape, no fun because you have no energy, unable to keep up with your kids, and constantly complaining about doing something about those extra pounds. Or would your spouse secretly be happy that you're doing the right thing for yourself and want to come as well?

### I can't afford to join a gym!

Joining a gym is the equivalent of one cup of coffee a day at a typical coffee shop. Joining a gym for a month is less than one pack of smokes a day, less than one night at the movies with the kids, less than a couple of pizza home deliveries a month and less than a movie rental or two a week. And out of all these things, isn't feeling good about yourself more important than any of them. Come on, put down that second cup of coffee and get yourself a gym membership.

### I don't know if I will stick with it!

You only have to participate in a fitness program a couple of days a week to enjoy the benefits. If you add a few walks at home, take the stairs at work, and keep moving, getting fit just happens. You don't have to change your life to get the benefits of fitness, but you do have to make the decision to start moving a little each day and make it a part of your life.

## [Your Logo Here]

Figure 18-12. Fitness excuses

# [Your Club Name Here]
### Need a specific solution to a specific training problem?

We have the answer if you:

- Encountered those wobbly legs on the ski slopes last year and want to hit the mountains this year in shape and ready to go

- Are tired of your buddies blowing the ball past you on the golf course

- Need to drop a few pounds and get in shape fast for a special event in your life, such as a wedding or trip to the beach

- Want to run a road race or triathlon and need a coach to get you trained and ready

- Need any help with any sport or specific training problem

**[Your Club Name] Sport-Specific Training Program
1 session for $75 • Multiple sessions for $50 each
All sport-specific training lasts between 1 and 8 weeks**

Who is sport-specific training for?

- Anyone who wants to get ready for a specific sporting event or who is trying to solve a specific problem in their life and has a timeframe that needs to be considered

How does it differ from personal training?

- This type of training is for someone who wants a set answer for a set problem. All sport-specific training has an expected outcome and provides a solution to a problem you are trying to solve. Those using traditional personal training usually are looking for an ongoing relationship with a trainer and the motivation that goes along with that type of training.

# [Your Logo Here]

Figure 18-13. Sport-specific training

Many owners say, "We are so proud of the things we own that you're going to see all my stuff no matter what." But every club has stuff, and while your stuff maybe bigger or better than the other guy's stuff, stuff isn't what sells the most memberships.

Answer the following question early and often—"What's in it for me as the consumer?"—and you will start selling a lot more memberships. The selling stations help you present the club to the guest in a consistent manner so that he will receive the full impact of the services and programming you have to meet his needs as a new member.

> The selling stations help you present the club to the guest in a consistent manner so that he will receive the full impact of the services and programming you have to meet his needs as a new member.

## Step 8: Review at the Table

The next sales step is to bring the guest back to the information table after the tour. The salesperson would then review what the guest just saw, which is the third step in the sales presentation—tell him what he just saw. In this case, you sit your guest at the table again and thumb through the Welcome Guide one more time, quickly pointing out the things he just saw.

*Salesperson:* John, here is the class schedule I mentioned on the tour. Here is a layout of the club that will make more sense now that you have seen it. And here is the information on the personal coaching program that we discussed at the training center.

This quick review ties the tour to the Welcome Guide, so when John gets home he will have that added connection of being able to associate the material in the book with what he saw that day on the tour. This connection is important because it fills John with the sense that a lot more things were going on in your club than in any of the others he visited that day.

If you have a small facility, you can still create a sense of total support and service by filling your tour and Welcome Guide with all the training options a person has with you. Many people who aren't familiar with fitness think that working out is just working out and that everyone does the same thing.

Your goal with the smaller clubs is to create the individual approach to fitness so that everyone who belongs to your facility is getting personalized fitness designed just for them. Your potential members also need to know that you have group classes in golf conditioning, for example, which might be something they didn't even know existed but sounds cool when they are sitting at home reading your Welcome Guide on the couch. Reviewing the Welcome Guide and telling the person what he saw is also a great transition tool to help move the guest to the next sales step, which is the presentation of the prices.

# Step 9: Present the Prices

Once you have the guest seated at the table and have reviewed what he saw using the Welcome Guide, you are ready to give a formal price presentation. An old adage, however, must be understood before you get down to the actual price talk. This little saying is a strong way of putting the salesperson's role in presenting the prices to the guest in the proper perspective:

*You can scratch my car,*
*You can kick my dog,*
*You can slap my girlfriend (or any significant other),*
*But if you mess with my money I will kill you!*

Yes, this saying might seem a bit harsh, and no, this book is not advocating that you beat people or abuse animals, but a line should exist in your business that, if crossed, leads to a sad time for the salesperson that crossed it. This line is all about money and how it has to be explained to the guest. When it comes to that final few paragraphs that explain the prices to the guest, no deviation should occur from the pre-approved script that the salesperson had to memorize.

Salespeople get tired. They get hungry. They break up with people and have bad days. So when it comes to talking about the club's money, you need to eliminate any chance that any of these factors might affect how the salesperson talks about what it costs to join the club.

Use a structured price presentation coupled with a printed closing sheet. The price presentation is always less than one page long and has to be memorized by the salespeople, who should be tested monthly to make sure they aren't slowly drifting away from the original presentation.

This verbal price presentation is recited while the salesperson goes through a matching closing sheet with the guest. Using this method, the salesperson covers an auditory person and a visual person at the same time.

## The importance of printed materials

It wasn't too many years ago that no one in the industry wanted to use preprinted price information. Each owner stated his own reasons, but none of those reasons stand up to today's market.

The main reason cited was that you always wanted the ability to change the price depending on who was sitting in front of you. Most sales guys in those days had ranges rather than actual prices that they had to stick to, so putting a set price in writing prevented them from wheeling and dealing with the guest.

> **The price presentation is always less than one page long and has to be memorized by the salespeople, who should be tested monthly to make sure they aren't slowly drifting away from the original presentation.**

Another reason was that you never wanted the person to get to the prices ahead of you. If you wrote the prices out as you spoke, the guest stayed with you during the presentation and you both got to the prices at the same time. The belief was that if he saw the price he wouldn't listen to you, but instead begin the, "Can I afford this?" process in his head.

The third reason is that you didn't want your competitors to have any type of formal price sheet with your club's name or logo on it that they could use during their closes. "What do you mean you want to check out other clubs? Well, I can tell you right now what the guy down the street charges because I have his price sheet right here."

In the era of the more educated and sophisticated buyer, all of these reasons collapse. If you pull out the old yellow pad and start to write out your prices, the buyer knows you aren't legitimate and that he is probably getting swindled. "What's this idiot do, make up a new price for everyone that comes through the door?"

**As an owner in today's marketplace, you just can't risk the illusion of doing anything that could be construed as wrong or sleazy.**

As an owner in today's marketplace, you just can't risk the illusion of doing anything that could be construed as wrong or sleazy. Writing out the prices as you go creates a barrier that is hard to overcome for most buyers. More importantly, many states now demand that you have a printed price sheet listing all membership options available to the consumer, which helps keep clubs honest.

It's doubtful that anyone has ever proven that the consumer stops thinking and listening to you when he sees the prices printed out on a nice closing sheet. In addition, the reward versus risk is probably stronger for clubs that use a classy closing sheet that presents the club in the best possible light.

Finally, who cares if your competition knows your prices? The wrongful assumption is that everyone is driven by price and if your competitor pulls out your sheet and undercuts your price you'll lose the sale to him. More educated owners would probably like to see the standard in the area, and if your price sheet scares your competitors so intensely, then the consumer is probably going to want to at least see your club first.

Also remember that if the price is over $39 per month per member, 70 percent of the people who visit gyms will need two or more visits to make a decision. That "drop the price and slam the buyer today" philosophy doesn't hold up anymore.

The recommendation is to use a high-quality preprinted closing sheet that gives the club a touch of class and puts the buyer at ease that you aren't doing something that is not in his best interest. A sample closing sheet is presented in Figures 18-14 and 18-15. Consider the following rules that will help you build your own closing sheet:

- Only list two or three options on the front of the sheet.
- List what's included with the membership either on the side or across the bottom.
- Include all of the alternatives to your annual membership, such as short-term memberships or daily drop-in fees, on the back.
- Clearly show what it takes to get started today.
- Put the club contact information on the sheet.
- Have a line for the salesperson to sign so that you know who gave the presentation if the guest walks back in later with the sheet in hand.

The recommendation is to use a high-quality preprinted closing sheet that gives the club a touch of class and puts the buyer at ease that you aren't doing something that is not in his best interest.

---

# Workout America Memberships

## All of our memberships include:

- Guaranteed renewal option
- Unlimited use of our fitness facilities
- Unlimited use of our group exercise programs
- Access to our special club fitness offerings
  (limited access for an additional fee)

## Membership options at Workout America

If you join as an individual:

**$59** **one-time membership fee**
**Monthly dues of $49 per month**

This membership assumes the easy-pay EFT option.

**$59** **one-time membership fee**
**Monthly dues of $54 per month**

This membership allows you to write a check each month.

### Our renewal guarantee program:

We guarantee all members that your membership rate will never go up in the future as long as you stay a current member or renew your membership within 30 days of expiration.

---

Figure 18-14. Sample closing sheet (front)

# Workout America Memberships

**Other membership options:**

- Our short-term membership at $229
- Our daily fee of $20
- Our member/guest fee of $10
- Punch cards are available at $120
  (a savings of $30 off the daily fee)
- Our VIP week @ $49, which includes a full week offitness, three free shakes, unlimited tanning for the week, and a club T-shirt.

**More from Workout America during April . . .**

Refer a friend who joins this month and pick from one of these gifts:

- 2 free months added to your membership
- 1 month of unlimited tanning
- 2 free personal-training sessions

Specials this month:

- Intro to Personal Training — 3 sessions for $99
- Buy 2 get one FREE — Apex Supplements

Figure 18-15. Sample closing sheet (back)

**The power of a memorized price presentation**

As stated earlier, you don't want variation when it comes to presenting the prices. Developing a uniform price presentation requires that you write a less-than-one-page script that details the basic memberships and options. The following sample, which includes a number of options that can be built in, can be used as a model. When you develop a final version for your business, make sure you practice out loud so it sounds normal and doesn't come across as too overdone.

Now_____, let me show you what it costs to join the gym. An individual membership at [club name] is on an annual basis and has a one-time membership fee of $_____ and monthly dues of $_____.

This monthly payment is based upon our Easy Pay plan, which allows the club to automatically deduct the payment each month from your chosen bank account or credit card. If you wish to pay each month by check, simply add $5 to the monthly payment. It costs the club a little less to process the Easy Pay plan each month, so we pass those savings along to you.

At the end of the first year, we guarantee that your monthly rate of $_____ will never go up for as long as you wish to be a member. All we ask is that you simply stay current or renew within 30 days and we will honor your rate for any successive years you wish to be a member. All you need to get started today is your one-time membership fee of $_____. Your first month's payment is not due for a full 30 days from the day you join the club.

*(Open-ended membership option—use only if it is needed in your market)*

[Name], we also offer a month-to-month, pay-as-you-go membership plan. We have a number of members who like the freedom to come and go as they wish without having to commit to a membership.

The one-time membership fee for this membership is $_____ and the month-to-month fee is just $_____. This membership does not, however, have a guaranteed rate in the future and is subject to any increases the club might choose at a later date. If you plan to be a member of the club all year round, and would like to save $120, then we still recommend the annual individual membership, with its monthly dues of only $_____.

*(18-month option for price-sensitive markets—list at $10 lower than your annual plan)*

[Name], we do have one other membership option you might want to consider. Some of our members are concerned about fitting their monthly dues into their budget, so we do offer a saver's program. This program is based upon an 18-month membership and you can save $10 per month with this plan. Your one-time membership fee for this plan is

$_____ and your monthly dues are just $_____ for 18 months.

*("Two adults at the same address" option—do not call it a couple's membership—don't offer it unless you get a "yes" to the following question)*

[Name], do you have additional family members who you want to join the club with you?

*(If yes, continue here)*

In that case, we also have a special plan for two adults living at the same address. Our one-time membership fee for these two people is $_____ and the monthly dues are just $_____. This membership is also guaranteed for as many years you wish to be a member.

*(Family option)*

[Name], we also have a family plan available. This membership is for any members of your family living at the same address and whom we offer services or programming for here at the club. Your one-time membership fee for the family option is $_____ and your family rate is just $_____, again based upon an annual basis.

*(Cash option)*

If you wish to pay for your membership all at one time, we charge you the same total price as our regular individual membership, but we do add two free months, valued at $_____, to your annual membership. Your rates are also guaranteed in the future with this membership option.

---

**Do not offer endless options unless you get a nod from the guest that he might be interested in hearing about them.**

Do not offer endless options unless you get a nod from the guest that he might be interested in hearing about them. Many club salespeople routinely explain everything, such as the family plan, when it would be better to focus on the guy sitting in front of them who is trying to join today. Keep it simple and focused and keep the options to a minimum.

## Step 10: Buy the Sale

Once you present the prices, one further step must be completed before you ask for the sale. Remember, you always enhance and never discount. At this point in the sales steps, you present the Trial Gift Certificate.

The trial certificate is a closing tool used by the salesperson to help the guest make that buying decision today. You don't discount the membership fee, but instead buy the deal using gifts.

**You always enhance and never discount.**

These gifts add value to the sale instead of insulting the more sophisticated buyer by trying to pretend that you are really going to knock off $50 today if he joins right this minute, but if he comes back tomorrow he'll have to pay full price. Review Chapter 15 before you work through this particular step in the sales process.

Where you are in the sales process at this point:

- You have toured the guest and are back at the information table.

- You have reviewed what he saw both verbally and by using the Welcome Guide.

- You have presented the prices using the closing sheet and by using a memorized price presentation that matches the information he is looking at while you speak.

- You are now ready to use the Trial Gift Certificate as an added benefit.

*John, before you decide which one of those memberships you would like, there is one further benefit to joining the club that I'd like to show you.*

*(Pull out the trial certificate and lay it on the table. Do not put it in the Welcome Guide.)*

*We realize that you have choices when it comes to joining a fitness facility and as a way of saying thank you for selecting us as your gym, we'd like to start you off with some gifts from the club. If you are already comfortable with the club and are planning to join during your first visit, we'd like to offer you our special premiere package of gifts and incentives.*

*(Review the incentives listed on the Trial Gift Certificate.)*

*If you need more time to experience the club before you commit to a membership, we'd like to offer you the following package that is yours any time during the first seven days of your trial membership.*

*(Review the incentives listed on the Trial Certificate.)*

To get the most power out of the Trial Gift Certificate, keep the gift bag on the table loaded with goodies so the guest can touch it and play with it if he wants. Don't forget the doers who like to experience things and will want to pick up the bag and see what's inside.

**The Trial Gift Certificate should be a work of art suitable for framing.**

Also, don't forget that the Trial Gift Certificate should be a work of art suitable for framing. Don't be cheap and copy something you made yourself on your computer in the middle of the night in your underwear. Make it nice, since it will represent your brand outside the club as your trial member shows it to his significant other or friends at work.

# Step 11: Ask for the Sale

Now you're ready to ask for the sale. To review, you are at this point in the sales process:

- You have toured the guest and are back at the information table.
- You have reviewed what he saw both verbally and by using the Welcome Guide.
- You have presented the prices using the closing sheet and by using a memorized price presentation that matches the information he is looking at while you speak.
- You have presented the Trial Gift Certificate as an added benefit and have gone through the gifts and shown the guest the loot bag on the table.
- It's money time!

At this point, everyone falls apart. Some people are more able to kick a kitten down the stairs than ask for money from someone who came in to actually buy a membership and start working out.

Jeffrey Fox, a noted business author who is well worth reading for the small business owner, states that 95 percent of all salespeople never ask for the sale. In this business, that number is probably accurate, but salespeople don't believe it because everyone feels that they did ask for the money at the end. However, the following phrases are not closes and if you use anything close to these words you aren't really asking for the sale—you just think you are:

- So hey, what do you think?
- How's that sound to you, man?
- So, is this something you want to do?
- Do you think this is something that sounds good to you?

You aren't closing here. You're babbling, and the difference is defined by how many of anything you sell. None of these phrases would be effective and most give the guest a way to walk away.

## When it comes to the close, learn one go-to line that you master.

Learn one line and use that line over and over again, because one line is all you need to really be good at asking for money. Start with this one first:

*Well John, I've shown you the prices and I have also shown you the special gifts we'd like to offer you as a new member as our way of saying thanks. Let's pick the membership that is best for you and get you started today.*

The first line is just the setup for the second line, which is all you really need to get it done. Simple, clean, and direct is always the way to go when you ask for money.

## The old sales gizmo that you still need

You should learn this old sales trick, which still works today and is brilliant in its simplicity: Once you say the line, whoever speaks next loses. Just say your line and look at the person with a gentle, hopeful smile on your face, but don't say another word. Just wait.

Most new salespeople can't stand it and have to fill the silence. They will say the line correctly but have to follow it with something to keep it going:

*Let's pick the membership that is best for you and get you started today. (Quickly followed by) Well, John, what are you thinking about?*

Silence is good and usually means that the person is processing the information he just received. Jumping back in too soon forces him to stop processing and then the safety word jumps out: "No." Give the person time to think and the answer will more often be "yes," but rush the decision by intruding on his thoughts and he has to say a quick "no" to give himself room to maneuver.

## If at first you don't succeed... ask again.

You should always ask for the sale twice, but keep in mind that begging is not closing, so you need a set plan if you get a "no" or indecisive answer the first time, such as: "Well, I don't know. I think I'd like to go home and give it some thought tonight and I'll get back to you tomorrow." A safe follow-up line that can be used by pros and rookies alike is:

*John, what did I miss showing you today that might have helped you make the decision to get started?*

Sometimes you truly miss things or the guest is so overwhelmed with what he is seeing that he just overlooks something important to him. Asking this question often brings good results. For example, he might answer as follows:

*Guest:* Well, I thought your weight area was kind of small and I didn't see enough benches, so it must be tough in here during prime time.

*Salesperson:* John, I don't think you noticed everything. We actually have two weight areas in the club and the second one is a softer area for members who like to stay out of the main weight room. Let's go look again and make sure you aren't confused before you make up your mind.

> Simple, clean, and direct is always the way to go when you ask for money.

The salesperson would walk the guest back one more time to make sure he had really seen everything. Many times this extra effort will get the deal because the person is simply overloaded and missed a key part of the tour.

## Ask twice nice and then back off.

Once you gain experience, you might want to break this rule, but don't forget the power of the trial membership. Entire books have been written about how to handle objections at this point, but mostly the salesperson just ends up really making today's potential member angry and wanting to walk out the door.

The trial membership is designed to cover all of the major objections in advance. The three classics—time, money, and spouse—all are absorbed by the trial. Consider these three examples:

*Guest:* Gee, I don't know if I have the time to do this.

*Salesperson:* Well, why not try it free for 14 days and see if it fits your schedule over the next two weeks?

*Guest:* I don't know if I can afford this membership.

*Salesperson:* Well, why not try it free for the 14 days and see if you can start fitting it into your budget over the next two weeks?

*Guest:* I really need to ask my wife before I join.

*Salesperson:* How about a 14-day pass for her, too? Even if she doesn't join, she might feel better about the club and your new membership.

Once you gain experience, you can move on to handling some of these objections a little more aggressively at the point of sale. Some are simple, such as the money issue, which can be handled by keeping a nicely printed sheet listing what can be purchased in your area for the equivalent of your monthly membership.

This idea has been mentioned elsewhere in the book, but it's worth mentioning again in this context because it represents a larger issue. If you get these types of objections, why not anticipate them and build them into your Welcome Guide and sales presentation instead of trying to teach new salespeople how to be old salespeople?

This takeaway approach is strong because it puts the responsibility back on the client to work through each one of these issues on his own. For example, the spouse objection can be handled nicely with a page in the guide that talks about working on fitness for yourself as well as for others in your life. By making fitness both personal and for others, you kill the objection before it even comes up by simply showing the person the page while he is sitting in front of you.

> The trial membership is designed to cover all of the major objections in advance.

This type of anticipation builds a system that is dependent upon the salesperson knowing where the page is versus trying to teach young salespeople how to think and double-talk like they were selling cheap cars.

## Sometimes they are faster than you are.

Sometimes, the potential member is moving faster than you are in the sales process, and you ruin the sale by backing up. For example, the person says, "How many days a week should a person be working out when they start?"

A new salesperson may not pick up the clue he was just given, however, and remain back at the selling part. "John, fitness is a lifetime commitment and it starts today with you taking the first step and buying a membership."

The potential member already sees himself as a new member and is asking how many times a week he needs to be there when he starts, and the salesperson is still pitching and answering the wrong question. The lesson to learn from this scenario is that salespeople are often so intent on selling that they don't listen. In this case, the person has already put himself into the gym and the salesperson failed to see that he had moved beyond the sales part into the membership part.

> Salespeople are often so intent on selling that they don't listen.

## Don't forget the old rule of dating.

Two women are sitting in a bar. Both are good-looking fitness women who are 7s, but they are talking to guys that are 5s. One woman keeps looking over the guy's shoulder, watching the door for the next guy who is a 10 to come in so she can upgrade, while the other is in deep conversation with the guy in front of her. The woman watching the door leaves by herself, while her friend leaves for a nice dinner and night out with her new friend. The moral of the story: Get the sale in front of you and stop worrying about buddy sales, family members, and upselling the person—not to mention the two other people you just noticed at the front counter.

It is easy to lose the deal in front of you while you're watching everything else in the club or trying to sell the guy in front of you a family membership instead of just getting him done and started today. You are always better off taking care of the business in front of you first and worrying about the other things after that membership agreement is filled out.

# Step 12: Make Sure No One Leaves Without a Membership

Either the person leaves as a real regular member or as a trial member, but he has to leave with at least one of these two options. "Be-backs" are another old term that caused a lot of angst in sales training in the past. If you believed in

**Either the person leaves as a real regular member or as a trial member, but he has to leave with at least one of these two options.**

be-backs, which is a term for someone who went home to think about it and said he would be back tomorrow, you probably also believed in Santa Claus, the Easter Bunny, and honest politicians. You would be punished if you told your supervisor that you missed a deal, "But don't worry, he'll be back tomorrow and I know I'll get him for sure." The theory was that if you didn't do everything possible to get the person today, including embarrassment, harassment, and brutal pressure, then you weren't doing your job.

Prices have gone up for memberships, people have more choices, and they will leave. But they will come back if no undue pressure was placed on them during the first visit that kept them from wanting to see you again.

Mike Grondahl, founder of the Planet Fitness chain and an astute marketing guru who has studied what it takes to get and keep members for years, says, "Let them walk. If you blame the competition, the economy, or gas prices for people who don't sign up today, then you have no confidence in your product." He goes on to say that a much larger percentage of the population in this country would belong to clubs if it wasn't for the "don't let them leave until they are crying" horror stories of the past.

In this system, people are not necessarily signing up today, but they still leave with a commitment to the club, and to come back, due to the trial membership. In either case, it's your job to make sure that the new member leaves with everything he needs to take that next step with your club. Following up leads is covered in Chapter 21. This step only deals with what you should be doing to make sure that a person who leaves with either type of membership has a set next step to keep him in the system.

## The regular new member

It is important to get your new member completely grounded in the system as quickly as possible. Members are very vulnerable during their first 30 days and they will quit if you don't get them into the club and working out. The following things should happen immediately to keep the member staying longer and paying longer:

- If you can't afford the loot package included with the trial membership, make sure he leaves with at least a T-shirt. You have to let him know that you appreciate his business.

- He should leave with an appointment card for his first training session.

- He should be introduced to every staff member on duty before he leaves.

- The salesperson must walk him to the door and thank him again for his business.

- If you are offering the full package with the Trial Gift Certificate, load the guy up with one of everything. Once he receives his gym bag or backpack, walk him past the counter and give him a munchie bar, sports drink, soft drink, muffin, key chain, etc. Make him feel good about what he just bought and send him home with some good stuff.

- The salesperson has to send him a "thank you" email before he leaves the parking lot. The sample for this email is included in Chapter 21.

- You must mail him a handwritten, hand-addressed "thank you" note the same day he joins the club, so that he receives it the next day. The script for this letter is also included in Chapter 21. Make sure a pair of one-day guest passes are in the envelope as well.

- Add him to your regular email list immediately. All members should get a weekly email every Monday at 4:00 p.m. This email has one motivational page that keeps the person wanting to work out that week, one page that includes information highlighting a new program, class, or party in the club that week, and four coupons that have to be used in the club by that Sunday. If you touch the member weekly through this email system, the person will stay longer and pay longer.

- Also send him a copy of your previous electronic newsletter. At this point in time, you should not be sending any paper newsletters due to the waste and cost. All newsletters should be electronic. Make sure you send the new member the last couple that you sent to your regular members. Don't worry about that small percentage of old, anti-tech holdouts and earth people from the 60s that don't have email yet. Just remember the dinosaurs and what happened to them.

**All newsletters should be electronic.**

- At the end of his first week, he should receive a nice letter from the owner or operating manager thanking him for becoming a member of the club. The copy for this letter is also included in Chapter 21.

- At the end of 30 days, send him another small gift in the mail, such as a nice coffee cup like the metal car cups from Starbucks®. You can bulk order these cups for a few bucks each and get the entire package, including 10 single guest passes stuffed inside, for less than five dollars each. Just when the new member thinks that he is lost in the pack, surprise him one more time by validating his decision to go with you with another nice "thank you."

## The trial member

- The trial member should still get the "thank you" email.

- He must leave with the appointment card solidifying his next contact with the club.

- Add him to the same email "tip of the week" list as you would a new member.

- The trial member also gets the handwritten card.

- The new trial member should also be given a temporary membership card, be added to your software system, and have his picture taken and put into the computer. If your software system can't do these tasks, get a new system that can. If you treat the trial member like a real member, he will become a member. He should check in just like every other member does.

- He must leave with a Welcome Guide, the Trial Gift Certificate, and the closing sheet with the prices. It is worth mentioning again that 70 percent of your guests need two or more visits before they buy. What do you want in front of the person when he is sitting at home thinking about which gym he wants to try or join? Load him up and you will not only get him, but his significant other and maybe a friend as that package travels through the neighborhood.

- Start collecting interesting fitness articles and make copies to give the trial members, or join a service that provides an online library of fitness-specific articles. A number of clubs access these services and print specific articles relating to the trial member before he leaves from his first visit. For example, he mentions that he has diabetes and that his doctor recommended he start working out. While he is with the salesperson, another person on the staff can pull up two or three articles related to diabetes and fitness, print them out, and send them home with the guest.

In summary of this step, the trial membership gives you an option past owners and salespeople didn't have at their disposal. If someone left without a membership in the high-pressure days, he wasn't coming back, because anyone beaten that badly who left without a membership would never set foot in that club again.

**The trial membership is the bridge that builds a connection between the guest and the club that continues even if he doesn't buy a membership the first time.**

The trial membership is the bridge that builds a connection between the guest and the club that continues even if he doesn't buy a membership the first time. He now has a low-pressure alternative to come back and try the club without feeling bad about the experience. In this system, everyone leaves with a membership, either a regular membership and all the support that goes with it, or a trial membership, which is still packed with support and incentives to keep moving forward.

## Check These Things to Increase Your Results

You can add a few more things to your sales act that will help you be more effective over time. Some of these points are mentioned elsewhere in this chapter, but they are worth mentioning again because each one is a key to making more sales than the guy down the street.

*Ask permission.* Always ask permission and use courtesy:

- With your permission, may I show you our club?

- If you have a few extra minutes, may I buy you a smoothie?

- Thank you for stopping by our club today. I'd be happy to answer your questions.

- Thank you, we really appreciate your business.

No one should really have to remind you to say thank you when someone gives you money, but people seem to lose their sense of business over time and replace it with the classic quote: "This business would be great if it wasn't for those darn members." Courtesy sells because it is so unusual these days.

**Courtesy sells because it is so unusual these days.**

*Use the assumptive approach.* Don't sell, assume. This rule means that your conversation with the guest is always based upon the assumption that he is already a member. For example:

- As a member, you will want to get here a little early for that particular cycle class.

- Are you going to be working out in the morning or after work, John?

- You need to move a little every day to stay fit. Sometimes that activity will be with us, but for those days that you can't get into the gym, take a long walk or even a jog when you're ready.

*Remember the alternate close question.* "Which one of these options is best for you?" This question is powerful, but only if you keep your choices at the point of sale limited to two or three.

*Ask for the sale.* The biggest mistake made in all sales is the failure to ask for the sale. Remember that the person sitting in front of you came to you seeking help. You are the expert and you are selling the help he needs to change his life. Simply say, "Let's get you signed up today."

*Follow the steps.* The steps of the sale were designed to go in the exact order in which they are presented in this chapter. If a wandering guest, club emergency, or other happening knocks you out of order, try to get back in the right sequence and keep going. Your sales will be stronger if you can master the steps as they are presented and then follow them during each tour.

## Key Points From This Chapter

- Set systems are easier to teach and allow you to quickly develop good salespeople.

- The 12 steps should be done in the same order every time.

**The most important part of the tour is when you don't sell.**

- Use the best tools you can afford. Print everything with class and quality, mind the details, and make sure everything you give the guest is the best possible representation of your business.

- Everyone who visits your club sees everything you have to offer every time.

- The information is neutral ground that makes for an easy starting point for your tours.

- The most important part of the tour is when you don't sell. Spend at least two to four minutes just getting to know the person and what he wants from his membership. You don't have to be a hardcore salesperson, just a nice person who cares.

- Present the prices in exactly the same way each time. You'll get better results and it is easier to train people if everyone is following the same script.

- You always enhance, and never discount. Buy the sale with class and by using tools designed for a more sophisticated buyer.

- No one leaves without a membership. A person is either a regular member or a trial member, but he is indeed a new member of your club.

- Ask for the sale. Failure to ask is the biggest mistake that salespeople make in any field, but especially in the fitness industry.

---

**Tip of the Day**

# Read and listen.

You don't find too many people who are successful that don't read a lot or listen to an audio series of some type. Your goal should be to read a book a week for the rest of your life. If you're not a reader, try to read one book every two weeks or get some audio books to listen to. Don't forget the Internet. A few quick clicks and you can find hundreds of articles that will help you grow as a person and in your career.

You don't always have to read business books either. Read motivating books, such as biographies or great novels that inspire. Hundreds of magazines and websites will give you more than enough information about hundreds of subjects.

Readers are smarter, more interesting, and have more successful careers than nonreaders. And you don't have to have a great deal of formal education to read. Educating yourself can make you just as smart and just as successful as someone with a degree, but you have to take personal responsibility.

# 19

# The Rhythm of the Sale

Every sale has a rhythm to it. Once you get experience, you can actually feel if you're in sync and on your way to getting the sale done or if your rhythm is slightly off and closing will be tough that day. Using selling stations as your set tour path enables you to get control of that rhythm, something salespeople weren't able to do in the past because the tour was freestyle and based on the whims of the salesperson.

For example, if you have 15 selling stations in your club, you should know exactly where every salesperson is on the tour, how much time it took to get to that point, and approximately how much time he has before he gets back to the information table. If your average tour takes 40 minutes, and Kristen, your salesperson, is halfway through, you know as a manager or owner how much time it will take her to finish and when she will be available for the next tour.

Knowing the average time also allows you to troubleshoot your sales. If Kristen is struggling with her sales, for example, and is consistently finishing in less than 30 minutes, while your successful salespeople are taking approximately 40 minutes for each tour, then you know that she may be rushing the sale and not spending enough time with the guest.

## The Perfect Pace of a Sale

The magic timeframe for most sales is 30 to 40 minutes. It should take you somewhere between 30 and 40 minutes from the time you meet someone at the door (the meet and greet) until you walk him back to the door with his finished paperwork.

This timeframe takes into account most club sizes up to approximately 60,000 square feet. If your club is larger, your sales encounter can stretch to approximately 45 minutes. Owners of smaller clubs will often find that their salespeople (or the multipurpose owner who does everything) will take the 45-minute route with most sales due to the individualization of the presentation.

In a smaller club, you don't have a lot to show and are actually forced to do what everyone else should do, which is spend time with the guest talking about what he wants, who he is, and how you can help him. These owners have less to show and end up taking the time to really get to know the guest. When you have a larger facility, you lose that magic and end up spending too much time showing stuff and not enough time finding out how you can help the potential member succeed.

Sales in women-only clubs often are closer to 45 minutes as well. Many guests in this type of club are a little more nervous and need more reassurance than someone who might have more fitness experience. Again, you are forced to do the right thing to cater to the nature of the guest, which is to slow down and get to know the person you are talking to at the moment.

Another way to look at the time needed to get a sale done correctly is to look at what the perfect tour might look like in the future:

*Yes, we have everything you need to get in shape in this club, but before I show you what we have to offer, let's spend 30 minutes just sitting here so I can find out how I can best help you get what you are looking for in a club. Now tell me, what are you doing to stay in shape now?...*

When you spend the optimum time with someone, you are actually accomplishing the ultimate sales goal, which is to hit the magic combination of getting to know the client well enough to demonstrate a caring attitude, presenting the club in its best light, and earning money for the business—all accomplished with a rhythmic flow that takes approximately 40 minutes for a trained salesperson in most fitness businesses.

## What Happens When You Go too Quickly?

The more experience you get, the faster you go. The faster you go, the less effective you get. The less effective you get, the more nervous you get and the faster you go. The following statement is the ultimate sales tip of all time:

> **Slow down and take the time to care.**

> **Sales managers and owners will find that the most common mistake the staff makes in term of sales, besides not firmly asking for the sale, is rushing the entire process.**

Sales managers and owners will find that the most common mistake the staff makes in term of sales, besides not firmly asking for the sale, is rushing the entire process. If you spend less than 30 minutes with a client, you have not spent enough time to build a relationship, and without a relationship the sale will be much more difficult. It is a pretty solid rule that if a salesperson is back in less than 20 minutes, your chance of getting that sale is very low.

In traditional club sales, if you don't use selling stations as markers you'll find it very difficult to fill a full 40-minute presentation because you don't have the tools to develop the rhythm. The salesperson walks the guest to the back of the club, points out a few rooms and the cardio equipment, strolls through the free-weight room, and then tries to do everything that should have been done upfront in too short of a time period while sitting across a desk. This tour never develops a relationship, and without the relationship you're down to throwing high-pressure tactics at the person.

Selling stations provide the structure that gives the tour its pace and allow the salesperson to keep that 40-minute time a reality. In other words, it forces the salesperson to spend enough time with the guest to build the relationship of trust that will lead to the sale.

The takeaway point in this section is that as an owner or sales manager you need to start timing all of your sales and developing averages for each person and times of success for the team. If, for example, your team averages 35 minutes per sales encounter, but your best salesperson averages 42 minutes, then the rest of your squad might be rushing their tours. Simply slowing down the process might increase your numbers.

This advice is just the opposite of what many sales managers believe. The old standard was, "Get him up, get him down, and move on to the next person, because we're busy turning numbers in this club."

That style might have worked in the days of big volume and little competition, but in today's market, where you are fighting for you life against many good players, you must change how you think about the sales process in general. Your new philosophy is, "Get to know them, tour them carefully, and close them gently by using the relationship you have developed over the past 40 minutes."

## What Happens When You Go too Slowly?

You can take too much time. Tours that run close to an hour or more usually don't turn out well in most sales encounters. These tours are usually done by your more talkative salespeople, who end up telling too much of their own stories and not listening nearly enough to the guest.

Exceptions exist, of course, such as when you hook up with someone you really like and with whom you have a lot in common. Those sales encounters sometimes take a legitimate hour to do, but they also usually end up with a sale.

> In today's market, where you are fighting for you life against many good players, you must change how you think about the sales process in general.

The reality, however, is that if you spend too much time you are probably talking the person out of the sale instead of into it. It's going on too long and you may be seriously boring the person to a slow sales death. Owners and sales managers need to watch the salespeople who go too long just as closely as those who rush too much, although the biggest error will still always be rushing too much.

**Find the effective sales time for your club and then use that number as the measuring stick for the team.**

In summary, find the effective sales time for your club and then use that number as the measuring stick for the team. Look for those who rush and finish in less than 20 minutes, but also keep an eye out for the hardcore talkers who take an hour or more for each sale. Your starting point should be in the 30- to 40-minute window, but some clubs will find that 45 minutes is the optimum time for the most effective sales encounter.

# Key Points From This Chapter

- An optimum time exists for a membership sale.
- Start your planning in the 30- to 40-minute range.
- Selling stations provide the structure that provides the rhythm.
- Rushing is the biggest killer of most sales.
- Slow down and care and your sales will increase.

**Tip of the Day**

## Save a little money.

When you are young, you think you will live forever. Who knows? You might, but who says you have to live broke?

Start your career by learning to save money. No matter how old you are, set up a retirement account and throw at least $50 per month into it, and then add more as you make more in your career.

Start early enough and you will be wealthy when it counts. Saving also shows the discipline you need to run someone else's business. If you can manage your own money, then you might do well managing someone else's, but if you can't budget and save what you have then investors or owners will say, "No way can you handle my money."

The fitness-business trail is littered with hundreds of owners who were successful and then for some reason lost their ability to make money in their clubs. Most of these people had never saved enough to get out of their businesses or to take a chance doing something else. Money gives you the freedom to live your life at a higher level and that freedom starts today with your first deposit into your new retirement account.

# 20

# It Is Time for Fun and Games and the Misery That Goes With Them

If you can't do something in practice, then you probably can't do it at all. Every owner has heard the lame excuse that role-playing and practicing is stupid, "And besides, I can do it when it counts out on the floor." No, you can't, because if you can't put together a smooth presentation in front of your teammates, you won't be able to hold up under pressure during a busy night with a lot of prospects.

Practice is when you work on your delivery, polish your words, work on the small nuances, such as how you stand or shake hands, and most importantly master the material it takes to become an effective salesperson who can be counted on to get the job done. The hard part for most owners is not the practice; it is making time to practice that kills them. The question is, "What is more important than finding time to practice the most important skill in the fitness business, which is the ability to generate new revenue through sales?"

## How Much Time Is Enough?

When you first switch over to a new sales system, or to try to completely rebuild one that isn't as effective as you'd like, schedule two complete days to practice, set up the new materials, and get the group comfortable with using the new system on the next business day. These two days do not have to be back to back, but could be on two consecutive Fridays, for example.

After you install the system, you should use at least one four-hour block a week to constantly review and improve all the basic steps and systems. This training would work best on a Friday, when most clubs are slow anyway.

The sales manager should be in charge of these training sessions, but the owner should be involved as well. You could also bring in outside trainers at least once a month if time and budget allow.

# Who Gets the Training?

**Everyone on the staff, including childcare providers and janitors, should get sales training at least once a month.**

Everyone on the staff, including childcare providers and janitors, should get sales training at least once a month. Your Friday training sessions should include as many full-time employees as possible.

> Most states allow you to pay training wages for employees who come in just for training. For example, if an employee gets $10 for being on the clock but comes in for training when he is not scheduled, he can be paid $7 per hour for hours spent in training. You have to keep your training wage standardized across the board and be fair to everyone, and these wages must be listed in your employee manual.

It helps the entire sales effort if your counter people are trained in sales along with the sales team. First of all, you might find that next superstar who you hadn't noticed yet. Secondly, you might find competent people who can fill in for sick days and vacations. Your team will also do better when everyone gets an understanding of what his teammates do for a living. Also, people are more likely support something that they feel they are a part of while at work.

Most sales managers overthink this training when they first get started by trying to do too much in each block of time. "Do less and master more" is a good thought to keep in your head if you are in charge of training people in your club. Consider the following four-hour sample lesson plan that illustrates the "less is more" principle:

12:00–1:00—Answering the phone (Review the basics and role play with all staff):

- Expected outcome—to master the greeting and how to handle inquiry calls
- Tools needed—two fake phones and a tape recorder

1:00–2:00—Working the handoff with the front-counter person:

- Expected outcome—a smooth transition between the counter person who first meets the guest and the salesperson who will give the tour
- Tools needed—none

2:00–3:00—Filling out the inquiry sheet without looking at it:

- Expected outcome—the ability, of both the salespeople and front-counter people, to fill out the inquiry sheet from memory to keep the process sounding more natural
- Tools needed—stack of inquiry sheets and fake phones

3:00–4:00—Reviewing the membership agreement and recent errors we can improve upon:

- Expected outcome– to improve the quality of our work, as we have rushed the membership agreements recently
- Tools needed–membership agreements and recent examples of ones that could have been better

Daily five-minute sessions are also very productive. Pick the point of the day and spend five minutes with every salesperson or key staff member and pound in that point. Use the same format as the four-hour training in terms of the expected outcome, but keep it simple. Consider this example:

> Point of the day–Answering the phone by the third ring and using the welcoming statement

- Expected outcome–get everyone back to answering the phone more quickly and reemphasize the value and power of the welcome statement for the desk and phone

## Using Games to Train

Role-playing is the normal way you train for sales, but most role-plays are often based upon experience that may not yet be developed in your new salespeople. If you want to develop role-plays that drive revenue back up, you must first break down the main point you are training for that day into smaller components and practice those components first.

A good example is an owner who wants to work on greeting the guest at the door and moving toward the office (or information table). He might tell the staff member to walk up, shake hands, introduce himself, and then invite the person to the table.

> If you want to develop role-plays that drive revenue back up, you must first break down the main point you are training for that day into smaller components and practice those components first.

## The Steps of Good Training: What, How, Why, Show, and Practice

In the role-playing example, the owner told the staff what to do, but then he stopped. Most employees will struggle with this directive. What he didn't do was tell them how to shake hands in a professional manner, how to introduce yourself and take the lead in the conversation, how to transition to the table, or how the handoff from the counter person is supposed to work. In other words, he told them what to do, but he didn't tell them how to do it.

> If you want to be successful in sales and in life, remember the following rule:
>
> **Everything counts.**

The money is in the details, and the owner and salespeople who practice the how will beat the cheap beer out of the team that just works on the actions without a plan.

The money is in the details, and the owner and salespeople who practice the how will beat the cheap beer out of the team that just works on the actions without a plan. How you shake hands sets the tone for the sale and is not a random act. How you walk up to the person sets an image. What you are wearing, your hair, and even your breath form a first impression, either positive or negative. The money is in the details, and you should practice and train for these details in everything you do.

If you want more out of your employees, master these four words—what, how, why, and practice—and how they relate to training. Many of you may have been forced into being a trainer but really haven't had the training yourself or the experience to develop and motivate a staff. This basic system can give you a great deal of strength as you begin to build an effective sales machine.

---

## The Story

A guy thinks he is a good skier. He has never had a lesson, but he can get down most of the hills on the mountain and thinks he is pretty darn good.

He takes his girlfriend, who has never skied before, on a ski trip. He knows they have only a few days, so he tells her that she doesn't need lessons, and that he'll teach her himself. He also doesn't want to waste his day on the bunny slopes, so he drags her up to the top on the first run.

"It's easy," he says, "just make a big wedge with your skis and snow plow down the hill." She starts out slowly but then picks up speed. He skis behind her yelling, "Turn, turn, turn."

She doesn't turn and hits a tree. She is unhurt but scared, and he is mad. "I told you to turn," he says. "I tried, you schmuck," she yells back.

An hour later they are in the ski school. A nice, patient instructor sees runny makeup from crying and a feud underway. "I think I can help," he smiles, and for a mere $350 for a private lesson he leads her off to a nice gentle slope. An hour later she is making nice round turns coming down a beginner's run and two hours after that she is on a gentle intermediate run and holding her own.

The ski instructor also skied behind her, but his plan was different than the boyfriend's method of teaching. The instructor told her to turn, but he also had patiently told her how to turn before she tried it. And he also demonstrated a good turn before she tried it, in the way it would look as she would do it for her level, not as it would look if someone more advanced did it. Later that night, the instructor found himself in a hot tub with a grateful student and they lived happily ever after.

The moral of this story is that to be an effective trainer you have to cover all five steps with any of the training you do. These steps are as follows:

- Tell the student *what* to do
- Tell the student *how* to do it
- Tell the student *why* it is important
- *Show* him what it looks like when it is done correctly
- *Practice* and coach for results

The following sections apply these steps to a typical training situation in the club. You have a new counter person who is learning how to answer the phone. The trainer in this example is working on the welcome statement and answering the phone by the third ring. The counter person's name is Julie.

## What

*Now Julie, part of your job is to answer the phone at the club. We always answer the phone within three rings and we always use the welcome statement: We're having a great day at the Workout Company.*

## How

*Always listen for the phone. It gets pretty loud in here and sometimes we get busy and think someone else will get it. There is a phone here, but there is another one on the other end of the counter in case you're working with people at that end. The welcome statement really sets the tone for the caller and you should say it with enthusiasm and some pride in being the best club in town.*

**Many of you may have been forced into being a trainer but really haven't had the training yourself or the experience to develop and motivate a staff.**

## Why

*Our club is known for customer service and that service begins when you answer the phone. For many of our potential members, you are the first contact, so in some ways you have one of the most important jobs in the club. If you are enthusiastic and courteous on the phone, then the caller's first impression of us is going to be good. And if a member calls, who is someone who is paying us each month, he or she expects good service as part of every contact with the club. So your role is important in that case as well, since you are part of our member-retention plan.*

## Show

*I'm going to have Billy call from the office and pretend that he is potential member. Listen to how I answer the phone and see if I sound like I'm having fun and this is a great place to work out. We'll do that two or three times and you'll see a pattern start to form, I hope.*

### Practice

*Okay, now it is your turn. Just remember that each time you practice this technique it gets better. And don't forget about the third ring. We have to practice the details to get good at providing our members and guests with great service.*

This training session might last 30 minutes or less. The trainer had a plan and worked through it one step at a time. Most trainers don't have an expected outcome or a step-by-step method of training for results. The training you do for any employee will be more effective if you work through the steps listed in this section. Remember, less is more and train in small chunks.

# Some Games

**Games are useful in that they break harder concepts into digestible parts.**

Games are useful in that they break harder concepts into digestible parts. Games are also fun, and no rule states that training has to be boring. Each of these games represents some aspect of the system, which will be mentioned along with how to do it. Literally hundreds of other training games are included in books for trainers that you can find at any good book store. These games are just a few to get you started today.

### The hand-off

- Expected outcome—The counter person should smoothly hand over the guest to the salesperson.
- Why this step is important—You want to be known for your customer service and it begins here. If this step is done well, it will also make the sale easier for the salesperson.
- Tools needed—The script for the counter person to memorize
- How—Let the counter person practice the lines while handing off a real person to the salesperson.

This game is more of a role-play than a game, but it is based upon practicing a set skill using a set script as follows:

*Hi [salesperson], I would like to introduce [guest] to you. He is here to get some information about the club. [Guest], this is [salesperson]. She is the best person in the club to help you with that membership information. By the way [guest], it was a pleasure to meet you. My name again is [counter person] and if you need any help in the club please come find me. I am usually here during the evenings and you can almost always find me here at the front counter. Thank you for coming in and we look forward to having you as a member.*

You need three people to role-play this game. The counter person should be given the script at least 30 minutes prior to the training session so he has time to memorize it. Also, have it written out in large type to use in the training.

Whenever you can, practice in the place where the action will actually take place. The staff members pick up cues from the environment that make them more successful with the training, which will be more effective more quickly.

The extra players will also benefit from the training. If you are using a real salesperson, he or she will gain experience from working with the counter staff and will be able to help them out if they get in trouble when it is busy.

## Shaking hands

- Expected outcome—Everyone on the staff should learn how to professionally shake hands and greet someone.

- Why this step is important—The sales encounter begins at this point, and how you greet someone sets the tone for expected customer service.

- Tools needed—None

- How—Rate each other's handshakes on a 1 to 5 scale, with a 5 being a great, professional handshake.

First impressions are more important than even your mother told you they were. The first impressions in most fitness facilities are poor. The staff is too young and undertrained, the clubs are too loud or too quiet, the staff is dressed in poorly fitting T-shirts or worn-out golf shirts, and too much clutter is around the front counter.

**First impressions are more important than even your mother told you they were.**

One thing you can do to make a difference is work on the first impression your staff makes, which starts with the greeting. Handshakes seem simple, yet how much training have you, or your young staff people, had on this basic business skill? It may be a lost art for some, but it is still a fundamental business tool for the professional.

The handshake game is simple. Get everyone to stand up and shake each other's hands and then rate that shake on a 1 to 5 scale, with 5 being the best. Look for weak shakes, sweaty hands (cured by wearing pants with pockets and drying your hand on the way out), grips that are too strong, and guys that try too hard.

The real key is not necessarily to find the perfect handshake, but to make your staff aware that it is an important act and that they are judged partially on how well they perform something that simple. Awareness is a lot of what training is about, and making your staff aware that this detail is important is a good first step to mastering it later.

## The distance game

- Expected outcome—Learn that how far apart you stand when you greet someone makes a difference in how leadership is perceived.

- Why this step is important—The sales encounter begins at this point and how you greet someone sets the tone for expected customer service.

- Tools needed—None

- How—Experience the difference between a normal greeting distance and the "power zone."

Pick a partner. Extend an arm straight out, with fingertips extended and barely touching your partner's chest or shoulder. Then step straight in until the distance is decreased to where your wrist is even with your partner's arm or shoulder and then step out again. When you're at the fingertip length, you are at the normal adjusted safe level. When you step in to wrist distance, you are entering the power zone. Step in and then step out to feel the difference and then let the other person try.

People usually operate at a safe distance when they greet someone, staying far enough apart that they really don't connect. The power zone is a little closer and is where someone who is perceived as a leader would stand. When you shake hands with someone, step into the power zone during the greeting. The other person normally makes a small, subconscious adjustment and then you begin your two- to four-minute meet and greet. Just by stepping into that space, you take a leadership role in the conversation and are assuming the lead role.

**When you shake hands with someone, step into the power zone during the greeting.**

If you are a shorter person, simply extend your arm to the taller person's side when you practice. Again, this game is just an awareness game to illustrate how to use your body as part of the sales presentation and how powerful small gestures can be.

## The stance of involvement

- Expected outcome—Learn how to position your body when you shake hands so that you don't accidentally intimidate someone. You also learn how to use your stance as a tool to make someone feel more comfortable when he first meets you.

- Why this step is important—The sales encounter begins at this point and how you greet someone sets the tone for expected customer service.

- Tools needed—None

- How—Practice the proper body language to be used during the greeting in a stepwise fashion.

Pick a partner. As you step in to shake hands, do the following things one at a time at first and then all together as you learn the steps:

- Step in with your left foot slightly forward of your right and turned out slightly to the left.

- Your right foot should be turned out slightly to the right. Done correctly, your feet are comfortably under you with the left out in front and both feet forming an "L" with the right foot being the shorter base of the "L."

- Your hips are turned toward the right. You don't want to square your hips straight at the guest. This position is challenging and intimidating for smaller people and women.

- Your shoulders can square up more with someone your own size and can be turned away slightly to the right if you are talking to someone who is smaller than you. Either way, keep the feet in the "L" position.

- Your head should be upright and straight ahead when greeting people your own size, but let it lean slightly to the right and forward if the person is smaller. It seems like an odd detail, but when your head is slightly forward and leaned just a little to the side it looks like you are conveying sincere interest in what the person is saying. Body language is powerful and everything counts, so be aware of the power of how you stand and face someone.

- Once you have your feet planted, shoulders in position, and head at the right angle, you can shake hands. Since your left foot is forward, you shake hands with the right your arm coming across your body, which again is a move that is designed to offer friendliness and avoid intimidation.

Practice the steps in order, but once you think about each part just step in and do it all at once. In all likelihood, when you shake hands with someone without this training, you are using an entire series of actions all at once, but these actions are random and done with little if any thought and no practice. Everything you do with your body during a sales encounter sends a message, and while you may not think practicing these things is important, you are sending a message with your handshake and body position whether you intend to or not. Why not think about it and try to make sure that what you do sends the positive image that you are hoping for when you meet someone?

## Finding your voice

- Expected outcome—Your voice is another tool in your sales kit. Learn how to control it to fit the sale.

- Why this step is important—The sales encounter begins at this point and how you greet someone sets the tone for expected customer service.

**Everything you do with your body during a sales encounter sends a message, and while you may not think practicing these things is important, you are sending a message with your handshake and body position whether you intend to or not.**

- Tools needed—None
- How—Learn the power of your voice by expressing various emotions.

Pick a partner. Sit on the floor with your legs crossed and your knees touching your partner's knees. You act as the moderator by saying an emotion, such as anger. Your partner responds by saying your name with that emotion in his voice. Each time the emotion is given, his voice should change to fit what he is trying to convey. The goal is to realize that your voice is a tool and that you can change the way you project yourself to others by changing your voice. Use these emotions, in this order, for your practice:

- Anger
- Happiness
- Extreme happiness
- Sadness
- Lust (Sneak this in. It always gets people laughing.)
- Professional (End on this emotion, as you are trying to find your professional voice.)

**Your voice should match your guest.**

Your voice may be your most powerful tool, yet most salespeople really don't know if they have that pleasing sales voice that is soothing, yet professional, or that voice from the inner circles of hell that makes you want to run two minutes after you meet them. The important thing to remember is that your voice should match your guest. When you practice the greeting statement, try using your voice strongly for someone your own size or age and then use a softer version for someone who is smaller or more nervous.

## The greeting

- Expected outcome—Put it all together and be able to greet a person with a strong handshake, the right stance to match your guest, and a practiced voice.
- Why this step is important—Get this moment right and the rest of the sale is easy.
- Tools needed—None
- How—Practice all components of a properly conducted greeting.

This game is where all of the other games come together. You step in, shake hands, and say, "Hi, welcome to the club. My name is...," and off you go on your sales encounter. Get this moment right and you make the rest of the process much easier. Get it wrong by mumbling, not shaking hands, or leaning back against the counter and you've got nowhere to go but down.

As an owner or sales manager, you should visit other clubs and note how you are greeted and then compare those greetings to a banker, lawyer, or other business professional. You are in the business of helping people, just like they are, and you need to emulate some of the things that make the best of those professionals successful.

Pick a partner. Step in while thinking about your distance, your handshake, your body position, and your voice, and say, "Hi, welcome to the club. My name is [name], and you are... [pause/get name]. [Repeat name], what brought you into the club today?"

Your practice partner responds by saying, "Well, I'd like to get some information about your club."

The salesperson should go one line further and ask, "[Name], have you ever been in the club before?"

It is good to practice going through the first question. Many rookies who just practice the greeting will say it and stop because they have never really worked beyond that point with a smooth transition.

## The five Ws, how, and have

- Expected outcome—Learn how to talk to someone for two to four minutes without selling by mastering the basic question involved in conversation.

- Why this step is important—Most club salespeople sell from the beginning, which is too much too soon. You need to include a few minutes of helping the person feel comfortable before you go after the sale.

- Tools needed—None

- How—A number of games used for practicing this skill are presented in this section.

*Say a word/make a question*

This game is very simple. Gather your staff in front of you, either sitting on the floor in a half-circle or on chairs. Say one of the key words and the staff person you point to has to come up with an appropriate question using that word. For example:

- The leader says "how" and points at someone.

- The staff person should respond, "How did you hear about us?" or some other appropriate "how" question.

It is good to write these questions down as the game progresses because you will find that only about 15 to 20 of them will make sense and are the ones that your staff needs to know and memorize. Just for review, the key words are as follows:

> Most club salespeople sell from the beginning, which is too much too soon.

- Who

- What

- Where

- When

- Why

- How

- Have

This game can be accelerated as the team gets some practice. You can, for example, eliminate anyone who stumbles and then buy lunch for the last person standing. Keep it fun, but pound these questions into everyone's head.

You can also progress to pepper ball, which is the speed version of this game. You shout out the word and the person has to blast back an answer. The goal is to speed up the game to the point where you are shouting out words and you have two or three people answering at almost the same time.

*Football (a listen-and-respond game)*

Once you have the questions under control, you can move on to the next level. Learning the questions is good, but salespeople also have to learn how to listen to the answers and respond to what the person is saying. Remember the cycle that was mentioned in Chapter 18. It looks as follows if it is done correctly:

### Ask—listen—respond—listen—ask another

The ask part of that sequence comes from the five Ws, have, and how. The next step is to learn to listen to those answers, respond to what the person says, and then keep the circle going. The football game is designed to develop this skill set.

Arrange the group in a half-circle—or full circle if you have enough people—with you in the middle. You play the role of the guest in this game. Start out by saying, "I'd like to get some information about your club please," and then point at someone in the group and toss a small Nerf® football to him. The staff person then must ask one of the key questions and toss the football back to the leader. The football going back and forth represents the circular motion of a good conversation. If someone stumbles, it is a fumble and the ball is thrown on the floor and everyone shouts, "fumble!" This game is goofy, but effective.

You respond to the person's question, but then point to another team member. In this case, you are the potential member and all of your staff people are playing the combined role of one salesperson. This scenario forces them not only to listen to you for your next question as a guest, but also to each other, since they want to keep the conversation going and not ask the same

> Learning the questions is good, but salespeople also have to learn how to listen to the answers and respond to what the person is saying.

question someone else did. This game might look as follows (you can either assume that the greeting has been done or practice it):

*Leader (You):* I'd like to get some information about your club please.

*Team Member A:* Of course, I'd be happy to help you. Have you ever been in our club before?

*Leader:* No, I just received a mailer today and it sounded interesting, so I thought I'd check you out. (points to someone else)

*Team Member B:* Yes, those mailers do bring in a lot of new guests. What part of the mailer got your attention?

This practice session is going well. When you start these games for the first time, they won't go this well, which validates the point that you do need practice. When someone stumbles, stop and fix it, and keep moving. Try to keep the rhythm going and complete at least two minutes worth of conversation.

## The circle game (a listen-and-respond game)

If you have enough staff members, put them in a circle on the floor and stay on the outside. You start of the game by saying to someone, "I'd like to get some information about your club please." The person does not respond to the leader, but instead turns her head to the person sitting to her left and says, "Of course, I'd be happy to help you with that. Have you ever been in the club before?"

That guy does not respond to the woman who asked that question, but instead turns to his left and gives an answer to the next person, who then turns to his left and gives his answer. Think of this game as getting your information on the right but passing it on to the person on your left.

The fun part is that you really have to listen because your role may change from playing the part of the guest to being the salesperson, depending on the number of people in your group. The goal, of course, is to get all the way around the circle without any stumbles.

You can add another level to this game by starting two different inquiries at opposite sides of the circle. This scenario forces everyone to slow down and listen to the person who talks to them, since they have to respond directly to that question, which has nothing to do with the other conversation going around the circle at the same time.

## Role-playing

Basic role-playing is the next step after the group has an understanding of the question/listen/respond dynamic. This game is nothing more than role-playing

> Basic role-playing is the next step after the group has an understanding of the question/listen/resp ond dynamic.

an entire meet and greet, from greeting at the front door, moving to the table, and then starting the tour. Focus the largest amount of your training on this part of the sales process, because it will be the strongest differentiator between you and your competitors. The process would go as follows:

- Greet at the door using the welcome statement.
- Set up the transition to the information table.
- Work in the trial membership.
- Present the Welcome Guide.
- Ask the final questions before the tour: "What is the single most important thing you want from a membership at this club? Why is that important to you?"
- Ask for permission and tour.

You should also work in the handoff if you have counter people in the training session. Don't forget that your counter people are the first-impression people in your business and if they are comfortable and professional the sale will be easier for the rest of the team.

> **Practice until they are beyond tired, and practice some more after that point.**

It is absolutely essential that you get to the point where all salespeople can get through the entire meet and greet and transition to the tour without stumbling. Practice until they are beyond tired, and practice some more after that point. Practice now is money in the bank later.

Of course, many other games could be used to teach sales. The games presented in this chapter are old but proven games that build awareness as well as teach the fundamental concepts of this sales system.

## Key Points From This Chapter

- Nothing is more important in your business than training your staff to be effective in sales. Find the time.
- Everyone on the staff should get sales training at least once a month. Salespeople should be trained as a team once a week. Individuals on the team can be trained daily.
- Train for the details, because everything counts. If you don't train for the greeting, for example, then where did the team learn to do what they are currently doing in your business?
- Training involves explaining what to do, how to do it, and why it is important, showing the person what it looks like when done correctly, and then practicing. Most rookie trainers just focus on the "what" and aren't aware of the rest of the steps.

- Games build awareness. Unless you point out things such as body language, voice, and stance, your people will not discover them on their own.

- Not one staff in the history of the fitness business has ever been overtrained.

---

**Tip of the Day**

# Learn to dress.

You may be styling, but you still look like you just rolled out of bed and crawled two miles to work. A huge difference exists between business-appropriate dress and casual clothes that you would wear out to a club or party, and the two should never meet. Most young employees don't know the difference and some that do don't care because they would rather look cool than look professional.

Your ability to dress for success as a professional will play a big role in your future success in almost any field you choose. Unless you are a future rock star, then you'd better spend some time figuring out what it takes to dress for your job.

A key point to remember is that you should always dress a little more professionally than the people you work with in your job. You want to stand out and professional business dress is the quick route to accomplishing that task.

Professional dress does not mean ties and business clothes. Professional dress is a nice shirt, usually tucked in but perhaps worn out if it was designed to be worn that way, pressed pants, and shoes that are neat and clean. Take pride in your clothes and dress for success every day and save those casual clothes for the bars.

---

# THE LOST ART OF FOLLOWING UP ON A LEAD

**Section Four**

# 21

# The Art of the Follow-Up

Following up does not mean calling up a guest who visited your club and harassing him at home during dinner, asking why he didn't come back and when you can set that next appointment. Follow-up has devolved rather than evolved during the past 20 years in the fitness industry. Most sales teams are down to nothing more than a few desperate phone calls that are made because the sales manager makes the salespeople do them, and only because he had to make those calls when he had that job.

Phone calls are the lazy person's method of choice. You look busy while making calls, but you really don't get anything done and you can always blame those darn voicemails and answering machines if the boss sees you not talking to anyone.

As an owner or manager, it's all a game of numbers and efficiency. Take your best people, put them to work doing the things that have the highest probability of success, and you will likely make some money. Have that same group of talent do inefficient tasks, for example, and you won't get the results you want and it will not be the team's fault.

For example, you put your best salesperson into an office on Monday night at 6:00 p.m. to make 40 follow-up calls to guests who had been in the club during the past 30 days. Remember that this guy is your best salesperson, the one with the most experience and training. How many people will he actually talk to in a one-hour phone session?

Experience and research points to a 10 percent effective rate, but for the sake of this example, assume that he does a great job and has a success rate of 20 percent. In a one-hour period, your best guy on the sales staff will actually talk to eight people from that list (40 x .20 = 8). Don't forget that he is off the floor during the club's prime time for an hour as well, but he has to make the calls during that time period because that is when most people are actually at home.

If you were using a more effective follow-up method, such as email, your best guy could go into the office, hit "send" with preprogrammed auto-responses, and be back in five minutes with a 100 percent effective rate. And, you have the guy on the floor where he belongs during prime time for 55 minutes out of the hour.

Phone calls still have to be made, but depending on the phones as your major follow-up tool for missing leads is simply not cost-effective. You can use better tools to stay in touch with your former guests.

An additional issue affects your ability to use the phone to chase missed guests. "Do not call" lists are empowering the consumer to say no. In this case, the club does have a relationship with the consumer that justifies the right of the business to generate the call, but the consumer still may not want to hear from you. People usually get on those lists because they don't want any calls from any business annoying them at home.

When the club calls, the guest is not happy and does not expect a phone call at home, even when he relented and gave the club his number. Some guest might give his number out of the pressure of the sales situation, but doesn't really want that contact at home.

It's like buying a car. You may stop at the lot, check out a few cars, and even give your number as the salesperson fills out the paperwork, but do you really look forward to the salesperson calling you at home? In your mind, aren't you really saying, "Look guy, if I wanted to buy a car I would be down there and you calling isn't going to make me want to buy any faster." If you feel this way, then how does a guest at your club feel? "Hey, if I wanted to join a club I'd be back already without you having to call me at home during dinner."

## You Never Gave the Person a Reason to Come Back

**Potential members who check you out and don't come back do so because you didn't give them a reason to come back.**

Potential members who check you out and don't come back do so because you didn't give them a reason to come back. In fact, most sales systems make it almost impossible to come back through the door at all.

Discounting during the first visit is an all-or-nothing shot based upon getting the guest to buy during the first visit. If this technique fails, no backup plan exists. The old sales guys have close-out parties on the last day of each month and invite everyone they missed that month to come one more time and get the discount they used to slam them in the first place:

*"Hey Bill, it's Freddie from the club. You know when you were here last week and I told you that if you signed up that day you'd save $100? Well, since you didn't join that day, I'd like to invite you to a close-out party this week. We buy 50 pizzas and have a party in the club and invite all of our*

*guests to come and get a second chance at saving that $100. We know that some people change their minds and wish they had said yes, so we're going to offer you one more opportunity to get started."*

This plan sounds logical, but does it work? The guest probably left feeling pressured and hammered by the salesperson who offered $100 off "today, and today only," to force the sale. The guest left without buying and obviously had no reason to go back because the salesperson put up the barrier of the $100 extra charge that would have to be paid—assuming that the guest even believed the salesperson and didn't just laugh at him for using sales techniques that are probably older than he is.

Another issue is that the club's credibility is questioned because the salesperson told the guest one thing, couldn't get the sale, and now he is changing the tune a little to try to buy the guy again. Potential customers start to think, "If you lie to me a little now, you'll lie to me a lot later." This statement is a common response to this method and is a hard way to start the long-term financial relationship between the club and a new member.

This system bets everything on one sales encounter, so all of the follow-up techniques have to overcome the negativity of the high-pressure drop close. You lied and then you have to clean it up with other pressure techniques, such as endless phone calls and invitations to parties where the customer knows he is going to be pressured again.

Keep in mind that during this process the consumer has never really seen the club or worked out beyond perhaps his initial freebie during his first visit. In other words, the salesperson is trying very hard to sell a product that the potential buyer has very little experience with and no emotional connection with at all. It is hard to sell someone something if they don't even know if they really want it or not.

> It is hard to sell someone something if they don't even know if they really want it or not.

## The trial opens the door to come back again.

The trial membership turns the all-or-nothing close into an either/or close. The theory behind offering a regular membership, accompanied by a trial backup, is much the same as using the alternate close when you present memberships.

Instead of telling the guest that he has to but this membership today and here is the deal he will get to force him to make the decision, you're telling the person that the club offers two choices: one for people who are ready to go today and one for people who need a little more time before they decide. Do you as an owner really care if the person buys tonight or works out a few times and then buys? At the worst, the trial delays the purchase by a week or so, but you still get the membership at the club, which is all that should really matter.

The trial also dictates a different type of follow-up, which is very important to understand when you first make the shift to using trials in your marketing.

You don't have to call the potential member and beg him to come back and sign up. He is standing in front of your sales guy checking in for his workout that night. He is in the gym, so your salesperson has another chance to service and chat with the person in a way that should lead to a membership sale. Your follow-up with the trial is nothing more than building the emotional bridge between the potential member and the club through planned contact involving every tool you have available, such as emails, electronic newsletters, special mailings, and even the phone to leave messages of support and information.

The Trial Gift Certificate is your new leverage tool that you use to buy the sale over time. Leverage is still a powerful tool to wield, but a difference exists between negative leverage, such as the drop close, and a more positive application of leverage represented by enhancing the sale with gifts and incentives.

Out of all motivators, such as prestige, elitism, and value, fear of loss is the only one that makes sense over time and it is also the hardest for your competitors to take away from you. Value, for example, which is defined as going for the cheap price, is impossible to defend in a marketplace of businesses all offering pretty much the same service. If you offer $19-a-month membership, why can't the gym down the street offer one for $15?

Fear of loss, however, is harder to take away, especially if it is tied to the trial membership. Fear of loss in this case is the development of an impressive trial certificate package and then taking it away if the person doesn't join.

This technique sounds the same as a drop close, where you lower the price by $100 if the person signs today. That scenario creates fear of loss, in theory, but in reality the consumer knows that the $100 never really existed in the first place, so there really is no loss to consider.

**Using fear of loss is part of the follow-up process when you are working trial memberships.**

Using fear of loss is part of the follow-up process when you are working trial memberships. "Hey John, I see you're in the fifth day of your trial membership. Don't forget about that great gift package we offer if you become a member by your seventh day. I'd hate to see you lose all that great stuff and then sign up anyway next week." The important point to remember is that the leverage in this case can be applied as slowly as needed, and as the person becomes ready to commit.

People sign up at different times. Some do so during the first visit because a friend referred them while others need a few workouts to make sure the club has what they need. Others may take a full week or even two, especially if they aren't fitness people. The key to the follow-up with trial memberships is that every buyer can make the decision regarding when he or she is ready and a good follow-up system can easily be devised to keep the salesperson involved in the process over time.

The final point to consider is that you can't escape the numbers. If your price is $39 per month per member, then 70 percent of the people who visit your club will need two or more visits before they will make a buying decision. It's simply a large enough number that it requires some thought before the money is spent.

A traditional sales system and follow-up by phone don't work for this group, because these potential members just aren't around for that second or third visit. The all-or-nothing slam during the first visit creates the barrier that keeps these folks from ever getting to that second workout and beyond. The door was closed hard during the first encounter, and they aren't interested in opening it again.

Theoretically, this statistic is probably why the big chains struggle so much, especially the old-style groups that still use high-pressure techniques on the first visit. If you only have the chance to close approximately 30 percent of all the real traffic through your business—those people who will buy on the first visit because of referral, previous gym experience, or a lack of sophistication that causes them to fall for the pressure trap—then you can't buy enough leads, no matter how much marketing money you spend to overcome the 70 percent you lose every.

The moral of this story is that as an owner or manager, you need to find a way to sign up the most new members you can during their first visit, and get the highest percentage of those in the 70 percent who need more experience with your business to sign up as well. That goal is the real purpose of this book, as well as of the follow-up system detailed in this chapter.

## A Follow-Up System Anyone Can Live With and Use

The most important rule that you can learn about follow-up is:

**Do fewer things, but do them well and do them every time.**

Most club owners live off the first wave of memberships that their team signs during the potential member's first visit. After the initial hit, they might sign up another 5 percent per month from their missed lead pile. Operating in this way leaves a lot of potential membership dollars on the table at the end of each month.

> Most club owners live off the first wave of memberships that their team signs during the potential member's first visit.

Follow-up done correctly, and coupled with other tools such as the Welcome Guide that keep the emotional connection going after the person visits the club, can add 15 to 20 percent to the club's overall annual sales. In other words, the typical fitness center only closes approximately 38 percent of the qualified leads that come through the door each month on annual memberships. Your potential is 55 to 60 percent, but to hit this number you have to embrace new tools and think differently about follow-up.

Systems are everything and steps to follow are the dream of every employee who has ever been told to do something but was never told "how" and had to figure it out for himself. Employees won't, and shouldn't have to, figure it out for themselves. Your job as an owner or manager is to create exact steps, along with the supporting materials and tools, that any staff member can follow, even if he has only been on the job for a week. Remember, don't teach anyone to think. Instead, teach them to follow the steps.

### The first step is to put someone in charge of all follow-up.

That person, of course, is the sales manager. Individual salespeople are responsible for their own leads, but the sales manager is accountable for ensuring that each member of the sales team is keeping up with his own work. The follow-up process should follow this sequence:

- The salesperson tours a guest.
- A matching guest profile/inquiry sheet must be complete at the end of the tour, whether the guest is qualified or not (Figure 21-1).
- All guest profiles are turned in to the sales manager after each tour.
- If the guest is qualified, he leaves as a member or a trial member.
- All guest profiles are put into a notebook for the month on the sales manager's desk. Think low-tech and just have a three-ring binder with a sticker on the side for whatever month you're working in at the time.
- The sales manager attaches a follow-up cover sheet to the guest profile and initiates follow-up. It is the sales manager's job to make sure that the salespeople are doing their part.
- Two separate follow up tracks are used: one for a new member and one for a trial member.

**The key to following up is to touch the person at least three times during the first 24 hours after visiting the club.**

The key to following up with this method is to touch the person at least three times during the first 24 hours after visiting the club. If he is a member, then you want to solidify the deal and make the person feel good about what he just bought. Happy people are buddy-referral people and this contact validates the buying decision.

The trial member might still be shopping other clubs and you want to be the one to touch him the most, but in a professional manner. Three phone calls won't do anything but irritate the person, which is not what you want.

Owners also forget that many of the guests who responded to a trial offer aren't your regular gym-head people. Many might even be first-time folks for whom that visit to your facility was their first visit to any club. Taking that big step and joining truly takes several days. The question is: What do you want in front of the person during the next few days after they visit your club and are in that, "Gee, I don't know if I can really do this?" phase.

**Guest Profile**

Today's date _____     Date recorded by manager _____

Did the person:   ❑ Visit the club   or   ❑ Phone

**Guest's or inquiry's name:** _____

Have you heard about our trial membership? _____

Before we get started, may I offer you a gift from the club? _____

How did you hear about us? _____

Do you know any of our members? If so, who? _____

Have you ever been in the club before? _____

Do you work or live near the gym? _____

What type of workout are you doing now? _____

_____

**How would you classify yourself as an exerciser?**

**❑ I currently work out.**

What are you doing? _____

How long? _____

How many days a week? _____

How is it working? _____

What are you looking for that your current program doesn't provide? ____

_____

**❑ I used to work out.**

What did you do at that time? _____

Were you consistent? _____

How did it work? _____

Why did you stop? _____

How are you feeling since you stopped? _____

How long have you been thinking about getting back to a regular program?

What's kept you from getting back in the past? _____

Is that still a problem?_____

**❑ I don't work out.**

What has gotten you interested in working out?_____

How do you feel about your health and condition?_____

What was the best you ever felt?_____

What was different at that time?_____

How long have you been thinking about getting into a fitness program? __

_____

What's kept you from getting started in the past?_____

Is that still a problem?_____

_____

Figure 21-1. Guest profile/inquiry sheet

**We've found over the years people that who want to join a gym and begin a regular exercise program usually fall into one of three categories. Which one of these is your primary goal?**

❑ Improve your appearance

❑ Improve your health

❑ Improve things in your life, such as energy level, or reduce stress

**Keeping this goal in mind, what is the single most important thing you want to get out of a gym membership?** _____

_____

_____

**What are some other things you would like to accomplish with us?**

How would you like to change your body? _____

_____

Is your weight something you are concerned about? _____

What's the timeframe you've set for your fitness program? _____

On a scale of 1 to 10, how important is it for you to reach your personal fitness objective? _____

Is that enough to get you started and keep you coming to the gym on a regular basis? _____

**Now that I have a little information about you and what you're looking for in an exercise program, may I show you the club?**

Profile notes so we can best help our guest: _____

_____

**Most of our guests or phone inquiries want to know more about what we do here. May we have your email address so that we can send you ongoing information about the club as well as our electronic newsletter?**

Email address: _____

To thank you for taking the time to visit the club, we'd like to send you a gift. May we have your address? _____

_____

_____

What is the best phone number with which to reach you? _____

_____

Office use only:

Club representative _____

New member _____

Trial member _____

If you use the follow-up sheet in Figure 21-2, the person will get an email before he gets home, a handwritten thank-you note from his salesperson, and already has a Welcome Guide full of fun facts and motivational articles to keep him on the right mental track. It is worth mentioning one more time that the last thing you want that person to leave with in his hand is a price sheet and a group schedule.

You can also email the new trial member one of your electronic newsletters and the fitness tip of the week. Contacts are okay, as long as they aren't harassing or irritating.

Phone calls can be added if you like, but try to restrict the content to something positive. If you have a Happy Hour, as some clubs do, and give away free beer and wine every Thursday night, leave a phone message inviting the trial member to visit the club that night and experience the social aspects in addition working out.

As you can see on the guest follow-up sheet, two tracks are available to the sales manager: the first for the trial member and the second for the new member. A third section of general follow-up affects both groups. Some of these things were briefly touched upon in Chapter 18, but are detailed in this context along with supporting copy.

## Trial membership follow-up

- Send the email before the guest leaves the club (Figure 21-3). He should see you first when he gets home to check his messages, or might even find you on his Blackberry® while still in the car.

- The handwritten thank you is a retro touch (Figure 21-4). Anything you find in your mailbox box that has a handwritten address is usually opened first. This letter has to be sent the same day the person tours the club.

- On this follow-up sheet, the club is using a 14-day trial and the Trial Gift Certificate, which offers the loot packages for becoming a new member. The five-day follow up reminder lets the guest know that if he doesn't get into the club in the next two days he will lose all the loot (Figure 21-5).

- At the end of 30 days, send the person a real check (the more authentic, the better) made back to the club for $45 dollars that he can use toward any program any time in the next 12 months (Figure 21-6). If you don't get him with this technique, then no one is going to get him. The check is a reminder that he has free money waiting at your club anytime he wants it.

> Contacts are okay, as long as they aren't harassing or irritating.

# Guest Follow-Up Sheet

Club representative who will do follow-up  _____

Date guest visited the club_____

**The guest's name and address:**

Name  _____

Street  _____

City  _____

State  _____  Zip  _____

Email  _____

Phone  _____

**Trial member follow-up:**

**Same day as member visit**

❍ Email thank you sent/added to auto-response file     Date  _____

❍ Handwritten thank you sent/with two one-day
   guest passes                                        Date  _____

❍ 5-day follow-up certificate reminder/email and phone Date  _____

❍ 30-day check/letter sent/mail                        Date  _____

**New member follow-up:**

**Same day guest becomes a member**

❍ Email thank you sent                                 Date  _____

❍ Handwritten thank you sent/with two one-day
   guest passes                                        Date  _____

❍ 7-day thank you letter from owner                    Date  _____

❍ 30-day thank you letter from owner with gift         Date  _____

**General follow-up:**                                       _____

❍ Email thank you sent                                 Date  _____

❍ Added to the club's database if guest doesn't become
   a member                                            Date  _____

❍ Added to the Fitness Tip of the Week                 Date  _____

❍ Added to the club's electronic newsletter            Date  _____

❍ Monthly call and email follow-up                     Date  _____

❍ _____            Date  _____

❍ _____            Date  _____

❍ _____            Date  _____

❍ _____            Date  _____

Figure 21-2. Guest follow-up sheet

---

**Trial member e-mail thank you**

For this email to be effective, it should be:

- Sent the same day the member visits the club
- Signed by the salesperson who toured the club

*Dear,*

*Thank you very much for becoming a trial member at [club name]. We realize that you have other fitness choices and we truly appreciate a chance to earn your business. If you have any questions at all about your trial membership, or if you are interested in bringing a guest with you to the club, please feel free to call me personally at [club number] or email me at [email address]. Thank you again and I look forward to working with you in the future.*

*Sincerely,*

*[Sales person's name]*

Figure 21-3. Suggested copy for sales follow-up

---

**Trial member handwritten note**

For this note to be effective, it should be:

- Handwritten
- Hand-addressed
- Sent the same day the guest visits the club
- Preferably signed by someone other than the person who toured the guest and signed the email in Figure 21-3. For example, the salesperson could sign the email and the club manager or owner could sign this note. In small clubs, it is okay for the same person to sign both notes.

*Dear [trial member],*

*Thank you for taking the time to visit our club. We really do appreciate you taking the time to come see what we do at [club name]. We would also like to thank you for becoming a trial member. We realize that you have choices when it comes to fitness and we are grateful that you have given us a chance to become your gym. If you have any questions concerning your trial membership, please call the club at [club number]. Thank you again and I look forward to seeing you soon.*

*Sincerely,*

*[Club manager or owner's signature]*

*P.S. I've enclosed two guest passes for a friend or relative. Please let me know if you need more.*

Figure 21-4. Trial member handwritten note

---

For this email to be effective, it should be:

- Sent exactly two days before the trial certificate expires. For example, if you are using a 14-day trial membership and a trial certificate that gives the member an incentive package during the first seven days, this email would be sent on the fifth day after the member visits the club.

*Dear [trial member],*

*We hope you are enjoying your trial membership at [club name]. As a reminder, don't forget about the great gifts we are offering if you decide to become a member anytime during the first seven days of your 14-day trial membership.*

*If you plan on becoming a member, please call or stop by the club during the next two days to receive the $285 incentive package detailed on the gift certificate you received as part of your trial membership information.*

*If you can't get to the club in the next day or so, please call me personally and I'll reserve your package for you so you won't be left out. Thank you again for your business and we hope you are enjoying your membership with us.*

*If you have any questions, please call [club number] or email me at [email address].*

*Sincerely,*

*(Sales person's name)*

Figure 21-5. The five-day email

## New member follow-up

- The email and handwritten thank-you notes serve much the same purpose as the ones sent to trial members (Figures 21-7 and 21-8). You say thank you and enclose two guest passes.

- The seven-day letter is a formal letter from the owner or senior manager thanking the person for supporting the business (Figure 21-9). This type of thank you validates the buying decision and adds a touch of class to the business.

- The 30-day thank you is a gift sent to the member that rewards him one more time just when most members think you have forgotten about them (Figure 21-10). The 30-day mark is a crucial time for a new member and a second wave of regret sometimes occurs at this point in their membership. This gift, which should cost under five dollars, including mailing, is designed to alleviate some of that latent buyer's regret.

For this tool to be effective:

- It should be sent to any trial member who did not become a regular member

- It should be sent 30 days after the trial membership began

- The enclosed check should be on real check paper with fake numbers at the bottom. As part of the numbers it should state "nonnegotiable."

- The check should be made out to the club, not the member, and may be applied toward any membership the club has to offer any time during the next 12 months.

*Dear [trial member],*

*Thank you for taking part in our trial membership program. We appreciate you giving us a chance to earn your business and we are also disappointed that you decided not to become a member during your trial visits.*

*During the years that we have offered trial memberships, we've learned many people who try the club like it, but for some reason becoming a member just wasn't right for them at the time. Sometimes it's job commitments and often it could be an issue with children or other time-related problems. If this is the case for you, we'd like to extend an invitation to come back any time during the next 12 months.*

*To help make the decision to come back when the time is right easier for you, we've enclosed a check made out to the club for $45. This check may be used toward any membership we offer any time during the next 12 months.*

*Thank you again for giving us a try and we hope that sometime in the future you'll give us another chance by becoming a member of our club. If you have any questions concerning the check, please call us at [club number] or email us at [club email].*

*Sincerely,*

*[Club owner or senior manager]*

Figure 21-6. The 30-day check/letter package

For this email to be effective, it should be:
- Sent the same day the guest joins

*Dear [new member],*

*Thank you for becoming a new member of [club name]. We realize that you have other choices in fitness in the area and we truly appreciate your business and your faith in our product.*

*If you any questions concerning your new membership, please feel free to call me personally, or anyone at the club at [club number]. You may also email us at [club email]. Of course, you can always find someone on the staff during any of your visits who can help you with any question you might have connected with being a member.*

*Thank you again and we look forward to having you as a member.*

*Sincerely,*

*[Club salesperson]*

Figure 21-7. New member email

For this note to be effective, it should:
- Be sent the day the guest becomes a new member
- Be handwritten
- Be hand-addressed
- Include guest passes

*Dear [new member],*

*Thank you for becoming a member of [club name]. We understand that you have other choices when it comes to fitness in the area and we truly appreciate you giving us your business.*

*You will probably have many questions about your new membership during your first few weeks with us. Please feel free to call anyone at the club any time at [club number] with any problem or concern you might have. You may also email us at [club email].*

*Thank you again for your business and we look forward to seeing you in the club soon.*

*Sincerely,*

*[Club owner or manager]*

*P.S. I've enclosed two guest passes for a friend or relative. Please let me know if you need more.*

Figure 21-8. New member handwritten note

For this letter to be effective, it should be:

- Sent at the end of the member's first week in the club
- Signed by the owner or senior manager

*Dear [new member],*

*We'd like to send you a formal thank you letter as recognition of your new membership at [club name]. Deciding to spend time and money with us is a very important decision and we would again like to thank you for your business and your faith in what we do here.*

*An important thing to remember is that any type of fitness program is always a work in progress and never really ends. During your membership, you will achieve personal goals and then move on to the next step and next level of fitness that's right for you.*

*If you need help with anything beyond your basic membership at the club, please feel free to see anyone on the staff. After our years of experience, I am sure we can put the right combination of services and offerings in the club that will help you get the most out of your membership with us.*

*If a question arises about your membership, or if there is an issue that concerns you, please call us immediately at [club number]. We want to help and we want to make sure your membership is going well, but there is nothing we can do unless you take the first step and express your needs or the point out the problem you are encountering.*

*Thank you again for your business. Members like you have allowed us to build a great gym and we truly want you to know that we don't take your patronage for granted.*

*Sincerely,*

*[Club owner or senior manager]*

*P.S. I've enclosed additional guest passes for your friends or relatives. Please let us know if you need more or if you have any questions about the club's guest policy.*

Figure 21-9. The seven-day thank you letter for new members

## The general follow-up

The general follow-up is based upon getting the new trial or regular member tied to the club's electronic contact tools. These contacts add to the emotional bridge that is so important in getting people into the club as members and getting the actual members to stay longer and pay longer.

The general follow-up is based upon getting the new trial or regular member tied to the club's electronic contact tools.

For this tool to be effective, it should:

- Be sent at the end of the member's first 30-day period
- Include a letter from the owner thanking the member one more time
- Include a small gift such as an oversized coffee cup with the club's logo on the side in a gift box
- Include 5 to 10 nicely designed passes to the gym

*Dear [new member],*

*Congratulations! You have reached the end of your first 30 days as a new member at [club name].*

*By this time, you should be well-established in a workout routine and be making regular visits to the gym. This 30-day anniversary is an important one for anyone just beginning a consistent workout program. This is the time when you start reaping the benefits of your work by feeling better and you should also start noticing those first results in how you look. Be patient with your program, because the best is yet to come.*

*We would also like to thank you again for being a member and for being part of our club family. Once again, we appreciate your support and the money you spend with us.*

*As a small token of our thanks, we've enclosed a gift from the club. We've tried a number of gifts over the years, but the oversized coffee cup is the one the members seem to most appreciate and get the most laughs from when they open the box. Thank you for your business and we hope you enjoy the gift.*

*On a side note, look for [add a few small things you expect to do in the near future, such as add equipment, paint, or improve something in the gym— remember that small things count] coming in the near future. We constantly try to improve the gym and most of the ideas for those improvements come from members like you. If you have any suggestions for the club, please stop by the desk and let us know.*

*If you need help with your program and would like a quick review, please bring this letter to the gym and schedule an appointment at the desk. We want you to get the most from your membership and a review at this stage will keep you focused. Don't forget that we also offer personal and semi-private training, as well as a nationally known weight-loss program if you're not getting those results as quickly as you want. Personal attention may be just what you need and a little personalized guidance may help you get to where you want to be that much more quickly.*

*Thank you again and we look forward to serving you during the rest of your first year with us.*

*Sincerely,*

*[Club owner or senior manager]*

*P.S. I've enclosed additional guest passes for your friends or relatives. Please let us know if you need more or if you have any questions about the club's guest policy.*

Figure 21-10. The 30-day thank you letter with a gift

# Going Electronic

A number of software systems are designed for sales follow-up and tracking. Some companies, such as ABC Financial Services, the largest third-party financial-service company in the club industry, offer this software as part of their software management packages for clubs. Other companies, such as Activtrax, offer automatic call systems and auto-response email as part of their total package.

At some point you will gravitate toward going electronic, but when you first start, go low-tech for at least six months. This hands-on approach to follow-up, including the handwritten notes and personalized emails, is designed to create individualization, which is often neglected in many automated systems.

Another thing to remember as an owner or manager is that if your follow-up system is on the computer, then your salespeople will get on the computer and play. What should take 10 minutes will often take 30, as the person checks his email, does a little shopping, and looks at the sports scores. Start low-tech and master the process before you move up. Remember, it is not the system that does the work; it is your people using a system that will drive sales.

## Web pages

Web pages are necessary in today's market, but you should remember that a web page is B-level marketing. Many owners get caught up in developing their pages, and what should be a small project becomes a work of art with cartoons, figures dancing across the screen, in-depth video tours of the club, and page after page of useless information.

Web pages should be simple and clean for the user and have an expected outcome of inviting potential members to call or use the trial membership they print off the computer. The following components should be part of a solid web page:

> **Web pages should be simple and clean for the user and have an expected outcome of inviting potential members to call or use the trial membership they print off the computer.**

- It should have a capture on the front page. A capture is a tool used to get the person to respond by asking for more information or something free in exchange for his email address. Your capture should be centered on offering a free 14-day trial. The browser says, "Yes, I want my free 14 days" and hits the button. He is then taken to a short questionnaire and once he completes it, he receives his trial membership to print out or he may just come to the club when he is ready. The questionnaire goes automatically to the sales manager's computer. An auto-response should be built in that instantly acknowledges the site visitor and lets him know that someone real will be getting in touch with him.

- Your web page should also have an auto-response system built in to handle all of your sales leads. These systems allow you to dump all of your leads into the computer, design email templates, and then have the system send out these emails automatically at predetermined times each day according to when you want them to hit.

- Information on the trial should also be detailed. Some visitors to the site will want a lot more information before they hit the capture button. Make sure your site is designed with the first-time-experience person in mind and that you are not showing off for gym rats who will be impressed with your equipment lists. Don't forget that the real gym people will find you anyway. Design the web page for people who have little practical experience in fitness centers of any type. Keep it safe, simple, and inspiring, and let anyone looking at the site know that they can do it and that you are here to help.

- You can also add a members-only section. Once a person is a member, he can be given a code to access the members-only pages where you post schedules, club information about happenings, and motivational articles. The secret is that your members section has to change daily to work. The goal is to get that guy who is killing time at work to log in and see what is going on at the club that day. This type of contact is invaluable to your member retention in the coming years because you are touching the person and keeping him in contact with the club without spending any real money or time.

- You might also consider adding a shopping cart. People are not yet buying a lot of memberships on line, but that time is coming. Adding the ability to buy online was a major production not too many years ago, but now it is relatively cheap and easy. Marketing companies such as Susan K. Bailey Advertising are doing full-service web pages for as little as $800 to set it up and $150 a month for maintenance, including daily copy changes. In this type of system, you can modify certain areas to keep them relevant to your club with little pain or effort.

### It is all about the daily contact.

How do you build the emotional bridge to someone new to your business? Answer this question and you will get many new members and keep more of the ones you already have in the system. Daily contact done positively builds that bridge and makes the person feel like he is a valued part of your business.

Trial members still don't know if they belong in your business. Follow-up based upon steady contact is a way to slowly absorb someone into your business over time, when he or she is ready to join, and after they develop the feeling that you are the answer to their problems.

New members are still nervous and most are quickly forgotten in today's turn-and-burn membership mills. Your future is based not only on attracting as many new members as possible, but also keeping as many as you can over time.

*Follow-up based upon steady contact is a way to slowly absorb someone into your business over time, when he or she is ready to join, and after they develop the feeling that you are the answer to their problems.*

People who stay develop this emotional bridge and a commitment to your business, and your job is to keep this bridge alive by staying in contact as often as you can without spending a lot of money. The follow-up and contact systems that begin with your trial members, and that overflow into your new members, are the same ones that will build you the strongest retention base over time.

## Key Points From This Chapter

- Traditional sales are either all or nothing. You get them today or lose them forever.

- Trial memberships are the either/or alternative, meaning that if the person doesn't buy the regular membership he can leave with a trial and feel good about coming back to the club again the next day.

- Most follow-up systems are based upon trying to recover from the damage done by the high-pressure first-visit sales close.

- A higher level of follow-up is done by maintaining a steady stream of contact that entices the person to come back and builds an emotional bridge with the club.

- When you develop a follow-up system, do fewer things but do them well and do them consistently.

- The sales manager is ultimately responsible for all follow-up with every guest as well as the follow-up needed for new members during their first 30 days.

- Fear of loss is still the biggest motivator to take action. The Trial Gift Certificate, which is based upon buying the sale with gifts and incentives, utilizes this motivator since the prospect loses the stuff if he doesn't join.

- Drop closing doesn't meet the fear-of-loss criteria, since the money the customer supposedly saves was never real in the first place.

- Electronic tools are necessary to perform the daily and weekly contact that you need to develop long-term relationships with your members.

**The follow-up and contact systems that begin with your trial members, and that overflow into your new members, are the same ones that will build you the strongest retention base over time.**

**Tip of the Day**

# Try working out.

Here's a concept: Try working out. You don't have to be a ripped fanatic beyond normal comprehension, but you do have to be a work in progress at all times if you work in a fitness facility.

You are not a role model, but you do have to be on the same journey as everyone else in the club. Many of the members struggle with their weight and with finding time to work out, just as you do. However, you must lead the way and show that it can be done.

The same is true for all employees. They can't be fired for not working out, but those who don't walk, run, lift weights, or participate in group classes should go home, because they don't really understand what this business is all about.

The same goes for the closet smokers who take their breaks behind the club dumpster and the party guys who show up still drunk from the night before with diesel fumes pouring out with every breath. These people cost you business and no place exists for them in your fitness center.

You are in the lifestyle business and people do watch and judge. It may not be fair, but it is the reality of your business. Besides, a few workouts might just change your attitude about this business anyway.

# THE PHONE IS WHERE YOUR BUSINESS IS MADE OR LOST

Section Five

# 22

# The Phone Rings Every Day, So You Must Train on the Phone Every Day

---

**The Ugly Phone Fable—A Story About Another Failed Club Owner**

A young owner opens a new, exciting fitness business.

He runs marketing to get new members.

The phone rings and everyone is excited.

The staff is undertrained to handle calls, resulting in few people coming through the door.

The owner blames the marketing and spends more money.

The phone rings again, but still no one shows up.

The owner panics and runs crazy price-driven ads because he is desperate.

The phone rings again but still no one shows up.

The owner closes the club and is now an insurance guy in Buffalo.

---

If only the hero of this fable had trained his staff on how to get the most out of every phone call. This owner spent $4000 to $5000 per month on marketing, which worked in that the phone rang, but how much time did he spend training the staff members that took that phone calls?

An old saying states that the goal of marketing is to get the phone to ring or the door to swing. Good marketing is supposed to get someone excited enough to want to find out more, and most people just pick up the phone and call the number to get their questions answered.

As a side note, most club marketing doesn't work because whoever designs it begins with the wrong expected outcome. Most club ads have too much information and in essence try and sell the person a membership at home rather than just get him excited. You can always spot these ads, because they all contain the same things: bullet points listing all the club's classes and equipment, pictures of big rooms full of equipment, and cheesy, semi-naked model shots.

These ads are functional in that each one tells the reader everything the club has to offer. Without leaving his chair, the guy at home knows how many classes you have, the type of equipment you feature, all about your locker rooms, how many trainers are available, and even what you charge for childcare. Unfortunately, the ad never gives him a reason to want to know more, since he now knows everything about the business and what it offers.

**Good ads tease the reader and make him want to know more.**

Good ads tease the reader and make him want to know more. He should want to see what the business is all about. Done correctly, the guy at home says to himself: "Hey, this looks interesting. I'd like to know more about what they do there."

The trial membership is the bait that gets most people to want more information. The thought behind the trial is, "Come try us. We won't hurt you and you don't really have any risk either."

If your ads work, and the phone does ring, then you have to move on to the next step, which is to get the person in the door and in front of the salesperson. The technical name for this move is: Get more butts in seats.

Another way to interpret this statement is that the expected outcome of that phone ringing is to get the person on the other end to ask about membership prices and visit the club. That is truly the only goal—to have that person come and see the club and meet a salesperson. Forget about his wife, his friends, and his dog; just concentrate on getting him through the door as soon as possible.

## What Is Your Phone Strategy?

Your phone strategy is exactly the same as the meet-and-greet portion of the tour. Whoever takes the call will spend two to four minutes getting to know the person and finding out what he wants. He should also invite the caller to the club using the trial membership as the bait:

*"Hey, I could talk about this club all day, but would you like to try it for 14 days with no risk, no obligation, and no money up front? We're proud of what we do here and we do believe that we have the best club in town, but everyone you call will tell you that. Please try our club before you buy, come meet our staff and the other members, and give us a chance to earn your business over a full 14 days."*

The trial is the ultimate phone tool because it covers all objections and sets the bait to see more without any risk or obligation. What you are saying to the caller is, "We know that you are checking out other clubs, but why not come and experience this one before you spend any money?"

This option also makes your sales training easier, because even the newest phone dummy can get excited and invite someone to work out for free. Getting someone in to meet a salesperson in the old systems is hard because you don't have any bait. Getting someone in on a trial is easy because you're giving the person something of value for free with no risk and no money up front. It's just not that hard to give away free stuff, and the skill set needed to offer a trial versus what it takes in a traditional sales system can be a lot lower.

The trial is the ultimate phone tool because it covers all objections and sets the bait to see more without any risk or obligation.

## What Does a Sample Call Sound Like if Done Correctly?

Look at the following sample call and the rhythm that goes with it. Several key points are worth noticing. First, 99 times out 100, the caller will times ask about the prices as the first question.

If you think about it, what else would he ask? What would you ask if you called and didn't know anything about fitness or the club? Even if you have experience, wouldn't you still ask the price question first?

*Hello, I'd like to get some information about your prices please.*

This statement is safe and gets the conversation going, which is what the caller is trying to accomplish. No one wants to look stupid and if you don't really know anything about the business you are calling, then you would play it safe and ask the question that is least likely to get you in trouble, which is always the price question.

Most of the time, the salesperson can take the lead, move past this question up front ,and get to it later in the call. But don't forget the Plummer 99/1 rule. You will always get that one freak that shouts: "Just give me the damn prices—and I mean now."

He might be having a bad day. He might have called one of those old chain clubs that still don't believe in giving the prices on the phone. Or he might just be the biggest jerk in the city, and it's just your day to take his call. No matter what, you have to give the prices on the phone.

> **It's the 21st century. Don't live in the 1950s.**
> **Give the prices on the phone.**

**Nothing—nothing!—angers someone more than wasting time calling a business to get information and then having some jerk salesperson not give it to them.**

Nothing—nothing!—angers someone more than wasting time calling a business to get information and then having some jerk salesperson not give it to them. In the olden, but not so golden, days of the fitness industry no one gave the prices on the phone. The theory was that you didn't want to scare the person off if your prices seemed too high or if he was shopping other clubs and your price was higher. It was also believed that if you kept the prices hidden you added a little magic to the club, and the person just couldn't wait to come see what you did.

The bad news is that the buyer has grown up and you have to as well. Sophisticated buyers don't want to waste their time. If you don't give them the price on the phone, they will be off to another club that will within seconds of hanging up on your out-of-date mentality.

> **Always give the price, but always give it with value.**

You have to give the price, but you should never do it without giving value. In the following example, the salesperson gives the price, but she comes right back with the value proposition as well:

*"Well John, as far as the price goes, our monthly dues for an individual are $49, but as you mentioned earlier, you haven't seen the club yet. Once you try our trial membership, do a few workouts, and meet the staff and our members, I guarantee that price won't be your deciding factor."*

Review the following inquiry call, which features Sarah as the club's salesperson and John as the caller:

*Sarah:* Hello, we're having a great day at the Workout Company.

*John:* Hello, I'd like to get some information about your prices please.

*Sarah:* Of course, I'd be happy to help you with that. By the way, have you ever been in our club before?

*John:* No I haven't. I just received a mailer today and thought I'd call and check it out.

*Sarah:* Thank you for calling us. What caught your eye about that mail piece?

*John:* That trial membership sounded very interesting. I just moved here and was looking to try out a few new places to work out.

*Sarah:* Yes, that trial is something unique to our club. Oh, I'm sorry, I didn't introduce myself. My name is Sarah, and you are? John, I apologize, we're busy here and I didn't even give you my name. Now, about that trial, we're very proud of our club and feel that we have the best club in town, but everyone you call will probably tell you the same thing. We are, however, the only club in the city that will let you try it absolutely free for 14 days with no risk, no obligation, and no money up front. We'd like you to come meet our staff, meet the other members, and try the club before you consider buying a membership. We feel that if you work out for 14 days, and we haven't earned your business, then we don't serve to have you as a member. How's that feel to you John?

*John:* I like that.

*Sarah:* Good. By the way where did you move from John?

*John:* I just moved here from St. Louis. This is my first week.

*Sarah:* You'll like Denver, John, especially if you are an outdoors person. Where do you live in town?

*John:* I live on lower Alameda.

*Sarah:* That's good news. You're only about a mile from the club. If you're free, would you like to stop by now and let me get you signed up on your trial?

*John:* I think I might. Could you tell me what it cost first, though?

*Sarah:* Of course. Our monthly fee for an individual is $49 and we have a number of additional options if you are interested in personal coaching or some of our other services. But as I mentioned with the trial John, once you come try us I guarantee that price won't be your deciding factor. May I set a time for you to come by today?

*John:* Sure, how about 5:30.

*Sarah:* Okay, 5:30 it is. John, let me make sure you know where we are. We're at...

And let me ask you one more thing. Are you near your computer?

*John:* Yes, I'm at work.

*Sarah:* With your permission, I can send over an email with an attachment that will give you some more information on the club and the trial and it has a few fun pictures of the club, too.

*John:* Sure, that sounds nice. I am at John@aol.com.

*Sarah:* Okay, I just sent it over.

*John:* Yeah, it popped up already.

*Sarah:* Good, pull it up and I will quickly review it with you.

**Sophisticated buyers don't want to waste their time.**

You can learn a number of things from this scene:

- The person answering the phone used a strong welcome statement.

- She used the words "of course," which are good customer-service words. She also could have substituted, "absolutely."

- She did not give her name when she answered the phone, but waited for two questions and worked it in as if she forgot. Doing it this way allows you to get the person's name gently without the feeling that you are coming on too strong too early.

- The trial was also explained completely. The trial is a strong tool to differentiate your club from the competitor's and Sarah took her time and gave a thorough explanation about how special the trial is and why the club offers it.

- Sarah also use the five Ws, have, and how, listened to the answers, and then responded to what John said.

- When she gave the price, she also gave value by mentioning the trial a second time.

- She used the immediate-response tool, which is a preset email with attachments, to instantly get information in front of John. This tool is discussed again later in this chapter.

- She invited him to come in right away. Always invite the guest in now, then tonight, then tomorrow, but always start with, "What are you doing right now John?"

**Many more of your borderline calls will go well if you practice the basics and know what a good call is supposed to sound like when done correctly.**

Obviously, not every call goes this smoothly, but you will find that many more of your borderline calls will go well if you practice the basics and know what a good call is supposed to sound like when done correctly. Study this scene carefully, because as a trainer of staff, one of the hardest things to grasp is what good work looks or sounds like when an employee does get it right.

If you don't have an expected outcome, then training is more difficult, because you're not really training to meet any specific goal. Your employees will also respond better to the training when they have something to model after as they work through the various games and exercises. In summary, always show the group the exact thing you want to have happen when they get it right by doing a demonstration or by using written scripts, such as the one just reviewed.

# Using the Immediate-Response Tool

You can find almost endless information on the web about consumer buying habits, citing everything from how much guys spend while shopping on a Saturday to classic works such as Paco Underhill's *Why We Buy: The Science of Shopping*. One of the more interesting theories is that today's consumer just won't spend the time shopping and comparing products in person that he might have in the past. For example, in the 1990s, it the average person would visit 3.8 businesses before making the buying decision, but today the average person only shops in 1.6 places.

What does this statistic mean to you as a fitness business owner? If you don't get them into your business first, you most likely won't get them at all.

In the earlier scene, John is at work. He is probably busy with his new job, but is taking a few minutes on his break or during lunch to get some quick information about local fitness facilities. The question is, how many clubs will John call before picking one to visit after work? Would it be two, three, or all the clubs in the Yellow Pages? Or will he call from the mailer he received, and if the person is informative and professional, stop start there and get back to work? If it was you, and considering how busy you might be in your business, how many would you call? Keeping all of this information in mind, Sarah has to not only be patient and answer questions well, but she also needs to take John out of the shopping market as quickly as possible to prevent him from even wanting to call any other clubs.

Enter your power tool, the trial membership. If John knows he has a real 14-day trial to use without paying any money at all, and that the club is near where he lives, which is the first thing someone looks for when checking out clubs, why would John consider looking any further? He is done, he is coming to see Sarah, and it's time to get back to work.

You still want to nail him down, however, and you do so by using the immediate-response tool. This tool is an email that is prewritten and that has a number of attachments that give a quick, but professional, overview of the club, including a lot of information about the trial.

> The immediate-response tool is an email that is prewritten and that has a number of attachments that give a quick, but professional, overview of the club, including a lot of information about the trial.

The goal is to get your information to the prospect now—instantly—and take him out of the hunt for another club. Waiting for him to come in tonight is still too long. Mailing him a cheap brochure takes too long. You have to get quality information to him now, even while he is still on the phone talking to the salesperson.

Don't try to take him to your website, however, since you can't really wait while he pulls it up and then you have to help him navigate to the right pages. Also remember that John is at work and he might not be able to surf the web while on the job.

The answer is an email with attachments that focus him on the key points you want him to see about your business. You can also include a link to your website that he can reference later, but that's not where you want him to go during your first contact with him as a potential member. Again, look at part of the sample scene to see how it might be worked into a conversation:

*Sarah:* Okay, 5:30 it is. John, let me make sure you know where we are. We're at...

And let me ask you one more thing. Are you near your computer?

*John:* Yes, I'm at work.

*Sarah:* With your permission, I can send over an email with an attachment that will give you some more information on the club and the trial and it has a few fun pictures of the club, too.

*John:* Sure, that sounds nice. I am at John@aol.com.

*Sarah:* Okay, I just sent it over.

*John:* Yeah, it popped up already.

*Sarah:* Good, pull it up and I will quickly review it with you. First of all, there is a letter from our owner that tells you why our club is different from most clubs in this area and why we offer the trial membership. You'll also fine some information about our services and pricing and there are a few testimonials in there too, just so you know you won't be our first member. That last page details everything you might want to know about the trial membership and how to use it and there is even a map to make sure you can find us tonight. Do you have any questions on anything that might have caught your attention?

John may not go into too much depth with Sarah about what he received at this time, but the important thing to remember is where John is in the process. He called from a mailer, spent time with a knowledgeable and patient salesperson who invited him to try the business for free with no risk and no obligation, and before he got off the phone he had four or five pages of information in front of him about the business and why it is the only one in town willing to stand behind its service by offering a trial membership.

If John has experienced all of these things, why would he call a random business out of the Yellow Pages? The goal is to lock him down to only responding to your business and Sarah did a nice job in this scenario by using some sophisticated tools. The following items should be in your immediate-response tool:

**The first thing the person should see is a letter that positions the club in the market compared to the competition, written by the owner or senior manager.**

- The first thing the person should see is a letter that positions the club in the market compared to the competition, written by the owner or senior manager. People like to hear the story and most folks want to support that local business guy on a mission rather than that nasty national chain. On the other hand, if you're a chain club, position yourself as the national expert who brings the experience of a hundred clubs or more to the business and explain that the person would be better off with you than at the local mom and pop store. Your goal either way is to develop a storyline that defines what your business is and whom it is for in the market. A sample of this letter is presented in Figure 22-1.

- You should include two or three pages of information about your services and memberships, and yes, you should include the prices.

Detail what the person gets as a member, list briefly in one paragraph or so the various service and amenities that are available, and give an overview of everything the club will do to support the new member.

- Add at least one article that is inspiring about the benefits of working out. If you are an IHRSA member, you can attain some good copy from them or just clip out good articles that you like in fitness magazines and scan them into your computer. Make sure these articles are focused on the people who aren't yet fitness people. It is an easy mistake to put advanced articles and training tips into this tool that would scare the novice, which is your real target market in this situation.

- You should include one full page of dollar-bill-sized testimonials (about four) as well.

- The last page should be devoted to just the trial membership. What is it, how does it work, who is it for, and where does the customer start?

The format of this tool is just a simple email with attachments. The customer will feel good about opening it because it is coming directly from a salesperson who is still on the phone, which decreases the virus fear factor. You should also include at least one line on the last page that lets the person know that if he would like he can forward the email to a friend who may join him as his guest when he comes for his first workout. The best way to make this tool work is to have a dedicated computer in the sales office where the sales manager can do all of the follow-up and the sales team can get information to clients quickly and efficiently.

## How Good Do You Have to Be on the Phone?

As always, you need a standard of performance to compare your team against. The trial membership dramatically increases the number of people who actually show up as promised on the phone.

> You need a standard of performance to compare your team against.

The old term "no shows" told exactly what happened to most of your phone appointments. You booked appointments on the phone with a bunch of people, and no one showed up at their scheduled times. It is frustrating as a salesperson to spend an hour on the phone working for that appointment, and then the person doesn't show up or call. This factor alone may be why it was so hard to last very long as a salesperson working in the old high-pressure days of sales.

The show rate is much higher when you offer a trial membership on the phone, since the person is coming to get something valuable for free, as opposed to stopping by so you could pound him into submission in a sales office. They know what goes on in a club and few people voluntarily want that beating.

Welcome to our club!

We realize that you have other choices when it comes to fitness and we'd like to thank you for choosing our business as your place to explore acquiring a gym membership.

We believe that we have the best club in the area with the most attentive and knowledgeable staff, great members, equipment that sets us apart from all the other fitness businesses, and a club that is truly clean and comfortable. Talk is cheap, however, and all owners in the area are equally proud of their businesses.

What sets us apart from our competitors is that we are the only [or first] fitness business in the area that will let you try before you buy with no risk, no obligation, and absolutely no money up front. Come meet our staff, hang out with our members, try a few workouts, and evaluate our service. At the end of our 14-day trial membership, if we don't earn your business, then we don't deserve to have you as a member. It's that simple, with no strings attached and no fine print. If you live in our market area, then we will stand behind our business by letting you try us absolutely free for 14 days with no risk to you, except for the fact you might actually get in a little better shape during your trial membership.

Our club has been in business for [number] years and we understand that making a decision to commit to working out is difficult and that picking the right club for you is even harder. Will I like the gym? Will I like the other members? Am I going to get service in this business after I become a member? Will I be able to get any help? These fair questions can only be answered by trying our business before you become a member. Remember, it isn't hard to hide the flaws during a single visit, but it's impossible to hide bad service and a poor business over an extended trial membership. We feel that we can stand up to this test and we invite you to take the trial and see what we are really all about.

One of the most important things that we want you to know about our business is that we are solution based, which means that there is only one really important question we need to ask you: What's the single most important thing you want from your fitness experience?

Based upon your answer, we will recommend anything from a full membership to a simple weight-management program. Think of us as your fitness resource. If you know what you want to accomplish, we can help find a solution tailored just for you.

Another thing that makes us unique is that we treat every member in this club in the same every single day. In other words, we don't make deals with one person and not offer our other members the same thing. We also understand that you have choices when it comes to fitness and as a way of saying thank you for choosing us, we offer substantial gift incentive packages presented with our trial certificate to every new person who is considering becoming a part of our business. If you have any questions about our gift incentives, please call us immediately.

If you have shopped other businesses in the area, then you will note that we are one of the more expensive gyms in town. We do this by choice. To us, poor service, unclean facilities, and lack of service all go hand-in-hand with being the cheapest price in town. You simply can't be the best and the cheapest at the same time in any service business. It also means that our gym is not for everyone. If you appreciate quality, then we're the club for you. If price is your deciding factor, then you won't be happy with us and won't get the most out your fitness experience.

Thank you again for your trust and we look forward to serving you as a member in the future.

Sincerely,

[Owner or manager]

Figure 22-1. Sample letter from your immediate-response tool

# Numbers to Expect With the Trial as Your Phone Strategy

Six out of 10 of your phone appointments will show up if you're training on the phone consistently and following the suggestions in this chapter. This number assumes that the calls are qualified, meaning that the person lives in your area and is over 18 year old. The following numbers are typical of a club offering a free trial on the phone:

- 100 calls
- 80 appointments
- 60 people show up

# General Phone etiquette

The business phone is a mysterious tool to many of your employees, especially those raised on cell phones and who spend hours talking to their friends in those strange phone languages that have developed in the last 10 years or so. For example, a cell phone rings and you overhear the following:

*Dude:* Yo dude, you go, you called.

*Dudette:* Party happen' late.

*Dude:* Yeah baaaabby, party time. Location, location , location.

*Dudette:* Me, mine, and at nine. Bring the boys, there's plenty of girls.

*Dude:* Be there, gotta go, another fan is trying to reach this rock star baby. (Flash) Yo dude, you go, you called...

The dude depicted in this scenario is your new hire from last week who is currently being trained to answer phones at your front counter. He has never seen a business phone in action and all of his phone habits have been developed through years of talking on his cell with his friends.

Everyone on your staff who comes anywhere near the phone should start with several hours of training on phone etiquette. Start with the basics and always return to the point that the phone is where the money-making process in your business begins. Tips for your new team members are included in this list, as well as some general phone-improvement suggestions to give your business the professional edge:

- You always answer the phone by the third ring.
- Never, ever use an answering system. The person called for service, not to be placed in voicemail hell. Answer live and professionally.
- Use a strong welcoming statement.

> Everyone on your staff who comes anywhere near the phone should start with several hours of training on phone etiquette.

- Ask permission and wait for the response before you place someone on hold.

- Use a company such as Voicescapes to provide on-hold messaging. Do not let them listen to dead silence or lousy music. On-hold messaging is part of your sales efforts and should be treated as such.

- Thank every caller at the end of each call, no matter the subject.

- No gum, ever, is allowed in the gym. Yes, the person can hear you popping that gum on the phone and it sounds like you're 12 years old.

- Put a mirror by the phone and check yourself while you're talking. If you're not smiling in the mirror, then you are being perceived as miserable by the caller.

- All calls from members have to be returned within the hour. No exceptions.

- It is easier to pick up the phone and say no than it is to see a stack of messages pile up that you won't call back anyway.

- Develop a professional screening system. The worst is: "Who is this please? Let me see if he is in." Customers know that in most clubs, "he" is standing behind you whispering, "Who is it?" The safest screen that doesn't insult is: "He is in a meeting with a member. May I take a message please?"

- Return general business calls at a set time each day. Get in the habit of returning all call between 1 and 2 o'clock p.m., for example, and work that time into the phone scripts.

These tips are some general guidelines. A number of good books have been written about phone-based customer service that should be added to your library in the club. Just remember the key word, "professional," and that the phone is the first step toward making money in the club.

## How to Practice for the Phone

The phone rings every day, so you should practice every day.

The phone rings every day, so you should practice every day. The phone is your first line of contact with the outside world, and the impression you make on the phone is how you are perceived by the buyer outside the club.

Many owners will spend thousands of dollars each month on marketing and then train their staff at the front counter on how to take the call for just a few hours a month. Adhere to the following guidelines for phone training, which you need to apply immediately, even before you install or update your sales system:

- Train for at least four hours in one block for two weeks when you first start to make changes in using the phone. This number includes time for sales training on the phone as well as general phone etiquette. Remember, you have to make money from inquiries, but you also have to service your existing members who call, so be sure to train for both scenarios.

- Block out at lease one hour per week, every week, for phone training with your sales staff. You should do two hours a week with all the counter people who answer the phone, even if only part time.

- When practicing sales calls, use old phones as props and make sure the two people who are role-playing are sitting back-to-back. If they can see each other they pick up visual clues that wouldn't be available on the phone.

- Script out everything. Put want you want to be said in writing and practice off the scripts. Write out key lines, sample conversations, and trouble calls and how to handle them. Many owners spend too much time trying to teach everything verbally, but it is easier if you just work off the scripts in their employee notebooks.

- You can consider taping calls. A number of marketing firms will rent you an 800 number for your advertising that rings through your regular phone lines. These firms also tape each call, with the proper warnings to the consumer on the phone, so your management team can analyze how each call is handled. This system gives you focus points for your training that isn't available from normal role-playing.

## Key Points From This Chapter

- Marketing gets the phone to ring, and phone training gets the door to swing. Without good phone training your marketing dollars are wasted.

> **Marketing gets the phone to ring, and phone training gets the door to swing.**

- Your phone strategy is the same as the meet-and-greet step of the tour. You spend two to four minutes getting to know someone and then invite them to the club.

- Almost every inquiry call will start with: "Hello, I'd like to get some information about your prices please." Learn to master the call from that point forward.

- Give the prices on the phone, but always give value when you give prices.

- Script out what a good phone call sounds like so the staff members can learn the words and the flow.

- Train for general phone etiquette as well. Your members are important and need good service as much as the inquiry caller.

- The trial membership gives you a much higher percentage of guests who show up for their appointments. Instead of trying to get someone in just to get pitched, you are now offering that person something of value for free.

- Spend much more time training for all aspects of phone service than you think might be necessary. Money in your business begins with that first phone call.

**Tip of the Day**

# Learn to speak.

Most of you have no idea how you sound, but you're pretty good at laughing at other people who have funny or unusual voices. What if you are really one of those "other" people?

If you're going to be a true professional and make your living with your voice through sales, then you should get a voice coach. Most clubs would even benefit from hiring one for the day. They aren't very expensive and can provide some training for your entire team.

Your voice is one of those things that you take for granted, but the person who is listening might be truly overwhelmed by what he hears. Think about people on cell phones, for example, and how loud and obnoxious some people sound, seemingly oblivious to those around them. Maybe they are just rude and don't care, but it is more likely that they have no idea how loud or abrasive their voice can be.

A good voice coach will tape you and teach you how to use your voice as a tool. Your coach will also help you get the most out of what you have, even if your voice is unusually soft or harsh. It is important that you realize that your voice is another tool in your arsenal that has to be developed like any other skill you might possess.

# THE SECRET TO BUSINESS IS DRIVING REVENUE

**Section Six**

# 23

# Geting a Plan in Place to Drive Revenue

Making money is not a random act left to sales gods who magically drive revenue through your door at the end of each month. If you want to make the most money possible in your business, then you have to start thinking about creating systems that keep your key players focused on your goals on a daily basis, rather than waiting until late in the month to see where you stand and then scrambling to catch up to pay your bills.

## Thinking About Money in Smaller Chunks

Chapter 14 discussed how to project revenue for the month and how to break it down into weekly and daily goals. Once you have these numbers, you have to create a vehicle to drive those numbers each day.

Knowing the numbers is only half of creating revenue. The other half is building a plan that can be carried out by the team. Think of knowing the goal as the "what" and the plan as the "how." In other words, knowing the number or the goal is not enough, because you still won't hit this goal unless you create a plan to achieve it.

### The daily meeting focuses on the "what" and the "how."

The daily meeting is the focus tool you use to create revenue in the club on a daily basis. Once you've established your targets for the week, you can use the team to drive those numbers.

The daily meeting is just what it sounds like. Get your key staff together once a day and talk about the money you need to make, what each department can generate, and the plan everyone has to reach the goal.

You also have to understand that almost anyone can figure out the number you need to hit. The money is made, however, from being able to build a plan

**Each department, meaning each department head, should have an exact number to hit each day.**

that tells you how you will make the money and what you need to do to get it done. Knowing the number is a start, but knowing how you will hit that number is more important. Each department, meaning each department head, should have an exact number to hit each day. Consider the following example, which features Sammy as the lead salesperson:

*"Sammy, how many sales and how much revenue are we going to get from your department tonight?"*

*"Well, we should be able to do three new sales and about $300 in the register."*

Sammy just gave the wrong answer. If you're going to hit numbers consistently, you have to set an exact number and then figure out the plan to get it done. In this case, Sammy is guessing, which gets him off the hook tomorrow if he doesn't come through tonight. A more effective exchange between the manager and Sammy might look like as follows:

*"Sammy, how many sales and how much revenue are you going to put on the board tonight?"*

*"Well, we have five appointments. Also, it is Monday and we have been averaging 12 trial workouts on Mondays. Out of those 17 possibilities, our team will put six new sales on the books and we will put $420 in the register."*

Sammy has been trained to understand the potential of the business. In this example, he knows exactly how many possibilities he has in front of his team and he knows what he has to do to score that night. Guesses don't lead to money; knowing your potential and going after a set number is how revenue is made.

The staff of each department has to understand the potential in front of them and how to exploit it. The head of the training department (Sarah), for example, would have a different exchange with the manager:

*"Sarah, what's coming from you and the trainers today?"*

*"Well, we have 14 training appointments tonight, but only two are in their last two sessions. We will rewrite one of those for sure, which will give us $500. But I also have two extra trainers tonight, so we are going to grab some members and take them through a functional group-training class. If they take a group of six each, we should be able to generate at least one package per group, which would give us another $600. Put our department down for $1100 tonight."*

Sarah is doing two things well in this example. She understands the potential of her business for that day and she also is offering a plan to generate revenue on a slow night. Many owners and managers who are reading this book are saying to themselves, "I can never find people like Sarah to work in my business."

You're right, you can't find them. You have to train them and develop them yourself. Good employees aren't made; they are developed from good people who want to do the right thing and then they are paid well for their work so they stay.

## The basic rules for the daily meeting

The daily meeting is one of the tools you use to coach and guide your team through the process each day. Daily meetings help people understand the potential of the business and the responsibility they assume in making the numbers happen. Consider the following basic rules of a daily meeting.

Set the meeting for the same time each day, between noon and 4 o'clock. Never deviate from this time, don't change it just because you feel like it, and make it the most important part of your staff's day.

All full-time managers must attend, including your manager, sales manager, lead trainer, lead counter person, lead weight-loss person, and perhaps your group-exercise manager. Set the time so that most of these people are at work, but you may need to change schedules to make it a part of everyone's day.

Run your business from Monday through Sunday. For example, if your projections determine that you need to do a $1000 per day through the register to make your goal, then you have to do $7000 for that week. If you have any experience at all in the business, you know that you will make most of your money early in the week and then hope that the Sunday person can make enough to cover his own salary that day. For example, you might generate $4000 on Monday against a weekly goal of $7000. If you recalculate, you then need $3000 divided by the remaining days in the week ($3000/6 = $500). In other words, the daily number dropped from $1000 per day for the week to $500 per day for the remaining six days. By looking every day, and recalculating every day, the team stays focused and the numbers seem attainable.

Use segments to keep your meetings consistent and to make it simpler for you to do each day. Using segments also keeps you from wandering off track and keeps your meetings quick and effective. Start with the following segments and modify as you get more experience. Each segment is about five minutes long.

*Segment 1: Where you stand right now.* This segment is a recap of where the business, and each department, stands in their efforts to reach their monthly goals. Never start a meeting without letting everyone know exactly where the company is as of that moment.

*Segments 2 & 3 (two segments lasting five minutes each): Set a goal with each department.* Each department should report on where they are for the month, how much their team will put up that day, and how they will hit those numbers. No one works without a plan and everyone has to know what he is being held accountable for each day in the business.

> Daily meetings help people understand the potential of the business and the responsibility they assume in making the numbers happen.

*Segment 4: Review something that can be done more efficiently.* Remember that one of the most important rules in developing staff is that you always praise in public and criticize in private. Never use the daily meeting to chew someone out in front of his teammates. However, you can make the group aware of some things as a whole if they will improve the business.

For example, assume that the sales team is rushing while filling out the memberships and errors are being made on the addresses. This segment could be used to bring in four or five copies of contracts that were not done well, with the errors circled. "Okay team, note here that we're missing apartment numbers and we're not getting zip codes. Note on the samples from the last two weeks where the holes are. We need to slow down and get full addresses, because without them we can't process the memberships." In this example, the entire membership team is being cross-trained in case they need to help out or fill in for each other.

*Segment 5: Teach them something new.* Use at least one segment to teach the team something new. In five minutes you can introduce new supplement, review a new program, talk about a ad that will be running or anything else that will make them more effective in their jobs.

*Segment 6: Review the goals one more time.* "Okay, let's wrap it up. Sales, you're down for six memberships and $420. Training, you're down for $1100. Front counter, you're down for ..." Always leave with the goal fresh in their minds and an exact plan of how they are going to reach those goals.

Get your team back together at 5 o'clock for a focus minute. During this quick meeting, you should the following:

*"Remember why we're here tonight. We all have goals to hit and since it's Monday we're going to have around 500 guests through here. Let's put on a good show and make some people happy, and don't forget our mission statement: We're the best part of their day every day."*

> **The fitness business is hard, and you have to work to keep your team focused on making money and remind them that they are part of the show.**

Put your hands in a pile like the high school football kids and then spread out and make some money. Sounds kind of old-fashioned and you're just too cool for it? The fitness business is hard, and you have to work to keep your team focused on making money and remind them that they are part of the show. You get them together, get them focused on what's important in your business, and then you all spread out and make some money. As one owner said in a staff training session, "If it made me money, I'd wear a diaper on my head and water skis to work. Slapping hands and making people feel like part of a team just isn't that hard."

When the day ends you have to ask the final question: What did you do today to make this company money? Always finish the day with accountability. What did you do today as a team leader to keep this company growing? Ask that question at the end of each workday before your team leaves, so they understand that it always will come down to their personal accountability for the numbers they agreed to in the meeting.

The example presented in this section is for a total team meeting with the managers. The sales team should have its own meeting using the same format. The same basics also have to apply:

- Use history and trend line for the monthly projection.

- Set a goal for the coming month.

- Break it into daily and then weekly goals.

- Every projected sale has to be assigned to an individual.

- Use the same segment format described earlier for this meeting.

## Paying People to Do the Work

Good employees do the work first, and then bonuses and commissions are awarded for that work. Lousy employees who will drive you insane and make you wish you were a landscape guy with no employees constantly claim that they could do better if only the money was better. In other words, they withhold their talent unless you throw more money at them first. Owners and managers will also discover that there isn't enough money in the world to get those people to work hard, because no matter how much you offer another excuse will surface. Your job is to either be one of these people from the first group or find and hire them.

Finding these people isn't as hard as you think, but owners often look in the wrong places. The right people usually aren't working in other fitness centers and haven't had a lot of bad training from one of the national chains, but it is hard to resist looking for that experienced salesperson who doesn't need the training or any supervision to do his job. While you are looking for the perfect salesperson for your team, you also might as well see if you can pick up the tooth fairy and a leprechaun too, just in case you need some cash down the road.

The right person to look for is probably working for someone else, but doesn't necessarily have fitness sales experience. Your job is to create a sales system within your business that can be easily taught to someone who brings the right experience and traits to the job.

Managers from the Gap®, real estate people, strong customer-service people, and experienced women with some past business experience all make great salespeople if a system exists for them to follow. If they have practical business experience working with the customer, almost anyone can be made into a fitness salesperson. In fact, these nontraditional people often make the best employees, especially if they have interest in fitness and being in shape, because they can relate to so many of your members, which is something a male in his mid 20s, the typical club salesperson, often can't do.

**While you are looking for the perfect salesperson for your team, you also might as well see if you can pick up the tooth fairy and a leprechaun too, just in case you need some cash down the road.**

Nontraditional people often make the best employees, especially if they have interest in fitness and being in shape, because they can relate to so many of your members, which is something a male in his mid 20s, the typical club salesperson, often can't do.

## The sales manager

The sales manager should be on a salary, plus bonuses for hitting the target number for the month. This person should never get paid for individual sales, because you take the incentive away for him to train his staff if they competitors.

The starting base salary for this position is usually approximately 60 to 75 percent of the manager's salary, based upon experience. The bonuses are based upon hitting the month's target goal and you should always use a three-step incentive system based upon the target, the incentive, and the boom-boom. For example, assume the sales manager's goal for the month is 70 new sales, which was determined by using history and trend line. The incentives might look as follows:

- The target is 70—The sales manager receives $350 if the club hits this goal.
- The incentive goal is 75—The sales manager receives $700 if the team hit this goal (just the $700, not $700 plus $350).
- The boom-boom is 85—The sales manager receives $1275 if the team hit this goal.

The target number is the first level that is based upon the calculations using the target and trend line discussed throughout this book. But if you want to drive the big revenue, you need to set goals for the month that will provide the necessary incentives for the manager to take his team past the first-step goal. In this example, the manager is paid a bonus equivalent to approximately five dollars per sale.

The incentive goal is the second step and is always just slightly beyond the first-step goal. In this example, the manager is paid the equivalent of approximately $10 per sale, which is quite an incentive compared to the $5 for the first level and is teasingly just beyond the first step.

The boom-boom is the big step and is a full 10 memberships beyond the second step. In this example, the boom-boom is a big jump and the sales manager can pick up the equivalent of $15 per sale for hitting the big number.

Boom-boom, by the way, is an old sales term from the 1970s that is still cool to use and say. "Give me the boom-boom" made the staff laugh then and still does today. Weird terms and goofy sayings are fun and keep boring jobs from becoming too frustrating. As an owner or manager, it's always fun to tell an employee who wants more money: "Give me the boom-boom and you can make all the money you want in this place."

Everyone wins if the sales team hits the boom-boom, because the club owner was only targeting 70 sales, the sales manager was getting a decent incentive for 70, and everything beyond that number benefited the owner and the sales manager. Whenever you have a win/win situation, the chances of driving more revenue is higher.

The negative, however, is what happens if the sales team doesn't hit the target number (first step). You should have a bailout number that represents approximately 80 percent of the target. In this example, the first-step target is 70 sales and the bailout number would be 56 (70 x .80 = 56). If the sales manager fails to hit the target, but at least reaches the bailout number, then you can set a small incentive, such as $1 per sale.

The three-step system should be applied to all goal-setting and works for any team member in the club. If for some reason a staff person goes beyond even the boom-boom, then immediately set another goal for whatever time is left that month. Always keep some incentive dangling in front of that person and if he overperforms then you have to overcompensate.

> **The rule to remember is that you don't compensate for failure (less that 80 percent of goal), but you should overcompensate for success beyond the target number.**

Another part of this rule is that all employees are not created equal. Some people work their little fit butts off for you every day, while others are perfectly happy doing a steady job and making less money. If you have that driven employee, then this system of compensation rewards him for the work he does compared to his fellow team members. If he blows past your goals, then set new ones and let him make all the money he can, because you and the club win anyway.

**All employees are not created equal.**

## The individual salesperson

Pay flat commissions only and stay away from anything that resembles a percentage of sales. You are not developing car salesmen. Pay a flat wage and a flat commission for salespeople on your team. Salespeople should make approximately $2 to $4 more per hour than what it takes you to hire a front-counter person in your area.

For example, if you can hire a front counter person in your area for $8 per hour, which is what is called your local minimum wage, then you should start your salespeople at between $10 and $12 per hour plus commissions.

This salary may seem high to you, but my grandmother was right: If you pay peanuts you get monkeys. In the old systems, the owners paid a smaller base and put everything into the commissions. This system worked in the 1960s and '70s because most salespeople were young males and commission sales was the way to go in those days.

In today's market, you must use a higher base to attract a higher-quality person. A lot of status resides in your base hourly wage, and a better base will get you talent in most markets. Women especially appreciate a higher base salary, because kids are often involved somewhere in the process. For a single mom, for example, a higher base provides a bit more security when it comes to raising a child or two on her own. The base pay is also a status symbol to some people. The number one motivator for women in the workforce, for example, is recognition, and a higher base is a strong recognition factor for what they bring to the job.

> The number one motivator for women in the workforce, for example, is recognition, and a higher base is a strong recognition factor for what they bring to the job.

The number one motivator for young males is money, mostly because they always seem to be broke. Although no scientific research exists to support this assumption, employees who are constantly broke and don't manage their money well are the worst employees you can have, because no matter how much you pay them they are always mad at the owner and the club because you aren't paying them enough to pay their bills.

As a side note, many employers have begun asking for credit reports from anyone who is working in a management position. If you can't manage your own money, then you probably can't manager someone else's.

Commissions are regional in nature. In the South and in smaller, rural markets elsewhere, a club owner or sales manager can offer $10 to $15 per new annual membership generated, while other markets in the North or in major metro areas have to offer $20 to $40 per membership to get and keep good salespeople.

Rule of thumbs are hard to come by for this situation, but if you want a quick number, try paying the equivalent of approximately 50 percent of your monthly payment for an individual membership. For example, if your monthly payment for one person is $49, you are probably safe paying approximately $25 in commission.

These commissions are based upon selling an annual membership. If you want to set commissions for other types of options, set your annual number first and then adjust downward. You should not offer larger incentives for paid-in-full memberships because the whole goal is to drive the receivable base.

Most club owners have also gone to separating two-person memberships. If you offer a membership for two people living at the same address (you cannot call it a couples membership anymore; see Chapter 17), then you might want to write separate agreements for each person.

It is the way of the world today that people keep their own last names, use separate checking accounts or business accounts, and often get divorced. To increase your chances of collecting the most money from the most people, write separate agreements by simply dividing the total in half and then pay the salesperson two commissions, one for each membership he generated.

Renewals should be turned over to your best person, and he should handle any of these accounts that aren't automatically renewed by your third-party billing company. Any salesperson or staff member who handles a renewal should receive a full commission for that membership.

# Using Action Plans and Performance Contracts to Drive the Numbers

People perform at a higher level if the ownership of the goal is transferred to them. Giving a person a goal for the month and receiving a positive shake of the head from your staff person is not going to get that goal accomplished. You may think that you have agreement, but on the way out the door the person is saying to himself, "Where did he come up with that nonsense? It must be nice to be the boss and have time to do drugs all day, because no way is anyone is going to hit those ridiculous numbers."

You as the owner think your employee is on the way to hitting the established goal, but the employee has already set a secret number that he thinks is right and that will be the number he hits no matter how often you beat him or yell at him. Without buy-in, you have nothing, and no one is going to hit your goals.

Action plans and performance contracts are the first steps to transferring the ownership of the goal to the employees. These tools allow the employee to accept responsibility for the final goal and, therefore, commit to getting it done.

**Action plans and performance contracts are the first steps to transferring the ownership of the goal to the employees.**

You can use the following steps to transfer ownership of the goal. These steps should be followed at first with just your managers, but eventually every employee should go through this process during the last week of the month for the coming month:

- Set the goals for the coming month during the last week of the preceding month.
- Break the goals into smaller chunks that are assigned to each manager for his area of responsibility.
- Each manager should be given a performance contract for the number he agrees upon and commits to hit for the month.
- Each manager should give even smaller pieces of the goal for their department to individual employees. For example, the sales manager would work on goals for each member of the sales team.
- Each member of the sale team would sign a performance contract for the month.
- Each day, all managers and staff members have to fill out an action plan for the day.

## The performance contract

The performance contract is a simple agreement that clearly puts into writing what the person in question agrees to do for the month and what he gets for hitting the goals (Figure 23-1). Note that the three-step incentive plan mentioned earlier fits this situation as well.

By signing this document, the employees are agreeing to ownership of those goals that are transferred to them. "Hey, you signed this contract at the beginning of the month, agreed that these goals are what you could hit, and this is the loot you get if those goals are met." If it is in writing, then it is real. And if the employee signs it, then it is no longer a piece of fiction that the manager or owner created; it is a formal working business document.

Again, fill these documents out during the last week of the month for the coming month. Start with the managers only and then each month add more employees as you gain more experience.

Also note that a place exists at the bottom of the agreement for the 80 percent minimum-performance goal. This number should be established each month along with the target numbers and higher-level goals.

## The action plans

People work better when they know exactly what is expected of them each day, and action plans clearly state that if you do this work for the day, then you did a good job.

Action plans are tools that you use daily to keep people focused. People work better when they know exactly what is expected of them each day, and action plans clearly state that if you do this work for the day, then you did a good job.

The manager should fill this form out in the morning and give it to the owner if applicable. Department heads should fill one out either the night before or first thing in the morning and turn it in to the manager. No one should be allowed to work without first filling out an action plan. Action plans set specific goals for the day, and without goals making money turns into a random act.

Lower-level employees should be given action plans already filled out. Managers should then review the plan with them when they start work each day. Even your front-counter people should not be allowed to work without a plan to make money each day.

Four samples are presented in Figure 23-2 through 23-5, for the manager, the sales manager, the front-counter manager, and a front-counter person.

I, _____, agree to meet the following goals for the month of _____, 200_.

**Goal for the month:**

- _____
- _____
- _____
- _____
- _____

If I meet the agreed-upon goals, I will receive the following incentives in addition to normal commissions for the work performed.

**Additional incentives:**

- _____
- _____
- _____
- _____
- _____

I also understand that I am accountable for a minimum level of performance based on the following numbers. If I don't reach the minimum level, I understand that it will be documented according to the company's policies listed in the Employee Manual.

**My minimum level of performance:**

- _____
- _____

Staff member_____

Date _____

Team leader_____

Figure 23-1. Employee performance contract

Note that each one has focus points for that day, which can change weekly and are used by the manager as a tool for training. The manager might also add points that he is working on that week with that particular employee.

For the day of: _____

Club: _____

## The numbers we need to hit today:

Daily usage goal          $_____

Daily number              $_____

New annual memberships _____

## Paperwork that must be finished before the day begins:

___ Daily Production Report

___ Manager's Action Plan

## Daily meeting/time: _____

## Anticipated revenue and source for the day:

- _____
- _____
- _____
- _____
- _____

## Internal promotions for the day:

- _____
- _____

## External promotions for the day:

- _____
- _____

## Daily basics:

Complete at least three atmosphere checks.

Set Action Plans with each department head.

Set three staff training sessions for the week.

Question of the day: Am I doing the important things that will make this business money?

## Summary of the day:

Daily usage number achieved:                    $_____

Daily number (total deposit for the day) achieved: $_____

Annual memberships sold:                        _____

Other memberships sold:                         _____

My plan for tomorrow:

Figure 23-2. Manager's action plan

For the day of _____

Annual contract and cash goals:

Our cash goal from new sales for this week is $_____

Our cash goal from new sales for the month is $_____

Our annual contract goal for the week is _____

Our paid-in-full goal (memberships) for the week is _____

**Other sales/specials:**

Our cash goal from other sales for this week is $_____

Our number of other/special sales for this week is _____

**Promotions for the week:**

- _____
- _____
- _____
- _____
- _____

**The Sales Manager's review of the week:**

- Set daily production with department team members.
- Coach performance by using action plans.
- Train and coach throughout the week as the numbers dictate.
- Finish the daily production sheet through the previous day before starting your day.
- Walk through the club for an atmosphere check at least three times per day, concentrating on the music, temperature, the overall cleanliness of the club with an emphasis on the locker rooms.
- Set three staff trainings for each week by the end of the workday Monday.
- Always remember that 95 percent of what you do is sell somebody something every day.

**Summary of the week:**

Weekly cash flow                      $_____

Weekly goal +/-                       $_____

Weekly annual membership goal  $_____

Weekly goal +/-                       $_____

**If your numbers weren't made, please describe the plan for next week:**

Figure 23-3. Sales manager's action plan

For the day of: _____

**Basic tasks that you are responsible for each day:**

- Prepare the front counter area for business.
- Make sure the front counter has adequate staffing.
- Promote of the club's profit centers.
- Make sure we hit our front-counter profit-center goals each day.
- Understand and help prepare for the club's in-house promotions each day.

**How are we going to promote profit centers at the front counter this week?**

- Monday
- Tuesday
- Wednesday
- Thursday
- Friday
- Saturday

**What are your sales/program goals for the week?**

- _____
- _____
- _____

**What are your goals for each profit center for the week?**

- _____
- _____
- _____
- _____
- _____

**What are your plans to meet these goals?**

_____

_____

_____

**Daily summary:**

- Sales $ _____
- Sales $ _____
- Sales $ _____
- Sales $ _____
- Sales $ _____
- Sales $ _____

Figure 23-4. Front-counter manager's action plan

Name of employee: _____   For the day of: _____

Club: _____   Shift hours: _____

**Basic tasks that you are responsible for each day:**

- Greet every member by name and welcome him (or her) to the club each visit.

- Make yourself aware of the daily promotions and your roles during your shift. Refer to the employee continuity book (the notebook kept at the front desk with notes from the manager and previous shift workers telling the next person coming into work about important things he needs to be aware of to help him do his job more efficiently) before you begin each shift.

- You must answer the phone within three rings and use the company greeting.

- Check members in promptly and with courtesy. Also make sure the photo always matches the person presenting the card. If you cannot find a photo in the computer, make sure one is captured during the member's visit.

- Promote house charges and the club's credit systems to all members who buy something from the club's profit centers.

**Today's promotions and sales:**

**The daily sale is:**

_____

_____

_____

**The weekly special is:**

_____

_____

_____

**Your daily goals are:**

- _____

- _____

- _____

**Your plan to achieve this goal is:**

_____

_____

_____

**Summary of your day:**

Daily goals hit: _____

Daily goals missed: _____

Figure 23-5. Front-counter person's action plan

# Summary

**You need to have a formalized, written plan to make money each month and that plan has to be given to your employees.**

You need to have a formalized, written plan to make money each month and that plan has to be given to your employees. The daily meeting keeps your key players focused for the day. Performance contracts shift the ownership of the goal to the employee. Action plans set a goal for individual performance for the day. All of these tools combined give you, as the manager or owner, the ability to run your business with objective numbers rather than subjective responses when you're not making the money you hope for each month.

## Key Points From This Chapter

- Break your target deposit for the month into 24-hour chunks.
- The daily meeting is the most important tool you have in your arsenal to keep your team focused and on goal.
- Each meeting should have a set format that can be reused based upon simple segments.
- Sales managers should be paid based on the production of their departments and not for individual performance.
- Individual salespeople can be paid flat rates and flat commissions.
- Learn to use the three-step incentive program for all employees.
- Action plans set daily goals for each employee.
- Performance contracts transfer ownership of the goal to the employee.

## Basic courtesy isn't dead, just heavily wounded.

Courtesy still sells, but it is truly a lost art in this business. One of the first things you might want to do as an owner when it comes to hiring and developing new staff is to introduce the concept of basic courtesy during the first day of training.

"Please have a seat." "Thank you for waiting." "May I put you on hold?" These simple statements just aren't used much in this business. In fact, most of them have been replaced with grunts and rude statements such as, "Sit over there and someone will be with you in a little while."

Some of your younger staff members will actually be embarrassed to use these phrases with people their own age, and they should be trained or replaced with people who can get it done. When people are trying to support your business, you should pay them the respect they deserve by being courteous and polite.

# 24

# Six Things You Can Do Now to Increase Your Sales

What would a sales book be without a chapter on shortcuts? One of the most often asked questions in our seminars over the years has been: What can I do now—today—to get sales going in my club?

This chapter lists six things you can do now to get control of your sales and increase your chances of scoring in the future. These ideas form the basis of much of the other material in this book, but they are listed in this context as a global view for those people who need things explained in a shorter format.

## Number 1: Get a Designated Sales Manager

Many owners fight the system when it comes to this point. "Hey, we're too small for that yet. Maybe in the future we can go there, but for now there are so few of us that everyone has to do everything."

The reality is that without a dedicated salesperson your business will never be as successful as it can be and you will be stuck being small forever. People who have three or four jobs in the club, called "slash" people because their job is something along the lines of salesperson/trainer, are less effective than people who specialize in specific tasks.

The real benefit of specialization, however, is that in the business world no success occurs without individual accountability. Someone, at some time, has to be held accountable for the total number of sales generated that month in your business. Even if you are so small that it's just you and one other employee, then one of you has to be responsible for driving production and acquiring business for the company.

# Number 2: Get Control of Your Leads

In almost all cases, more potential business is available than is recorded in your typical fitness business. The staff, due to neglect, laziness, misrepresentation, or merely because they are trying to hide the fact that they blew a tour, will not count all the potential traffic that comes through the door.

The inquiry sheet is your tool to count leads. Visit your club at unusual times. Send fakes. Have relatives call. Give small bonuses for every sheet that is filled out correctly. Do whatever it takes to find out how much real potential business is being generated each month, but realize that leads are underreported by at least 10 percent in the typical club.

Keep in mind that by not knowing your true business potential, you put a huge burden upon your marketing. Most owners who don't know their real leads will think their marketing is failing, when in reality the marketing might be working, but no one has control of the lead process. Marketing is too expensive to not know if it works, so get control of your leads immediately when building a new sales process.

> **Most owners who don't know their real leads will think their marketing is failing, when in reality the marketing might be working, but no one has control of the lead process.**

# Number 3: Send Them Home With Something Besides a Price Sheet

Your price sheet is the last thing you want in front of a prospective member who is sitting at home reviewing the materials that he grabbed while visiting clubs. Who knows the real percentage, but it is the rare club that sends the person home with something besides a price sheet, a beat-up aerobics schedule, a business card, and perhaps a cheap three-fold brochure.

You spend thousands on marketing, so why wouldn't you spend a little more to increase your closing percentage each month? The Welcome Guide is a 70-page story about your business that includes a list of services, descriptions of who uses the club, pictures of your last party or social event, and fun, motivating fitness articles that are designed to keep the person's excitement about your club going at home.

The key question is: What do you want in front of the person when he is making a buying decision? Do you want a cheap presentation based on a handful of loose paper, or do you want the person to have a three-ring binder that tells the story of your club to compare against what he got from your competition? Do it big and don't cheap out. Developing a quality Welcome Guide is one of the most important things you can do to dramatically affect your sales in a short period of time.

## Number 4: Slow Down and Talk to the Person as if He Is a Friend You Are Trying to Help

This recommendation probably should be the number one tip for rookies. Stop talking about the club and what it offers and ask a few questions about the person. What do you want out of fitness? What kind of workout are you doing now? What is the single most important thing you want from a membership at this club? Why is that important to you?

In a world full of lousy service and rude people, someone who demonstrates a caring attitude and takes a few extra minutes to get to know the customer and what he wants before showing him around will get more sales than anything else you can do. Slow down, take a breath, and remember that the person in front of you is an individual and not another sales number. If you remember this fact each time, you will sell more memberships than you ever thought possible.

## Number 5: Offer the Trial

When you drop close at the point of sale, meaning that you are applying the old-style, "I'll knock off a hundred dollars if you buy today but tomorrow the price goes back up" technique, you absolutely kill any incentive for the person to come back the next day. And you need the person to come back, because drop closing just doesn't buy enough sales to support a fitness business anymore.

Try as you might, today's buyer is more sophisticated and he is either insulted that you attempted such nonsense or just can't make that big of a decision without thinking about it overnight. If your price is $39 per month or higher, 70 percent of the people who visit your club will need two or more visits before they buy—and all the drop closing in the world won't change that statistic.

If the person leaves without buying, and you kill his incentive to come back tomorrow by using too much pressure to sign him today, he will buy a membership somewhere else before you figure out how to get him back in using fake closeouts and other antique tools. Your goal is to figure out how to close the most people possible today and yet make the rest want to come back tomorrow on their own. The only tool that achieves this result is the trial membership, because if he doesn't buy today he still has a reason to come back tomorrow or take the salesperson's call later in the week.

> **Your goal is to figure out how to close the most people possible today and yet make the rest want to come back tomorrow on their own.**

## Number 6: Buy the Sale

You still have to buy the sale to get it done, but today's strategy is based upon doing it with style and class. The Trial Gift Certificate is a tool that offers the person valuable gifts, such as a free gym bag or backpack, and club incentives, such as training sessions and gift certificates for a special person in his life.

The cost, however, doesn't change. The gifts vary in their worth, with the largest package offered on the first visit. The person still feels good, however, about coming back for the trial tomorrow if he doesn't buy today, because the price is the same and he hasn't been penalized concerning the membership.

Learning to buy the sale will add a strong point of differentiation in the marketplace as well as increase your overall closing rate, because you are treating your potential members with respect. For example, your script at this point might read as follows: "Thank you for considering us. We realize that you have choices in the market and we'd like to say thank you for giving us a chance to earn your business. If you are already comfortable with the club and would like to get started today, we'd like to offer you…"

Saying thank you and offering gifts as a way of conveying that feeling of appreciation is much more powerful than offering to whack a fictitious $100 off a membership fee that you never really charged anyone anyhow. The new consumer is smarter than the old one, and your strategy has to change to sell memberships in today's market.

## The Key Point From This Chapter

**Small things make a difference when it comes to sales.**

Small things make a difference when it comes to sales. Slowing down, sending people home with the proper materials, and showing respect to someone who is giving you money by saying thank you with gifts are not revolutionary thoughts, but these methods are powerful sales tools that will buy you more business.

# Take responsibility and develop yourself.

At some point, you move beyond your teachers, your parents, and others that drive you to learn and grow. The responsibility to continue to grow as a person then shifts to you.

Don't wait for your boss to tell you to learn something new. You should force yourself to grow as a person each day by learning a new skill that will help you somewhere in your life. Work on how you dress. Work on how you talk. Work on a business skill you need. Learn to sell and present yourself, which is a fundamental skill for almost anything you want to do in your life.

Many young staff people get out of school thinking that they know everything, but the harsh reality is that once you leave school your real education begins. If you want to be successful as a person as well financially, it's what you learn after you get out of school that counts, and you must take personal responsibility to learn those lessons.

It would seem that after thousands of sales books and literally millions of tours through health clubs, someone should be able to come up with the perfect sales pitch. This ultimate pitch would score every time by making the potential member feel that he just can't live without your business.

This magic pitch is actually already known, but the tendency in this industry to make things harder than they have to be masks the simple, yet perfect, things you need to make the most money from the most members. The consumer has lost value over the years as an individual and has been turned into a sales number, a paid-in-full, a telephone inquiry, or a walk-in, and the industry has suffered because of this loss of sensitivity for the individual who pays the bills. So what is the perfect pitch?

*Hello, welcome to our club. My name is Sarah and you are John, I see.*

*John, before I show you around, let me find out more about you and what you want from a fitness program and a membership at our gym. Yes, we have everything you could possibly need to get in shape here, but before I show you anything, let me find out how I can help you so we don't waste a minute of your time.*

*So John, what kind of workout are you doing now...?*

Relationships sell memberships and the art of building a relationship is a lost skill in the fitness business. Slow down, get to know the person, ask questions that show you are sincerely interested in both getting to know the person and in providing the help and leadership he is looking for from a club, and you can sell more memberships than anyone else in your market.

As competition increases, the need for sales is going to become even more important. But before you build your sales process, always return to the magic close, which is nothing more than spending a little time letting your guest know that you truly care about what he wants and needs to reach his goals.

Epilogue

Thomas Plummer has more than 25 years of experience in the fitness industry. He is the founder of the Thomas Plummer Company, which currently has eight full-time employees and does approximately 22 major seminars per year. He has also founded the National Fitness Business Alliance (NFBA), a group of industry vendors and suppliers who, with IHRSA, have banded together to provide education and tradeshows to the independent club owner.

Thomas Plummer is in front of more than 4,000 people a year, through numerous speaking engagements as a keynote speaker and event host. He is also the author of four books on the business of fitness, which have remained the bestselling books in the industry for almost 10 years. Due to the number of people who attend the seminars, coupled with the popularity of his books, many industry experts feel that Thomas Plummer is the most influential person working in the fitness industry today.

From 1985 to 1989, he became the vice president of marketing for American Service Finance, the largest third-party financial-service provider in the industry. Soon afterwards, he became the executive director of the National Health Club Association from 1989 to 1990, which was founded by the owner of American Service Finance to capture the independent market.

He created Thomas Plummer and Associates in 1991 and started a limited tour with industry sponsorship. In 2003, he reformed the company and moved it to Cape Cod, Massachusetts. The NFBA, which was founded in 2006, is currently the largest provider of education for the independent owner in the world.

Thomas attended Western Illinois University and then attended graduate school at the University of Arkansas. He started working in the martial arts (taekwondo) in 1976. He worked as a ski instructor in Colorado for 10 years, raced bicycles in the 1970s, reached a third-degree black belt in the 1980s, and loves hiking, music, and books. He currently lives on the Cape with his family, travels extensively, and is currently working on his next book project.